Kartemquin Films

Kartemquin Films

DOCUMENTARIES ON THE FRONTLINES
OF DEMOCRACY

Patricia Aufderheide

UNIVERSITY OF CALIFORNIA PRESS

University of California Press
Oakland, California

© 2024 by Patricia Aufderheide

Library of Congress Cataloging-in-Publication Data

Names: Aufderheide, Patricia, author.
Title: Kartemquin films : documentaries on the frontlines of democracy / Patricia Aufderheide.
Description: Oakland, California : University of California Press, [2024] | Includes bibliographical references and index.
Identifiers: LCCN 2024000468 (print) | LCCN 2024000469 (ebook) | ISBN 9780520401655 (cloth) | ISBN 9780520401662 (paperback) | ISBN 9780520401679 (ebook)
Subjects: LCSH: Kartemquin Films. | Documentary films—History. | Independent films—History.
Classification: LCC PN1995.9.D6 A944 2024 (print) | LCC PN1995.9.D6 (ebook) | DDC 070.1/8—dc23/eng/20240314
LC record available at https://lccn.loc.gov/2024000468
LC ebook record available at https://lccn.loc.gov/2024000469

33 32 31 30 29 28 27 26 25 24
10 9 8 7 6 5 4 3 2 1

publication supported by a grant from
The Community Foundation for Greater New Haven
as part of the **Urban Haven Project**

Contents

List of Figures ix

1. Kartemquin Films: A Shared Story — 1
2. How Kartemquin Thinks — 19
3. Cinematic Social Inquiry, 1962–1970 — 36
4. Feminist Voices and Revolutionary Cinema, 1970–1978 — 62
5. Confronting Neoliberalism with Workers' and Women's Stories, 1978–1985 — 104
6. Kartemquin in the Filmmaker Public: Making Not Just Media but the Media Landscape — 126
7. Filmmakers Become Artists, Art Becomes Experience, and *Hoop Dreams* Changes Everything, 1985–1995 — 147
8. Making Broadcast and Cable Stories with Integrity, 1995–2008 — 179
9. Becoming a Media Arts Organization, 2008–2022 — 213

| 10. | Crisis to Crisis | 250 |
| 11. | Documentary for Democracy? | 289 |

Acknowledgments	297
Appendix: Interviews	299
Notes	303
Further Reading	313
Filmography	321
Index	325

List of Figures

1. Gordon Quinn with a 16mm camera. 3
2. *Home for Life* showed meetings of the elderly with administrators. 43
3. *Inquiring Nuns,* inspired by the cinema verité classic *Chronique d'un été.* 56
4. The building at 1901 W. Wellington Avenue in Chicago, Kartemquin's home base for half a century. 67
5. Collective members Gordon Quinn, Judy Hoffman, Sue Davenport, Sharon Karp, Jenny Rohrer, Betsy Martens, and Sue Delson. 71
6. Collective members Jerry Blumenthal, Sue Delson, Sharon Karp, Sue Davenport, Gordon Quinn, and Vicki Cooper mid-meeting. 72
7. *The Chicago Maternity Center Story.* 87
8. *Trick Bag.* 94
9. Gordon Quinn and Jerry Blumenthal interview a worker in *Taylor Chain II.* 111
10. Jerry Blumenthal, Judy Hoffman, and Gordon Quinn shooting a demonstration of unionized workers for *The Last Pullman Car.* 115
11. A sketch for *Women's Voices: The Gender Gap* by Nicole Hollander. 122

LIST OF FIGURES

12. Gordon Quinn and Jim Morrissette at the Library of Congress after their presentation to the Copyright Tribunal. — 145
13. Gordon Quinn, Leon Golub, Judy Hoffman, and Jerry Blumenthal relax after shooting, for *Golub*. — 158
14. Steve James, Peter Gilbert, and Fred Marx shooting for *Hoop Dreams*. — 169
15. A *New Yorker* cartoon by Nurit Karlin on display above the toilet in a Kartemquin bathroom. — 173
16. Steve James talks with editor Susanne Suffredin in the kitchen. — 185
17. Joanne Rudnick and Justine Nagan. — 187
18. American and Vietnamese war veterans share a moment, in *Vietnam, Long Time Coming*. — 192
19. Director Steve James with Gordon Quinn and Adam Singer in *Stevie*. — 197
20. Maria Finitzo. — 200
21. The *New Americans* team at the Wellington storefront doorway. — 209
22. The team expanded during Justine Nagan's tenure. — 219
23. Public screening of a rough cut of *'63 Boycott*. — 243
24. Kartemquin's archives. — 246
25. Kartemquin's fiftieth anniversary year included awards. — 249
26. Ameena Mathews, a lead participant in *The Interrupters*. — 261
27. The 2018 Diverse Voices in Documentary cohort. — 269
28. *Minding the Gap* director Bing Liu. — 272
29. Gordon Quinn and Tim Horsburgh in unaccustomed tuxedos. — 274
30. *Unapologetic* participant Ambrell Gambrell. — 277
31. Gordon Quinn's farewell roast. — 287

1 Kartemquin Films

A SHARED STORY

Kartemquin Films, formally launched in 1966 in Chicago, is perhaps the most long-lived, continuously productive, independent, social-issue documentary production house in the United States. It is also a national leader in shaping the history of independent social-issue documentary. And its history is, to some degree, the history of the field.

How has it managed not only to endure but to assert such influence? After all, for most of its history, it lacked much formal structure. True, there was continuity. One of its founders, Gordon Quinn, continued through the decades to provide vision and leadership to the organization, in collaboration with others.

What it did have, above all, was mission. The philosophy that Quinn and his colleagues brought to the organization—one of using media to spur better conversations for a more open society—has infused it throughout. That philosophy was only partially articulated in words. More often, it was enacted in relationships, in work conversations that were guided by shared core values, and in an ethos that brought enough joy to the job that it compensated for often- miserable working conditions.

Kartemquin has been honored in many ways. Kartemquin's films have received awards at every level—multiple Academy Award nominations,

Emmys, Peabody Awards, and Sundance Film Festival awards, including its audience award for documentary. The festival awards for its films are myriad. The organization itself has been celebrated, too. Kartemquin was a charter recipient of the MacArthur Foundation's "genius" grant for nonprofit organizations. At the time, the head of the MacArthur Foundation, Jonathan Fanton, noted, "To call Kartemquin Films only a production company would be to understate its impact on the critical societal issues it addresses as well as the documentary art form it has shaped." Kartemquin also won a 2019 Peabody institutional award for "its commitment to unflinching documentary filmmaking and telling an American history rooted in social justice and the stories of the marginalized."

All this in spite of the fact that Kartemquin's films are notoriously unsellable. They lack celebrity, true crime, and even easily blurbable stories. In fact, they are nondidactic, unsentimental, deliberately complex works, with a paucity of villains, looking at the human struggle inside unjust systems.

Kartemquin is and has been for decades a leading site in US documentary for character-driven, humanistic real-life dramas around central problems of our time. Perhaps Kartemquin's hallmark work is *Hoop Dreams* (1994), and its director Steve James, with two Oscar nominations, its most well-known figure, with many more award-winning films. But Kartemquin has also been a home for many more artists of note. Kartemquin is the place to come when you want to make a film about climate change as seen in a couple of Chicago neighborhoods (*Cooked* [2018]), when you want to look at ambition, creativity, and diversity among tween girls (*5 Girls* [2001]), when you need to share the stories of homeless high schoolers (*The Homestretch* [2014]). It is the place for untold stories worth telling to audiences who themselves aspire to democratic agency.

Kartemquin was an early trend-setter in the genre of socially engaged, character-driven, long-form documentary narrative films that now occupy the top-prestige roster of documentary filmmaking in the US. With *Hoop Dreams,* Kartemquin showed that its kind of generous curiosity about how and why and to what effect people take agency in harshly constrained lives could be a marketplace success. Just as Michael Moore had done a few years earlier when he burst through commercial barriers to social-issue documentary with his first-person narrative *Roger and Me* (1989),

Figure 1. Gordon Quinn with a 16mm camera. Early on, Quinn imagined cinema verité as a way to foster stronger democratic publics, as proposed by philosopher John Dewey. Source: Kartemquin Archives.

Hoop Dreams in 1994 demonstrated to a cynical business that stories about ordinary people carving out spaces of dignity in their lives were sellable.

Kartemquin also honed the miniseries documentary format, with multiple stories interwoven in each episode. Its 2004 *The New Americans* was followed by *Hard Earned* (2015), *America to Me* (2018), and *City So Real* (2020). The streaming environment that naturalized this format was not even imagined when the ambitious team that put together *The New Americans* decided that each of its six family's stories should be interwoven rather than stand-alone. What was once a creative gamble is now a format.

Kartemquin's storytelling styles have never followed a formula, but the spirit of humanist storytelling for a stronger democracy that it inspired has infused entire sectors of programming. It is seen most pervasively in US public TV's documentary series, including *Independent Lens*, *POV*, and sometimes *Frontline*. Not all character-driven humanist stories carry the commitment of Kartemquin's filmmakers to celebrating and nurturing democratic agency. The approach can easily slip into sentimentalism, uplift, moralism, and sensationalism. But character-driven narratives about hitherto unheralded lives are now a default expectation in documentary viewing. Kartemquin pioneered the form and gave it the gravitas it now has, when done well.

Kartemquin has also been more than its films. Kartemquin modeled how artists and creators can participate fully as citizens, using their professional expertise to inform public policies. It has always been a center of activism around the relationship of film and democratic life. It has affected media policy both in Chicago and nationally. Kartemquin's policy work, often led by Gordon Quinn but actively engaged by many in its network, has consistently supported media production for democratic life. Kartemquin has been the Midwest leader in national media policy initiatives, including public broadcasting and on fair use. It has also been a leader in initiatives to carve out new opportunities for Midwesterners to participate in mediated storytelling, for instance in public access cable, in partnerships with and through pressure on local broadcasters, and in the creation of new resources for marginalized makers. Kartemquinites have participated in the work of local, state, and federal arts and humanities councils. This activism has been a feature of every generation of Kartemquin, and it has been transformative. Kartemquin's efforts were essential, for example, in the creation of the Independent Television Service (ITVS) launched in 1989. Kartemquin's unstinting educational efforts around fair use contributed to a sea change in how documentary filmmakers use third-party material in their films.

Kartemquin has, furthermore, been a site of building artistic community. Throughout its different phases, it has developed an enduring network of filmmakers who consider themselves not just friends but part of a Kartemquin "family"—a word that came up consistently throughout my interviews with people who have worked there, in all areas. People used phrases such as "it was a place where I could be my whole self" and "I learned who I really was there." "I love Kartemquin," filmmaker Gita Saedi Kiely said. "I feel like I grew up there." Karen Larson, who was finance director at one point, said, "I will never work again with a group of people as creative, smart, funny, and engaged. It was hard, and it was the high point of my working life." The great exception was the choreographer Bill T. Jones during the making of *A Good Man* (2011). He said the term "family" didn't apply, because families were dysfunctional, and this group worked well. Many who passed through the doors of Kartemquin took its spirit with them into the rest of their lives.

People referred to Gordon Quinn and his longtime business partner Jerry Blumenthal as second fathers, as family, as dear lifelong friends. "Jerry and Gordon were like brothers," recalled Marcy McCall, who worked there in the 1980s. "Gordon had this affectionate way of calling Jerry, he called him Blume. And Judy Hoffman was like a sister to Jerry." They developed friendships that lasted throughout their work lives. Many people have left Kartemquin, but most have maintained relationships and periodically returned. It has been an artistic second home for people who loved film and wanted an ethical way to practice their storytelling. It has also been an incubator for many people who continued to work in ethically grounded storytelling and for social change. Kartemquin has been an anchoring node on an ever-growing network of tough-minded, generous humanist storytellers.

And yet, while Kartemquin is a bright spot in Midwest film culture, it might also be one of the least understood film institutions of its era at a national level. Its star directors, especially Steve James, garner journalistic coverage and some academic analysis. But when journalists and academics focus on its filmmakers, typically Kartemquin is not even mentioned. When it is mentioned at all, the focus is on its early history, not the last thirty years. Kartemquin has been a blind spot for much documentary film studies scholarship. For instance, Angela Aguayo's definitive work on social-issue documentary projects over the last fifty years recalls Kartemquin's early phase but not its later ones. In 2000, when the pathbreaking scholar Patricia Zimmermann wrote a landmark book about independent film as "a counterdiscourse to both transnational and nationalist media and their de facto privileging of commercial exchange values," she never mentioned the then thirty-four-year-old Kartemquin. The legendary Erik Barnouw, in his classic history *Documentary*, never mentioned the group. Michael Chanan, the lead British scholar on political film, similarly ignored Kartemquin in his comprehensive overview *The Politics of Documentary*. A hefty textbook, *A New History of Documentary Film*, merely spends a page discussing Kartemquin as a collective, although it was only a collective for a few years of its six decades.

This absence of a major documentary film organization from leading scholarly histories has many possible explanations. As a Chicago institution, Kartemquin has not been fully linked into the typically bicoastal world of independent film. As well, Kartemquin's work has deliberately avoided a celebrity model. Its longtime ramshackle economic structure prioritized making the work, not developing a brand. Quinn, as the continuing figure throughout the decades, is notoriously self-effacing and resistant to marketing. Finally, Kartemquin has always eschewed any kind of political ideological rigidity or political sectarianism, fully embracing the concept of citizen-led democracy, and it has striven to reach relevant working-American audiences where they find their media. These choices have sometimes meant that scholars who study filmmaking that they describe as politically progressive, dissident, radical, resistance, or alternative look past it. Meanwhile, it is not on the radar of the chroniclers of the celebrity-proximate world of commercial documentary. The very collaborative mode of Kartemquin, its avoidance of promotion and celebrity, its insistence on mission—all have contributed to effacing its large role in the history of documentary filmmaking in the United States. It is time to place Kartemquin back in the mainstream of documentary history.

KARTEMQUIN IN THE HISTORY OF SOCIAL-ISSUE DOCUMENTARIES

Kartemquin's history is nested within many others, including the history of documentary filmmaking.[1] When Kartemquin Films was founded in 1966, "movies" never included "documentaries." Documentaries had evolved, out of lantern slideshows and photographs, as a show-and-tell medium for many other purposes than the engrossing and diverting entertainment that Hollywood promised. After some big theatrical hits during the silent era, they mostly became educational tools, whether for training new military recruits or for kids in schools. Governments used them for propaganda. Even when they were designed as entertainment—for instance, as a trip to an exotic locale or culture, or as a wildlife adventure film—they were expected to teach you something. So many documentaries were produced in a tedious, top-down, lecturing style, particularly for schools, that people often assumed all documentaries were boring. You saw them mostly in places you went because you had to—school, work, church. A theatrical documentary was a real rarity.

By the 2020s, everything had changed. Documentaries had developed explicitly entertainment genres—standup comedy, music docs, sports docs, and true crime topped the popularity list. But celebrity profiles, animal docs, IMAX spectacles, and more also added to the burgeoning economic value of the documentary form. The number of theatrical documentaries tripled in two decades. Entire cable channels were dedicated to what people were increasingly calling "factual" programming, a term that extended to reality TV. Miniseries and long-running documentary programs became major hits. Documentary became the fastest-growing genre for streaming. Streamers employed documentaries to compete with each other for market share, prestige, and awards. Documentary was hot.

In this evolution from obligatory to diverting, Kartemquin Films charted its own course, while always working within the commercial realities of the film business. From the start, for Kartemquin documentary was a tool—in this case, for democratic discourse. It was also, from the start, an art form. It was a reality-expanding device in its ability to bring other experiences into the viewer's vision. To do that, the films, no matter their style, had to be made *with*, and not merely *about*, the people whose reality was being depicted.

This approach, grounded deeply in American pragmatic philosophy (discussed ahead), was distinctive even within the subgenre of social-issue documentary. The social-issue documentary form had some roots in government-funded documentaries in the 1930s. The British documentarians led by John Grierson produced portraits of British daily life designed to reinforce government messages, primarily to persuade the British citizenry that British democracy was functional. American and German government-funded documentaries were similarly designed around propaganda needs. Those efforts produced striking stylistic and technical innovations, around deeply conservative missions. The form also drew from a countermovement of scrappy, left-wing activist documentaries in the 1930s, some of it fed by political movements including the Communist Party.

After World War II, many liberatory movements mobilized, including anticolonial, civil rights, feminist, student, and youth movements worldwide. That energy was refracted in a diverse documentary filmmaking movement. From many perspectives, filmmakers revolted against both propaganda and the often-patronizing perspective of the filmmaker toward the people they focused their lens upon. The term *cinema verité* eventually became an umbrella term to refer to filmmaking that eschewed allegiances to the state, didacticism, and the staging and scripting that went along with both. This movement, discussed ahead, developed in tandem with filmmakers' resistance to authority.

In the United States of the 1960s, documentary filmmaking became a form for activists—typically liberal or leftist—looking to change the way people think about an issue or problem, which shift in thinking is an agent of change for reality itself. Why was it the preserve of left-of-center makers? Documentary was a genre in a prestige art form, but relatively accessible, compared with fiction; costs were lower, and equipment was increasingly available. National mass media, especially TV networks and prestige dailies, maintained a cozy relationship with power, and the government's anticommunist politics tarred anyone who critiqued power with that brush. Right-wing organizations had funding to buy ads, start and fund think tanks and journals, buy endowed chairs at universities, and lobby for their issues. They did not need documentaries, which struggled to find audiences in an era when filmmakers' best hope for a public screening was often to rent out an independent theater.

But people with something to say, and possibly a trust fund to go with it, made films that found audiences in the few theaters that accepted independent work, and sometimes, if they had the right connections, even occasionally reached broadcast TV. Cooperatives and collectives sprang up alongside the political movements of the 1960s, often working to serve social movements. With the advent of video, makers explored new ways to connect with their publics, including through participatory work.

The advent of US public television in 1967 brought new opportunities for dissident filmmakers to find audiences and funding. Gradually an ecology developed, with private funders on one side looking for ways to support their agendas, communities on the other striving to be engaged, and filmmakers in the middle. An entire business developed to do "outreach" and "impact," fueled by people with strategic communication skills. Small businesses emerged to assist filmmakers in designing strategically useful work and engaging audiences with it.

Social-issue films aimed at target audiences were often persuasion projects or organizing tools. Meanwhile, participatory filmmaking was often designed less for the product than for the process of engagement with communities. By contrast, broadcast-ready work often phrased its perspective well within mainstream discourse. It raised issues in ways that could enter the slipstream of current conversations; the films were, therefore, often character-driven stories carefully unlinked from direct public action.

Kartemquin has done all three kinds of work: advocacy, engagement, and theatrical film and television program production. Each has a distinctive design stemming from the intellectual formation of the organization. Kartemquin films feature stories of people you could sympathize with. They do not hide their perspectives. At the same time, they are not designed to force compliance with the filmmaker's viewpoint. Even the most pointed Kartemquin films, such as *Trick Bag* (1974), *The Chicago Maternity Center Story* (1976), and *The Last Pullman Car* (1983), treat audiences with respect. Nor are they hagiographies of their subjects. These films display a cultural curiosity with parallels to sociology and ethnography. The point is to show you a complex reality so you can see a familiar world as socially created, or an unfamiliar one as a cultural reality you can enter. You see why people make the choices they do, and within what constraints. The film's participants may be marginalized or unusual, but they are never victims. For a Kartemquin film to succeed, the filmmaker and subjects have to work together. The viewer is invited into that story. Kartemquin eventually adopted as its identifying slogan "Democracy through Documentary," an original aspiration of the organization. That link to the project of engaging publics in the democratic process has run through all three forms, and all eras of the organization.

A SHARED STORY

The story I tell here is also a personal story for me. When I arrived at the democratic-socialist newspaper *In These Times* in 1978, one of the first people to bend my ear was Gordon Quinn, one of the founders of Kartemquin Films, already a Chicago arts institution. He wanted to talk about art, culture, and politics, and the job of democratic journalism.

I had already found, in the newspaper, a political and intellectual home. Led by James Weinstein, the noted New Left historian, it was nonsectarian—nonaligned with any political party or rigid dogma—and realistic about the American two-party system. At its founding in 1976, Weinstein had written, "Our overriding commitment is to democracy, to socialism as the means to its attainment, and to the inseparability of the two in modern industrial society." Democratic socialism was a big-tent philosophy, seeking a society that prioritized human welfare above profit. The newspaper was interested in up-and-comers like a socialist city council member in Burlington, Vermont, named Bernie Sanders. Jimmy, as we all called our editor—he had an impish demeanor and a wry humor—had left the Communist Party in crushing disillusionment in 1956, along with many others, after Khrushchev's revelations about Stalin's brutalities and the brutally quashed Hungarian uprising. He had joined with members of the New Left and the intellectuals around the *New Left Review*. He leveraged a tiny family inheritance into a weekly newspaper speaking to the parts of the American left that hadn't shredded themselves through internal conflicts or been silenced by relentless federal surveillance, prosecution, and even murder. Quinn and Kartemquin, a left-leaning film production house, found in Jimmy a reliable friend and interlocutor.[2]

Jimmy had chosen Chicago deliberately, as a place to ground a newspaper designed for the working left. Its value to the *In These Times* project was as a working-class city, where union locals were active and likely to push back on complacency in union leadership. The greater Chicago area was, and is, a huge production hub, with the third-largest and most diversified workforce in the country, and was the second- or third-largest financial center in the US. Chicago's wealth came from manufacturing, food processing, scientific/engineering production and research, medicine, and publishing. Its ethnically diverse, working-class population included postwar Latinx immigrants, Black Americans whose families had made the "Great Migration" from the openly segregated South to what they hoped (with sadly partial success) would be more equal terms of work in the Windy City, and Eastern European (especially Polish) and Irish communities that had been part of the huge migration of working poor to Chicago in the nineteenth century. Chicago was a "city of neighborhoods," in polite parlance, or to put it another way, a set of ethnic enclaves with boundaries not always set by their residents. European American communities both clung to ethnic heritage and formed a patronage constituency for government jobs, excluding Black people and people from later waves of migration.

From a left perspective, and important personally for Jimmy Weinstein, who was thirty years older than the student and post-student activists who swelled the ranks of the left in the late 1960s, Chicago was a step removed from performative, youth-led leftism seen in other cities such as Boston, New York, and San Francisco. In Chicago, progressive organizing occurred around labor issues, racial injustice, and poverty, and it was grounded in physical community at home and at work. Chicago was where Saul Alinsky's Industrial Areas Foundation (IAF) had organized the working poor to defend their interests and their rights. New Leftists loved his organizing primer/manifestos, the 1969 *Reveille for Radicals* and 1971 *Rules for Radicals*, which distilled his hard-boiled left pragmatism about working to change systems of power. (The political right eventually loved them too, and used it to organize right-wing populists in the Tea Party movement.) Paul Booth, one of the cofounders of the Vietnam-era Students for a Democratic Society, and his partner, Heather Booth, were co-organizers of the Citizen Action Program, an outgrowth of IAF, and soon founded the Midwest Academy, to train organizers. (The academy was launched with money Heather won from a National Labor Relations Board decision after she was fired for organizing on the job.) Chicago was where Fred Hampton, the young Black Panthers leader, initiated the

"Rainbow Coalition," coordinating activity between groups representing different working-class, ethnically identified communities. The Young Lords, a Latinx-rights (as it might now be called) group, developed in Chicago out of street gangs. The New American Movement and the Democratic Socialist Organizing Committee, both inheritors of the Vietnam War–era student movements, were active in Chicago when Jimmy launched *In These Times* in 1976.

Chicago was also home to a vibrant and complex intellectual community, which was why Gordon Quinn had decided to settle there when he graduated from the University of Chicago in 1966. This towering, self-important institution in a city rich with higher education was founded in the late nineteenth century with Chicago's robber baron–era wealth. Along with resources from oil king John D. Rockefeller, it attracted funds from many notable wealthy Chicago businessmen including department store mogul Marshall Field. Its fifth president, Robert Maynard Hutchins, had made its undergraduate program into a kind of temple of the liberal arts, with a "Common Core" of knowledge to study and a heavy emphasis on academic achievement (getting rid of college sports was part of his reorientation of priorities). Idealistic undergraduates flocked to the University of Chicago, to think with their fellow nerds. In the 1960s, the nerds started asking unnerving questions, and then organized to protest everything from curriculum design to the Vietnam War. While the university was roiled by student unrest, it was also becoming the central academic site of the neoconservative revolution in economics, with Milton Friedman and his acolytes eventually dominating the economics department.[3]

The University of Chicago was where Quinn met most of the people he worked with for the first decade, and who created the core of Kartemquin Films. The university was also the reason why I ended up in Chicago, following my partner, Stephan Schwartzman, who was studying anthropology there. (Steve ended up making his life's work rainforest protection and climate-change mitigation, in collaboration with peoples of the rainforest, at the Environmental Defense Fund.)

The city also boasted a flourishing arts and entertainment sector. The vibrancy of its Black culture marked, among other things, the Chicago music scene. Chicago was famous for the blues, captured on vinyl by Chess Records, situated on the South Side. University of Chicago students like

Quinn frequented the South Side clubs; Quinn also loved the Paul Butterfield Blues Band, whose white band leaders attracted Black alums of Howlin' Wolf's band, and eventually Mike Bloomfield as well. The Paul Butterfield Blues Band was basically the university's house band. Chicago's theatrical scene was second only to New York; the Steppenwolf theater company was recognized as top-tier in the theater world. Second City, a notable incubator of comic talent—it was a feeder to *Saturday Night Live*, for instance—proudly took a name that referenced Chicago's chip-on-the-shoulder attitude toward bicoastal culture. The Art Institute of Chicago downtown hosted a world-class film screening program showcasing world film culture. A scrappy art house on the North Side, Facets, showed cutting-edge films from Eastern Europe, the "new cinemas" of Latin America and Africa, and work with an experimental edge, sometimes pulling in neighborhood residents as well as art lovers. On the North Side, Chicago Filmmakers, started in 1973 as a place for filmmakers to show experimental and art films to each other, showcased cutting-edge work. Chicago was also a major center of printing and publishing. It was the home base of the *Encyclopedia Britannica* and its Great Books of the Western World series. Its two major daily newspapers, the business-oriented *Tribune* and the more liberal *Sun-Times*, were both national prestige dailies. Their lead film critics, Gene Siskel (*Tribune*) and Roger Ebert (*Sun-Times*), eventually teamed up to start a nationally distributed TV program of film criticism that established the template for the form. A deep bench of advertising firms served both a national market and the huge market created by Chicago's industrial culture and the gigantic consumer base it generated. That, and the corporate film that had become essential to big companies, kept many creative professionals—writers, cinematographers, marketers, designers, and more—in rent money. Business-oriented filmmaking was crucial to the many independent film companies in Chicago, including Kartemquin Films, for the commercial work that paid the bills.

    This was the scene I stumbled into, more or less by accident, in 1978. I was living in a neighborhood that, while it bordered the white Daley stronghold of Bridgeport, was populated by North Mexican immigrants. I clattered north every day on the L, along a line of incipient gentrification to a Polish neighborhood for work. In the evenings, I went south through segregated Black neighborhoods to seminars on symbolic anthropology in

Hyde Park. On weekends, I strolled down Maxwell Street, listening to the blues and eating *menudo,* and shopped at a farmer's market at the Robert Taylor Homes housing project. I wrote not only for my newspaper but for the *Chicago Reader,* one of the first free weeklies, and for those reviews I watched filmic wonders my friends at the Art Institute of Chicago and Facets had just found for us. Sometimes Roger Ebert asked me to review for the *Sun-Times,* when he thought I might be more charitable to a film than he could be.

I got there through other lucky accidents. My PhD in Latin American history from the University of Minnesota gave me a solid grounding in colonialism—while I was, like all my friends, organizing against the Vietnam War. I had floated through graduate school on federal government grants made possible by the Department of Defense's investment in professional knowledge about, well, almost anywhere. It was the American Century, after all. I was now restlessly in search of work where I wouldn't become part of a corporate or governmental machine, nor immured in an ivory tower. I started a community credit union in one of Minneapolis's working-class neighborhoods, using some of the last of the Great Society funding from the Lyndon Johnson era. As the antiwar movement splintered and many of my friends turned sectarian, joining or forming rigidly ideological groups, I became politically lonely. The Great Society era government jobs and contracts were drying up. When we moved to Chicago, my friend Harry Boyte, another activist intellectual, introduced me to the *In These Times* team, which was looking for a cultural editor. It was serendipity within the world of Midwest New Leftism, and I never stopped being grateful for that luck. With the staff at *In These Times* and the gang at Kartemquin, I was finally at home.

The challenge of my new job was, in some ways, the challenge we all faced as New Left intellectuals: How do we find and push forward movements for social change? At the time, we all thought of ourselves as "cultural workers." I imagined the newspaper's cultural section could explore the inner workings of cultural institutions, highlight systemic processes conditioning our popular culture, develop a shared critical language around art that addresses social action. I wanted to explore the workings of systems that created our national stories, fueled our escapism, created new memes and myths. I wanted to find people who were figuring out ways to tell untold stories and challenge dominant ones. My realities were considerably less lofty, since I was working, effectively, with zero budget and no staff, in an organization chronically on the brink of folding. But it was thrilling work nonetheless.

At *In These Times* and Kartemquin, I found fellow dreamers for a stronger democracy. The organizations balanced idealism and pragmatism. It was Jimmy Weinstein who introduced me to the intellectual giants of the cultural New Left, and to the heated discussions about the role of culture in social change that fueled debates in *New Left Review*. It was Gordon Quinn who gave me a distinctively American language and a theoretical framework for that approach, by introducing me to the American pragmatic philosopher John Dewey.

Since those days, I have followed Kartemquin's work consistently, joined forces with Kartemquinites in various political and policy efforts, and joined its first fiduciary board. I left Chicago by 1982 to work as an editor at the magazine *American Film* and then transitioned to public-interest work in media and telecommunications, for the United Church of Christ's renowned Office of Communication, a leader in public-interest media advocacy. By 1989, I was a professor in the communications program at American University, whose public-purpose mandate infused the goals of the communication program. I leveraged academic privilege to focus on the possibilities of media to serve public life. In that work, I regularly returned to my allies at Kartemquin, and deepened what became a lifelong friendship with Gordon Quinn and his wife, Meg Gerken, a photographer and professor. But I never did get around to writing about Kartemquin as an institution, until now.

My goal here is not solely to describe the evolution of this improbable American cultural institution. It is also to show how intertwined artistic projects are with the politics and economics of the moment, how interdependent they are with other cultural institutions and policies, and how important guiding ideas are in setting agendas. And of course, I am also describing a journey I took with these people, in sympathy with their sympathies.

In charting Kartemquin's evolution, as it grew from a small business started by college friends to a national media institution in sixty years, I have used a chronological structure, which stops here at 2020, although the history goes on. Kartemquin has been a very different organization at different times, while always guided by a vision of communication serving democratic discourse. The organization began as a film production house with one foot in scholarship, as a form of social research (1966–70). It became a political collective, linked to local social movements; that spirit informed Kartemquin's work with labor unions after the collective's dissolution (1970–85). Kartemquin then pivoted to work in television programming, with humanist storytelling (1985–2007). It restructured from a founder-owned business to a board-run institution, which confronted both harsh business realities and issues of race and privilege (2008–20). Its story continues beyond that point, but that requires other tellers.

These rhythms of its growth and change partook of and responded to political, economic, cultural, and technological trends. I consider political trends in two areas: in social movements, and in two-party politics at the local, state, and national levels. Economic trends—both society-wide and within the media sphere—had a direct effect on Kartemquin's business and its choices of subject matter. Kartemquin's historical evolution within all these wider trends demonstrates the constraints and opportunities it evolved within, and how the institution responded.

Technological trends, such as the advents of the VCR, the home computer, and the World Wide Web, are interwoven throughout. A note on technology: Like many filmmakers, Kartemquinites loved tinkering with technology. But technology in itself never led changes either in the immediate or wider context within which Kartemquin operated. For instance, when Kartemquinites played with new and better ways to do wireless sync sound with 16mm, it was in order to do something they already had in mind and were already doing more laboriously. Kartemquinites seized on video when it was enormously difficult to edit, because it offered other affordances, especially immediacy, that met their political objectives. The development of internet technology was driven by political and business priorities and in conjunction with other technological innovations; the ways Kartemquin leveraged it depended on the problems it could solve for them, not the existence of the technology itself.

I have also followed some thematic through-lines in charting the evolution of Kartemquin. The realities of confronting power and privilege, including class, gender, and race, are ever-present, both in its subject matter and within Kartemquin. The leaders of Kartemquin from the start thought that race, class, and gender were key sites of the injustices they wanted to analyze. These systems of oppression reflected the terms of, and enabled the capitalist project of, moving resources away from people who make the wealth and turning those resources into capital. How to involve people who had less access to privilege was a constant challenge at Kartemquin. I look, in every era, at who came to the project, what those patterns say about who didn't or couldn't, and what their opportunities and challenges were. This is a way of seeing the terms of cultural social-change work in the United States.

A closely tied question is how Kartemquin kept its doors open over six decades. In those six decades, it never had a financially secure business model. There was never sufficient staff. The physical plant was never adequate. And yet the organization stayed alive. The people who talked to me frankly about what it took to make the work, maintain the operation, and keep the dream alive provided the flesh on the bones of a stark reality: Kartemquin has historically depended on people who were willing to pay a financial price to accomplish their dreams, which were not only of making film but of making change with film. That choice has always been harder the more disenfranchised one's community of origin.

Finally, and centrally, I have followed the also-related through-line of the American pragmatic philosophy that informed the idealism that drives Kartemquin's work. I have asked how that philosophy informed the approach, aesthetics, and use of the films, and how they circulated in the world. I have asked this rather than questions that might seem more obvious: Does art for social change "work"? Does a film spark social change? The answer at an item-by-item, film-by-film level is not, in this case, the point. For all of Kartemquin's work, one can point to direct effects, which I will note. But the larger story is the creation of a cultural mode, a way of working designed to translate hope into expression.

Kartemquinites came to the institution with certain aspirations, and developed them there. They found collaborators and funders who shared their ideals, and when they left, they found other ways to practice those ideals. Their work has been marked by a nonsectarian, progressive vision of social change. Kartemquin has thus been not only a film production house, or an institution, but a node on a multigenerational, ever-expanding cultural network.

This work, then, draws from personal experience, ethnographic observation, interviews, and scholarly research both of the literature and in archives. Kartemquinites have generously shared their stories with me. I interviewed dozens of them, as well as reading other interviews and testimonies they created (the appendix lists them and explains my methodology). I used the still-in-formation Kartemquin archives, at the Washington University of St. Louis. Although the archives were uncatalogued, Kartemquinites had organized them to the extent that the archivists and me were able to select materials. I focused on paper files rather than the many, many in-process versions of the films, looking to reveal the human stories behind the projects. I read drafts of grant proposals, business correspondence, and interoffice memos. The extensive minutes taken by members of the 1970s collective were a treasure trove. Members took turns, and often were clearly bored. The doodling, side comments, and wry summaries of discussions (particularly the criticism-self-criticism sessions that typically ended the sessions) all helped me to step back in time. I also benefited from Kartemquinites' work in recovering the institution's history over the previous fifteen years, including the building of a website that provides information on each film, its makers, its festival appearances, and its awards.

2 How Kartemquin Thinks

Kartemquin Films was designed not just to make films but to contribute to shaping culture for a stronger democracy. There are long intellectual and practice traditions of seeing cultural creation as the shaping of public consciousness, within what scholar James Carey called the "battle for reality"—the constant struggle of different forces of power to control dominant or hegemonic narratives about what is real. This book draws from many thinkers on how culture is formed and how it changes. Documentary film scholars look at the roles of institutions, business, and political contexts in shaping expression; media industry scholars study the commercial ecology of television and film; labor scholars pay attention to the conditions of cultural work. (I provide some sources in the endnotes and in Further Reading.)

The traditions of cultural studies—the discipline whose central task is understanding how our realities are shaped and changed—have been especially important to me. Cultural studies, shaped by scholars such as Raymond Williams, Stuart Hall, and Eric Hobsbawm, places communication itself at the center of reality-making, and therefore as well of transformative social change in that reality. These scholars took inspiration among others from the work of intellectual and revolutionary Antonio

Gramsci. Sociologists such as Pierre Bourdieu have demonstrated how to analyze cultural production in fields of practice.

These thinkers are grounded in Marxist tradition, which asserts that capitalism is a world-system that shapes economics, politics, and culture. That tradition also argues that capitalism is inherently unstable because of its tendency toward inequality, causing cyclical society-wide upheavals and ultimately self-destruction unless checked. Marxists imagine how society could benefit more generally from the wealth generated by modern industrial economies, and they debate how that might happen. The intellectual vitality of Marxism has sustained political parties in democracies around the world, has created a rich body of political thought, and has informed movements such as the democratic socialism that informs the left wing of the Democratic Party in the US. Its concepts grounded the work of study groups in which the Kartemquin founders participated during the 1960s and 1970s.

At the same time, the invocation of Marxism by dictatorial governments around the world to justify authoritarianism and brutality has also created a bitter legacy. Meanwhile, generations of cultural production work by powerful elites and governments, particularly in the US, have demonized Marxist intellectual traditions in service to geopolitics. Rightwing political operators foment this demonization, too, for instance by associating any education about the racial inequalities baked into American history with a "cultural Marxism" that bears no relation to intellectual work that has long used that description. Nonetheless, concepts developed by scholars in the Marxist tradition are some of the sturdiest available when seeking to understand how cultural creation works to maintain stability in the narratives that organize our understanding of reality, and also, crucially, how those narratives can change.

The New Left intellectuals at the heart of cultural studies as it burgeoned in the United Kingdom in the 1960s and 1970s regarded culture as both conditioned by forces of power and an expression of power itself. They challenged those who argued that cultural production resided in the "superstructure" rather than the "infrastructure"—which was where the economic engines of capitalism were located, and presumably the organized workforce to transcend it. New Leftists argued rather that cultural production shaped all possibility, and that anyone who cared about making a better life for all needed to look at the work of creating culture—the stuff that makes the narratives that organize everyone's thinking.

The great pioneer of today's cultural studies, Stuart Hall, a professor and a leader of Britain's New Left, was very good at making these big concepts understandable. The biggest of them is that of reality itself. He argued that the act of communication—connecting our brains to share meaning—is the way our reality is created. We are confronted with a welter of sensory input about the world. Our shared understanding of these inputs is our reality—our interpretation of what all that data actually means. Reality, a social construction at its core, is never stable. It is a battlefield, as Carey called it, in a war that never stops. The stakes are control of meaning itself. People leverage the power they have to dominate the expressive acts of communication, toward reinforcing or changing consensus about how to interpret the world.

This basic concept has an enormous power, because it doesn't just explain intractable differences between groups of people. It also puts power for social change in communication itself, as a shaper of culture. Without it, earlier theorists of social change had been frustrated in trying to explain why so many people go along with things that should be intolerable. With it, they could turn to questions of how social institutions can be shaped to create hegemonic realities—the dominant version of reality, and through it, often, broad social acceptance of what should be unacceptable. They could ask how power embedded in institutions and even habits conditions and limits change, and how change occurs.

Political organizers have said the same thing in different language. For instance, the great Midwestern civil rights activist Grace Lee Boggs (one of Gordon Quinn's heroes), who was featured in a film by indie documentary filmmaker Grace Lee, famously said, "Conversation is revolution." That is, the revolution starts with what's inside your own head, as a result of interaction with others. The great public intellectual James Baldwin argued that we can't address racism unless we understand it not as an attitude but as a reality—in fact, what he called in his landmark speech during a Cambridge University debate, "a system of reality." A white supremacist isn't just bigoted, he argued. The Mississippi sheriff who can't imagine a Black person as a human being like himself is actually living in a different reality from the Black person whom he abuses. Their actions reflect the reality they act within.

New Left intellectuals found Italian Communist political activist, political prisoner, and intellectual Antonio Gramsci inspiring. He creatively and passionately saw his own work through the lens of cultural expression. He argued that the powerful held their power crucially through what he called "cultural hegemony," controlling discourse and culture. Rejecting a rigid Marxism that looked first to change in economic formations for social change, he saw education, the arts, journalism, and other cultural expression as crucial ways of intervening in power. If ordinary working people were ever to have any power, they had to also play a role in intellectual and creative life. He heralded "organic intellectuals," people who developed new ways of interpreting and understanding reality and were able to mobilize people behind those concepts. Social-issue filmmakers are organic intellectuals.

The basic concept of reality as a social construct anchored Kartemquin's founders, justifying the work of documentary storytelling itself. It is also a guiding concept for this book's recounting of the organization's history. The organization's leaders saw themselves as organic intellectuals, people who didn't stand divorced from the people they wanted to work for and with for greater justice and a stronger democracy.

Kartemquin as an institution both shapes and is shaped by its surrounding reality. How do we understand that dynamic? Many scholars have provided ways to understand how to describe and analyze cultural production, how culture changes, and how hegemony can be challenged. French sociologist Pierre Bourdieu was among those who thought about how to describe the forces of power, especially through institutions, which structure what kinds of expression can happen. He spent his life working out how power and expression, mostly the kinds we do unconsciously (like choosing the kinds of rugs we put in the living room, what kind of music we prefer, our holiday rituals, even our bodily stances), are linked and conditioned by forces put in place by previous cultural architects.

The name he gives to the reality we inhabit in networks and communities of practice is *habitus:* a set of normalized expectations about what the world is, which forms one's reality. People who do different kinds of work, and associate with others in a specific part of the socioeconomic spectrum, and share different kinds of experiences, experience reality differently. Habitus provides stability in one's understanding of what reality is, and it cultivates among its inhabitants certain dispositions—ways of behaving that they don't even think about. These dispositions, distilling what seems like common sense, also keep people within their spot in society, and sometimes enforce the keeping of others in theirs (for instance, implicit bias resulting in racist behavior). Habitus is a term that reminds us that our reality is constructed in a web of social, political, and economic relationships. When Kartemquin filmmakers entered the cultural universe of the people they made their films with and about, they introduced their viewers to the habitus of that world. In so doing, they expanded the imagination of their viewers, to see other realities as (in Baldwin's words) a "system of reality," not just attitudes. Only when you understand that can you understand how and why people make the choices they do; only when you understand that can you understand what must change and how.

Bourdieu, like British cultural Marxists, was concerned with how cultural power maintains things as they are, through the work of what he called "symbolic violence," shutting out access to the means of expression of marginalized voices. Furthermore, he was curious about how cultural power can work to change our culture, especially when the less powerful act together. To understand how simple reality (hegemony) gets fixed in place and how it changes, Bourdieu looked particularly at aesthetic expressions.

Bourdieu's insights help us understand why it's so important to consider, in the process of cultural work, the structures that channel power around us. Here are some obvious examples. For documentary filmmakers, the economic structures of the media, whether public television, commercial cable, or streaming, condition their choices. Also important are funding sources—the private foundation world created through tax policy, governmental cultural funders, equity investment, revenue streams through commercial channels. More generally, welfare policies matter. Affordable access to healthcare is a policy structure that changes what anyone can do. Labor policies matter, and condition whether filmmakers can get a living wage or safe working conditions. Housing policies matter, because they affect where filmmakers can put their offices, and whether they can even live in places where they are likely to get work. Women and people in marginalized groups may benefit from policies that require parity of conditions, and from social mobilizations that encourage inclusion. If filmmakers regard inequitable, harsh working conditions as normal, and treat them as the terms of the profession (their professional habitus), they may not join other working people, even in their own circles, in asserting their rights and their needs for better terms. Region matters; location is related to opportunities and networks. Changing political winds, the formation of new social movements, and the advent of new technological options all do as well.

These kinds of insights about how patterns of practice are normalized into a felt and shared reality informed Kartemquin's vision. But they were often felt more than expressed. From the beginning, the leadership built the goal of contributing to a stronger democracy into Kartemquin's way of participating in their profession. Kartemquin leaders—especially cofounder Gordon Quinn—saw themselves explicitly as members of a filmmaker public. This vision became an expectation for Kartemquinites. They consistently took on the "good citizen" role of participating in activism to shape the working conditions of the field. Whether it was demanding more funding and airtime from public TV, helping create and sustain public access cable TV, participating in decision-making panels of arts and humanities agencies, or working on copyright policy issues, Kartemquin members understood that affecting the flows of power which conditioned their realities was part of their work.

The final thinker informing this work, and also the most important to the work of Kartemquin Films throughout its decades, was the American pragmatic philosopher and social activist John Dewey. A towering figure in the first part of the twentieth century, he was not a Marxist; his life work was imagining how people could have a stronger democracy, and he knew how aspirational that goal was in light of the US's highly imperfect one. At the same time, he was horrified by the fundamentally antidemocratic, despotic Stalinist regime in the Soviet Union. Still, he admired Marx as a sociologist and political analyst, and found considerable conceptual overlap with his own vision. Dewey put culture-making at the center of democratic aspiration, believing that education and art were key to building democratic practice. He thought conversation across difference, toward the goal of common problem-solving, was crucial to the ability of democratic publics to form and act. His concepts were both central to Kartemquin's formation and to my own life work as a critic and scholar.

John Dewey was the intellectual to whom Gordon Quinn turned most often for inspiration. Pragmatism as a philosophical position argues, like cultural studies scholars do, that reality is a social construct, created through communication. It says that there is no essential meaning to anything, and you judge the value of concepts by their utility in context. How do you judge the value of a concept's utility? Dewey's grounding concept for judging value was democracy, for its mechanisms to represent publics—the people throughout the society affected by the actions of the powerful. Democracy was, for him, the best way historically to rein in unaccountable power and its inevitable abuses, even though it was frail because accountability comes only from actions of the public. Governments can become corrupt in service of maintaining power, and corporations are unaccountable to the public unless regulated. Only the public can demand accountability of either government or corporations. And this essential social formation, the public, is a frail entity, even as it is essential.

The public is so frail because it has no institutional base; it arises out of commonly shared problems to be solved through organizing into a public. It also gains power from its very lack of structure, which means power doesn't become vested in formal channels. Such institutionalizing then sets in motion the priorities for continuity and growth that create a need for accountability. "The public," in a Deweyan sense, is any group of people who are united by a common problem. What they share, to become a public, is that their own lives have all been negatively affected by some organized force in society. Maybe there's a chemical plant dumping hazardous waste, a practice that benefits the plant's bottom line but poisons everyone who lives in the area. Then the central public would be neighbors in the community. Maybe there's a corrupt local government where embezzlement means that roads aren't being repaired. Then the public would be everyone who uses those roads, but especially those people in the local jurisdiction. Maybe it's a public university that increases tuition in ways that make it harder for working people to attend. Then the public would be students, prospective students, and their families. Maybe it's a workplace that refuses to give employees safe working conditions, or where institutional racism is not challenged. Then the public would be the workers, their families, and other people who depend on their paychecks to make a living. Ultimately, of course, publics extend outward, since all our actions touch someone outside our inner circle, but the most immediately affected people have the greatest motivation to mobilize to form publics.

How does a group of people who don't necessarily even know each other turn into a public? That happens, as Grace Lee Boggs said so succinctly, with conversation—with efforts to identify common interests among all affected, and to talk about the issue. Focusing on the shared problem means that publics can form among people who otherwise may disagree on many other things. Among those who might put such a process in motion is an "organic intellectual," someone who stakes a claim to the community of people affected, who may see or understand something others may not, and who communicates that to foster conversation toward action.

How does a public act for change? Again, the answer is contextual. In a society where the rule of law obtains, there may be antipollution laws, or anticorruption laws, or labor laws. The public may pressure political systems to work, through publicizing the problem, protesting, or otherwise forcing accountability. The laws don't self-execute, after all, and typically government works for its citizens reliably when citizens demand that it does. It is rarely a single person who can do that. People together, as publics, make it happen.

Deweyan publics depend on communication processes to form. Some of those processes are direct, person-to-person. Others result from interacting with media expressions, whether news, entertainment, flows of social media, or other cultural work. Person-to-person and mediated communication constantly interact. The Deweyan concept of the public joins with the cultural studies notion of reality as constructed, the sociological concept of culture and subculture as habitus, and the Gramscian notion of cultural hegemony as power, in the phrase "democracy through documentary." This phrase has been Kartemquin's banner slogan for more than a decade, and its guiding vision throughout its existence. For filmmakers, documentary becomes an agent of public-making, of culture-making, of change-making.

Those same conjoined concepts also guide me in what to look for in describing and explaining the evolution of Kartemquin Films as a Deweyan documentary film project over more than six decades. Kartemquin filmmakers have begun conversations, cultivated publics, contributed to social change, built institutions and networks, and against the odds persisted as a small business through political, social, and economic turmoil.[1]

CINEMA VERITÉ WITHIN KARTEMQUIN'S PHILOSOPHY

Kartemquin's work has always been informed by the thinking that inspired its founders. They founded a filmmaking company to strengthen the work of democracy itself, motivated by two general ideas: the revolutionary ferment in filmmaking encompassed in the general term cinema verité, and the arguments of John Dewey. Understanding the work of Kartemquin starts with understanding how those two themes intertwine.

Kartemquin has always embraced the filmic notion of capturing lived experience in a way that allows the viewer to believe they are experiencing it with the participants. This form has loosely come to be referred to as cinema verité, after a turbulent period in the 1960s when competing filmmakers and filmmaking entities staked rival claims to innovation, using different labels. Experiential filmmaking has now become so ubiquitous that it has lost its distinctiveness. We now expect any documentary to provide at least a frisson of experience. But cinema verité remains a widely used term to refer to filmmaking that seems to capture events as they are happening. From the start, Quinn and Gerald "Jerry" Temaner, two of the Kartemquin founders, as well as Jerry Blumenthal, who came soon after, always used the term cinema verité to refer to this general style and to what inspired them.

When Kartemquin began, the notion of filming experience at length was still an electrifying new concept, a break with the traditions of staging, full lighting, and tight scripting that had characterized much previous documentary work. But the style of cinema verité was not in itself what made it a natural language for the work of the Kartemquin founders. It was that this experiential style seemed appropriate to the mission guiding Kartemquin's evolution. That mission was one of "cinematic social inquiry." We know this because Temaner and Quinn wrote it down, and then generations of Kartemquinites read their manifesto.

The 1960s was a time of meetings and manifestos, articulating the values and political positions of anticolonial independence movements, civil rights, youth movements, and more. Filmmakers worldwide asserted the importance of cinema in changing the social narrative. In Italy, scriptwriter and critic Cesare Zavattini as early as 1940 called for a realistic cinema that told real people's stories. His ideas helped to inform the transformative and profoundly influential film movement of Italian postwar neorealism, built amid the wreckage of Italy's society and its film industry. The European "New Wave," which swept across political boundaries to capture artists in both Western and Eastern Europe, also caught the new spirit of often-youthful rejection of disgraced, unjust, or inherited authority. Postwar British, North American, and European filmmakers threw off the expectations of didactic and propagandistic documentary into which governments had poured money in the interwar and war periods. These were artists catching the whiff of social ferment. The decay of aristocratic grip on government in the UK; the success of anticolonial movements worldwide; rising demands for civil rights of oppressed peoples worldwide, including in the US; the coalescing of an international diasporic culture around *negritude*, with Paris as its hub; resistance to Cold War anticommunist conformity in the US, often in cultural expression—these were only some of the earthshaking movements that buoyed filmmakers who aspired to make work not only to be fresh and uncompromised but to participate in changing the world.

Filmmakers experimented with form in ways variously called "Free Cinema," cinema verité, observational cinema, *cinema direct* or direct cinema, and even "Candid Eye." These terms all depended on the promise of showing lived experience to viewers, but could refer to differences in both style and aspiration. For instance, the "Free Cinema" of the UK, which began before new technologies made any of it easy, referred to freedom from Griersonian earnestness, didacticism, and allegiance to state objectives—indeed, freedom from any need to be socially relevant. The French *cinéma vérité* imagined a cinema of political provocation and confrontation. Observational cinema makers claimed that they blended into the environment and so simply captured experience. Some filmmakers who used the long takes, natural lighting, and lack of narration characteristic of the form, such as, famously, Fred Wiseman, simply denied they were participating in any kind of filmic trend. But in the end, all these different approaches came to coexist under the broad, diffuse terminological umbrella of cinema verité.

Many filmmakers seized upon cinema as a tool of social change, and manifestos emerged. A 1963 conference on cinema verité in Lyons, France, resulted among others in a manifesto by the veteran social-action documentarian Joris Ivens, warning not to worship forms in themselves but to ground decisions in the ability of the form to execute social-action missions. In newly Communist Cuba, Julio Garcia Espinosa wrote "For an Imperfect Cinema" (1969), calling for a less commercialized, ultimately more participatory art form. In Argentina, Fernando Solanas and Octavio Getino wrote their manifesto, "Towards a Third Cinema" (1969), imagining a decolonizing cinema for revolution. These manifestos often grew out of furious discussions within political parties, at conferences and film festivals. This spirit of rebellion, of telling truth to power, of telling truths of the marginalized, of using the camera to reveal what was routinely ignored, also inspired anticolonial and postcolonial filmmakers, and launched movements now familiar as the "new cinemas" of Asia, Africa, and Latin America. Those filmmakers' work in turn inspired filmmakers throughout what was then called the "First World," who hoped that their own work would contribute to anticolonial or social justice work. A 1968 film exhibition in Paris, provocatively called "Cinema as a Gun" and showcasing anticommercial work in Latin America, also engaged filmmakers from around the world in discussions on the purpose of cinema.

The early stirrings of what became these furious conversations filtered into the experience of Temaner and Quinn through the University of Chicago's liberal arts programs. In founding Kartemquin, they both saw themselves as independent intellectuals, and they imagined cinema as a way to explore previously unarticulated social realities. They imagined themselves less as activists than as researchers for social justice and social change. They imagined combining ethnographic methods, including long-term observation; sociological research into the larger issues and patterns touched on by the subject matter; and a filmmaker's search for characters, story, and location—all processes intertwined. Filmmaking, for them, was a mode of research into social behaviors. "Our tool, cinematic social inquiry, is a continuous process wherein filmmaking and research become identical and the natural result of the process is a presentation," they wrote. The goal was to create a document—a film—that was rich enough in insights to be used for a variety of purposes, including social reform, because it was not advocacy but insight.[2]

CINEMATIC SOCIAL INQUIRY

The goal of cinematic social inquiry was developed in a creative relationship between the founders. Gordon Quinn, in his undergraduate career at the University of Chicago, had produced a senior thesis, "*Cinéma Vérité* in a Democracy." The work was astonishingly prescient. In it, he drew upon the work of John Dewey, who among his many achievements had once been a professor at the University of Chicago.

Dewey's *The Public and Its Problems* captured Quinn's attention, although it had nothing to do with film or even art. It was a book of political philosophy, which challenged the notion that in a highly technologized, industrial society, democratic institutions were better or even necessarily run by experts and representatives than with input and participation from the general public. In the book, Dewey argues for the centrality in democracy of informally constituted publics, formed around commonly experienced problems in order to address them.

Quinn also was impressed by how extensively, in other works, Dewey addressed the role of art, as a synthesizer and intensifier of the experiences that can empower people as members of publics. In *Art as Experience*, Dewey argued that it is the relationship of both artist and user to an art project that creates that critical experience, making art a rich contribution to community. "The real work of art is the building up of an integral experience out of the interaction of organic and environmental conditions and energies," he wrote. He also did not want to draw a line between "fine" art, circus performances, gardening, and cooking. Art could make reality more real, rich, full, and actionable. And it could help people imagine something better than today's reality while doing so.

As a twenty-year-old, Quinn was also excited by this new kind of filmmaking people were loosely calling cinema verité as a facilitator of public-making conversations, more immediate and intimate an experience than reading an essay, and a step closer to the face-to-face meeting experience that mobilizes publics. Like Dewey, he imagined the arts playing a vital role in democratic political life. He imagined filmmakers as having a responsibility to help shape public life. In this work, he was mentored by Temaner, a graduate student at the University of Chicago whom he met in French class. They shared a passionate curiosity about this innovative form of cinema verité.

He was particularly curious about the possibility of documentary film documenting social reality. He focused on its ability to chronicle behavior, drawing upon phenomenological philosopher Merleau-Ponty. Among the filmmakers he drew upon for his undergraduate thesis's argument were artists who were cutting-edge and not yet part of the canon: French sociologist Edgar Morin (as codirector of the pathbreaking *Chronicle of a Summer* [1961]), French filmmaker Jean Rouch both for his work in France and for his work in collaboration with Africans, the Russian revolutionary Dziga Vertov, the French avant-garde filmmaker Chris Marker, Emile de Antonio (*Point of Order* [1964]), and the now-iconic cluster of cinema verité pioneers in the US: the Maysles brothers, Donn Pennebaker, Robert Drew, and Richard Leacock. He referred to work at the National Film Board of Canada, which was undertaking experiments in collaborative filmmaking with subjects dubbed Challenge for Change, often using cinema verité (which the Canadians called "Candid Eye," a term that never caught on). He believed socially oriented cinema verité was destined for TV, because TV was a ubiquitous medium.

Decades before the field openly raised issues such as documentary ethics or impact engagement, Quinn addressed the filmmaker's responsibility to the participant, and the challenges of using a film to help form a community through conversation. Finally, and presaging his later activism on public access and public TV, he noted the constraints of commercial TV, which is wedded to scripted productions and subject to control by network executives: "This centralization of control of the news media is obviously dangerous to a democracy, particularly when the networks feel that their primary duty is to resolve issues, rather than to define problems." He even proposed, two years before the creation of today's public TV, "It would be wise to learn from the experience of the Canadians and British who have, in their state-supported television networks, an outlet for a medium of communication as essential to a democracy as cinéma vérité."

"Cinematic social inquiry" turned out to be a terrible business model, in practice. But it was a compelling idea and a driving motivation for Kartemquin Films over generations. It was attractive to others as well. The acclaimed Northwestern University sociologist Howard Becker would sometimes bring his graduate students to Kartemquin's offices to brainstorm with the filmmakers about this technologically enhanced, ethnographic approach to social inquiry.

This was also the era of "film culture," in which pre-internet students turned to on-campus film societies for the heady experience of international high culture. "Film culture" was a rite-of-passage experience for students, who could move beyond their own parochial experiences and be challenged by complex art in a form they had usually until then only encountered as commercial entertainment. These were not just movies but an introduction to mind-altering other realities. Releases—of the latest films by European masters such as Federico Fellini, Ingmar Bergman, and Pier Paolo Pasolini; of world-culture artists such as Satyajit Ray, Alejandro Jodorowsky, Yasujirō Ozu; of behind-the-Iron-Curtain artists like Jerzy Skolimowski, Dušan Makavejev, and Sergei Parajanov—vied for attention with retrospectives, including of the famed Soviet early cinema (later repressed by Stalin), the Italian neorealists, and American genres such as film noir. Quinn, Temaner, and others belonged to a University of Chicago club, Doc Films, which boasted of being the oldest student film group in the US. In it, they not only saw the classics of film culture and the latest festival films but also programmed and used them as inspiration for their own.

The beginning of Quinn's college career was also a moment of consolidating television's grip on American popular culture. While still a tawdry also-ran to the more prestigious film culture, television had become a ubiquitous element in households and daily routine. The number of households with a TV set grew from almost nothing after World War II to almost 90 percent by 1960. By the time Quinn graduated, almost everyone in America had a TV set. They were usually tuned to one of three national networks, which had relationships with local stations; stations aired local programs outside the prime-time (morning and evening) network viewing slots. Network lowest-common-denominator programming, and news produced in close step with political elites, were uninteresting to college students like Quinn.

But the networks also produced expensive, polished, long-form documentaries, sometimes cautiously addressing world affairs as part of their stations' trade-off for getting access to public airwaves, or spectrum. These documentaries concerned everything from corruption among federal contractors to modern poetry, Mardi Gras, strip-mining, and urban development. The network-ready documentaries of Wolper Productions were nicely calibrated to the tone of network news more generally. They projected, as scholar Joshua Glick noted, mostly a reassuring portrayal of a healthy democracy, while also encoding conflicts within the liberal politics of the time. It was these documentaries that cinema verité pioneers Robert Drew, Richard Leacock, the Maysles brothers, and D. A. Pennebaker attempted to disrupt, with their work for ABC. Last-place in audience ratings, ABC was the network outlier willing to take a risk on independent filmmakers.

Television was both an agent and example of cultural conformity, for Quinn, Temaner, Blumenthal, and other college students. Indeed, Federal Communication Commission chair Newton Minow would decry its shallowness and crass entertainment offerings, saying in a famous speech, "I invite each of you to sit down in front of your television set when your station goes on the air and stay there for a day without a book, without a magazine, without a newspaper, without a profit and loss sheet or a rating book to distract you. Keep your eyes glued to that set until the station signs off. I can assure you that what you will observe is a vast wasteland."

Television would also eventually present some opportunities for these young filmmakers. Although public TV was still in the future, educational channels existed, typically starved for programming. Quinn seized the chance to make episodes for a show, *Student Journal,* on the local educational TV station, WTTW. Another student, Larry Buchman, who would become a broadcast network journalist, ran the show. Quinn chronicled stories such as a high school jazz band, a University of Chicago Russian exchange student, and Sonny Liston's visit to a gym on Chicago's West Side. Eventually, the public television that came into existence in 1967 with federal legislation would become Kartemquin's most dependable distribution ally for decades, and a site of activism for a stronger public resource for public knowledge and action.

In Chicago, the moment in which Quinn, Temaner, Blumenthal, and others in their network were growing into their expertise was also one of profound social turmoil growing out of large social forces. The decades-long Great Migration, during which millions of Black Southerners left the brutally racist South for what they hoped would be a more welcoming environment elsewhere in America, ended for many in Chicago. Their arrival profoundly affected Chicago culture and geography. Maxwell Street, on the near West Side, which Quinn was to focus on as an apprentice for one of his first film projects, was a vibrant site of mixed and melding cultures drawn from the South. The Chicago blues style, an anchor of the Chicago music scene, was drawn from rich Southern musical traditions. The migrants and their children faced serious challenges, in a city where racism structured reality and realities reinforced racism. Richard J. Daley, a Democratic Party boss and Irish Catholic raised in Chicago's Bridgeport neighborhood, became mayor in 1955, and he went to work creating many ways to formalize the city's segregation. By the mid-1960s, the civil rights movement had reached northward to challenge that segregation.

Chicago also saw other signs of ferment during Quinn's college career. With the Vietnam War heating up, the draft was generating ever more demonstrations and protests, as well as waves of conscientious objectors. Quinn himself was at risk of being drafted, and he used the protection of his college-student status self-consciously. Student protests focused on antiwar activities, which inevitably also focused student attention, including Quinn's, on Cold War geopolitics more generally.

The philosophy that would shape Kartemquin up to the present day was thus forged in the tumultuous years of protest and action to expand citizens' rights and challenge Cold War geopolitics. Kartemquin's philosophy rejected the goals of vanguardist revolution, i.e., a small group trying to trigger change with radical and often violent actions. It avoided sectarianism, or rigid ideological or party affiliation. Rather, it found in a Deweyan framework a commitment to trust the capacities of audiences to see complex realities and act upon them together.

The cinematic style that Kartemquin established evolved over time, but it has been anchored to the goal of leveraging storytelling for public formation. In a 1981 retrospective of Kartemquin work at the School of the Art Institute's Film Center—a premier destination for film culture—curator Barbara Scharres's astute comments could serve as a summation of the Kartemquin aesthetic. She writes, "The films do offer emphatically the philosophical and filmic conviction that people are to be respected at all costs, and in that they are radical films." She notes that there is a "profound humanism" in the style, seen in the rapport between filmmaker and subject, in which no one pretends the filmmaker isn't there and the camera represents the eyes of the filmmaker interacting with the subject. The filmmakers listen well: "No one is ever cut off . . . People's ideas are given the duration needed for completion." Kartemquin's films are in "partnership with the subjects of their films in achieving political and human goals . . . They have chosen not to victimize anyone for the sake of a cause."[3]

3 Cinematic Social Inquiry, 1962–1970

Kartemquin's first years featured intersections with characters such as cinema verité pioneer Richard Leacock, legendary Chicago author Studs Terkel, and Bob Dylan. They were made possible by connections with Chicago-area universities and by commissioned work. Protests and the Vietnam War affected their choices of what to film and where to work. As their first work out of college, the Kartemquin founders finally pursued their lofty dreams of being in the business of ethnographic artistry, relying on cinema verité approaches to gain insight into social change. And they found that they couldn't make a living. But in the process, as political unrest and protest movements grew, they also found community in left-leaning filmmakers and issues.

The founding of Kartemquin came after a catch-as-catch-can apprenticeship in filmmaking for Quinn and his friends. He had no sooner gotten to the University of Chicago than he joined Doc Films, the club started in 1947 by students who were World War II veterans. One of their first projects together had been a documentary on housing problems of veterans. But by the time Quinn got there, the fascination was with auteur theory and film culture, including studying the great masters of early Russian cinema, Italian neorealism, and the French New Wave. He and others, including graduate student Gerald Temaner, wanted to revive the interest in documentary film so evident in the club's founding. Quinn organized film series to showcase documentary classics in the city-symphony tradition that had flourished in the 1930s. and to explore cinema verité. He was taken completely by Joyce Chopra and Richard Leacock's *Happy Mother's Day* (1963), now a cinema verité classic, about a North Dakota family that had birthed quintuplets. The parents become instant sensations on television news, but they still faced the iron cruelties of poverty. ABC had contracted the filmmakers to make a television segment on the event; *Happy Mother's Day* looked coolly into the terrifying challenge the farm-family parents faced raising five new children, and how the town fathers exploited them for publicity. ABC recut the footage into something executives thought more suitable for broadcast.

Thanks to Temaner's connections in Montreal, Quinn went to the Montreal Film Festival, with his soon-to-be college girlfriend Carol Brightman. (Brightman broke up with Quinn after she left for New York the next year, and went on to be a noted feminist writer; they stayed friends.) They both were entranced with *Lonely Boy* (1963), a Canadian cinema verité film that pioneered the rock star profile genre. They loved its intimacy, sense of immediacy, and the camerawork and editing. At a coffee shop, an affable Englishman approached them—"probably because Carol was tall and blonde," Quinn later surmised. It was Richard Leacock, the cinema verité filmmaker whose *Happy Mother's Day* they had both so admired.

They were both stunned to find out he hadn't liked *Lonely Boy*. He argued that the film looked down on Paul Anka, the teen pop star, snidely cutting between a scene of Anka doodling out a tune on the piano and his manager's claim that Anka was one of the world's greatest composers since Beethoven. "I never forgot that lesson," Quinn said. "Ricky said you should never make a film about someone you don't care about or respect. And at Kartemquin, we make movies where we can care about the people whose stories we're telling." More fundamentally, Quinn's experiences at the Montreal Film Festival convinced him of a career choice: "I thought, 'Now I know what I want to do with my life—I want to make documentaries.'"

Quinn and Temaner also convinced the university to pay for some actual filmmaking, by setting up a subunit of Doc Films. The university sometimes hired them to record events, via the film workshop they had started on campus. After one of them, Temaner and Quinn held onto the camera they used long enough to catch a major moment in Chicago grassroots organizing, using both leftover stock and some donated by friends. With others, including fellow students Stan Karter, Carol Brightman, and Danny Auerbach, as well as Mike Shea, they caught a unique moment, which would become a film almost fifty years later.

In 1963, Chicago erupted with protests about the separate and unequal treatment of Black students in the public school system, headed by a staunchly segregationist superintendent. Parents and children organized a one-day boycott; two hundred thousand students, almost half the student population, stayed home and tens of thousands demonstrated. Temaner and Quinn filmed the boycott, a decision with one immediate outcome. They sold nonexclusive rights to the footage to Canadian filmmakers doing a program on grassroots organizing, and then had a bitter awakening about institutions; the entire $500 payment had been taken by the university's communications unit. But this footage eventually became material for a 2017 half-hour Kartemquin film, in which the original footage was supplemented with current-day interviews with participants, *'63 Boycott*.

Temaner and Quinn also convinced an alumnus to donate funding for a film about the University of Chicago's undergraduate unit, *The College* (1964). (The Paul Butterfield Blues Band makes a brief appearance.) Temaner brought in Vern Zimmerman, an experimental filmmaker who later became a Hollywood scriptwriter and director. He took the film in an experimental direction. Local photographer Mike Shea (who later was director of photography on one of Zimmerman's Hollywood films) did some shooting, to get practice as he transitioned to documentary production. Temaner brought a style of filmmaking that he eventually named "cinematic social inquiry." Zimmermann tried to claim authorship and copyright, which Temaner protested; administrators agreed with Temaner. But administrators also hated the film, which focused on student protest. Nonetheless, it drew a large local audience, especially of students.

Still as a student, Quinn took on part-time work with Mike Shea, a picture-story photographer turned documentarian. He did sound work on Shea's passion project, the 1965 *And This Is Free*, a film about the lively blues scene on Maxwell Street in downtown Chicago. A teenage Mike Bloomfield, soon to be a music superstar for his sensational guitar work and promotion of the blues, was music liaison. Howard Alk, one of the founders of Second City, edited the film, beginning a two-year editing mentorship for Quinn. Maxwell Street was the beating heart of the Great Migration in Chicago. The film still communicates an electric energy of the weekend market, where immigrants, hustlers, Delta blues singers, and gospel groups commingled. With Shea, Quinn tried to convince the local educational TV station, WTTW, to carry *And This Is Free*, but the effort failed. It was not shown on the public TV station until almost a half-century later, long after Kartemquin had become a leading Midwest cultural institution.

Gordon Quinn participated in other ways in the social ferment at the University of Chicago. The university was located in a neighborhood that had become increasingly Black and crowded, as the Great Migration brought many people north. Students discovered that the university owned segregated apartment buildings in the area; Quinn tried to record an interaction with a segregationist landlord, but the device he had hidden in a student's purse failed. At the ensuing 1962 interracial sit-in protest, joined by Quinn and his friend and future photographer / filmmaker Danny Lyon, then college-freshman Bernie Sanders spoke. Their paths would cross again, when footage caught by Quinn became useful to the 2016 Sanders campaign.

Quinn attempted to stay in college, looking to avoid conscription for the Vietnam War. The university finally forced him to graduate at the end of his fifth year, in 1965. He was classified 1A, the most likely to be sent to war, after a failed attempt to win conscientious objector status. He was never called up to serve, though—possibly, he thinks, because he had put up so many obstacles and delays to the process that they recognized him as a troublemaker. (About half of all draftees were not called up.)

After college, he followed Howard Alk to New York, as his assistant editor. Alk had owned a nightclub in Chicago, after leaving Second City, and still knew many musicians. It was through those connections that Quinn had a close call with early fame, and also was instrumental in finding the director for the film *Dont Look Back* (1967), about Bob Dylan. Alk had connections to Dylan, who wanted a film for his upcoming European tour.

Their first thought for a cinematographer was Mike Shea, but he, a jazz buff, disliked Dylan's music. Quinn then recalled meeting Richard Leacock, and cold-called him from a phone booth.

Leacock welcomed Quinn, Alk and his wife Joan, and Dylan's manager Albert Grossman genially, and showed them some films. But it soon became clear that he thought they were talking about Dylan Thomas, and that he didn't even know who Bob Dylan was. They had to explain that liking Dylan's music was a *sine qua non* for the job. Leacock turned them over to his partner, D. A. (Penny) Pennebaker, one of Robert Drew's original team at ABC. Pennebaker couldn't believe his luck; he loved Dylan. The result, his film *Dont Look Back*, remains an icon of the form.

Quinn was on the edge of joining the team, but the process stalled until he took another job, with Mike Shea. Then Alk called him back to help edit Murray Lerner's film *Festival* (1967), about three years of the Newport Folk Festival, at one of which Bob Dylan had rocked the folk world by using electric instruments, with members of the Paul Butterfield Blues Band backing him. The work turned into eighteen intensive months of training in sound and editing.

HOME FOR LIFE (1966)

Jerry Temaner, now an all-but-dissertation philosophy student and ever in search of ways to combine academics and filmmaking, had won a $15,000 contract (almost $150,000 in 2023 money) to make a cinema verité "social inquiry" about aging in a Chicago seniors home, with funding from a donor to the home. The film was to be the showcase of a fundraising gala for the place, which was widely recognized as one of the best of its kind. Quinn took him up on the invitation to work on it, moving back from New York, and they became codirectors of *Home for Life* (1966)—Quinn on camera and editing, Temaner on sound. When Temaner took a job as a sabbatical substitute for the noted documentary scholar Jack Ellis in Northwestern University's film program, they also drew on Northwestern's equipment and Northwestern students' talents. As well, Temaner's friend from Doc Films at the University of Chicago, Jerry Blumenthal, worked briefly as camera assistant on the film.

Closely following the innovations of Pennebaker and Leacock, Quinn was fascinated by the technical challenges of the kind of filming he wanted to do. Cameras at the time were ponderous, and if you wanted sync sound, you had to manually connect the camera and sound recorder. Kartemquinites, like many cinema verité pioneers, were tinkerers. Quinn was envious of the pricey, $20,000 camera Shea acquired. This was a revolutionary design from the Leacock-Pennebaker team, which was portable and allowed crystal-controlled, wireless synchronized or sync sound.

They purchased instead a refitted Auricon newsreel-style camera, at almost a tenth of the price. University of Chicago physics doctoral student Danny Auerbach rigged a crystal-controlled, battery-run power supply, lighter than the Leacock-Pennebaker version. Then Quinn went to New York, and convinced Albert Maysles to sell him a short finder-lens, which was critical to balancing the camera on the shoulder. Auerbach's innovation, lighter than the original but less elegant, was never patented or marketed. The camera filmed most of Kartemquin's first film, *Home for Life*. After its retirement, it was resurrected in time for the fiftieth anniversary gala and installed in Quinn's office—an homage to Al Maysles, who had his original camera permanently on display. (It was also featured, with Quinn's technical explanation, in a five-minute Kartemquin short on YouTube, *Kartemquin's First Camera* [2012] by Black filmmaker and eventual Triibe cofounder Morgan Elise Johnson, an intern at the time.)

Portable sync sound helped them film richer cinema verité scenes, but it didn't solve an ongoing problem: They only started filming when they saw something worth filming, and that was always after something had started. Temaner began recording sound—far cheaper—before the camera started running the expensive 16mm film, to provide material for later editing. Eventually, Jerry Blumenthal adopted and refined the technique; viewers would be convinced they had seen the scene from the beginning.

For this first work, *Home for Life*, they chose to film in a highly rated seniors facility, with the goal of exploring questions of how Americans treat their elders. The Drexel home was, as an administrator recalled at a 1992 reunion, "an early provider of the now common meals on wheels service, communal living and residential pet therapy. It was the first to establish vacation programs for the vulnerable and frail elderly living in long-term care facilities, and was the center for many studies that contributed to better understanding the problems and needs of the elderly and their resolutions." The facility wanted them to film, confident that they had a top-line home. The makers wanted to depict a high-quality home, to allow an inquiry into the structural problem—what are society's solutions for eldercare—rather than an exposé. In that film, they operationalized for the first time the concept of cinematic social inquiry. The project of making a record of social inquiry in the film dictated their filming choices:

> We did not pretend that we were filming through a one-way mirror. Sometimes we would stand back and record the intensity of an argument almost unobserved by the participants, but at other times we would move in and participate in the argument ourselves. In a number of situations, the cameraman or soundman initiated responses. In a few cases, we modified the situation by arranging meetings between people who did not ordinarily meet, or by arranging that a topic of interest to us be discussed at a residents' meeting. Twice, we showed people films of themselves or others and filmed their responses. In all of these cases when they were used, we included these stimuli in the screen presentation of the situation.

They admitted that this method was not a social science "case study," and that they were acting as "social artists": "Cinematic social inquiry . . . is a way of trying to assure that the basic meanings and values which are the stuff of the maker's imagination, out of which a work's form and matter emerge, are primarily derived from the situation. Further, as you surrender yourselves to the situation, the situation surrenders its meanings to you."

Temaner and Quinn filmed many residents, but in editing selected two people to follow over a month as they entered the home: Bertha Weinberg, who arrives with her son after having lived for years in her son's and daughter-in-law's home, and William Rocklin, who reluctantly opts for the home after his wife's death, knowing he is increasingly disabled. (The filmmakers believed they were deluged with material, shooting at a less than 4:1 ratio, but today's ratios can be 1,000:1.) The two elders had vastly different issues in adapting to their new environment. The film is a series of closely observed, uncommented vignettes, often framed by the tersest of narration by an anonymous narrator: "After lunch." "To confront old age, life requires medical support." This sparse use of narration ran

Figure 2. Home for Life showed meetings of the elderly with administrators as an exercise of public life within the eldercare facility. Source: Kartemquin Archives.

against the advice of the filmmakers' academic advisory board, which was demanding explanations. Quinn remembers telling them, drawing on his reading of Dewey, "Everyone is sophisticated about interpreting human behavior; it's what makes us human. Let the viewer experience the scene and they will come to their own nuanced conclusion."

The new arrivals encounter an enormous staff of doctors, nurses, social workers, aides, and fellow residents. Residents participate, sometimes cantankerously, in committee meetings with the senior staff. The staff's care for their psychological, social, and physical welfare is manifest; so is the pain and frustration of being old and sidelined by society.

The film went majestically overbudget. The codirectors quickly ran out of money—eventually the film cost perhaps five times the funding—but fortunately, both Temaner and Quinn had other work to pay the bills. The 82-minute film even today holds attention, for its close and dispassionate eye on the process. The confused-but-cooperative mom, the bossy daughter-in-law, the new roommate, the bustling staff—all interact in ways that provide a critical and provocative view of this solution to care for the aging.

The final version was launched at the senior home's annual gala. Perhaps a fundraiser was not the optimal venue for the film's debut. "At the big fundraiser, the board of directors was absolutely horrified," recalled Quinn, "because the film is honest about what it's like. They tried to have the film destroyed. They wanted it never to be released." What saved the film in the end was the support of the home's director and senior staff. They believed that it was important and valuable. They were convinced that anyone in their field would recognize quality care. They understood, Quinn recalled, the difference between an analysis of the institution of eldercare and an attack on their own business.

"That was our first experience with finding out that not everybody wants to hear the truth," Quinn recalled ruefully. Kartemquin was also lucky that, years later, the Drexel home reverted ownership of the film to the company.

Their "cinematic social inquiry" work was not intended for theatrical consumption so much as for public knowledge. It was used for that purpose. In the case of *Home for Life*, the administrators of the eldercare home changed some of their practices after viewing the film, and the film was shown at conferences of anthropologists and social scientists, as well as winning festival awards and theatrical venues. At the 1992 reunion, an administrator noted that it was "used extensively throughout the country to train other professionals, boards, students, and volunteers."

Although its primary audience was not the general public, the film caught the attention of a rising local film critic who was the filmmakers' own age, Roger Ebert. He praised it to the skies. "Their cameras allow participants to speak for themselves—but they also allow the observer to see a great deal that is not spoken aloud," he noted. Another Chicago notable, the author Studs Terkel, whose ethnographic work chronicled the realities of working life in America, loved it. (He eventually became a stalwart Kartemquin ally, as well as a hearty supporter of *In These Times*.) He wrote: "*Home For Life* is the most moving and gently penetrating film I have seen, dealing with the theme of old age in our society. It is, in a sense, a hymn to life; yet, it presents a challenge to us to face up to one of the most pressing problems of our day—our attitude towards the aged. In its own way, it is a work of art rather than an artful work." *Variety* called the film "extraordinarily moving."

Quinn took a short leave of absence. Howard Alk had called him to Woodstock, New York, to help edit with Bob Dylan on *Eat the Document* (1972). The film was a record of Dylan's 1966 European tour, a year after the one chronicled in *Dont Look Back*. It too was directed by Pennebaker. Its editing was delayed by Dylan's motorcycle accident, but on his recovery, Dylan was determined to edit it himself with Alk. It was Quinn's job to take the shots that Dylan had selected and edit them into coherence, at his direction: "It was kind of amazing, because Dylan had a very powerful mind. At first you would think, this doesn't make any sense. But if you worked with it a little, it would." But Quinn had to leave the project, because he had a draft hearing scheduled; he had decided he would go to Canada if necessary. He left, possibly, one trace on *Eat the Document*. A widely believed rumor says that Dylan invoked Quinn's name when he wrote "Quinn the Eskimo (The Mighty Quinn)." The film, originally commissioned by ABC, was ultimately rejected as incomprehensible and only shown occasionally by Dylan, although Martin Scorsese used scenes from it in his 2005 documentary *No Direction Home*.

THE TEAM FORMS

With their first film complete, Temaner and Quinn finally got around to forming the film company they had been talking about, along with another University of Chicago alumnus and photographer, Stan Karter, who had also been in the Doc Films club. They settled on the name Kartemquin by pulling letters from each name, selecting the combination to echo the name of one of the iconic films of film culture, *Potemkin* (1925). Their original agreement specified that they would make films "of the sort we have agreed upon," and that their partnership was "not primarily to maintain Kartemquin as a financial venture but to maintain and develop it as a company producing this sort of film." Karter's association ended quickly, however, and he went on to other work, including graphic design and car repair.

Temaner and Quinn got an office in a southside Chicago building in Hyde Park. The building was largely occupied by doctors. Quinn was fascinated by the doctors' magazines he found in the trash, and made a small collection of them, little knowing they would become the raw materials for collages featured in a Kartemquin film critical of commercial consolidation of medical care, *The Chicago Maternity Center Story* (1976).

Jerry Blumenthal soon joined Kartemquin, abandoning graduate school when Temaner convinced him to join in 1967. He had just finished his first film (with other students), a short documentary called "Shulie." The film profiled a charismatic, obstreperous art student named Shulamith Firestone—long before her later feminist fame. (The film became a kind of underground success over the years, partly because Firestone disliked it so much; Blumenthal himself diplomatically chose never to distribute it, in deference to her concerns, but it circulated in many unauthorized versions.) Blumenthal was also already well under the philosophical tent that Temaner and Quinn had erected. In one of his student papers, he had written that "cinema-verite is a way of using film making as a process, or method, of inquiry into human affairs . . . film making becomes a kind of research whose aim is find out something new about the subject chosen; something that can be discovered by the film maker only in the act of film making . . . and by the audience only in the act of viewing." Among the filmmakers he mentioned were Flaherty, Eisenstein, Grierson, Leacock, and Rouch, demonstrating a solid understanding of film culture. He also specifically cited Dewey's *The Public and Its Problems*. Blumenthal, who had a wry, sharp sense of humor, later wrote that he was happy with his decision "to dedicate himself to a life of penury & pleasure."

Quinn later said, "I learned how to be Jewish when I encountered edgy, urban Jewish humor through Temaner and Jerry." Quinn had been raised with limited exposure to Jewish culture, except for a brief stint in Sunday school, in segregated, suburban Virginia outside Washington, DC. His mother was a homemaker active in community organizations, and his father had leaned left and secular. His father had worked in the Roosevelt administration's Department of Labor, but earlier membership in the Communist Party brought too-close scrutiny during the McCarthy era, and he left government to start a direct-mail business. Quinn had early rejected Jewish religious education, to his mother's distress and his father's approval. Quinn now relished his introduction to distinctively Jewish culture in his work with Temaner and Blumenthal.

Blumenthal's big dream had been to be a poet, and he saw himself as a creator first. One of his mentees, Jim Fetterley, remembered, "Gordon's take was that art is for the people. Jerry was first of all really into art." Blumenthal also brought a working-class anger at wealth, privilege, and pretention. His combination of artistic vision, emotional immediacy, and working-class outrage combined interestingly with Quinn's middle-class, analytic, quietly stubborn approach. Over many years, they melded into a sibling-like team.

Another early arrival was Jim Morrissette. Morrissette's family had moved to Chicago when he was a child, so his father could take a professorial job at the University of Chicago. Morrissette, who had a passion for the technical side of filmmaking, had finished his undergrad career at what was then University of Illinois at Chicago Circle (now University of Illinois at Chicago), and then gone to work for Temaner, who told him he had to meet Quinn. He was another one of those technical tinkerers who were crucial to early cinema verité. He recalled being in awe of Quinn's cleverness. For instance, the group provided crews for medical industrial filming, but this meant filming in a hospital with gruesome fluorescent lighting. Quinn worked with a sheet metal company to rerig a lighting stand, so that it could hold a bank of fluorescent lights to match overhead lighting and provide targeted light. With correction in postproduction, this avoided flicker and offered warm brightness. "And we never broke a tube," Morrissette recalled, because the portable stand was padded with foamcore. Commercial equipment providers later built on his prototype. Morrissette was hooked. He worked episodically with Kartemquin over the next two decades, before coming on full-time in 2000 and staying for the next twenty years.

This small group with big ideas was sustained with commercial work—not just filmmaking but also equipment rental, equipment procurement and installation, and freelancing. Kartemquinites more often worked for other small companies than they competed with them. They worked with Chuck Olin, with Mike Shea, and with Mike Gray. Gray ran a production house with an adman, Lars Hedman. During the increasingly politically turbulent years of the 1960s, Olin, Shea, and Gray joined forces as The

Film Group, with Bill Cottle as legal and accounting support and sometime involvement from Hedman. Gray invited Howard Alk to join them; Alk had an off-and-on-again relationship with heroin but had unparalleled editing skills and an impressive set of connections. All of them were work friends of Quinn, Temaner, and Blumenthal.

POLITICAL POLARIZATION

Everyone's politics, and particularly that of Gray, were moving steadily to the left, with the increasing polarization of the times and partly as a result of long, passionate discussions with Quinn and the openly leftist Howard Alk. Chicago was a city in political turmoil, the site of major riots between 1965 (the year of the murder of Malcolm X) and 1968. The Black Panther Party, with a Marxist ideology and with class struggle as an organizing principle, had a Chicago chapter within two years of its 1966 founding in Oakland, California. The National Council of La Raza (now UnidosUS), which grew out of organizations representing Mexican Americans / Chicanos, by 1968 had offices in Chicago. The Young Lords Organization, growing out of a Chicago street gang and with a strong Puerto Rican base, were particularly vibrant in late 1960s. White, working-class, Marxist organizations also arose, including the Young Patriots (from Appalachian migrant families) and Rising Up Angry (working-class youth on the North Side).

As leader of the Chicago chapter of the Panthers, twenty-year-old Fred Hampton put forward a vision that embraced them all: a "rainbow coalition." (Much later, Jesse Jackson borrowed this term, without Hampton's political meaning, for his movement.) He argued that various groups shared common concerns: poverty, government corruption, access to basic rights such as voting. His proposed Rainbow Coalition was, he said in 1968, a movement led by Black youth that respected "ethnic communities of all kinds." Class struggle united them. The coalition, which lasted after Hampton's 1969 murder until 1974, but whose effects have rippled down into the present, addressed police brutality, political corruption, and racist and classist urban development.

The decisive moment in which The Film Group sharply shifted to the left for its own authorial work was the 1968 Democratic Convention, in the wake of Robert Kennedy's murder in June. The convention was a brutal moment of confrontation both within and beyond the Democratic Party. President Lyndon Johnson's announcement that he would not run for reelection and would initiate peace talks with the Vietnamese—in the midst of increasingly violent opposition to the Vietnam War and deep divisions in the Democratic Party over his support for civil rights and poverty programs—threw the primaries into a fierce contest. Robert Kennedy had been a liberal front-runner, supported by anti Vietnam War activists who did not back the more progressive candidates Eugene McCarthy and George McGovern. His votes were unallocated when he was assassinated, and McCarthy and McGovern supporters argued over them. Hubert Humphrey inherited Johnson's delegates, making him the insider front-runner, but without some crucial support.

Inside the amphitheater the convention was dominated by bare-knuckled racial and pro / antiwar politics, while outside unfolded a bloody scene of chaos, which was exactly what everyone expected to happen. Chicago's Mayor Daley, committed to notoriously racist policies in Chicago and regarding the convention as a chance to showcase his leadership of a major city, ruthlessly shut down dissent. He faced not only left political leaders like Tom Hayden of Students for a Democratic Society, as well as ten thousand incoming antiwar protesters from throughout the US, but the performatively leftist group the Yippies, including Abbie Hoffman and Jerry Rubin. Yippies used ridicule, scatology, and other challenges to social mores to gain attention; they threatened to clog the toilets at O'Hare airport, and to lace the amphitheater's water with LSD. This all vastly raised Daley's paranoia. Demonstrators were banned from the event, and refused a permit to congregate. The amphitheater was ringed with barbed wire. Not only the Chicago police's notorious "Red Squad"—a unit that targeted protesters—but FBI and CIA operatives were called in. Black community activists, including from the South Side's powerful street gang Blackstone Rangers, were arrested.

Tens of thousands of protesters banned from the convention gathered downtown, in Grant Park among other places. Among them were Gordon Quinn and his girlfriend, Meg Gerken. Quinn had met Gerken at the University of Chicago. Reintroduced in New York by mutual friends, they both migrated back to Chicago. Quinn and Gerken weren't filming. Quinn had been filming protests for years, slinging a hugely heavy 16mm camera on his shoulder. This time, they had decided to be part of the protesting crowd. Gray and his associates were filming. Quinn and Gerken also hosted demonstrators at their home, including, accidentally, members of two different factions of the left-wing filmmaking collective New York Newsreel.

Gray's filming of the protests around the convention turned him into a radical. Hedman, always more conservative, eventually left for Los Angeles and Hollywood work. But Gray stayed, although he eventually also went to LA, cowriting the screenplay for the antinuclear movie *The China Syndrome* (1979). That film built on his own experiences shooting commercials in nuclear power plants, and on his training as an engineer.

What Gray had captured, and what galvanized him, was some of the intense, aggressive police brutality that caused delegates inside the convention to denounce it from the floor. Senator Abe Ribicoff called it "Gestapo tactics"; Daley's response, according to lip-readers, was "Fuck you, you Jew son of a bitch." The chair of the Colorado delegation called it "police state terror." National media figures, some of whom were roughed up themselves, also decried it. The police and National Guard, who outnumbered the protesters more than two to one, rampaged openly, and flooded the entire downtown area with tear gas.

The convention had other effects as well. It triggered a decision by José Cha Cha Jimenez, leader of the Young Lords, to join other groups in the Rainbow Coalition being led by the Black Panthers. And of course it increased the attention focused on all such efforts by the FBI's Cointelpro program, which often worked locally in conjunction with Chicago police.

Quinn and Gerken spent a day of the protests downtown, among other things stopping to chat with Chicago-based filmmaker Haskell Wexler, a fellow leftist who was filming material he would use in *Medium Cool* (1969). (Wexler's verité eye was eventually highly prized in Hollywood, where he won two Academy Awards, although he never left behind his fierce working-class activism.) On their way home, they were caught in the clouds of tear gas floating over the highway from the Yippie encampment in Lincoln Park; along with many other drivers, they had to pull over because they could no longer see. Weirdly, as a National Guard Jeep passed them, the Jeep stopped to leave behind one sole gas-masked Guard.

The young Guard, surrounded by angry, shouting protesters and no doubt terrified, cocked his rifle and made to fire. The protesters got back into their tear-gas-filled cars, to wait it out and eventually go home. When Meg and Gerken got back to their apartment building, National Guardsmen were taking sniper positions on the roof.

Gray and his colleagues decided, in the wake of that eye-opening experience, to quickly make a self-consciously revolutionary film: *American Revolution 2* (1969). Gray brought Howard Alk back from New York to coedit and codirect. The film used the violence at the convention as a moment to focus attention on endemic violence against Blacks in Chicago, and the formation of an unprecedented alliance between a white, working-class group, the Young Patriots, and the local Black Panthers, led by Fred Hampton. Alk had the contacts to the Panthers; indeed, it was after Alk's screening of *American Revolution 2* for the Panthers that Hampton publicly adopted the phrase "rainbow coalition." One scene, in which Panther Bob Lee features, showing the young white group their common concerns (grasping landlords, police brutality, bad schools), is particularly riveting. It appears to have provided material for a similar scene in Shaka King's 2021 fiction film about Hampton's murder, *Judas and the Black Messiah*. The Film Group made several short "trigger" films for community discussion out of the longer feature, an early example of outreach-and-engagement filmmaking.

That connection to the Panthers also led to another film project at The Film Group. The film was to be a profile of the Black Panthers' social and community projects, such as breakfast programs, anti-addiction programs, and community education. Howard Alk's wife, Joan, often worked sound at the film shoots. Quinn, who was already working on a commercial project (for Eli Lilly) at The Film Group, was pulled briefly into the Panther project. He filmed, among other things, a scene in the resulting film, where Hampton challenges an organizer who wants to start small businesses, but who can't articulate how that helps a revolutionary agenda.

Everything changed on that project on December 4, 1969, when police in league with the FBI broke into Hampton's home and shot him and another Panther dead. Gray and Alk made the decision to turn the film into a procedural, investigating the police murder. What became *The Murder of Fred Hampton* (1971) is a two-part film. The first part features the oratory and actions of Hampton, who at twenty-one was a highly charismatic leader. The second part exposes the postmurder investigation of the police action as a whitewash, using among other things footage taken the morning after the murder by Alk and Gray. Quinn recalled providing editing consultation as Alk, who had relapsed into his heroin addiction, struggled with the job. "Mike Gray deserves an enormous amount of credit for finishing the film," Quinn recalled. The film was designated in 2021 for the National Film Registry.

The murder also drew Quinn and Gerken into its immediate aftermath. Another leading Chicago Panther, Bobby Rush, was widely regarded as the next police target. "We were all stunned, and afraid for Bobby," Quinn recalled. Within a day of the murder, his lawyers contacted Quinn, probably through Joan Alk. Quinn and Gerken lived in a six-room, low-rent, Lincoln Park apartment that the Alks had once rented and had passed on to Quinn. Lawyers were looking for a place for Rush to hide out from the police, until they could arrange for him to turn himself in safely. Quinn and Gerken immediately said yes, although they didn't know Rush personally. "I wasn't worried about it," Quinn said. "We were both horrified at what had just happened and we knew where our loyalties lay. I was also close enough to the film to know what kind of organization the Panthers were. They were about community programs and building their base. There wasn't any ambiguity about what had gone down." This chance favor ended up getting repaid in unexpected ways two decades later. By that time, Rush was a congressman, and Quinn and colleagues successfully asked for his support for the creation of the Independent Television Service, a documentary production unit of public broadcasting.

As the political atmosphere heated up, Kartemquin continued in its efforts to conduct "cinematic social inquiry," rejecting all forms of sectarianism and extremism. Quinn in particular was viscerally averse to sectarianism, especially the kind that led some to violence. Among the notable local sectarian groups that fell into that category was the direct-action group Weather Underground, some of whose members were based in Chicago, but which had no connection with Kartemquin at the time. Other local groups included the Trotskyist Spartacist League and the cultish Revolutionary Communist Party, both of which did attempt to engage the group. Kartemquin would become instead an organization dedicated to revealing and enriching a culture of dialogue about critical conflicts and problems facing a democracy.

THE CATHOLIC FILMS

On the strength of its arguments for cinematic social inquiry and the execution of *Home for Life*, Kartemquin made several films for the progressive organization Catholic Adult Education Center. CAEC was created in the spirit of the Catholic movement that would come to be known as, variously, liberation theology (especially in Latin America) and Black theology (especially in the US). That movement, heeding the Second Vatican Council's concluding call in 1965 to engage with modern and secular life, argued that social justice needed to be central, with officers of the church making a "preferential option for the poor." CAEC formed a media production group, Intermedia, Temaner later recalled, because they were influenced by Marshall McLuhan's argument that "the medium is the message."

That group was concerned with issues such as the generation gap and antiwar sentiment. They wanted to engage communities with "trigger films," or discussion starters; the agendas for the films they wanted to do were set by the conversations that were needed. The War on Poverty and related government activities, such as Lyndon Johnson's assistant secretary of labor Daniel Moynihan's report, *The Negro Family: The Case for National Action* (US Department of Labor, 1965), had focused media attention on Black urban poverty and on white poverty in rural areas such as Appalachia. One of the Black organizers from the communities served by the Catholic Adult Education Center pushed back on the notion of the typical victim-portrait approach, in which urban Blacks were routinely featured. He urged a focus on white working-class families. Quinn recalled, "He told us, 'We know what the problems are, we know we have rats and roaches, we don't need a film like that. What we need is a film about racism, and racism is in the white community.'" That critique heavily influenced the projects' design. So did opportunities that emerged with the Catholic group's relationships.

Among the works Kartemquin made in 1968 were *Thumbs Down* (101 minutes, following young people who form a youth group and organize an antiwar mass as they grapple with the distance between the moral teachings of the church and the world around them) and *Parents* (20 minutes, the same youth group on their intergenerational conflicts). The original version of *Thumbs Down* was three 45–50 minute segments, to be used by the Catholic organization in a six-week course. When that length proved unworkable, Quinn cut the three into one long film, "which was still too long," he later commented.

The shared goal of CAEC and Kartemquin was to draw people in and let them make up their own minds. Jerry Temaner recalled, "This was why we wanted the films to be cut long. We got a lot of hostility from other filmmakers for the length. But we could say, you want people to have the material. They could generate real issues based on the material."

The white working-class teenagers in *Thumbs Down* can be boisterous, pompous, and arrogant as they struggle to find autonomy, respect, and a way to make their Catholic faith relevant to their concerns about peace and justice. But they are also earnest and genuinely interested in engaging adults, although they aspire primarily to teach them "liberal ideas." They are a world away from the middle-class "hippies" they find exotic and irrelevant. They and their priest are engaging directly with ideas in Vatican II, including having masses in English rather than Latin. Their priest patiently negotiates between their righteous passion and the fact that his parish is all-white, working-class, second- and third-generation immigrants. A lot of the dads worked as firemen and police, who had fled increasingly racially integrated neighborhoods. They were only living at the far northwest edge of Chicago, rather than the suburbs, in order to qualify for their public-sector jobs.

In *Thumbs Down*, the members of the youth group conduct a youth mass, deliberately challenging their conservative elders with antiwar talk (in spite of promises otherwise to the priest). The mass is filmed *in extenso* because, Temaner and Quinn later explained, they wanted people to be able to analyze the process. It was more "social inquiry" than "cinematic." At the end of *Thumbs Down*, some of the teens' parents join them for an open, if ultimately stymied, conversation about values, war, and resistance. The two films, both closely observed and uncommented, provide a respectful, curious, and kind look at the challenges of working-class white teens in a time of social turmoil. The film also takes their parents and their parents' frustrations seriously.

"There were other people making films about the antiwar protests," Quinn recalled. "New York Newsreel made agitprop films and distributed them to the activist movement. We on the other hand were always interested in reaching a wider audience. Our question was, How do you speak to people who don't already think like you do? These Catholic kids are struggling with their own questions about value and family. That was a way to reach out to people who didn't already think that the Vietnam War was a bad thing."

Thumbs Down was highly topical. The complexity of the human interaction it documented was undeniable; the goal of getting beyond easy condemnation and dismissal was met. CAEC used it in six-week sessions in different parish communities. The filmmakers often accompanied the educators to screenings, discussions, and conferences. The film was also the opening-night film at the Festival di Populi in Florence. In an indication of the volatile politics of the moment, its screening was interrupted by demonstrators protesting against elitism in festivals.

Inquiring Nuns (1968) (66 minutes) was also a CAEC project. A direct echo of a scene in the famed cinema verité film by Jean Rouch and Edgar Morin, *Chronique d'un été,* the film features two young nuns asking random strangers if they are happy. "We were influenced by *Chronicle of a Summer,*" recalled Quinn in an interview available as an extra on Kartemquin's DVD of the film. That 1960 film featured young people asking the same question. "So in proposing projects, we thought, 'How about two nuns? That makes it Catholic.'" The film is designed in two parts. In the first, the fresh-faced, excited nuns get basic training in use of the microphone. Then they head out to churches at the end of mass, to city streets, and to museums. The nuns quickly become savvy interviewers, and their on-the-street interviewees mostly say they're happy about their personal lives. One woman is happy because her children "can stand on their own two feet"; another celebrates her own good health. A Catholic university's football team was victorious: "Notre Dame won today!" Several people worry about Vietnam and wish for peace, and praise the solace of religion, but no one mentions one of the most divisive issues of

Figure 3. Inquiring Nuns, inspired by the cinema verité classic *Chronique d'un été*, explores the concerns of Chicagoans going about their daily routine. Source: Kartemquin Archives.

that moment—racism and the struggle for Black human rights. In the second part, which dives right into the interviews, people mention economics, and lack of balance in their lives. But in front of churches, parishioners both Black and white express gratitude for religion in their lives. The nuns find a cross-section of good-humored and often thoughtful Chicagoans, disarmed by the nuns' charm. Their interchanges allow viewers to reflect on their own lives in turbulent times.

The film became one of the most popular of the series. Upon its rerelease in 2016, it had a mini-theatrical run. "It's always a crowd pleaser," Quinn said. Sometimes people want to know what happened to the nuns; like many other novitiates, they both eventually left the order.

Marco (1970), 80 minutes long, about Temaner's and his wife Barbara's then-controversial choice for natural childbirth, was completed in 1970. Feminists were demanding to take back their bodies and choices from the medical establishment. At the same time, Catholics favored natural childbirth as part of the child-centered family, and the funders saw a connection in its theme to mission. Catholics also supported breastfeeding, and indeed the founders of the breastfeeding advocacy group La Leche League were all Catholics. La Leche Leaguers believed that it was a way for women to follow the natural law theory espoused by Aquinas. *Marco* was a perfect fit for the CAEC, and it was also a film aligned with that phase of the feminist movement, which was reclaiming women's autonomy over their own bodies.

The film begins with a montage of perspectives, including Barbara's and natural-childbirth advocates but also of doctors who firmly oppose both natural birth and having a husband in the birthing room. (All Chicago hospitals banned husbands from birthing rooms at the time.) Quinn explained later that the doctors were not included to give it balance. Rather, "The people who were pro-natural childbirth had their back up a little bit. To understand why, you have to understand what they're up against. So we realized that we have to show what they have to contend with." He also recalled how crushed they were when they succeeded in filming a doctor completely hostile to breastfeeding and natural childbirth—and were then denied a release. But it turned out such doctors were not hard to find: "We found another guy to do an interview, and he's even crazier than the first guy!" Temaner, always the deliberate, understated one, quietly observed in response, "The medical establishment didn't want to give up their power."

The bulk of the film is occupied with the birth itself. The couple need to drive ninety minutes away, to Wisconsin, to avoid Chicago's laws. Barbara quickly discovers that despite her Lamaze training and the claims of the pro-birthing advocates, the process is quite painful for her. Her husband encourages her through it, and the actual birth is filmed facing Barbara's vulva, from the vantage point of the doctor delivering the baby. Quinn later recalled his anxiety about potentially missing the birth, given the eleven-minute size of the camera's magazine, and his immense relief that he got the shot. The film ends with the new family's drive home. Over the credits run the words, "All people should have their babies the way they want to." Then Temaner personally apologizes, within the credits, to his mother (who phoned as they were birthing) and his landlord (whom he had called a monster for underheating their apartment, but who "turned out to be a friend"). The three end-credit announcements make the film both intensely personal and also an act of advocacy.

The film was used by the CAEC network, and also affected Marco's own identity. Marco said, at the age of forty, that he always gave the film to friends having babies, watching it with them, and had probably seen it thirty times. His sister also was inspired by her mother's choices, and decided to have a natural birth herself.

The Catholic work brought Kartemquin from inquiry to action. It was impact filmmaking before its time. The Catholic educators prepared related materials for discussion to accompany the films, including a six-week course for parishioners. The Kartemquinites enthusiastically brought their artistic cinema verité purity and social-inquiry commitment. All of the films featured Quinn's uncommented cinema verité camerawork, which tracks the emotional flow of the action. *Marco* and *Inquiring Nuns* both featured discreet musical elements created by Philip Glass, who was a personal friend of Temaner's. As far as Quinn could remember, they paid Glass a token amount. The cinema verité commitment, combined with their belief in the power of long-form observation to spur insight, made the films extraordinarily long for their purpose. The Catholics had wanted a discussion starter, and they got extended vicarious experiences instead. That limited their usefulness as triggers for discussion. Sales to parishes were low, possibly because of the Catholic group's liberal politics and also possibly because of their length. The Kartemquin filmmakers' learning experience with the Catholics was their first exposure to change-making with films.

OTHER PROJECTS

There were other short projects, with nonprofits. Among them was a course in which University of Chicago students read John Dewey and made a film, *Hum 255* (1970). (The title referred to the number of the course.) The students themselves chose the project. They decided to focus on a 1968 student strike about the Vietnam War and the firing of a particular faculty member. They interviewed ex-students, who were expelled for their actions, interweaving their comments with footage of a takeover of an administration building. The strikers engage the students about the meaning of their own education and the social function of higher education more generally. The film was used by students both at the University of Chicago and elsewhere as a "movement film," an organizing tool for growing protest movements.

Perhaps most striking of those early years, though, were the projects that didn't happen. Kartemquin's earliest projects imagined the kind of collaborative filmmaking that later became a cutting-edge practice of grassroots groups. One early project Quinn and Temaner proposed was to study the world outside the window of their offices in Hyde Park, where Black and white people interacted. The project reflected Temaner's long-standing interest in an ethnographic approach. He wanted to look at the unforced, casual daily interactions of people around the various businesses on the street. Furthermore, the study was imagined as participant-observation, as a collaboration with the people in the film. The group conducted a number of audio tapes—still in Kartemquin's archives—for the study, but it was never funded.

Another project demonstrated the kind of curiosity that would become essential to Kartemquin's style, particularly in *Hoop Dreams*. The group proposed following, in collaboration with physicists, the process of an experiment to create a first-level molecular accelerator. Danny Auerbach, the tech guru who built Kartemquin's first camera, was the lead graduate student researcher. The group won a National Science Foundation grant to start filming, but ultimately had to decline it because the University of Chicago refused to accept the money. The group had run afoul of university development policies; the university did not want to compromise its chances for its own NSF proposals by accepting that one. Still, the group shot enough for twenty minutes of a story that was ultimately about the failure of the experiment. After two years of work, the experimenters realize that a simple calculating error has ruined their results. Although the device was ultimately useful, it failed at its original purpose. "To me it was a real interesting story, about science and what scientists go through," Quinn said. "They were very emotionally engaged. It was a way for people to understand what the nature of science is. If you put all the emphasis on success, you don't understand. Most scientific experiments fail."

Yet another unfulfilled dream film was the one that Quinn still thinks about the most. Kartemquin proposed to spend a year in two neighborhood schools, in the Black neighborhood of Woodlawn, focusing on the social inequalities in education. The group developed a working partnership with the School of Education at the University of Chicago, the Woodlawn Organization, and the Chicago public school system. They met with the Blackstone Rangers, a local gang, and the Hyde Park based Guerrilla Theater Group.

A draft of an undated proposal from the era written by Temaner describes Kartemquin well in terms of defining its mission. Writing it, he said, was difficult because "we have discovered that we are part educational filmmakers, part political filmmakers, part artists, and part social scientists." They hoped their closely observed inquiry would provide "living documents embodying the human consequences of a social problem. They should provide the public, inner-city communities planners and government officials with a dimension of the inner-city school problem necessary for enlightened political action." Furthermore, he said, this would be "social research," although not replicable social science, because their method was "a hybrid of art and social sciences."

The group audiotaped a number of observations, wrote a script, and took still photos, but could not ultimately raise the funds to do the film. A script, written in the form of a play, called *Some Are / Summer Learning* and Stan Karter's still photos were all that resulted from the ambitious proposal; the script chronicles the grossly unequal learning outcomes of summer school classes in Chicago's Carnegie Elementary, and the difference good teachers can make.

This was only the first unmade educational documentary Kartemquin proposed. In the early 2000s, Kartemquin developed a huge NEH proposal, with development funding from tech philanthropist Paul Allen's production company. The filmmakers and the investors, however, fell out over where the focus should be. Kartemquin proposed centering the story in the teachers—as usual, finding the sociological nexus of the story. The investors wanted it to focus on cognitive science discoveries and potential tech solutions. The educational focus on teachers and students finally did take hold, in 2018 with Steve James's ten-part series about racism and inequality in an Oak Park high school (Oak Park was explicitly founded as an interracial community), *America to Me*.

The first Kartemquin era ended with the recognition that the founding members could not become the public intellectuals they imagined themselves to be by partnering with academic organizations and finding research funding. They had encountered, among other things, the closed system of the academy in the University of Chicago's refusal to accept grant funding that might conflict with other institutional priorities. They had encountered the realities of doing commissioned work, with pushback from Drexel's board members for too much truthfulness. They now knew how much time freelance work for hire actually took. But at the same time, the founding members found themselves riding a radicalizing tide that led them to partner with an organization—a liberation theology infused religious group. That group wanted their approach to stimulate better conversations for a better world. As well, the social movements pulled them into the orbit of organizations such as the Young Lords and the Black Panthers. The financial realities were daunting enough that Temaner, who had a family to support, took a job at University of Illinois at Chicago Circle, in a unit that produced curricular audiovisual materials and short films based on academic research there. Temaner could finally do at UICC what he had originally proposed to the University of Chicago. Quinn and Blumenthal continued to piece together paying work.[1]

4 Feminist Voices and Revolutionary Cinema, 1970–1978

In the 1970s, Kartemquin became a collective, making media in direct partnership with social- and political-action groups. The arguments and strategies of its feminist women members infused the collective. It morphed quickly into a sharply different version of the operation than the one founded by the budding philosophers of social inquiry and cinema verité. Its members now saw themselves as part of movements to overturn the core systems of race, class, and gender that maintained the structures of capitalism. But it was still propelled by the goal of experiential storytelling to expand the democratic agency of ordinary people. The team that had identified itself as filmic social researchers was now a group of people who called themselves cultural workers.

It was in step with the times. The late 1960s and early 1970s were experienced by some people as genuinely revolutionary. The rise in strength and diversity of ethnic organizations pushing for greater equality and rights was visible in Chicago, especially with the Rainbow Coalition that organized left-wing activists in Chicago's brutally segregated neighborhoods, openly calling for a Black-led revolution for all poor, working people.

For the all-white participants in the Kartemquin collective, the movements growing out of the student antiwar movement were a structuring reference, although Kartemquin also had active relationships with all the Rainbow Coalition groups. The movements mobilized by war resistance were in turmoil in the 1970s. Students for a Democratic Society had galvanized movements across the country, especially on college campuses, between 1965 and 1969, inspired by Britain's New Left. It had never been able to fully incorporate people of color or women, though, and it did not survive the end of the Vietnam War. Some activists joined the New American Movement (NAM), which in some locations strove for a community-based leadership, working-class representation, and a working-class agenda. Others joined the Democratic Socialist Organizing Committee (DSOC), which worked on the left of the Democratic Party. (NAM and DSOC eventually merged into Democratic Socialists of America, or DSA, the party of Representatives Alexandria Ocasio-Cortez and Bernie Sanders.) Some left for even more extreme movements such as the Weather Underground, and some joined sectarian Marxist organizations. The Cultural Revolution, in full flourish in China, inspired some, and Mao's "Little Red Book" was ubiquitous, even among those who did not aspire to the vision of grassroots socialism it purported to offer. Smaller factions were often isolated. The Communist Party had been almost entirely discredited in the US during the early years of the Cold War; Trotskyist factions were small and doctrinaire; the Revolutionary Communist Party, loosely affiliated with Chinese communism, was cult-like.

Other movements were rising both within and outside of political parties; "identity politics" was forming—movements on the basis of social / political identity, and common identification of oppression, taking inspiration from civil rights. The second-wave feminist movement was a national presence by 1970, introducing new words such as Ms, new inclusion standards, new healthcare expectations, hiring and labor standards, and much more. Socialist feminist movements arose, combining the politicization of the 1960s with the gender awareness of the women's movement. The environmental movement was launched, with the 1970 Earth Day. The gay rights movement in the US, eventually to become LGBT+, was stuttering into existence after the 1969 Stonewall riots, although organizing efforts had preceded it. Disability rights advocates were organizing.

While the left was fracturing, it seemed that left-wing values were entering the mainstream. Helen Reddy's "I Am Woman" dominated radio in 1971, topping Billboard charts. Prime-time television was suddenly twinkling with liberal-leaning programs. *The Mary Tyler Moore Show*, featuring a single, working woman with an ability to hold her own, debuted in 1970. The noted Hollywood liberal Norman Lear launched in quick succession a series of social-issue sitcoms: *All in the Family*, featuring a beloved but racist, misogynistic, working-class white dad and his critical family (1971), followed by *The Jeffersons* (showcasing a prosperous Black family) and *One Day at a Time* (which dared to show single motherhood). *M*A*S*H*, a sitcom poking fun at military culture and set in Korea (but widely read as about Vietnam) launched in 1972. In theaters, Hollywood briefly put countercultural talent in charge, starting with the 1969 *Easy Rider*, and with new auteurs such as Francis Coppola (whose *The Godfather* came out in 1972). Public television was pioneering programs showcasing Black perspectives, such as *Black Journal* and *Soul!* For members of the budding collective, and especially Gordon Quinn and Meg Gerken, these TV shows and films were all cultural furniture.

At the other end of the commercial spectrum, "film culture" was now electrified by political works. The New Latin American Cinema, a filmic kaleidoscope inspired by neorealists and driven by polarizing Latin politics, shocked and entranced audiences throughout Europe and North America, after a 1968 Paris showcase called "Cinema as a Gun." Postcolonial films from sub-Saharan Africa, North Africa, and Asia began to circulate, all with a sharply political edge. Kartemquin collective members watched the latest films together and debated their claims to revolutionary form. They watched a revolutionary work of New Latin American Cinema, Fernando Solanas and Octavio Getino's *Hour of the Furnaces* (1968). This film, which boldly intercut title cards, scenes of violence and exploitation, and pointed questions to the viewer, also was divided into sections suitable for action-oriented discussion. (The film was banned in Argentina, and both directors went into exile during the years of dictatorship.) Blumenthal remembered being thunderstruck by the film—"a revelation"—and finding in it inspiration for their own work. Indeed, Kartemquinites saw themselves as part of that movement and were seen by others in the same way; their own films were shown in a 1976 exhibition programmed by B. Ruby Rich, a feminist film activist and scholar, at the Film Center of the Art Institute of Chicago, "Revolutionary Films / Chicago." This same series also featured "new cinemas" of Cuba, Africa, Asia, and Eastern Europe.

In this tumultuous period in which social unrest and the toppling of cultural norms were intertwined, the Kartemquin social network was experimenting with new ways of forming family. They participated in what Chris Robé describes as the anarchist edge of the social movements of the time, in which communal living is a form of "prefigurative politics," practicing alternatives. Quinn and Gerken, already a couple, also explored relationships with other people. Jerry Blumenthal had married an artist, Shirlee Jensen, before he joined Kartemquin, and they adopted a son. Jensen ultimately left the marriage to live with her lesbian partner, although everyone remained close friends. Eventually the friends bought a farm in Wisconsin together, and then a house on Fremont Street in the Lincoln Park neighborhood of Chicago, big enough to house Kartemquin in the basement. The neighborhood was diverse and affordable; it is now hyper-gentrified.

Political mobilization was all around them. Gerken and Quinn had friends in the New American Movement, and once hosted a meeting at their house. Around the corner from their communal home on Fremont St. was the "Peoples' Church," a Black church where the Young Lords, the Chicago Latinx group that formed out of local gangs in 1968 as an anticolonial, pro Puerto Rican and Latinx organization, had their base and a health clinic. They also showed movies, including *Hour of the Furnaces*. At the time the group moved in, the Young Lords were actively fighting Mayor Daley's open attempts to displace them for white gentrification. The "Fremont Nation," as the roommates jokingly called themselves, joined in holding police to account when a Black teen was shot to death by police in their alley. They also volunteered as drivers when patients at the health clinic needed to go to the hospital.

Kartemquin's projects were divided into work-for-hire (mostly crewing for other film companies doing commercial work) and its social-inquiry work, which was now directly linked to grassroots politics. Work-for-hire covered the costs for social inquiry. Jerry Blumenthal once wryly referred to the arrangement as "schizophrenia." But he also was buoyantly optimistic. "'We've got the equipment, the ideas, the desire, the kindred spirits,'"

Blumenthal recalled as their naïve attitude. "'We know where to go to connect with progressive grassroots groups. All we'll need is a few rolls of film to begin telling the stories that need to be told.'" It was harder than they thought it would be.

Kartemquin began to take on contracts of its own. The work-for-hire ranged from local advertising contracts to PSAs, but only with clients they could "admit publicly we were working with," as Quinn said. Most of their work, though, was still with other film production houses, who subcontracted with them. Their idea of doing cinema verité commercials, like the superstars of cinema verité Al and David Maysles were doing in New York, did not work out in the more staid Chicago advertising market. Cinema verité was still too new for advertisers to appreciate its advantages, although that would change. Kartemquinites were also learning how to impress the companies that hired them. Gordon Quinn, notoriously phlegmatic, later recalled that as a cameraman, his usual laconic demeanor was losing them business. Finally he learned, he said, the magic answer to the question "How was that shot?" was "It was awesome!" For two years (1971–72) and twenty-six episodes, a contract to produce a sports series, *Sports-Action Profile*, kept the organization afloat, and it also drew in some of Chicago's best film editors—Blumenthal recalled David Szabo, Ron Clasky, and Brita Paretzkin.

Some of the profits were invested in Kartemquin's equipment base. By 1972, it owned four state-of-the-art Steenbecks, and rented them out. Quinn had spotted a demonstration model on the floor of an industry convention, and immediately saw the Steenbeck advantage; he bought the floor model. Optimized for 16mm technology, the Steenbeck was much easier to use than the Moviola, particularly for filmmakers working in long-form scenes typical of cinema verité. Where the Moviola was upright, with the Steenbeck you loaded film onto the table. Where the film went through the Moviola jerkily, the Steenbeck used optical technology to move the film smoothly, so that it was less likely to catch.

The growing collective outgrew its basement space on Fremont Street, and a devastating fire speeded the moving process. Kartemquin bought a two-story building in a working-class neighborhood, on West Wellington Avenue, which had been three apartments and a storefront. It became the organization's home base for the next fifty years. Technically, Temaner and

Figure 4. The building at 1901 W. Wellington Avenue in Chicago became Kartemquin's home base for half a century. The turret was the most prized real estate. Source: Kartemquin Archives.

Quinn were the owners, but Quinn always understood it to be the organization's. Purchased in 1971 for $21,500, it was appraised in 2023 for $600,000, during its transfer to the legally revamped Kartemquin.

Blumenthal became the sound man as well as editor at Kartemquin, and Quinn specialized in cinematography. Their next move was to provide teaching resources to activists who needed those skills to serve their revolutionary purposes.

FILM AND POLITICS

Even before the collective fully formed, Kartemquin films captured the social-movement moment. The 1970 short film *What the Fuck Are These Red Squares?* recorded a conversation among students at the Chicago

Institute of Art. Led by Jerry Blumenthal's then-wife, the strikers acted in response to the Kent State and Jackson State killings of young people on college campuses by police and National Guard. The students delved into hard questions about the art market, the function of art, and how they as artists should play a role in what they saw as a revolutionary time. (The title refers to a casual reference to a comment the Yippie Abbie Hoffman made during the 1968 Democratic Convention, as a marker for questions about how art works in capitalism generally.) The film proposed that art and politics were inseparable, and it was both classically cinema verité and social inquiry.

The filmmakers produced a closely observed, uncommented observation of an intense meeting. It was the film on which Blumenthal learned how to edit, under Quinn's tutelage; he would become Kartemquin's master editor. The film—conveniently short as a discussion starter—circulated among left-wing, activist teachers, and student groups, in an ad hoc distribution system. They, like other small, mission-driven film studios, were pioneering DIY distribution. A year later, the left-wing, independent-filmmaker collective New Day Films was founded by friends of theirs, including Julia Reichert, and from which Kartemquin would learn a lot.

Worldwide, film collectives had sprouted up in the 1960s, inspiring media makers in the US, where anti Vietnam War activism was mobilizing draft-age young people. The fertile "New Cinema" or "Third Cinema" movement in Latin America, the Arab world, and Africa inspired them too. In the US, Newsreel was launched in New York in December 1967, and in San Francisco in 1968, with Boston and Los Angeles following. The New York Newsreel organization was founded by wealthy young men, who wanted, in the words of cofounder Robert Kramer, to make films that "unnerve, that shake people's assumptions, that threaten," and even "explode like grenades in people's faces." This echoed with European claims for Third Cinema—that it was "cinema as a gun"—and with the claims of Argentine directors Solanas and Getino in *Hour of the Furnaces* (that influential film for Kartemquinites).

These political media collectives were notoriously unstable, both politically and personally. New York Newsreel soon split, with self-identified Third World members forming Third World Newsreel. Women challenged male leadership, and people of color challenged whites. San Francisco Newsreel also split apart, with the survivor becoming a distributor of films about labor and race issues. Kartemquin, by contrast, built a filmmaking community.

COLLECTIVE STRUCTURE

The collective that became the Kartemquin of the 1970s was loosely structured, informal, and grounded in relationships with local political movements. It grew along friendship network lines, as word spread that you could learn filmmaking skills there. The group made decisions collectively about their film work, but other than that, the collective was resolutely informal. It had 13–15 members, some intermittently, with stalwarts including Quinn, Blumenthal, Jenny Rohrer, Suzanne Davenport, Judy Hoffman, Vicki Cooper, Betsy Martens, Susan Delson, Sharon Karp, Teena Webb, Richard Schmeichen, Alphonse Blumenthal (Jerry's brother), Greg Grieco, and Peter Kuttner. In the spirit of the time some collective members formed personal intimate relationships with each other, while others found partners outside of the group; but no personal relationship ever threatened the collective itself.

While the group dedicated a lot of time to discussing its own structure, women—especially Jenny Rohrer, Suzanne Davenport, Vicki Cooper, and Judy Hoffman—became important voices. Blumenthal and Quinn were always the technical experts and the financial anchors. But the era of Kartemquin's collective was infused politically by socialist feminism, and the women who came to Kartemquin were the most influential in turning it into a collective.

Throughout its nearly decade-long history, the collective told stories both with and about working people and members of movements for social justice. The films were designed to be used by members of those movements, and to inspire others to join movements for social justice. Members of the collective, who were all young and had typically come from some kind of 1960s organizing, were committed to fundamental social change. Some thought they were revolutionaries. Several collective members recalled their expectations wryly at a recorded reunion decades later. (DVDs of the Kartemquin early years, produced in 2010 and available on Amazon, feature extras that include these recollections.) Sharon Karp, an editor, said that she still had her "Little Red Book," the Maoist tract that was ubiquitous in the late 1960s: "We used to read and discuss this every week." Director Teena Webb said, "I thought the revolution was going to happen." And when it didn't, "I was crushed, disappointed." Cinematographer Peter Kuttner said, "I fully expected we would be driving Jeeps down State Street [a major commercial avenue in downtown Chicago]." Feminist (and Maoist) Vicki Cooper said, "I thought I was gonna be driving a tank, and I figured out in 1976 that it wasn't gonna happen, that there weren't gonna be any tanks." She shook her head, remembering her disillusionment. Quinn, by contrast, never had the tank fantasy. "When tanks are in the streets, they're usually oppressing people," he said later.

But in spite of revolutionary dreams on the part of some of its participants, the collective never adopted a political ideology. The archived meeting notes of the collective carry the flavor of the group's deliberative style. Notes from March 25, 1973, summarize a lengthy discussion about mission:

> Kinds of political film we are trying to make
>
> a. Non-sectarian
> b. Films that are needed for political use—decided is a distinction not relevant at this point [this followed a discussion about the terms 'political films' and 'films needed for political use']
> c. We participate in the struggle for socialism.

Quinn emphasized, "Make it clear we are open to different groups to work with; we put energy into maintaining our openness." The organization's nonsectarian approach communicated well to others. The *New Art Examiner* noted, in 1976, "At times they quote Marx, but on the whole, their political orientation remains undecided. More than anything else, they sympathize with their characters and urge collective action."

Neither Blumenthal nor Quinn could abide sectarianism. But they did believe that unchecked capitalist priorities built structures that were

Figure 5. At the Wellington Avenue storefront sit, from left, collective members Gordon Quinn, Judy Hoffman, Sue Davenport, Sharon Karp, Jenny Rohrer, Betsy Martens, and Sue Delson. The women are laughing because the only man in the collective who showed up was Quinn. Source: Kartemquin Archives. Credit: Meg Gerken.

inhumane and unjust. Blumenthal, soon after the collective's end, recalled, in an interview with filmmaker Alan Rosenthal,

> Our politics were left politics, but independent left and nonsectarian. We were not tied to any particular line in any particular left group, but we were very interested in making films that could be used in organizing and teaching. We may not have agreed with one another specifically on a given Marxist line, but we all felt that a film had to have basically a left or socialist analysis of what the problems were in American society and how those problems were to be solved.

Peter Kuttner, in the same group interview, explained the collective's focus on white, working-class issues. "Our neighborhoods were delineated by this Rainbow Coalition," he recalled, referencing the coalition Fred Hampton had been developing when he was murdered. Hampton had encouraged

Figure 6. Collective members Jerry Blumenthal, Sue Delson, Sharon Karp, Sue Davenport, Gordon Quinn, and Vicki Cooper mid-meeting. Source: Kartemquin Archives. Credit: Meg Gerken.

different neighborhood/ethnic groups in the highly segregated "city of neighborhoods" to work within their own cultures for antiracist, anticapitalist change. "We were mirroring, taking leadership from the Black Panther party, trying to recreate it and working in white neighborhoods," recalled Kuttner. "We were working on changing our own communities, making films about our own communities." The collective, he recalled, would never have overstepped to make a film about Black people.

Most of the women came from the socialist-feminist Chicago Women's Liberation Union (CWLU), which was then in the democratic-socialist vein of *In These Times* and the Democratic Socialist Organizing Committee. Individual political perspectives of collective members ranged from the dogmatic, Maoist views of Vicki Cooper to the pragmatic democratic socialism of Jenny Rohrer to the eager naiveté of Betsy Martens, who later recalled her early self as a "tripped-out hippie" bringing her fascination with experimental film art into the collective along with a search for new skills.

The group rejected the notion that they were creating art; rather, they were "cultural workers." This term, borrowed from Maoism, was widely employed at the time. "Whenever anybody had an idea for a film, the first questions that we always asked were, 'What's it for and who's going to use it?' ... We tried to pick subjects that showed organizing situations," Blumenthal recalled in the Rosenthal interview.

For two years of the collective, the group organized film screenings throughout the year, organized by themes such as women, labor, geopolitics, and healthcare. They circulated invitations to the screenings to groups and individuals they worked with, and they held discussions after the films. It was, said, Blumenthal, a "way of encouraging people to use film more often in their organizing," as well as continuing education.

Drawing on the nonhierarchical experience of the women in CWLU, the group discussed structure, process, and purpose, toward identifying common goals and problem-solving. They formed study groups. For instance, in studying labor, notes show, they read a range of books, including *Labor's Untold Story* and *Strike!*, and asked questions such as, "What role did racism and sexism play in the development of the labor movement?" and "What were the economic and social forces within capitalism that held back the development of the working class?" Quinn also later recalled he and Meg Gerken reading *Capital* in the Sojourner Truth Organization study group, a "new communist" Chicago group that put issues of race at the center of analysis. (Gerken taught Marx in her humanities classes at Wright College, one of Chicago's network of public community colleges.) He also participated in a Maoist study group. But, he said, "I was always very careful to make sure sectarianism did not infect Kartemquin. You are a certain kind of organization, you're evolving in the historical moment, confronting specific social problems, and you have to change and evolve with it. You don't go down a narrow path, you want a back-and-forth from a more democratic perspective." This was very much a Gramscian perspective on the need for organizations to evolve as circumstances changed. At one point a zealot from the Revolutionary Community Party joined the group, but ultimately gave up. Among other things, members of the group—including Richard Schmeichen, who had not yet come out as gay—were repelled by the woman's antigay bias.

Several collective members addressed the organization's approach at the time, in an interview with scholar and *Jump/Cut* editor Julia LeSage, another Chicago media activist. She and her husband, Chuck Kleinhans, a Northwestern University film professor, had started the magazine with a left-wing perspective on film scholarship. In the group interview, Jenny Rohrer commented, "One of Kartemquin's priorities was not to wage some kind of internal struggle over politics, resulting in innumerable splits. Two of us from Newsreel found that'd happened all the time there. We wanted a group that would stay stable and broad enough so we could sustain ourselves and make films." Richard Schmeichen pointed to the politics of practice: "Our political thought and political struggle mostly went on in working on the films. As a group of, say, four people took on the primary responsibility for a film, based on their previous political experience, they'd struggle with and work out the politics of that film." Gordon Quinn stressed process:

> We started off fairly committed to not hammering out a line and had broad-based, progressive left politics. We talked a lot about making films for different kinds of groups that were doing political organizing, like women's groups and union groups, and taking our politics from the situation we were working in. That was good but also created some problems for us. In the last year or so we've put more energy not into actually hammering out a political line but into examining what our points of agreement are and what our politics as a group are. We've found that in some ways we were too broad in the beginning.

The finances of the group stayed informal as well. Most members did not draw salaries. The collective leveraged its assets—including rental of equipment and freelance commercial work that did not violate the group's ethics. Other members worked at jobs where they had skills, which ranged from teaching to bartending. Grants, which were rare, went to the costs of film projects, not salaries.

But the group quickly confronted the need for more structure. By 1973, it was having formal "Structure and Identity" meetings. Issues addressed, as one set of meeting minutes shows, included how to understand the role of the commercial work done by members in relation to what the group considered its "political" work. But also, what was political work exactly?

If the group was working with an organization paying them for the work, was it political or commercial? Or both? Should the credits only list the Kartemquin collective, or individual members?

The group grappled with the meaning of "mass work," i.e., working with movement organizations directly for social and political change. They found a conflict between the work of professional film production and movement participation. At one 1974 meeting, the group came to a temporary consensus, according to minutes, but as usual left substantial flexibility:

> NEW KTQ PRINCIPLE: We think mass work is a priority for everyone in KTQ. It means generally some serious, sustained work in political situations and / or organizations. (We will develop our definitions of mass work later—important priority to do so.) It can be internally through KTQ's screenings + other activities or outside of KTQ. People who are committed to and do this as well as take the other responsibilities at KTQ will be the leadership. Someone can be here working and not doing mass work for a while—but is not leadership at that time or until they do mass work. (Other priority for us is to figure out more about leadership)

How should skill-sharing work? At the outset of the set of relationships that loosely evolved into the collective, Quinn and Blumenthal committed to teaching activists how to make films, and in doing so also brought them along on shoots, even commercial ones. As more people arrived, though, this everyone-learn-everything approach proved unviable; among other things, commercial clients complained. Kartemquin film professionals decided that members had to pick a skill to professionalize in, and not try to do everything. In this way, many Kartemquinites did get valuable skills and entrée to the local film production community.

The structure debate culminated in 1974, and it was informed, as earlier discussions had been, by the women's feminist experience. The women raised the issue of what feminist activist Jo Freeman began calling, in 1970, "the tyranny of structurelessness." This critique argues that lack of structure masks informal authority, which can be harder to identify and challenge than formal authority. After some discussion, Quinn and Blumenthal, along with Jenny Rohrer, came to more openly assume responsibility for their expertise and their financial role, and were able to address more openly issues of inclusion and participation.

This change was greeted by some with relief. Meetings were often long. Basic issues of maintenance (what to do about the termites in the basement?) were interwoven with big-issue discussions about how to decide whether they were compromising their ideals in project design. Meetings always ended with a "criticism / self-criticism session," a feature borrowed from the Chinese Cultural Revolution, although they often involved irony and humor. One 1974 session ended with these notes, for instance: "We tried to figure out why the meeting was such a drag. We were bogged down in business and money shit and our relationships and purpose for being seems to be degenerating down to only that and we aren't finishing projects and aren't starting new ones, and don't do enough outside work." The notetaker also commented, "We are getting black lung of the brain (are we covered on our policy?)."

Quinn later recalled editor Sharon Karp—she was editing the era's landmark film, the socialist feminist feature *The Chicago Maternity Center Story*—bursting out at one point, "Can I stop coming to these fucking meetings, which are boring me to death? When you decide, just tell me what you want, and I'll edit it." Jerry Blumenthal was far less patient than Gordon Quinn. "He hated meetings," recalled Judy Hoffman. "He loved the work, and he did the work. He was the one who finished things. He mentored people; he taught Sharon Karp to edit. And he brought money into Kartemquin." Blumenthal also hated "mass work"; his attitude was that he contributed to political life with his filmmaking and film screenings.

The group sometimes looked more like family. Judy Hoffman recalled later struggling to recover from the trauma of a rape in 1976, and leaning heavily on women in Kartemquin as she got better. She also came to look upon Jerry Blumenthal, with whom she had a cheerfully scrappy relationship, as a "brother." Jenny Rohrer lived for years in an apartment in the Kartemquin building. Sharon Karp also was both a roommate and a colleague for some Kartemquinites. Several of the long-term Kartemquinites also developed their formative professional relationships in this era.

The very different backgrounds and foci of three active members of the Kartemquin collective—Jenny Rohrer, Judy Hoffman, and Peter Kuttner—are illustrative of the diversity and shared values of the group.

JENNY ROHRER

Jenny Rohrer, who with Gordon Quinn and Jerry Blumenthal became an anchor of the collective, came to it through a feminist organization's focus on the last at-home birthing service in Chicago. Rohrer was an organizer with training from the Midwest Academy, which was inspired by Saul Alinsky's hard-nosed organizing approach. She had dropped out of college to join the movement, but while there she was captivated by watching antiwar veterans using film to reach out to college students. "I saw that films could open up a reality that people hadn't experienced personally," she later said. She went to work at Chicago Newsreel, circulating political films to Chicago-area schools, colleges, and organizations: "It immersed me in how films work best, and how they work in organizing." So she entered Columbia College, a film school. There she teamed up with Suzanne Davenport, another student, to make a short film about the CWLU, and became a staffer there.

Rohrer brought her understanding and experience of feminist advocacy and organizing skills into Kartemquin's emerging collective. It was a key reason why Kartemquin avoided some of the painful divisions of other collectives at the time, as Quinn acknowledged to Julia LeSage: "Right from the start, when we became a group, we had women who were part of our leadership, part of the Women's Union, and sensitive about not being into the wrong kinds of roles. We didn't build up a backlog of bitterness about sexism or have to go through the nasty struggles about it, which have destroyed a lot of other groups." Women in the group further explained to LeSage that they did not share a common approach to women's issues or the feminist movement, but they did share a common experience of being less skilled than the men who had led Kartemquin when they came in. So their negotiations with them focused on skills acquisition.

Vicki Cooper and Jenny Rohrer, once best friends, fell out irrevocably over women's movement politics. Such political differences ultimately destroyed the CWLU, which Rohrer was then heading, but Kartemquin survived.

JUDY HOFFMAN

Another stalwart of the collective years was Judy Hoffman, who first encountered Gordon Quinn when he was picking up equipment from Temaner's office at the University of Illinois Chicago Circle campus. While studying there, she had applied for a work/study job with Temaner's office, hoping to acquire filmmaking skills. She had demanded the job, in fact, arguing that women were being shut out of film production—without realizing she was talking to a progressive. "He finally told me, 'I don't need to hear this anymore. When do you want to start?,'" she recalled later. She seized on the new-tech opportunity: "As a woman it was much harder to break into 16mm, and there were no rules for 1/2 inch videotape. It was easier for a woman to enter doing that." She had discovered her inner geek.

Hoffman had stumbled into the Portapak Revolution, which generated a kaleidoscope of projects, activities, and even organizations. Even before the Portapak, a portable video system, was introduced by Sony in 1967, two social movements were primed to take advantage of it. Both were driven by ideals of accessing grassroots voices, challenging elite narratives, and diversifying expression. One was the New York techno-arts scene. Nam June Paik seized the opportunity to use prototype equipment to film the visit of the Pope and show it later that night in downtown New York. The video-art movement launched organizations including Video Free America in San Francisco and Chicago-based Video Data Bank. VDB was launched by Kate Horsfield and Lyn Blumenthal at the School of the Art Institute in 1976, to collect and preserve this fragile art form, particularly women's work. The other movement was social activist video, in groups such as Raindance. These took inspiration from George Stoney, a veteran filmmaker of social-action films, who while in Canada worked for the legendary Challenge for Change program. Some organizations, such as Videofreex in New York, combined art and politics.

Hoffman, a veteran activist, saw the connection between video and the politics of grassroots expression. One of her mentors was Anda Korsts, a Latvian immigrant whose family was displaced during World War II and who was a leader in the Chicago video collective Top Value TV with Tom Weinberg. In the 1970s, TVTV not only made video programs but got them onto public TV. Korsts then founded the nonprofit Videopolis. Hoffman worked there to create a program, "It's a Living" (1975), based on Studs Terkel's book *Working*. Chicago public TV station WTTW showed it, as did other public stations. Hoffman also knew Jim Morrissette, an engineering guru, from when she worked in Temaner's office. Morrissette too was entranced by the possibilities of video, and became a pioneer of Portapak use and video editing.

Quinn met Hoffman when he showed up to borrow the Portapak for a workshop with labor activists, and then to record for the video he and Blumenthal were making, at the request of rank-and-file steelworkers—*Where's I. W. Abel* (1975)? Hoffman convinced Quinn that it was a serious innovation, and that Kartemquin should buy its own. Quinn always had a fond eye for new technology. He was immediately captured by the possibilities, even though the challenges of early video were enormous by today's standards. Video was still reel-to-reel and editing was still done laboriously in an analog linear editing deck (any changes would require starting over from the point of change, degrading the quality with every change). Hoffman would work with Kartemquin on several labor projects.

Hoffman brought a relentless curiosity about form, as well as a passionate commitment to social justice. She was inspired by the collaborative approach of legendary cinema verité filmmaker Jean Rouch, who acknowledged his presence on camera, honored his relationship with subjects as colleagues, and encouraged grassroots filmic expression. While working with Temaner's office, she had been given the opportunity to work with Rouch as his assistant during a three-week ethnographic congress in Chicago. It was at that conference that Temaner and Quinn presented "Cinematic Social Inquiry." Jean Rouch had evolved a filmmaking style that included working alongside the film's subjects, to do shared storytelling and skills transfer. He had become a mentor to many; the Rouch *Ateliers Varan* formalized this mentorship into training of filmic storytellers worldwide.

Hoffman became, she later recalled, both his assistant and informant, about the beating heart of Black, working-class Chicago, where he decided to make a never-finished film on a jazz big band. (They worked on it for years.) Besides the filmic inspiration, Hoffman treasured his friendship: "Rouch was an anarchist. We shared a lot of the same politics, and particularly the same sense of humor. He was a surrealist and was totally hilarious. So we were the bad kids at the conference [where they met]. Margaret Mead would come looking for us, to bring us back." Hoffman reveled in being the "bad kid" generally. During one Kartemquin meeting's criticism-self-criticism session, she initiated a round of irony, according to the minutes: "Judy criticizes the way Gordon dresses. Sharon criticizes Judy for dressing worse. All concur that Jenny is well-dressed and Peter is good looking—except Gordon and Peter."

Hoffman was concerned with craft, always looking for ways to improve the look of video, while using its immediacy for organizing. She was always technologically *au courant*. When 3/4 inch tape came in, she organized with others to create the Chicago Editing Center (funded by the MacArthur Foundation), which then became the Center for New Television. She also brought video editing to Kartemquin.

PETER KUTTNER

Peter Kuttner, a staunch collective member, knew Quinn and Blumenthal through Chicago Newsreel, where they had attended meetings. Through that connection, he had used Kartemquin, while it was still in Hyde Park, as a clandestine place to edit an interview with a Young Lords leader on the run. He became a longtime friend of Quinn's, and came to look upon Blumenthal as a brother. "We shared a sense of humor, we both had younger brothers, and we both liked to party," he recalled. "And his skills as an editor were brilliant."

Kuttner had radical credentials. He was a founder of the Chicago self-styled revolutionary group of working-class, young white people, Rising

Up Angry, which flourished between 1969 and 1975. But he distanced himself from the organization once it became explicitly vanguardist. He had also worked with Students for a Democratic Society, producing their newspaper. He was a middle-class Chicago kid who had failed at college but had learned filmmaking skills on the fly. "I grew up in a liberal family, no socialists. I was a wet diaper baby. [He is referring wryly to the phrase "Red diaper baby" to describe children of Communists.] I didn't know anything about socialism or any of these isms. I knew in my gut that wars are bad, people of color are good," he remembered. He had bumped into leaders of Newsreel while in New York. They persuaded him, reluctantly, to return to Chicago to work mostly on distributing left-wing films. Kuttner coordinated the filmmaking around the Democratic Convention that resulted in Norm Fruchter's *Summer '68* (1969), a Newsreel film still studied in film classes. He also learned about organizing by taking Newsreel library films to different political groups around Chicago.

By the time he joined the collective-in-formation in 1972, Kuttner was well known to the FBI. As part of Newsreel, he had hosted dozens of the people arrested during the Democratic National Convention—all of whom, apparently, gave his address as their Chicago residence. He and his girlfriend were constantly moving, because the FBI would warn neighbors about them. In 1970, the FBI visited his home, after the Weather Underground planted a bomb at the US Capitol. His girlfriend, meanwhile, had been arrested during an antiwar demonstration and was scheduled for release into her father's custody, in line with the pre-feminist tenor of mainstream culture. To ensure she wouldn't go back to jail or to her father, they married hastily and formally transferred "custody" to her new husband. Kuttner sued the Chicago police for brutality he experienced during a protest, and when he won a settlement, he split the money with Kartemquin.

Kuttner was also a cinema verité devotee. Twice he had had the good fortune to hire on to film production teams with the legendary Canadian cinema verité filmmaker Allan King. King produced closely observed studies such as *Warrendale* (1967), about a boarding school for emotionally disturbed children. Kuttner was impressed with King's ability to get ordinary people's stories on-screen.

PRODUCING WITH ORGANIZATIONS

Kartemquin's collective members fostered relationships with organizing efforts throughout the area. Their goal was to produce work that could be used by change-makers within those organizations. Since their work was designed strategically, and in combination with organizations' leaders, it was often effective within limited circles. More surprising to them was how quickly produced and sometimes crudely executed work proved to be effective and moving in other contexts.

This was a sudden and dramatic shift not only in method but style for Kartemquin. The founders had been ideologically committed to cinema verité as the way to provide the most reliable and responsible "social inquiry." They had agonized over how to represent their own questions and interventions in a shot. The newcomers wanted to use the expressive means that best achieved their sociopolitical objective. Narration? Fine, if necessary. Title cards? If it makes the point better. Remarkably, the founders welcomed this approach. They were not wedded to form but to purpose. The fact that the collective grew organically, in its membership, in its projects, in its style, went along with the fact that the mission of the collective years was iterative, developed project by project.

The organizations they collaborated with were distinctively local. Vibrant, contestatory, and complex networks of makers evolved in San Francisco, Los Angeles, New York, Boston, and Philadelphia. These impulses were also reflected in the film school and university environments of Chicago, as *What the Fuck Are These Red Squares?* showed. But the context mattered. The commercial film scene in Chicago was centered on industrials and corporate films, not on consumer-oriented production. The lived environment was working-class, manufacturing-oriented cultures and neighborhoods, and the social movements that responded to them. A small, regional activist film producers' network evolved featuring Kartemquin; the Community Film Workshop, which was focused on serving African American makers; the alternative television makers around the Center for New Television; the world of activist intellectuals around *In These Times* and *Jump/Cut;* and the activists around public access TV and Chicago Access Network. In an era when airfares were high and long-distance calls were charged by the minute, Kartemquin lacked the connections to develop a national reputation. This lack of national visibility lingered long after the collective era.

Kartemquin was also the heartland destination for bicoastal media activists. Out of New York, left-wing media activist Mark Weiss and Pacific Street filmmakers showed up when shooting the 1972 film *Red Squad*, about police and FBI abuse of citizens' rights. Later Blumenthal and Quinn shot Pacific Street Film's 1983 *Anarchism in America*. The left-wing, experimental indie filmmaker Jill Godmilow called Kartemquin when she was making *The Popovich Brothers of South Chicago* (1977). In the 1970s and 1980s, Julia Reichert and Jim Klein, located near Dayton, Ohio, in Yellow Springs, sometimes used Kartemquin as a base when they had business in Chicago. Their 1976 *Union Maids*, which has become part of the documentary canon, was partly shot at Kartemquin. In fact, Quinn and Reichert had arguments about the film, because the filmmakers suppressed the fact that all the interviewees were members of the Communist Party. "I felt that there were people who were organizers who weren't part of the CP, but all those women were, and they were able to do what they did because they had that support system. Leaving that out distorted the history; it didn't explain how they got where they did," Quinn recalled. "But not all of them wanted their connections to the CP in the movie. And really, the film wouldn't have been as successful with that in it." Later, Reichert came to believe, or at least assert (to me, among other people), that she and Klein were unaware of the CP connection while making the film.

Kartemquin members formed a presence at the historic 1979 Alternative Cinema Conference at Bard College, a gathering of cultural workers in film from around the country; there was an organizing meeting for it at Kartemquin as well. It revealed both the extraordinary flourishing of a phenomenon and also weaknesses of the New Left. Planned for two hundred people, the event eventually attracted some four hundred, including members of the Kartemquin collective and me as a reporter from *In These Times*. Like the field, it was heavily tilted toward the coasts, particularly New York and San Francisco. Panels and workshops delved into issues of production, distribution, and impact. The organizers of what became known as "the Bard conference" were mostly white, middle- or upper-class male New Yorkers, including Marc Weiss. Black filmmakers such as St. Clair Bourne felt either excluded or misunderstood. LGBT activists denounced male privilege; Richard Schmeichen was among those who insisted on an LGBT-focused panel, and only got it after pressuring the organizers.

The conference revealed two kinds of filmmaking: reaching wide, broadcast audiences, and media work for specific purposes and audiences. A report by several attendees in *Jump/Cut* described it this way: "The conference represented people who, in the wake of the fragmentation that ended the 60's movement, spent the 70's working in fairly restricted and separate areas defined by constituency and community, by sectors such as health and education, by issues such as anti-nuke and anti-imperialist work." This was also a good description of the group that had coalesced over that decade at Kartemquin.

For Kartemquinites, as Midwesterners, attending the Bard conference meant both seeing themselves as part of a wider movement of media for social justice, and seeing how different their experience was. At that meeting, they were members of a filmmaking public. Gordon Quinn recalled it as an important, coalescing moment in the field. Judy Hoffman, however, has never forgotten her sense of alienation from the coastal makers, who she experienced as careerist and cliqueish. "It was like high school for leftist filmmakers," she remembered. I knew what she was talking about; I often felt at sea in a group of people who already had networks in place, and I experienced some of their talk as pretentious and self-absorbed. But the conference marked the evolution of a field self-aware as a force for politically progressive storytelling, and it included people who built the next generation of documentary institutions, including the Association of Independent Video and Filmmakers, New Day Films, and Independent Feature Project. For me, it was the beginning of trust ties with people in the field I would depend upon both for my reporting and my own actions as a member of this filmmaking public, and it began my friendship with St. Clair Bourne, which opened the door to friendships with other Black filmmakers.

THE CHICAGO MATERNITY CENTER STORY (1976)

The largest project during the collective years was *The Chicago Maternity Center Story*, a socialist feminist critique of capitalist healthcare and a celebration of woman-centered maternity medicine. The center, launched in 1932, offered pre- and postnatal care, as well as birthing services in the home, mostly to lower-income women. Its maternal mortality rate was a third of that of Chicago-area hospitals, which generally were lower than the national norm. Once the largest such obstetric service in the nation, by 1970 it was the last. Medicine in the US had become big business, with a shift away from in-home to in-hospital services and specializations. What scholar Carolyn Herbst Lewis calls "medical apartheid" typified obstetrics. Nearly all births to white women happened in hospitals in the 1970s, but the majority of births to Black women were out-of-hospital, not attended by a physician. In CMC-related surveys, women overwhelmingly reported they chose CMC because of its high-quality, warmly humane, and patient-centered quality of care. But by 1971 the CMC faced closure because of loss of community foundation funding and of medical trainees, whose programs no longer supported at-home obstetrics. The CMC had come up against a fundamental shift in American healthcare delivery.

The CWLU, mostly white middle-class women, focused on women's health, and especially reproductive health. This was part of the broader white feminist health movement of the time, which linked health knowledge and decisions with wider environmental and social values. That movement was itself part of a wider revival of a movement for women's rights, buffeted and conditioned by the racial and class segregation of the society. White feminists rallied around autonomy, choice, and knowledge of their bodies. The publication in 1970 of *Our Bodies, Ourselves*, by the Boston Women's Health Book Collective, was a touchstone. Feminists also focused on rape as a violent method of social control, setting up rape crisis centers around the country. Black and brown women were often not part of these projects, in spite of efforts of leaders such as Gloria Steinem. She resolutely refused speaking engagements where she could not accompany a woman of color.

For the CWLU, the threatened closure of the CMC, which overwhelmingly had Black and brown women as its clientele, became a cause. The CWLU joined a coalition group, Women Act to Control Health Care (WATCH), focused on keeping the center open, and Rohrer and Davenport became leaders. Davenport, already aware of Kartemquin's work through her own focus on education, took the project to Quinn and Blumenthal, who embraced the idea. They were willing to train the women, and others, to document the struggle to save the CMC. The women were willing to find outside work, to fund themselves while raising grants for the project. Toward the beginning, the film won a small Illinois Humanities Council grant. Toward the end, the group received a surprise check from George Pillsbury, a scion of the flour fortune, who supported independent film.

The film project launched the collective and became its centerpiece. It took nearly six years to make, partly because of delays caused by the disastrous fire at the Fremont Street offices. It was released three years after the incorporation of CMC into Northwestern's women's hospital and termination of its home services.

Its style marks the height of Kartemquin's direct engagement with movement organizations for social change. The film is composed of two core elements: The cinema verité portrayal of one pregnancy and home birth at CMC, featuring Scharene Miller birthing her baby boy Djuane; and a didactic essay on the brutal consequences for women's healthcare of bottom-line executive decisions. The essay is illustrated with advertisements, newspaper clippings, magazine photos, and a 1939 Pare Lorentz film, *The Fight for Life*, which features the maternity center's work as an important advance. The film is punctuated by standoffs between feminist protestors fighting the center's closure and Northwestern hospital board members.

The cinema verité harked back to Kartemquin's social-inquiry commitment; the militant essay reflected the 1970s Kartemquin's social-action commitment, and to some degree the influence of radical films such as *Hour of the Furnaces*. Blumenthal told Alan Rosenthal that the departure in style had to do with the moment: "As the political situation in America changed, it became clearer to us as filmmakers and people who the enemy was. It became important for us to try to find the way . . . to communicate that kind of analytical grasp of the situation." Quinn often did camera on the cinema verité shoots, with Davenport doing sound. Rohrer often shot meetings, confrontations, and demonstrations, with Quinn as assistant camera. Blumenthal became more involved in the editing, as he mentored Sharon Karp and Rohrer. Quinn's collection of pages torn from medical journals, from Kartemquin's earliest days, finally proved valuable. Left-

Figure 7. The Chicago Maternity Center Story chronicled protests organized by socialist feminists to keep the center open. Source: Kartemquin Archives.

wing sociologist Barbara Ehrenreich and left-wing journalist Dierdre English's 1971 essay "Witches, Midwives and Nurses: A History of Women Healers," later to grow into a book, became the bible for the film project. Its historical analysis, which ends in action points, argues that women's medical expertise has been systemically suppressed in the service of capitalist, racist, and sexist priorities.

The film's part one, "Healthcare Worth Fighting For," opens in the center, with women celebrating the service. Rohrer as narrator explains the political fight about the center's future, over images of protests and a confrontation between organizers and officials. The narrator explains, over more montage, and with use of *The Fight for Life* (1940), that understanding the changing business of healthcare explains why Northwestern wants the center closed. We meet Scharene, and the narrator emphasizes that the success of the center is in its deep investment in prenatal care, thus avoiding unnecessary crisis. A fifteen-minute segment tracks Scharene's birthing process, which turns out to be in the one percent of births with complications. But nonetheless it transpires without incident. The section ends with the blissful mother and child, at peace. It shows what's at stake, in terms of one mother and child.

Part two, "The Struggle for Control," goes deeper into the changing economics of healthcare, and the fight to keep the center open. The narrator explains the sidelining of midwives, without providing any substitute for anyone but the wealthy. The center is a charity project of hospital board wives, until in the 1950s medical care becomes more about products than services. The narrator does not discount modern medicine: It "does have the potential to bring good healthcare to all people. In countries like China, it does." As we watch Scharene bring her baby in for a checkup, the narrator returns to the political standoff between WATCH and hospital board members. It's clear from a contentious meeting that the board members regard the WATCH women as a temporary nuisance. They offer figleaf concern, and even say there's no demand for the service. The center finally shutters, and the film closes with a glimpse at Scharene's baby boy, a return to the faces we met at the beginning of the film, and scenes of activism, accompanied by a rallying cry: "We're fighting together because only peoples' control of the healthcare system will guarantee that it meets everyone's needs."

Interestingly, the film's critique never touched on insurance. At the time, Medicare and Medicaid had just been passed, addressing the two largest groups (the poor and elderly) who were not covered by employer insurance, and the cost of healthcare was only beginning its dramatic climb upward. After that point, healthcare costs consistently grew faster than the economy and created an enduring national crisis around healthcare insurance.

The choice for a narrator and didactic exposition was a dramatic turn from the founders' style, but it aligned well with the focus of the collective on providing useable tools for social movements. Collective members debated whether the film should have a form that reflected its radical critique. Blumenthal recalled talking with Rosenthal soon after the film was released:

There were differences of opinion within the group on that question. Some people were more of the [avant-garde filmmaker Jean-Luc] Godard school ... What's important is to find a form that will communicate the ideas, and I think that that is what someone like Godard often forgets. He's not that interested in communicating ideas to the people who need the communication. He's more interested in satisfying himself and perhaps a few of his intellectual friends.

The film was also developed with substantial community input. Rohrer and Davenport screened versions of the film-in-progress for the CWLU group WATCH, for nursing classes and a health clinic, and at a Puerto Rican community center. "We wanted to make a film that continued to be *responsible* to the people who were in it and who would recognize its form. We didn't want them to say, 'That wasn't what we did,'" recalled Rohrer to Rosenthal. Thus, decades before public concern in the filmmaking community about "nonextractive" filmmaking, Kartemquin was collaborating with the people in the film and taking their feedback.

The film was self-distributed widely, through women's health organizing networks and with the help of CWLU, and also at festivals. The film had an electrifying effect on some. After a screening, one Florida women's group marched directly from the screening venue to a local hospital, to demand support for home deliveries. Among others, Judy Hoffman brought ties to the Young Patriot Free Health Clinic, which was aligned with the Black Panthers; and to Rising Up Angry, the working-class white organization, which also had a free health clinic.

The film also had a respectable life at festivals, due mostly to coincidence, since none of the makers knew anything about that world. In 1976, Quinn was working in France on contract on a film about Marc Chagall, with his old friend Chuck Olin. He had brought a 16mm print of *Chicago Maternity Center Story* with him, and he took it along when he attended the Rotterdam Film Festival, which showcases independent and experimental film. Quinn, entirely unaware of festival protocol, sought out the new festival's founder Huub Bals (it had just launched in 1972). Bals scheduled it right into the festival, leading to a screening at the Berlin Film Festival, which Rohrer and Blumenthal attended. "That event really opened up the world of festivals to us," Quinn recalled.

Europeans were fascinated with its analysis of corporate-run healthcare. Quinn later recalled his frustration at not being able to find a women's health network in The Netherlands to connect with around the film—until he realized that the country had socialized medicine. A film about the dangers of bottom-line capitalist healthcare was more of a curiosity than an urgent issue there.

Rohrer and Blumenthal were just as fascinated with a new film they saw at the festival, emerging from anticolonial, Third World film culture: the 1977 *The Perfumed Nightmare* by Kidlat Tahimik. That film whimsically chronicles the travels of a Filipino naïf who dreams of being an astronaut, and who finds out when he goes to Europe that progress isn't what colonialists claimed it to be. As devotees of film culture and as makers who saw themselves in the same filmic movement, they were thrilled to see it and to meet Tahimik.

The Chicago Maternity Center Story ended up being the only film that made money for Kartemquin in the collective years, and it was because of Rohrer's work with the new distribution collective, New Day Films. The film had a long tail in educational sales and community screenings. Amazingly, *The Chicago Maternity Center Story* continues to be shown. Quinn noted that he is always surprised at the age range of the audiences, all of whom connect with the material. Rohrer told me that made her furious, because it means the same issues are still urgent.

WORKING-CLASS GROUPS

In the early 1970s, the cultural workers at Kartemquin decided to make organizing films featuring white working-class people, and especially children. They saw that children of color appeared increasingly on television, although rarely in their own voice, but that working-class white children were absent. "'Let's do the thing that gets left out,'" Quinn recalled the group deciding. "Rising Up Angry was working primarily with white gangs trying to organize white kids against racism, and we were tied to them so it was like, 'Let's make some films about white working-class kids.'" Several films emerged from their bootstrapped efforts, which were assisted with a small grant from the Kohl Foundation; Kohl's was a

Midwest department store chain. The films exemplified the community-oriented, mission-driven work of the collective; they were coproduced by a number of collective members.

Gentrification was changing the working-class neighborhood around DePaul University in Lincoln Park at the time (Chicagoans today may be surprised that this area was ever working-class). Kuttner and Blumenthal both lived in the neighborhood, and they both employed a teenage girl there as a babysitter for their young children. That girl, Roxane Taylor, was a member of RUA. The 24-minute film *Now We Live on Clifton* (1974) follows Roxane's younger siblings Pam (10) and Scott (12) around the changing neighborhood. Pam narrates; Scott and his friends talk to and perform for the camera. Dad cooks dinner and leaves for work as a nighttime cab driver. Mom comes home from her secretary's job. Pam goes to karate class with Roxane. They play with their multiracial friends. "I like living here because all of my friends aren't white," says Pam. The film is still shown today, among other places in a geography class at DePaul University. Forty years later, when Kartemquin filmed an interview with Roxane and Pam (included on the DVD), Roxane was still in the neighborhood, and teaching at the high school where they filmed. They both mourn the decline of the neighborhood's diversity.

Winnie Wright, Age 11 (1974) was made about Gage Park, a neighborhood where Blacks were moving in, and whites were moving out. The Wright family came to Kartemquin through union contacts. Her father, an active union member in a can factory, had met his wife through political actions. They named their daughter Winifred, which means "win peace," because they were attending antiwar demonstrations at the time. Winnie provides an eleven-year old's perspective on her working-class family's struggles with low income, a possible strike, and pervasive racism. She says that the whites who moved did so "because they're prejudiced." As an adult (in an interview available on a Kartemquin DVD), she recalled the filming sunnily, and said she and her brother loved the attention they got. The film uses both verité and experimental approaches, with a pixelated opening by Teena Webb, and intertitles that Quinn thought would be in a "Brechtian," or confrontational and disruptive, style.

Winnie and *Clifton* were widely used in community screenings, and also received positive reviews. In *New Art Examiner*, Ralph Cintron noted a surprising lack of rhetoric. Rather than the work of determined politicos, these films contain almost as much restraint as conviction. By allowing their interviewees to speak for themselves Kartemquin / Haymarket [Haymarket was, briefly, the name of Kartemquin's distribution arm] has managed to avoid the trap of dogmatism which plagues most political filmmakers ... [B]y allowing the children to watch the world around them and talk about it Kartemquin / Haymarket has managed to make those films accessible to the public at large thus accomplishing much more than the militant purist.

Trick Bag: A Black and White Movie (1974) was made through Kuttner's RUA connections. In fact, he joined Kartemquin to make the film, after developing the idea at Chicago Newsreel and SDS. It featured RUA members who were in gangs, and who were Vietnam vets and factory workers. Originally, his idea was to produce a series of vignettes. Kuttner had started it in combination with a white mentor who had been a colleague of Stokely Carmichael. Carmichael had told him to develop projects with whites in the North.

When the TV series *All in the Family* came out in 1971, Kuttner saw it as amplifying stereotypes about white, working-class bigotry. He decided to fully develop a documentary narrative film that would represent working-class men positively. The participants perform conversations about the ways racism is used to divide them. The "trick bag" was the capitalist trap of making white people believe they were superior to others. Jerry Blumenthal fell in love with the people Kuttner had found—articulate young people who were white, Black, and brown, and who perceived racism as a threat to themselves and others. Jerry and he had, Kuttner recalled, long conversations about treating documentary like a fiction narrative, and emulating John Cassavetes, the independent filmmaker who used verité approaches in fiction.

In the end, the 21-minute film became five segments, which flowed into each other but could also be used stand-alone for discussion. In the first, white teenagers talk about racism in neighborhoods, and the racism they hear from their parents. One girl tells how she got evicted because her landlord saw her bring a Black friend home from work; within fifteen minutes of their arrival, he called saying two tenants had already called to complain. When she refused to throw her friend out, he gave her thirty days to move. The second segment addresses gangs. White, Black, and

Latino young men explain how representatives of different groups got together and agreed not to fight. One young man says, "They say there's a race problem between blacks and whites, but what there really is, is a class problem." The third focuses on racism in the military. Veterans describe racism from superiors and peers, and white favoritism. One white man tells a story of how his confronting of a superior's racism roused unsuspected sympathy from his Black peers, who rallied around him. "I see them come over and they tell the guy he's done [harassing the speaker for confronting him]. So it means less and less what color you are, and more and more where your head's at." The fourth segment is filmed in front of a Schwinn bicycle factory. Latino, Black, and white working men talk about white favoritism on the job, and a Black man suggests that Latinos get it worse than Blacks. A white worker says, "We are all being ripped off, all being exploited, and so long as they don't see each other much they can believe the myths . . . when you start seeing each other, you see you're living the same life, you're being fucked over by the same people." In the fifth segment, a mixed-race group of working women gather on a back porch, talking about workplace racism. One woman says media peddle white supremacy stereotypes, and they agree that management wins when it divides workers. A Latina worker says that white favoritism encourages them to fight for crumbs, "while employers make the big bucks." A Black woman says getting an education hasn't guaranteed her a good job. We have to "make the system change." Their arguments about racism being a strategic tool of worker division were core to RUA's position.

The film was extremely successful for its purpose: *Trick Bag* became a staple organizing tool for RUA. It continues to be shown, and to engender conversations on the issues that continue to be troubling today. The film also had a hyperlocal positive result. Kartemquin was constantly being tagged with graffiti from local youth gangs. Judy Hoffman befriended the Insane Unknowns, a subgroup of a neighborhood street gang. She threw a pizza party and showed them *Trick Bag*. Quinn recalled the kids being galvanized by some of the scenes, and angrily insisting, "It's like, true, true!" "It was like they thought we hadn't noticed," mused Quinn decades later. No one tagged the Kartemquin building again for years.

Viva La Causa (1974) was the project of Teena Webb, a teacher who came into the collective via feminist ties. The film focuses on the creation

Figure 8. Trick Bag, made with and for Rising Up Angry, a left-wing white working-class group, featured interracial conversations about the way racism divides working people. Source: Kartemquin Archives.

of a mural in a predominantly Latinx community south of Chicago's Loop, led by Latino artist Ray Patlán. The film focuses on this work as the latest in a tradition in Mexican art, reflecting the large population of immigrants and their descendants from (especially northern) Mexico. It explicitly links art and revolution, and captures a moment of growing Latinx consciousness.

The entire 12-minute film, with no synch sound, is either close-scrolling of existing murals or, at the end, scenes of young people making the mural. The audio features the artist Patlán, who is never introduced (although he is recognized in credits), working with young people, with comments from them and sparse narration. Patlán explains his own inspiration from studying Mexican murals and, from them, learning more about Mexican history and his own traditions. He describes the process of youth-made murals, and how the teens wanted to address a gang war with messages of peace in their designs. As the mural-in-progress comes to completion, we hear the teens debating its symbolism. "Murals can help me help the community, and develop my talent more," says a young man. "The work of art is really beautiful," says a young woman. In an open gesture to solidarity among Latinx groups, a young man declares, "The Puerto Ricans, their cause is our cause. In the US you tend to lose your identity." Another young man, in closing, says, "We can recover our history and our culture."

The films were shown in events cosponsored by the organizations with which Kartemquin worked. Kartemquinites brought them into schools and led discussions there. They sold them to universities. Their study guide plan was, sadly, never adopted in schools, nor were the films adopted into school curriculum, as Kartemquin had hoped. But the study guide plan later became a prototype for many such plans.

GRASSROOTS LABOR

Gordon Quinn had been attending regular workshops in the Gary/Hammond area, held by Staughton and Alice Lynd since the mid-1960s. Staughton Lynd was a democratic socialist, a pacifist, and at the time was a rank-and-file organizer with union locals. He had already had a brilliant academic career, which ended when Yale University fired him for political reasons; blackballed in academia, he turned to organizing. The writers' workshop he hosted in Gary, Indiana, a steel town next to Chicago, was populated with children of steelworkers, some of them steelworkers themselves, and all working for more democratic, less corrupt unions. It also included Vicki Cooper, soon to join the collective. Quinn found common cause in Staughton and Alice Lynd's resolute commitment to democracy.

The Lynds' concern with revitalizing the labor movement at the grassroots was part of a wider trend. Many people hoped to challenge both complacent union leadership and creeping globalization—some inspired by the movement to create the United Farm Workers, some by their experience with antiwar activism, civil rights, or feminist struggles, some trained at the Midwest Academy, others with Saul Alinsky's organizing precepts in their back pockets. The labor movement, which had a peak presence during World War II, had suffered a brutal corporate backlash afterward. Federal government retrenched labor rights dramatically with the Taft-Hartley Act of 1947, and prosecutions of corruption in unions resulted in more weakening legislation. Anticommunism contributed to shrinking labor's presence. Labor unions in industrial areas, prohibited from expanding, focused on parochial benefits for existing workers. They developed cooperative arrangements with the largest corporations to maintain peace in exchange for favorable contracts for core workers ("business unionism").

The new radicals of the later 1960s and 1970s faced entrenched union bureaucracies within the labor movement. Globalization was making the cooperative approach untenable, and labor's mainstream did not adapt. Globalization, with no check on international abuse of labor rights, also undermined the postwar industrial economy that "labor peace" produced through business unionism. Once real competition entered the picture—especially from Japan and Germany—labor peace turned to liability for business. Business reacted by breaking the "peace"—its agreements with unions to keep benefits rolling toward the union members. A recession triggered by the 1973-74 OPEC oil embargo became grimmer by the year, as inflation rose, and the term "stagflation" came into vogue. Smaller cars produced in Japan and Europe competed aggressively against heavier, larger American cars that used more gas.

At the outset of this process, the heady enthusiasm of 1960s social movements still pervaded the spirit of union organizing. Reformers worked in unions as varied as the United Electrical Workers, the Teamsters, the United Mineworkers, the Service Employees International Union, and a clutch of organizations working to organize informal sector and gig workers.

Out of the Lynds' regular meetings came Kartemquin's first union-related video, *Where's I. W. Abel?* United Steelworkers' president I. W. Abel had come to an agreement with ten steel firms not to strike, in a classic move of business unionism—without a member vote. At the same time, the steel industry was cutting wages and benefits, claiming that international competition threatened everyone's job without those cuts. To recruit worker support, the company and the international union had created a xenophobic and racist film, *Where's Joe?* (1972), about the danger of losing jobs to foreign workers, and the need for American workers to patriotically be more dedicated and accept less in order to compete. The film was shown in required meetings at workplaces. The half-hour video Kartemquin made is a point-by-point rebuttal of the film, by rank-and-file workers. The narrator is a member of the local, interviewing other workers and presenting evidence backed by research.

Clips from the xenophobic *Where's Joe?* provide the setup. (A copy of *Where's Joe?* had been sneaked to the team by a disgruntled worker.) That film is professionally made, and openly presents a jingoistic, anti-Japanese argument. The voice-of-God narrator argues that individual productivity—a "man-to-man showdown"—is the key to winning the battle against wily international companies whose workers "are after the lion's share... to put us right out of the big leagues." Responding to points clip by clip, in first-generation video, unionized workers argue that companies have refused to invest in modernizing and now want workers to solve their problems; that the productivity crisis is a "hoax"; that pitting US workers against international workers belies the fact that US companies are already using cheaper international labor; that already their wages are lowered and accidents are up. "The real worldwide contest is between workers everywhere and management everywhere," says the local rank-and-file leader. They then focus on Abel and their union. They argue that the international (the union leadership) sold out to the company; that the problems with having three-year contracts (which permit customers to stockpile supplies from foreign suppliers) are a self-created problem; that the right to strike is their only real weapon as union members; and that they need to restore grassroots leadership. It ends with workers singing union songs while protesting the international union's position.

The film was hastily shot entirely on half-inch video, and edited quickly, on a now-obsolete system. Quinn recalled, "We had been very proud of our craft, and we'd been editing in film to the frame, and so we thought, 'This video is absolutely terrible.' It was crude." Indeed, there are glitches, jerky editing, poor lighting, and some sound problems. Their fears were not warranted, in the end. The video was designed to speak directly to union members, and also to show union leadership the need to take grassroots voices seriously. Kartemquin used reel-to-reel machines and a hookup to the TV, to show the film in homes, bars, and meetings. "We had to explain to them, it's not being broadcast, it's just in your living room,"

Quinn remembered. It was hugely effective. "You could hear a pin drop, people were riveted to this movie, because they were gonna make decisions on what they would do and how they would vote based on this film," Quinn recounted. "It shows that you don't count all audiences the same. Someone who will watch a film because it'll inform their decision on their lives is different from the one watching the film in their Barcalounger."

Hoffman came into the collective to make another labor project: *What's Happening at Local 70* (1975). Unemployment compensation workers at one Chicago office were holding a wildcat strike, because they were working overtime on weekends and weren't getting paid appropriately. When they called Kartemquin for help, Gordon Quinn called Hoffman, who he'd been trying to get into the collective. She recalled, "I grabbed Sharon Karp and a Portapak and we went to their local office the night before the strike." They brainstormed with the strikers about why they were going on strike, and who to focus on. Hoffman edited in-camera on the spot and produced a 20-minute video that strikers watched that afternoon. Hoffman and worker colleagues set up screenings for the next nine weeks, finding bars or restaurants where workers at unemployment offices congregated, playing it on the establishment's TV set or a monitor.

The video is as simple, urgent, and clear as it is spontaneous—interviews with strikers about the conditions leading to the strike, the office's illegal retaliation, their need and hope for support from other locals. The stories are both highly specific and eye-opening. At one moment, management hired, right out of the unemployment line, seventeen Black job seekers to fill strikers' shoes. Strikers, including a Black woman, went to those workers and explained that they were breaking a strike, couldn't be punished for refusing to cross a picket line, and that they could ask to be relocated to other local offices. They did so, and ten of them also joined the union. Then management fired them, and the union helped to get them their jobs back.

The film proved a much-needed spark for organizers, and workers called a general strike for all unemployment offices, without union authorization. They marched together on the central unemployment bureau on Michigan Avenue, in the heart of Chicago's downtown. On that day, Hoffman showed the video, guerrilla-style, in Grant Park, the park between Michigan Avenue and Lake Michigan (the same one where in

2008 Barack Obama would celebrate his presidential win). In the end, the head of the Illinois unemployment bureau was fired and workers were hired back. Two weeks after the big downtown rally, the union called a meeting to censure the wildcat strikers. Hoffman and Quinn appeared with a Portapak and a TV monitor. As union members chanted, "Show the film!," they set it up and screened it over the objections of union leadership. The sentiment in the room changed, and the union voted to back the strike after all. "It doesn't get better than that," Quinn recalled.

Less immediately successful was Hoffman's 1975 attempt to chronicle the doctors' strike at Cook County Hospital, to protest budget cuts. While she was able to get the material on tape—including in the jail, where doctors were held for violating a back-to-work order—she lacked the time and resources to finish it. She showed rough takes at a meeting or two, and when the issue erupted again in the late 1980s, she reused the material successfully in that later organizing.

Gordon Quinn's labor connections led to the making of two half-hour films that have become classics of the genre, *Taylor Chain I: A Story in a Union Local* (1978) and *Taylor Chain II: A Story of Collective Bargaining* (1983). Vicki Cooper, whose focus was always health and safety in the workplace, drew Quinn's and Blumenthal's attention to a small chain factory in the Gary / Hammond area, where workers were defying their union's staffman (the national union liaison to the local) to protest dangerous working conditions. As the conflict evolved, the workers went on a seven-week strike for more pay and more safety language in the contract. The story became one of union democracy, and of rising militancy against stale union leadership.

Taylor Chain I is a closeup, intimate look at tense relationships within a union local. The evident trust of the participants is clear in the fact that the camera (run by Quinn) is nearly inside small groups as people argue. Quinn's and Blumenthal's ability to sense intuitively where the action will go and to move together toward it is also evident in these one-camera shoots, where the camera is tracking the emotional flow of the arguments. The two sometimes referred to this intuitive relationship as a kind of ballet.

The scene is set, and narrative advanced, largely with informational cards. We learn at the outset that Gary / Hammond is 97 percent Black, but the company is 98 percent white and 80 percent male.

The film opens with shots of the factory at work that echo the fascination with machinery of early "city symphony" films, which Quinn, Temaner, and Blumenthal had all studied in the Doc Films club. (They captured the footage by sending in a young team that represented themselves as students working on a student film.) Then we meet the international union's staffman and the local president. They're holding a meeting to discuss the upcoming negotiations. The staffman tries to manage expectations, as does the local head, but in the audience, members are clearly riled about plenty of issues: dangers in the workplace (a worker with a badly broken arm makes an excellent case), women's desire for more opportunity and fair treatment, young people's dismay at the passivity of older workers. The camera focuses in close-up on speakers, communicating their intensity. After early negotiations, the members meet again, and the members express outrage at the terms—both in terms of language on health and safety, and money. Local leadership leads them in a vote to strike.

Next we're on the street with the strikers blocking the gate, and inside their warmup trailer, where men have put up nude pinup pictures. By the next day, the women have retaliated with nude pictures of men. "That's where that women's lib comes in," says one man wryly. Everyone's trading strike stories. At the next meeting, we find that management has been trying to buy off key workers, and has cancelled their health insurance. Back on the picket line, the mood to reject the next deal is growing. At the next meeting, the staffman announces that callers have been harassing his family, and asks for respect; despite what they may think, he says, he cares about the local and always lets them vote. The negotiating committee is divided within itself about whether more can be won; in the end, the members prematurely call the vote, and apparently dissenters are swept into the almost unanimous call to reject. The strike is getting expensive for everyone. After two weeks, the company comes back with a little more money and better language. This time, the staffman starts the meeting by saying the local negotiators did all the work, and well. The local head claims responsibility. He tells them not to be intimidated, urging them to "be a man" (the group is dotted with women) and vote their conscience, without intimidation. After a thumbs-up vote, we watch people leave the building.

It's a quiet and undramatic end to a process that allows us to see the internal dynamics of difficult decisions, decisions that divide workers as much as they unite them. We've watched a local productively at odds with its international, in a relationship mediated by a sympathetic staffman. This is a film that depends both on a commitment to worker power and on the power of conversation about shared problems, in a Deweyan tradition. The drama is about whether people working out a solution to a common problem can do it. The filmmakers avoid easy hero / villain narratives, e.g., worker / company or local / international. The people they're following are all in good faith, coming from different positions and sometimes simply unsure of what's the best route.

The film took years to finish; the strike ended in 1974 and the film wasn't finished until 1978. It eventually aired on public TV in 1980, in the series *Matters of Life and Death and Other Matters*. That was a series provided by the Corporation for Public Broadcasting for a couple of years to placate filmmakers angry that public TV was not honoring a congressional mandate to showcase independent work. With the film about to go to air, the makers feared the reaction of the union's staffman, Jack Bierman. But Quinn recalled that he said, "I know you guys think I'm a stuffed shirt, but that movie is my life. That's what it's like."

The filmmakers wanted union support for distribution, but since the film told a story of member insurrection, that would not be easy. The staffman Bierman, though, arranged for Quinn and Blumenthal to meet in Pittsburgh with a United Steelworkers vice president. Quinn recalled that he argued for the film: "Yes, there's dirty laundry in this film, but you're seeing real democracy in action, not backroom deals. It's a pro-labor film, and if you endorse it that's how the press will cover it. If you oppose it, that will be the lead of every story." The argument worked, the Steelworkers publicized it to their members, and press coverage was sympathetic to the labor movement.

The film *UE/Wells* (1975) also resulted from personal contacts. A union organizer who knew Kartemquin's work, Guillermo Brzostowski, brought the project to them. A political refugee from Argentina's then-military dictatorship, he was a committed leftist. His union, the United Electrical, Radio and Machine Workers (UE), had a long leftist history. Formed in the 1930s with strong ties to the Communist Party and a commitment to socialism, it had been thrown out of the CIO (the Congress of Industrial Organizations, an industrial union federation) during McCarthyism; the CIO created an alternative union. The short, 15-minute film follows organizers interacting in Spanish, Arabic, and English with a highly diverse workforce. The organizers deal with employers' claims that the union foments strikes, is Communist, and is secretly run by Jews; they stress that voting for the union is just the beginning, and then the real work begins. One Arabic speaker says, "Here there is no difference between Arab and Jew. We are all human people, all working in the same place." Once the workers vote for UE, there's a heady celebration party, featuring a train-shaped cake—a metaphor for everyone getting on board.

While the film circulated in left union circles, in the larger labor movement there was deep distrust of the United Electrical Workers. UE's relative isolation as an openly left-wing union in the labor movement also meant that Kartemquin could not expect broader union endorsement for the film. Although a longer version was originally planned, fundraising proved futile. Then Brzostowski was beaten up and faced a death threat by a rival union's thugs during a different organizing effort; he left town.

The labor films and videos often succeeded in contributing directly to the movements of grassroots working people. Even when they were designed directly for advocacy, though, their focus was on showing how people deliberate together and successfully to address shared problems.

THE END OF AN ERA

The relationships established in the collective years would be carried into later work at Kartemquin. But by 1978, the group had begun to fall apart. No ideological divisions fractured the group. But the energy from the various 1960s civil rights, labor, ethnic, and feminist movements had dissipated, and not accidentally. Persistent FBI surveillance had done enormous damage to the Black Panthers and other organizations. Murders of civil rights leaders Malcolm X, Martin Luther King Jr., and Fred Hampton among others, as well as of presidential hopeful Robert Kennedy, who had become a civil rights ally, had sapped leadership. The police murders of students caught in antiwar protests at Kent State and Jackson State universities were a warning signal to many that the state would stop at nothing to repress dissent. Sectarianism hobbled some movements and organizations, such as the Chicago Women's Liberation Union. The Vietnam era's solidarity among the working-class youth affected by the draft had also collapsed with the end of the draft, and then the war. The labor movement was being corroded not only from within by "business union" policies but also by aggressive, neoliberal free-trade policies that threatened the labor movement itself.

So the terms of making a living in America did not change enough for members of the 1970s Kartemquin collective to create different kinds of opportunities to support themselves. As enthusiastic young activists matured and started families, financial pressures forced them to find other ways to support themselves. In a pattern that was to repeat itself, Kartemquin's economic stability was both sustained and undermined by its dependence on commitment beyond the demands of the marketplace. The collective era succeeded for almost a decade, on the back of political passion but also the camaraderie of people who shared a commitment to a nonsectarian dream of democratic socialism.

Kartemquin's projects had been designed to have the makers take responsibility for their whiteness. The importance of feminist movements in the projects they undertook brought female leadership. They saw the work they did as part of the working-class movements they supported. They all had confidence in and respect for the people they made their films for and with. They imagined a future where those people's voices could become louder in the national discourse.

The collective years paved the way for new career possibilities for many of the participants, and they took their idealism into union organizing, healthcare work, education, or more independent filmmaking. The majority of them continued to drift in and out of Kartemquin, project by project, and became part of an extended network of activist contacts. Finally, their years at Kartemquin left a legacy of widely shared commitment to social-change media.[1]

5 Confronting Neoliberalism with Workers' and Women's Stories, 1978–1985

Kartemquin's postcollective years were a turn toward professionalism, but not at the expense of the core Deweyan values that motivated the group. Kartemquin collaborated with grassroots organizations, especially rank-and-file labor and union locals fighting for dignity. It worked on projects that would support Democrats in elections, responding to and reflecting the grassroots Midwestern constituencies that supported them. The organization continued to depend on work-for-hire and equipment rental to keep the doors open, and creative and logistically talented women were crucial to the operation. The films Kartemquin made in this period reflected how working people in the US, including women and union members, experienced the fierce new wave of neoliberalism.

As the Chicago collective faded away, a new political era arose. With the election of Ronald Reagan in 1980, a sea change in politics was underway. Although the Carter administration had paved the way with its anti-Washington campaign rhetoric and its market policies, the Republican victors aggressively sought to remake government itself. Neoliberalism's political approach rejects state social programs, associates private enterprise with the public good, and minimizes regulation of even monopolistic businesses. The government institutions brought into existence in the

New Deal and in Lyndon Johnson's Great Society era weakened or fell under unforgiving scrutiny. This had repercussions in the arts: renewed Republican hostility to public broadcasting, attacks on the National Endowment for the Arts ending in the NEA's inability to give grants directly to artists, and attacks on the National Endowment for the Humanities for funding "liberal" projects. Meanwhile, the Reagan administration conducted proxy wars with the Soviet Union throughout the world, including in Afghanistan and Central America, some of it funded by covert weapons sales to Iran. When public broadcasters attempted to provide independent reporting on those wars, the administration used unrelenting pressure to minimize it.

Reagan had also come to office riding a tide of public anger over high inflation and a recession, which had been precipitated by a number of events: a geopolitically triggered oil embargo raising the price of gasoline and goods in the US, declining value of the US dollar internationally, and effects on the US labor market from international trade. Kartemquin's microeconomy was destabilized as well, but perhaps mostly due to the collapse of left-wing coalitions and movements, which left them without partner organizations for making activist films. Their work-for-hire work never flagged, though.

Kartemquin's relationship with the still-young venue of public broadcasting was becoming more complicated. Post-1980, public broadcasting, barely more than a decade old and already seasoned in political battles, tacked to changing political winds. By 1981, the Corporation for Public Broadcasting, which held federal taxpayer dollars, faced brutal hostility from the Reagan administration as it began negotiations for its two-year-in-advance funding for the 1984–87 triennium. The administration proposed to halve its budget. (Congress disagreed, although CPB still took a $40M hit for 1984.)

Independent filmmakers had firmly lodged themselves as a thorn in the side of CPB, while arguing that they were indispensable to public broadcasting's service to the American people. Organized out of the social movements of the 1960s and 1970s, as reflected in the Bard conference, they positioned themselves as proxies for the diverse voices of the American grassroots, located as they were in every state in the nation, and committed to telling stories of ordinary people. Kartemquin was an early and active actor in the movement, and an important source of the Deweyan core arguments for independent filmmakers' importance.

What would become a ten-year campaign to create the Independent Television Service had begun in 1978. Indies had won space on the national schedule—the public-affairs series *Crisis to Crisis*. But by 1982, the series had been retired, putatively because station programmers saw it as uneven in quality and subject; ratings were low, and so was system support. CPB, which still had a line item of some $20M for programming in conjunction with PBS (at the time, PBS was still a station cooperative), decided to sink most of its money into "superseries," such as *Frontline, Great Performances,* and *American Playhouse,* none of which were likely venues for films like Kartemquin's. Public TV executives were trying desperately to find mainstream, middle-class-pleasing ratings hits that could insulate them from congressional and administrative ire. They also wanted to court potential "underwriters" (advertisers under another name), including oil and insurance companies. Kartemquin still had a contract with TV Lab, the embattled experimental wing of CPB's program funding. This semi-autonomous unit of public TV, partly funded by Ford and Rockefeller Foundation money, was established soon after public TV's inception, in the early 1970s, by David Loxton. He was a creatively ambitious British executive at the New York station WNET, with experience in both broadcast fiction and nonfiction. (WNET was one of the few public TV stations that produced programs picked up by PBS.) With Kathy Kline, he not only nurtured new video artists but set up a small production fund, Independent Documentary Fund. But TV executives looking to attract upper-middle-class audiences with anchor programs featuring nature, culture, and British drama often now looked askance at TV Lab projects. TV Lab finally fell to Reaganite neoliberalism within public TV and closed in 1984; Loxton died of cancer in 1989.

Kartemquin would face new challenges and opportunities as the business continued to change. Viewing was still a mass media experience, split between two screens: television and film. One-to-one communication was by telephone, telegraph, or mail. But on the horizon were media technologies that would fragment and proliferate audiences. Cinematic tinkerers were not the only ones searching for new connections. The VCR, an expensive and clumsy consumer product in 1970, became ubiquitous and sleek by the mid-1980s. The personal computer was becoming a high-end office tool. Cable television, long an unglamorous connection that extended the reach of broadcast, would suddenly become national programming once satellites made national transmission of content cheap in the early 1980s. Kartemquin would become a place with computers, using VCRs for outreach, and building capacity to enter the cable era.

The Kartemquin team slowly grew. Blumenthal and Quinn anchored the business, and Hoffman and Kuttner were frequent participants. Jenny Rohrer returned in 1982, after a stint as a union organizer and international travel. Kartemquin cobbled together a salary for her. An eager young filmmaking recruit fresh out of college, Peter Gilbert, sought them out, too.

Gilbert had grown up in Chicago, his mom a professor of education and his dad a local builder who had ascended from poverty with a scholarship-enabled, University of Chicago education to a career as a builder of starter homes. "I first heard about John Dewey from my mom," Gilbert remembered. Both parents were civil rights activists, and Gilbert spent time at marches as a child. At the University of Wisconsin, he got an education at the film societies that at the time were the core of film culture. Transferring to New York University, he learned among others from Larry Silk, an editor on Barbara Kopple's films, and he studied *Inquiring Nuns* with fascination. Moving to Los Angeles after college, he worked for Haskell Wexler, who counseled him to get out of selling his cinematography services and to aspire to tell his own stories. Wexler also gave him another piece of excellent advice: Buy a camera, because that makes you the director of photography. Moving back to Chicago, Gilbert did buy a $125,000 camera, by putting down a $5,000 deposit and having his parents cosign a loan to be paid off over the fifteen years the camera would be useful. Confident of his progressive values, Gilbert also saw enormous opportunity in the commercial world of television. And he loved playing with new technologies.

He knocked on Kartemquin's door, and he wouldn't go away until he got to do something. The stripped-down operation welcomed him, especially since they were surviving on miscellaneous commercial jobs. But they could only fit him into projects occasionally. In 1985, because Quinn was too busy, Gilbert took a job working with Barbara Kopple on *American*

Dream, the story of a drawn-out strike in a Minnesota meatpacking plant that was finally released in 1990. The problems workers faced were emblematic of the problems of workers in that era, ones that Kartemquin too would chronicle. That experience deepened his skills and understanding of the kind of films that Kopple and Kartemquinites wanted to make. Gilbert never went on staff at Kartemquin, but he always regarded Kartemquin as his professional home. His mentors included not only the founders but also the strong women in the shop, particularly Jenny Rohrer and Judy Hoffman. He would eventually serve on the founding fiduciary board of directors.

Young Northwestern film graduate Marcy McCall, after reading a short piece about Kartemquin in the *Chicago Tribune*, showed up in 1983, hungry for an opportunity to hang around. She stayed for four underfunded years, first volunteering and then becoming essential to Kartemquin's business side. She never gave up her job at Crate & Barrel, which was essential to supplement her meager salary at Kartemquin. Like other Kartemquin employees, she saw the tattered file folder holding Gordon Quinn's college thesis, linking the philosophy of John Dewey with cinema verité documentary. She didn't read it, but she imbibed the spirit of the argument, she said, from the films, which the group would watch and analyze. "I think their films speak their philosophy," she said.

The group created a revenue stream by carefully chosen industrial work, including for nonprofits and unions. They also crewed on commercials, among others for Mama Celeste pizza. Kartemquin was by now known in the corporate world as the place for your promotional or training film if you wanted real people, a cinema verité look, a documentary feel. Blumenthal, Quinn, and Hoffman also worked regularly with the left-liberal production house Chuck Olin Association, on its contract with Encyclopedia Britannica Films. Olin had been part of the team that made *American Revolution II* (1969) about the 1968 Democratic Convention and *The Murder of Fred Hampton*. Dirk Wales's Rainbow Productions, an industrial-production firm, had a contract with Ohio Medical to produce training films for anesthesiologists. "It wasn't evil work, and at least you were working in the industry," Hoffman noted. They rented out their editing suites. Kartemquin also let rank-and-file members of a union, the International Brotherhood of Electrical Workers, in the factory nearby meet in the storefront for months; the union members eventually won control of their local, switched affiliation to the more progressive United Electrical Workers, and rented the space.

For one wild moment, Kartemquinites thought they had stumbled upon a liberating revenue stream. They agreed to make a film for the Illinois Caucus on Teenage Pregnancy (ICTP). Teens working with ICTP had engaged with Oprah Winfrey, who was yet to become a national figure and was still hosting a local TV show, to host an event: *Teens Speak Out to Oprah* (1986). With young people from Denise Zaccardi's Community TV Network as crew, the noted Chicago editor Bill Haugse edited the 16-minute piece, which featured rich emotional moments. It seemed like an item that would sell nationwide.

But the contract with Oprah gave her final cut. Oprah had just starred in the mainstream film *The Color Purple* (1985), and had also just signed the contract to do her now world-famous, national TV show. She had a new agent, production company, and lawyer, and the lawyer nixed national distribution. Kartemquin had already put money into a national marketing campaign, purchasing (in those pre-digital days) mailing lists with labels, and foresaw future profits for both them and the Illinois Caucus. But Oprah's agent drove a hard bargain, and ICTP didn't want to be on a collision course with Oprah. In the end, Kartemquin could only distribute in the state of Illinois. It was another near-miss in getting financial stability.

LABOR AND POLITICS

The labor connections made during the collective years carried over into the new era. Now, though, labor was in crisis, because of the relentless pressures of globalism and neoliberalism. People in crisis turned to Kartemquin for help, as the one place that embraced storytelling about rank-and-file labor issues.

Kartemquin was pioneering in its documentary focus on the organizing of rank-and-file workers facing neoliberalist deindustrialization. In fact, only a small minority of filmmakers focused on labor issues at all. Filmmakers at Appalshop, the media arts center started in the Great Society era in Kentucky, were telling labor stories, such as Elizabeth

Barrett's *Coalmining Women* (1982). Tony Buba's mournful memoir from a Pennsylvania Rust Bowl town, *Voices from a Steeltown* (1983), was a personal lament. Barbara Kopple's *American Dream* would continue the story of union attempts to resist ever-larger corporate control. Lyn Goldfarb, who worked within the Service Employees International Union in the 1980s, made films such as the 1984 *From Bedside to Bargaining Table*, about organizing in the service industries. Christine Choy and Renee Tajima-Peña's 1987 *Who Killed Vincent Chin?* also dealt with deindustrializing labor issues, but within the context of the murder of a Chinese American worker by other workers. Julia Reichert's work, in later life with Steve Bognar, focused on labor in the neoliberal context. But films about labor issues and organized workers were and continue to be more the exception than the rule. Kartemquin distinctively embraced rank-and-file unionism as the story of workers in the deindustrializing crisis forming Deweyan publics—finding common cause in their conditions and holding their organizations accountable.

The Taylor Chain factory's United Steelworkers Association staffman Jack Bierman returned to Kartemquin in 1981, almost a decade after the first film, saying he could get them inside a labor negotiation. The workers were desperate, with the company in peril and workers having suffered drastic pay cuts. They wanted Kartemquin to film the negotiation process from the inside. No one had ever made a publicly available film of a labor negotiation. Even in Barbara Kopple's *American Dream*, viewers only can see the union caucus, not the negotiations. (Quinn filmed that caucus.) Unlike in *Taylor Chain I*, the new management of the factory was amenable and cooperative in the project. It too was struggling. As the half-hour film reveals, the negotiation was taking place in a very different environment than the earlier strike. Times were hard for both sides. Both workers and management were caught up in the deindustrialization trend that was associated with globalization without regulation, and which turned swaths of America into postindustrial dead zones.

The resulting half-hour, 16mm film, *Taylor Chain II*, like other Kartemquin films shot *in media res*, captured in cinema verité style the issues and tensions at the negotiating table itself, as the process developed its own narrative arc. The film is told from the viewpoint of the workers and the union local. The new management permitted the film crew to film

Figure 9. Gordon Quinn and Jerry Blumenthal interview a worker in the Taylor Chain factory, in *Taylor Chain II;* they were allowed unsupervised interactions with workers. Source: Kartemquin Archives.

the negotiations themselves, something almost never captured in film, and unlike in *Taylor Chain I* gave them the run of the plant to film the remaining workers.

It starts with some harsh realities—the small factory is barely surviving a rough period, with a deep recession in the area, high unemployment, and closed businesses. The factory is under new management; for the first time in its history it is no longer family-owned. The new president explains that the family hadn't invested in modernizing; he had to replace the hugely expensive furnace. The workers have already agreed to a one-year wage freeze while management tries to rebuild the factory, and they now reluctantly have accepted a 10 percent wage cut. It hasn't stopped layoffs, though; half the workers have been let go.

The film moves into negotiations, inside a claustrophobic room at a Holiday Inn. The union's negotiating committee sits on one side of the table, managers on the other. Bierman, the USWA staffman who had to earn the trust of the workers in *Taylor Chain I*, is now a trusted partner of the local's workers. The union wants the wage cuts restored, with a 5 percent increase; a cessation of contracting with outside services, such as for janitors; and a discussion of health and safety issues. Managers say they can't give up the right to hire part-time and outside workers. The union local president, Winnie, who had been a sharp critic of local leadership in the first film, says sharply, "That's what we can't do." Bierman agrees: "We've done everything we can to keep that plant going, but—not that language." He goes on, "We're not going to give you a license to steal."

By the next morning, the plant manager, Jerry, has agreed: "I can live with the language of the contract as it is right now." Bierman is grateful, and says to him, "We [labor and management] need to be a team." A manager suggests that they have a one-year contract, and that they gradually raise the salary to what it had been, chiseling away at the 10 percent cut by 1 percent a quarter (so that in 2½ years it will be restored, although the contract will only guarantee the first year). Union members go away to think about it. In the afternoon, Bierman says to the company reps that they'll need 4 percent the first year. The company lawyer says, "I'm not rude, so I'm not gonna walk out. But [this] is the final position of this company."

When they meet again, the company says they can't raise salaries more than they have offered, but they will offer a month of insurance—if the bargaining committee recommends the contract to its members. The committee members discuss whether they can do it. Winnie says almost to herself, about the bargaining process, "It's not as easy as people think." Bierman reminds the group that with such high unemployment, a threat to walk off the job isn't credible. They finally agree to support the tiny concessions they have won. In the membership meeting, they explain the deal, and say they have done everything they can. Unlike the contentious atmosphere a decade earlier, the union local—apparently now more familiar with the union process and all too familiar with the grim economic realities—votes overwhelmingly in favor.

A year later, Winnie tells the filmmakers that the union has won another year-long contract under the same terms, but the factory is still struggling. In the epilogue, the narrator tells us that five months later, the factory declared bankruptcy and closed the plant. The workers kept their pensions, but lost their vacation time. A year after closing, half the workers were still unemployed.

The film is a sober and thought-provoking record of economic crisis brought home. The management team flounders with the challenge of resuscitating a small factory when high inflation makes loans pricey, globalist trade policy undercuts their efforts to stay competitive, and of course there's the recession. They're eager to show the workers they appreciate their efforts, but grim about their own prospects. The workers are thoughtful, realistic, angry about being in a corner despite their hard work, and worried. The union staffer holds out for respect for the workers, but also gives respect to good-faith gestures by management.

Taylor Chain II went inside a union negotiation with sympathy for the workers, but the film wasn't imagined or designed as an advocacy piece for them. It was designed for members of the public to understand what was at stake, at a crisis moment for working people whose lives had been upended by globalization. It didn't ask people to take sides in the negotiation, which involved two desperate parties. It invited people to consider what the workers and management were facing, and why they took the positions they did. What the film asked of viewers, in what was becoming a Kartemquin tradition, was to participate in the problem that the parties in conflict at the small chain factory south of Chicago faced. The film has become a staple in higher education, especially in law schools, and in unions, where it was received enthusiastically. It continues to be sold and used, particularly in labor-relations programs in universities. It has also been used by pro-management firms, to understand how negotiations take place. The problem-posing approach, about a public issue, is why the film was powerful then, and why it continues to be valuable long after the factory closed and all the participants' working lives ended.

The film's production was one result of Kartemquin's policy efforts to expand space for independent filmmaking on public broadcasting. It was made with funding from the Corporation for Public Broadcasting, through the Program Fund for the independent series *Matters of Life and Death . . . and Other Matters*. This was yet another of public TV's anthology series created to house stand-alone, point-of-view documentaries, a begrudging response to demands from independent filmmakers; it ended up as short-lived as *Crisis to Crisis*, but Kartemquin managed to leverage it while it existed. Funding also came from the Indiana Committee for the Humanities and a community foundation, The Crossroads Fund. The Steelworkers' union had provided the start-up money, with a $15,000 grant that came with a contract clause guaranteeing that it would have no editorial control. CPB, however, demanded that Kartemquin return the Steelworkers' money to avoid perceptions of conflict of interest. Very reluctantly, Quinn agreed to do that, while also grumbling (accurately) that CPB had much higher conflict-of-interest standards for labor money than it did for corporate money. Fortunately, USWA continued to promote the film and the broadcast.

When workers at the Pullman factory that made sleeper train cars and subway cars found their jobs in danger with a proposed factory shutdown in 1980, they also came to Kartemquin. They wanted the filmmakers to tell their story. Like the workers at Taylor Chain in the early 1970s, they were at odds not only with their employers but with their union, the Steelworkers. The story wasn't just their story. Workers throughout the Rust Belt and beyond were living the same drama.

Blumenthal and Quinn wanted to follow the Pullman story from the perspective of the rank-and-file. And for that, they needed to show the workers what they did to win their trust. So they brought a 16mm projector to the local's headquarters, and showed films to groups of 20–40 people. As well as their own work, Kartemquinites also showed *Harlan County, U.S.A.*, Barbara Kopple's Oscar award winning 1976 film, chronicling a miners' strike. The workers were fascinated; they had never seen films like that, Quinn later recalled.

The filmmakers followed the story for more than two years, until the plant was shut down. Quinn did cinematography, with Hoffman, and Blumenthal sound; they codirected and coedited. It was the last film that they coedited, though. Blumenthal became lead editor and the person who "taught everyone at Kartemquin how to edit," recalled Peter Gilbert.

Greg LeRoy, a white graduate student who had worked as an Amtrak sleeping car porter, was lead researcher on the history of unionizing in the railcar industry. The porter job had been his first out of college, and also his first experience of the Brotherhood of Sleeping Car Porters, which he quickly realized was "a historic institution, a Black-led union." He had studied its history, thanks to an NEA youth grant. A progressive archivist

Figure 10. From left, Jerry Blumenthal (with mic), Judy Hoffman, and Gordon Quinn shooting a demonstration of unionized workers against deindustrialization at the state legislature, for *The Last Pullman Car.* Source: Kartemquin Archives.

at what is now the Chicago History Museum had handed him a newspaper clipping about the Kartemquin project, and he immediately got in touch. By the time the film team was documenting the end of an era, LeRoy was working on his MA thesis about the Pullman porters. Jenny Rohrer also researched the labor history, and they accumulated a wealth of archival material. Rohrer and LeRoy were also associate producers.

They began shaping a story. Their work was helped by funding and consulting support from TV Lab. Another beneficiary of TV Lab assistance at the time was Kartemquin alumnus Richard Schmeichen, who with Robert Epstein made *The Times of Harvey Milk* (1984).

In the last days of TV Lab's short life, Loxton and Kline traveled to Chicago to consult with the filmmakers on the shape and storyline. They told the filmmakers how relieved they were that Kartemquin's filmmakers, unlike some independents, would listen to their advice; the filmmakers told them how grateful they were someone was paying attention to their work. The hour-long film eventually interwove cinema verité footage of the strikers' struggles with the history of the union local, the rise of monopoly capitalism, and industrial unions. Quinn and Blumenthal drew on their experience working on commercial work-for-hire contracts to get a key interview with a former president of the Pullman company. They also drew on their experience in the collective, working with social-change movements.

Rohrer's influence is evident in the film's core structure. Drawing from the experience with *The Chicago Maternity Center Story*, but integrating the analytical and cinema verité components, the filmmakers made the film a political and historical essay. As before, they used a female narrator and newspaper headlines, historical images and clips. The central part of the film provides a capsule history of American labor, intertwined with the workers' struggle to keep their jobs, and the film interweaves historical context and sequences of worker action throughout.

The film recounts the rise of monopolist railroad barons including Pullman, and worker efforts with Eugene V. Debs to form a nationwide industrial union and win the political right to organize. It signals the importance of the federal government, which twice (both during wartime) provided workers rights that it retracted or denied at other times. The film still shocks in its telling of federal troops and Chicago police murdering striking workers, and of Pullman's blatant racism in using Black workers as strike-breakers and threatening to fire them if they unionized. The film then turns to the crisis that occupies the film: conglomerization, capital flight, and the financialized world of mergers and takeovers. It shows the rise of neoliberal political justifications for refusing to leverage government on behalf of workers, or even for survival of American businesses.

This history contextualizes what happened to two thousand workers at the Pullman plant. The film begins with the workers' trip to the Illinois Statehouse, to argue for support for workers and to keep the railcar business in America. They are acutely aware of the need for labor strategies that can address the current business trends, and also that their union is not adapting to the crisis. One worker warns, "They better get off their duff." The local union head, John Bowman, makes cogent arguments to lawmakers about the need to support the people they represent, not corporations. Workers talking among themselves worry about automation, and they agree that the companies "don't care about anything but money." Their collective efforts beat back a right-to-work law in Illinois, but they don't get what they wanted—requiring a year's notice before closing, and compensation to affected communities.

A failed contract negotiation later, Bowman says they just have to focus on holding on to their jobs. But the union can't do that, as a historical interlude explains. Now Bowman is looking at a tiny local, of perhaps fifty workers, and a staffman who puts them under receivership. This means that the international union now controls the local. Workers plead with the staffman to use union savings to conduct a campaign to save the plant, but he's deaf to their pleas. Bowman says to workers around him, "If this is their answer to deal with plant closings in this country, the working man is in trouble."

When Pullman is sold to another conglomerate, the workers briefly hope their unit will be reopened. But the company offers a grossly insulting contract, then blames the union for why the company decides not to reopen. Workers in the meeting are outraged, and one sees a broader plan: "They're trying to break the back of labor."

At the last union picnic, young people play volleyball and veterans reminisce. One points out that in Europe infrastructure is well developed, while US rail infrastructure is outdated and even dangerous. Why, he wonders, couldn't government use the workers' talents to fix these problems? This is also a question for the film's viewers.

Like *Chicago Maternity Center Story*, this film provides an unapologetically political analysis. The film argues that workers cannot fight feckless international capital without both a strong union and a political party that is backed by and represents working people as workers. The film's perspective shows that the postcollective Kartemquin remainers had imbibed the political analysis of the collective years. The film is told from the viewpoint of the workers at the plant, and it showcases their capacity. Not only are they skilled and familiar with engineering issues—sometimes more than the engineers in charge. They also have an acute understanding of the politics of the labor movement, and the politics of bargaining. They are much more aware than the international union's officials of the need for nationwide campaigns and strategies, just as Debs argued almost a century before. They are facing a crisis of capitalism with knowledge and insight, and Kartemquin invites the viewers into the same process.

The most shocking thing about the film, at this remove, is that it was able to land a slot on public broadcasting's prime time, which scholar Erik Barnouw had with devastating politeness called "safely splendid" programming. That achievement in no small part was due to Loxton and Kline's expertise in managing the process. It also was distributed to targeted audiences. With Rohrer's help, Marcy McCall set up educational distribution through New Day Films. McCall learned the distribution business realities quickly. The entire Kartemquin collection, from *Home for Life* through *Chicago Maternity Center Story* and now the labor films, began being placed in university libraries throughout the country. In this period, educational sales were the most lucrative aspect of independent filmmaking, since libraries were willing to pay institutional prices up to hundreds of dollars for either film or video versions. Educational sales became crucial to Kartemquin's survival, and McCall became crucial to that side of Kartemquin's business.

Reviews largely praised the film for telling a neglected story from the workers' perspective. Staughton Lynd himself argued that it supported a workers' movement; labor scholar David Bensman called it "haunting," commending it for its educational value. The film was shown at film festivals, and it won the top prize at the Athens, Ohio Film Festival. And of course it showed on public TV, before going to cable's Learning Channel and into university libraries throughout the country. With LeRoy's help, Kartemquin won funding from the Illinois Arts Council and the National Endowment for the Humanities to write an extensive study guide, which helped with educational sales. Like the Taylor Chain films, Pullman had the ability to cross between disciplines—law, labor studies, economics, history, and political science. The union itself was thrilled with it, and this time, the filmmakers did not need to convince the international or other unions to use it themselves.

Sociologist Bernard Beck at Northwestern University argued that the three labor films from Kartemquin in this era "constitute a contemporary history of industrial workers undergoing rapid and painful change." Beck himself had been part of the early discussion groups led by sociology professor Howard Becker at Kartemquin's Hyde Park offices. Beck argued that their work had the quality of scholarly close observation, the vision that had launched Kartemquin:

CONFRONTING NEOLIBERALISM, 1978-1985   119

Kartemquin is notable for the care it takes to present subjects in context and to avoid manipulating the viewer's interpretation with its own commentary. When we see and hear union workers expressing opinions about negotiations with the company, we are also shown fully the place where they are speaking, the activity they are engaged in, and the other people present. Kartemquin is meticulous about the temporal sequence of events. This rich specification of circumstances gives us the opportunity to witness concrete events and does not palm off on us general impressions, atmospheric glimpses, or anonymous illustrations.

He argued that they behaved like "field researchers," who are on the side of their participants, intimately close to them. This observation harked back to Kartemquin's origins, in "cinematic social inquiry." It also evoked the Deweyan vision of engaging people as citizens, telling stories that both expose problems and the ability of people to address them together. *The Last Pullman Car* (1983) not only chronicled labor organizing but also the need for people to organize politically to demand more from their governments, to address industrial policy.

For Kartemquinites, one of the disturbing ironies of the labor work was that union-busting consultants also used the films. After all, the films chronicled, close-up, the brutal challenges union organizing faced. Talking about *Pullman*, LeRoy recalled, "But a point of the movie is to say that there's a historical reason why the union has less decision-making power than it should. As unions were purged of their left wing, a lot of power was ceded to management." As well, he noted, "It was a tragedy that there was no industrial policy. How could our country be so dependent on foreign capital?" When the project was over and he finished his MA, there were no more opportunities for LeRoy to continue with Kartemquin. As usual, the organization was running on fumes.

WOMEN'S VOICES: THE GENDER GAP (1984)

Kartemquin's other notable project in the postcollective years was an explicitly political one, a film designed to support a Democratic presidential win in 1984. In mid-1982, when Jenny Rohrer returned after traveling overseas, she immediately got involved in local Democratic politics. It was an exciting time for it. Longtime Democratic politician Harold Washington, a Black leader, was running for mayor, reviving Hampton's "rainbow coalition" concept. He was speaking to the people that Mayor Richard Daley had deliberately and consistently disenfranchised over his entire term (1955–76): the Great Migration generation, their children and grandchildren, who suffered most directly from his segregation policies and their legacy, including voter suppression. He also appealed to the so-called "lakefront liberals," white upper-middle-class and wealthy voters who skewed to the left. This was Washington's second mayoral bid; Kartemquinites had crewed on some Olin commercials for him the first time. Rohrer joined a small army of Washington supporters, including those mobilized by the Young Lords and by left-leaning groups targeting white liberals. The resulting hundred thousand new voters carried Washington to victory in the primary, and fought off a Republican challenger who was being helped by many Democrats.

In 1984, now part of the community of active Democrats in the city, Rohrer saw another political imperative: the presidential election. She was outraged, she later recalled, among other things by cutbacks to student meal programs, the gutting of Pell grants, and the open assault on women's reproductive rights. The Democratic hopeful, Walter Mondale, was running a campaign—ultimately doomed—against incumbent Ronald Reagan. Many political operatives thought the women's vote would be crucial, as the 1980 elections had revealed a marked "gender gap," with women disproportionately voting Democrat. (This also factored into Mondale's choice of a female running mate, Geraldine Ferraro.) Much was at stake. The first Reagan presidency had aggressively implemented its neoliberal agenda—union-busting, running roughshod over regulatory bodies, ripping holes into the social safety net.

So in January 1984, Rohrer came to the office with a new idea—a short film on the gender gap, to mobilize the women's vote in the upcoming election. A well-connected volunteer at Kartemquin, the social-justice-minded Nancy Meyer, agreed. While getting an education degree, she had come to have a reverential respect for the ideas of John Dewey, and used them in her work at a nonprofit for early childhood education. She also organized left-wing activist philanthropy, as one of a dozen cofounders of the social-justice foundation Crossroads Fund. Creating slide-tape presentations in her nonprofit work had given her the idea of making films. So she headed to Kartemquin, the most well-known indie production house in Chicago, and one founded on Deweyan principles. "I wanted a way to bring together my interests in history, activism and social justice, which was exactly what Kartemquin was about," she recalled.

Meyer loved Rohrer's idea, and she thought she was ready to use her filmmaking skills, honed by working on *The Last Pullman Car* and taking classes at Columbia College. She also helped the team get legal advice on creating a Subchapter S Corporation to raise money for a campaign film—not something Kartemquin could do. The filmmakers were able to leverage their Democratic Party connections to access Democratic lakefront liberals, especially women, and they quickly raised $125,000 for a 15-minute film. Now they were on a tight deadline, to deliver the film to Democratic Party activists by the National Organization for Women's June convention within four months. Meyer and Rohrer produced the film with Quinn (who also shot the film). Rohrer directed, with sound / editing from Blumenthal and Hoffman's assistant camerawork.

Women's Voices: The Gender Gap was an unusual video in the 1984 campaign. It demonstrated the Kartemquin conviction that ordinary working people's stories could be more effective than rhetoric and that ordinary people could identify problems commonly shared, as well as confirming its commitment to quality in production. So it did not sell an argument, but documented the commitment of voters to candidates who would support the concerns of women who worked in all aspects of the American economy. It was highly produced, on film and with cell animation. Its tone is set by cartoons by Nicole Hollander, a noted, nationally syndicated Chicago cartoonist—and the house cartoonist for *In These Times*—and a part of the extended Kartemquin community. Her cartoons, animated by the team of Sydney and Ron Crawford, featured her signature Sylvia character—a wiseacre of a fed-up feminist, who had an equally alienated and also wiseacre cat—as well as other snappy-comeback women.

The film opens with a jaw-droppingly sexist clip taken from a local TV morning news show, shown on a TV set within a Hollander cartoon. A female anchor describes the gender gap, and her male counterpart says, "Is there any way of knowing how many women vote for a male candidate

Figure 11. A sketch for *Women's Voices: The Gender Gap* by Nicole Hollander, among other things house cartoonist for *In These Times*. Hollander's sardonic drawings were animated and used throughout the film. Source: Jenny Rohrer. Artist: Nicole Hollander.

because they find him attractive?" The sullen cat, who has spread himself over the top of the TV set, dumps a jar of nail polish over the male anchor's head on the screen, in response. And so the film begins, with the title coming up over the spilled nail polish.

The animations alternate with unnarrated interviews and conversations with no-nonsense, confident, and thoughtful Midwestern women. They are Black, white, young, old. They are students, a farmer, an Avon lady, union members. The ex-head of the Republican National Committee decries the direction of the Republican Party, which she describes as throwing women under the bus with its anti-abortion platform. A woman narrator midway through explains the gender gap, with Hollander's funny animation illustrating her factual summary. The women give reasons why Reaganism isn't working for women (unequal pay, social safety net cuts, increasing militarism, shrinking support for education, hollowing out of the middle class), and they encourage voting. The film doesn't argue that voters should support Democrats, and it doesn't have to.

Given the planned wide distribution of the film, the team debated whether they should license the sexist TV news clip. Neither the time nor the money was available for that. Quinn, who watched TV news use unlicensed material every night, was sure they could use it unlicensed, and a lawyer agreed. Indeed, it was a clear fair use under copyright. Fair use permits unlicensed, unpermissioned reuse if the use is for a different reason/purpose than the market serves for the original, and the amount used is appropriate to that new use. It was perhaps the first time at Kartemquin that anyone considered these copyright issues, since earlier work, done before the 1976 revision of the Copyright Act (going into effect in 1978), occurred in a far more relaxed era for copyright enforcement. They received no pushback. Indeed, when the station that had originally aired the clip ran a story about a group of Democratic women watching the film, it used the opening segment of *Women's Voices* without licensing it. But the anchor was surprised to see that intro use news footage from his station. Quinn later recalled he said something on air like, "Where did they get that clip of us from?"

Although Kartemquin had thought that NOW and the Democratic National Committee would buy the film in bulk, the organizations did not. The filmmakers almost got a cable deal with Lifetime, but it fell through. So Meyer and a colleague, Barbara Tuss, leveraged every possible meeting chance at the NOW and DNC conventions, armed with colorful, fold-out, poster-size brochures for the film. Back in Chicago in July, Meyer and Tuss set up a frantic, homemade distribution operation, with 16mm, VHS, and ¾ inch tape copies going out and being returned every day. They set up a phone bank at Kartemquin, and used their phone and mailing lists to recruit on-the-ground organizers, until the November election. They were selling the copies as fast as they could make the calls, too. (Rohrer gave birth in the middle of the distribution campaign, which further complicated the process.) "People didn't know how they could show it," recalled Meyer, "and I had to say, 'Well if you have a home VCR and a TV you can put it all in your car, you can just set it up wherever the meeting is.' They had never thought of that." Ultimately the film was widely distributed, and Kartemquin and the investors almost broke even, but the filmmakers had hoped for more collaboration and support from Democrats and NOW.

The film has been shown in retrospectives at film festivals, and shown at the Museum of Modern Art in New York. It was selected for restoration by the New York Women in Film and Television's Women's Film Restoration Fund (NYWIFT) in 2012. The restored version was screened at Lincoln Center in New York, just before the 2012 presidential election. Nicole Hollander recorded a 2012 addendum addressing the Obama-Romney race, for the occasion. The updated and restored version is viewable on YouTube.

Looking back, Rohrer noted, "I'm really gratified that people are still interested in the films, but I am astounded and outraged that the issues are almost exactly the same, and in some cases they are worse. The issues on America's family farms are much worse than when the film was made. Pell grants and senior issues are still the same problem."

By the mid-1980s, as the neoliberal era became entrenched, Kartemquin came to an end of its period as a producer of engaged, often-short films, produced with and often for the people in the film. It had begun the process of taking its fully formed storytelling philosophy into the wider world. The Kartemquin ethos of engaged social inquiry, grounded in Deweyan faith in democratic agency, was now the character of the company, even for its work-for-hire projects. Kartemquin had faced and survived the brutal realities of making a living, while making work that challenged the very way that America worked.

The look of Kartemquin's work was shifting. Kartemquin films had mostly been made in the rich textures of black-and-white, which Gordon Quinn loved. As color became a possibility, but with aesthetic trade-offs and higher costs, both Quinn and Blumenthal stuck with black-and-white. They believed that the black-and-white imagery actually helped viewers pay attention to the interaction of the characters. But as television expectations switched to color, Kartemquin, however reluctantly, had to follow. Once they could work with color negatives, which allowed for better resolution, more range of color and contrast than the previous process of color reversal, Kartemquin embraced color, as they did in *Taylor Chain II*. As well, their films had also always been made in 16mm film. With the advent of video, 16mm would also become mostly—but not completely—a relic of the previous era.

Now the company was about to change the kinds of films it made, and the audiences for them. Kartemquin was about to become a player in the commercial entertainment film business, even though it would continue to tell stories that challenged Americans to participate in the democratic vision.[1]

6 Kartemquin in the Filmmaker Public

MAKING NOT JUST MEDIA BUT THE
MEDIA LANDSCAPE

At Kartemquin's pivot point between two ways of enacting the Deweyan vision of making documentary for democracy, we pause to focus on an enduring element of Kartemquin's work in every era: the work of forming and participating in a filmmaker public.

The work of making films was never neatly separated from the work of being a member of a filmmaker public at Kartemquin. Gordon Quinn put it this way: "From very early on there was a feeling that we had a role to play in making the media accountable and responsive to the needs of the democratic society. We wanted to make not just media but the media landscape." The Deweyan concept of publicness was situational, as were the core concepts of pragmatist philosophy generally. You are a member of a public wherever you collectively experience a problem that you could address together through pressuring the centers of power. Democratic structures putatively enable such pressure, although these channels can become disabled if members of the public do not mobilize to use them.

A filmmaker public, then, is one where filmmakers experience shared problems and share both experiences and ideas about how to address them. Kartemquin has both created and participated in the construction of such publics over six decades. Its external foci have included commercial broadcast TV; public TV; public access cable TV; cultural incentive programs of local, state, and federal governments; enabling filmmaker access to their rights to the copyright doctrine of fair use, a tool of freedom of expression; and the vitality and resilience of institutions serving the documentary field. Internally, Kartemquin has consistently structured opportunities to address power dynamics in the workplace, and most recently to address actively the chronic lack of ethnic diversity in its own operations, as well as in the field at large. Indeed, one of the reasons why Kartemquin did not, like many other organizations, self-destruct when questions or conflicts emerged within the organization was because its anchor personnel, and especially Gordon Quinn, recognized the relationship between power and publics at all levels of society.

Marcy McCall remembered Quinn's activism around public TV being a major theme at Kartemquin:

> Gordon saw public TV as a right of American citizens. There was a big emphasis on calling senators and congressmen. I learned about engaging in representation, because if you didn't no one would. I made the calls, and he did. There was a very practical aspect of defending the rights of filmmakers. And there was a bigger thing, to have an informed citizenry through media making.

That activism was part of a larger movement of media reform. The media reform movement was intertwined with other social movements of the 1960s and 1970s. Civil and human rights organizations understood the mass media as a potent channel of power, and both nationally and locally citizens organized with a range of demands. One of the high achievements of that time, the 1969 removal of an openly racist Mississippi TV station's license for failing to serve the public interest, resulted from civil rights and media reform leaders working together. The leader in that effort, the United Church of Christ's Office of Communication, employed me in the 1980s to work on communications equity issues in Washington, DC, where I worked on equal opportunity in employment, universal service in telephony, and broadcasters' obligations to serve the community. From that perch, I was able to continue my coverage of media reform movements in *In These Times,* and I routinely turned to Kartemquin friends for insights and allyship. That work also introduced me to public interest advocates in communication who have been part of my community ever since.

Media reformers had three foci: improving broadcast programming and employment diversity (including on-air); more citizen access to broadcast facilities; and expanding service alternatives to commercial and terrestrial broadcasting. Chicago experienced all three, and Kartemquin was involved in all of them. In Chicago, the Citizens Committee on the Media (CCOM), created at the height of that era's media reform movement in 1972, provided a gathering place for activists. It focused on better programming and more citizen access. Quinn brought his connections to groups with which the collective had developed relationships. With Latinx groups, CCOM demanded more minority and female staff at Chicago broadcast stations. Chicago had not even one nonwhite on-air news reader at the time. Quinn was happy to see labor activists in the group, including the Steelworkers' communication head Gary Hubbard, whom he had met earlier in labor groups. They were all able to pressure the stations directly because the FCC, addressing media reform demands, had in 1971 created a "community ascertainment" policy, by which a station owner had to learn about and respond to community needs and concerns. This requirement was rolled back during the first Reagan administration. Even in its prime, though, community ascertainment wasn't easy; for instance, members of CCOM were forced to hand-copy employment records at the station, in order to get the data they needed.

Quinn also depended on an evolving and deepening relationship with Community Film Workshop for media reform work. Quinn had met Jim "JT" Taylor, a Black photographer covering civil rights activism, when Quinn was still a University of Chicago student and Taylor would appear at events. During the collective years, Taylor served in an informal advisory role at Kartemquin. JT Taylor and Margaret Caples founded Community Film Workshop in the same year as Kartemquin, as part of a public-private initiative, with backing from the Ford Foundation, the federal Office of Economic Opportunity, and the American Film Institute. Its mission was to train underrepresented people to enter the film industry. Of the sites created by this initiative throughout the US, only two survived after program funding shrank in the Nixon era. Chicago's Community Film Workshop and Appalshop in Kentucky not only survived but made it past their fiftieth anniversaries. Both prioritized cultural production, not just job training, and once job training funding was pulled back, they received support from, among others, the National Endowment for the Arts and the John D. and Catherine T. MacArthur Foundation.

The MacArthur Foundation, based in Chicago, had a particular interest in Chicago-based arts organizations. Cultural program officer Woodward "Woody" Wickham met with Caples and Milos Stehlik, executive director of Facets Multimedia (at the time an art house, and later a distributor as well), as well as Quinn and other local film figures.

PUBLIC BROADCASTING

In the 1980s, media activists in Chicago and nationwide took on public TV as a focus. In 1967, the year after Kartemquin's launch, the Carnegie Commission Report, *Public Television, A Program for Action*, was published. It provided an optimistic blueprint for Congress to develop today's public broadcasting services, with legislation passed the same year. The commission found that public television (radio was a late add-in) should be created, as a middle ground between the entertainment of commercial TV and the instructional goals of educational TV. Public TV was needed to meet "the full needs of the American public," "an instrument for the free communication of ideas in a free society." The organization for disbursing public funds, the Corporation for Public Broadcasting, the commission said, should be amply funded through an endowment created by the federal government. There should be stations in every major population center, and also national-level programming that would offer high-quality, public-focused content to those local communities. (It was too expensive for local stations to provide their programming needs locally or regionally.) The commission imagined at least two national production centers, drawing on the talents of independent producers nationwide, showcased by local stations "responsive to the needs of local communities," on a networked national system. It further called for an experimental production center, to encourage innovation, and for local station production for regional or national audiences, as well as fellowships for emerging producers. It was a robust vision for a public-serving public television.

The commission had drawn, among others, on information garnered from public television's major national producing entity, the Ford Foundation funded NET (National Educational Television). NET produced highbrow cultural events, public affairs, and inaugurated live coverage of the State of the Union address with analysis immediately following. The commission also built on information from "educational" stations such as KQED in San Francisco. These early educational stations, launched in 1952 along with commercial TV as a result of a hard-won spectrum set-aside provision from a woman FCC commissioner stubbornly committed to public service, were chronically impoverished. Station managers and makers alike had great expectations for federal funds.

The Carnegie Commission's vision, fed in part by filmmakers, was genuinely electrifying to independent documentary filmmakers nationwide. The three-channel broadcasting universe was almost entirely closed to them. They knew about public broadcasting in other countries, for instance the United Kingdom's BBC and Canada's CBC, as Quinn's undergraduate thesis had referenced. The Ford Foundation had already primed the pump, once it failed to get commercial television to air public-focused programming, by funding NET to produce public-affairs documentaries for educational TV. But this vision was only partially executed in the 1967 Public Broadcasting Act, after congressional negotiations. Among the forces blocking the vision were legislators who feared a left-of-center network to join the three national commercial ones. As well, the Vietnam War and its political and economic costs had sapped the energy of Democratic negotiators.

Public broadcasting emerged in the Public Broadcasting Act of 1967 with a tiny federal budget, allocated triennially through appropriations rather than through the endowment the Carnegie Commission had envisioned. The small amount of federal funding meant that each station had to leverage that funding, which paid for the physical plant, utilities, and some salaries, to raise the rest of the money. The majority of their budgets would have to come from corporations, philanthropists, and crucially viewers themselves. Although they could not advertise, they could beg viewers to become members and they could accept corporate "underwriting"—on-air recognition for support. Corporate underwriting flowed into public TV, sponsoring programs like *Masterpiece Theater*,

Nature, Nightly Business Report, and *In Performance at Wolf Trap.* Meanwhile, as we saw in *Taylor Chain II,* labor unions were told that their sponsorship was a conflict of interest. Membership rosters quickly and unsurprisingly came to be dominated by white, older, professional, and female viewers, whose reasons to give often favored the "safely splendid" programming that worked so well during pledge week. The endless appropriation process guaranteed continuous political scrutiny, particularly from the right, while an endowment would have provided some editorial autonomy. It was launched without production resources or producer fellowships, making it impossible for it to offer opportunities to new or marginalized producers. And the Corporation for Public Broadcasting was banned from interconnection—the ability to provide stations with a network-like program service.

The drama playing out in Washington largely bypassed Kartemquin, which in the collective years focused on working directly with local social-change organizations, and producing work valuable to them. The Kartemquin collective did not see itself producing work for general audiences, but work targeted to activism. But locally, Kartemquinites were involved in the challenge of producing television sharing public issues and public voices. In 1975, Judy Hoffman, working with Videopolis, had actually gotten a program on the local public TV station, WTTW, based on Studs Terkel's book *Working.* But generally WTTW was unfriendly to independents. It had even spurned *And This Is Free* (1975), Mike Shea, Howard Alk, and Gordon Quinn's work on the richly multicultural site of Maxwell Street.

Independent filmmakers nationally had, from the start, butted heads with public TV over space for independent work and over the point-of-view documentaries seen as socially critical from the left. Within months of the creation of public TV, station programmers began meeting to create a way to share programming themselves: the Public Broadcasting Service, or PBS. This stand-alone nonprofit—carefully distanced from federal funds—was run, initially, as a cooperative of stations deciding annually on how to pool their programming money. The PBS leadership was dominated by more conservative stations. These leaders were also acutely aware of the fragility of public TV, particularly after President Nixon openly attacked public TV's federal budget. Nixon's ire had been triggered by an NET documentary that named one of his backers as a leader of a redlining bank (that is, a bank that systematically excluded entire geographical areas from loans). Nixon had not quite counted on the political power of all those stations whose congressional representatives were contacted, and of other supporters including the military, whose support had been recruited for a service that could become a site of technological experiment. After he failed to destroy public TV, though, Nixon had explicitly warned public TV about public affairs, urging programmers to stick to high culture. Many public TV executives had no problem with a demand for programming that did more "safely splendid" entertainment and less informing of the public about issues of public importance.

So independent filmmakers, who had by then developed a subculture and a business ecology, and who had come to see media as a site of political struggle, would have to use political pressure to get themselves airtime. And that is what they did. Partly through their national membership organizations, including the Association of Independent Video and Filmmakers (AIVF), partly with allies at the Ford Foundation, NET, and in the experimental studio TV Lab, they won spaces on public television. Along with ethnically diverse programs such as *Black Journal*, politically controversial programs aired on public broadcasting in the 1970s and early 1980s, even after Nixon's intimidation, including *Winter Soldier* (1972), a self-indicting war crimes tribunal organized by Vietnam Veterans against the War; *Union Maids* (1976), about several women union activists; and *Word Is Out* (1977), a personal-testimonial film about gay and lesbian realities.

After the Kartemquin collective dispersed, the remaining members worked to leverage the work they had, and they focused on public TV. Kartemquin's first big moment of intervention with public TV for its own films was over *The Chicago Maternity Center Story*. The New York station WNET's local series for independent work, *Independent Focus*—a project of media activist Marc Weiss, who also put together the selection panel— at first selected it. But the station rejected it, along with several others, for not meeting broadcast standards. In what would become a tradition of independent filmmakers taking on public broadcasting's program choices, filmmakers formed a coalition. The makers of *Finally Got the News* (1970), about Black workers in Detroit fighting union corruption, *A*

Comedy in Six Unnatural Acts (1975), a set of satirical sketches on social expectation of women's roles featuring a lesbian perspective, and *A Luta Continua* (1972), about postcolonial Mozambican socialism, joined with Kartemquin to protest to WNET. After much back-and-forth, in the case of *Maternity* the WNET curators found no fault with the facts in the film, all of which had been meticulously checked, as was standard for Kartemquin. They objected to the tone of Rohrer's narration; it sounded biased. "Yes," Quinn recalled himself responding. "She has a point of view, that of women's liberation. We're not pretending to be objective, and that's more honest than a voice-of-God approach." Quinn and Rohrer sent an outraged letter of complaint to WNET, one that catches the flavor of their approach to media activism at the time. It staked an unashamed claim to anti-elitist storytelling that could attract a working-class and minoritized audience:

> If WNET wants to expand its audience from the elite educated class, if it wants to deal with social issues from alternative perspectives, then these films from and about oppressed communities (women's movement, gay movement, black worker's movement, Third World movement) are what is needed.
> There is a great deal of cynicism among oppressed groups on the one hand and independent producers on the other, that Educational-TV has no interest in serving their needs. This incident can only confirm the attitude that many already have that Educational-TV is controlled by rich subscribers and corporate funders, and that those of us who use the "wrong tone" will not be allowed access . . .
> Our film . . . is made for and with the people who are suffering from the consequences of the dominant culture's view of technology. They cannot be asked to be "objective" about their own oppression. They cannot be dispassionate as they examine its historical sources . . .
> . . . If you honestly wish to deal with controversies and to broaden your audience to include minorities and oppressed groups, then you must examine the prejudices and limitations of your present programming procedures.

WNET was unmoved. In the end, the only film of the four that managed successfully to run the gauntlet in 1980 was *Six Unnatural Acts*, possibly because the LGBT+ community members rallied by the filmmaker were also a station membership constituency that WNET took seriously. In

Chicago, WTTW refused to show the film. During Kartemquin's fiftieth anniversary year, WTTW executives talked about showing it, during the station's celebration of Kartemquin, but plans fell through.

Quinn nonetheless pursued a relationship with WTTW, which had begun running a program showcasing independent work, *Image Union*. This program was the work of tireless Chicago media activists Tom Weinberg and Jaime Cesar. Weinberg programmed several Kartemquin films on *Image Union* over the years. Quinn continued throughout his career to broker relationships with the local community. For instance, in 1999, he wrote Judy Hoffman, suggesting that her film with Ronit Bezalel, *Voices of Cabrini* (1999), be submitted to WTTW. Cabrini Green was a largely Black housing project, where demolition and a transformation to a mixed-income neighborhood had begun. "It's refreshing to hear a story from the point of view of the people affected," he wrote. He explained that he and another independent maker, Jeff Spitz, had had a meeting with station executives: "They were talking about how they want to reach out to the independent community in some new ways beyond *Image Union*."

Kartemquin gradually became involved in a national movement as well, one of independent filmmakers that had begun in the early 1970s. Not just David Loxton and Kathy Kline but many of the same filmmakers who ended up at the Bard conference in 1979 saw public television as a crucial resource for them. The three commercial networks almost never took independent work. Their formats were rigid and those formats aligned with a cautiously center-right perspective carefully calibrated to political currents and often formed in consultation with political elites. And yet television was the road into every home in America. Public television was an extraordinary breakthrough, in that context. Indeed, public TV reached and reaches more homes in the US than commercial broadcast TV does, although daily viewership is far less.

Independents were up against some brutal political realities. Nixon's intimidation had done its work to make all decision makers—including the station heads who formed the cooperative PBS, and the CPB executives—aware of close political scrutiny of programming. The brash history of NET's documentaries, one of which had precipitated the Nixonian crisis, was there to remind them. The cohort of documentarians petitioning public broadcasting had emerged, like Kartemquin's collective, out of the social movements of the 1960s, as left-wing challengers of the status quo.

Filmmakers and their association heads who understood congressional politics, including the Midwest representative of the coalition Gordon Quinn, turned to Congress, arguing that independent filmmakers, dispersed throughout the US (i.e., in every congressional district), represented the diversity of views of America itself. Legislators, whether Democratic or Republican, liked the idea that their state's issues and filmmakers could be seen on public TV. By 1978, appropriation language included a clause demanding "substantial" dedication of program resources to independent filmmakers. This meant that filmmakers could invoke the power of Congress to demand space on public TV, in the three-year appropriation process that involved legislative actions every year to accomplish. This was what forced CPB to create its two short-lived series *Crisis to Crisis* and *Matters of Life and Death ... and Other Matters.* Independent filmmakers, CPB, and Congress entered into a tense, three-way, permanently conflictual relationship. To legislators, CPB trumpeted the fact that the program series PBS co-op members voted in, such as the science show *NOVA*, typically did employ independent filmmakers. Filmmakers argued that on those shows, they were just hired help; hiring freelancers to work on these executive-produced series, often with a strict format, was not the same thing as showing work created by those people in their own voice.

Between 1978 and 1988, the annual tussle between public broadcasters and independent filmmakers grew ever more intense. When *Frontline*, the public affairs documentary series, was launched in 1983 by a hard-hitting and celebrated South African producer, filmmakers doubled down on their criticism. *Frontline*'s founding executive producer, the politically savvy David Fanning, grasped the reputational problem. When leftist activists led by media activist Marc Weiss (one of the organizers of the Bard conference) came to PBS proposing a new series dedicated to indie point-of-view programming, called *POV*, Fanning embraced the idea. For him, having a series run by and for independents relieved the pressure on his series. Having Fanning, an award-winning international journalist whose work was beloved by station programmers, vouch for a group of people who had heretofore been seen only as left-wing rabblerousers made a huge difference. By 1988, he helped to broker the deal to a point where both activists and executives could live with it.

Something much bigger was in the works as well. Activists, particularly the executive director of the Association of Independent Video and Filmmakers, Larry Sapadin; San Francisco media activists Larry Hall and Jeffrey Chester; and distributor California Newsreel cofounder Larry Daressa, pushed the idea that Congress could stop being the man in the middle between indies and public broadcasters. Instead, Congress could create a permanent line item in the appropriations budget for a production service for independent producers. Kartemquin was the hub of Midwest support for the project. The activists, speaking on behalf of independent filmmakers nationally, grandly argued for 25 percent of the annual TV budget. What they eventually got in 1988, largely thanks to the brokering capacities of liberal Rep. Henry Waxman, a politically adept coalition-builder whose southern California district was full of filmmakers, was a permanent line item for what became the Independent Television Service, but at a far smaller amount. Furthermore, the line item allocated production funding, but no guarantee of access to the programming schedule. At the same time, any film using these funds had to be offered to public TV organizations first; only if none of them wanted it could it be shown elsewhere. Since public TV stations and its programming cooperative all had shown little interest in the perspectives and work of independent filmmakers, this was a big challenge to success. Nonetheless, indies now had a small and congressionally guaranteed slice of public TV's federal allocation.

Gordon Quinn was among those who went regularly to Capitol Hill, one of the few actual filmmakers who over the years followed the political drama, stayed with the arguments, and eventually helped to negotiate the details. Indeed, it was part of his organizing role to persuade me, as cultural editor of the *In These Times* newspaper, to make this issue one of ours. I did cover the entire decade of struggle, both in *In These Times* and in filmmakers' magazines such as AIVF's *The Independent*. I shared his view that public TV was a public service—and since it was paid for by taxpayers, unlike the commercial environment, filmmakers could ask from it a public mission. A core public mission in the Deweyan tradition was to provide a space for people living in a putatively open society to find other perspectives on a commonly shared problem, engage with them, and in a dialectic of conversation toward solutions, to find shared answers. Diverse, community-based, and non-elite storytelling could feed that process.

Archival records show that Quinn was a lead drafter of the missions and goals document for ITVS. He wrote that while geographic region among other kinds of diversity was important (particularly to him as a Midwesterner, he noted), board members' key mission should be "policies that will be part of opening public television to the innovation and diversity that all independents can provide." The board should be composed, Quinn and colleagues argued, of representatives from organizations, e.g., indie organizations, unions, women's organizations, and minority groups, not merely to represent their organizations' interests but to bring diversity—of the kind that Dewey had argued was critical to forming publics around problems—to addressing mission. In its pursuit of diversity and innovation, ITVS would, he imagined optimistically, "get away from market-driven programming and the ratings and numbers game."

Quinn also worked with other filmmakers and the leaders of the effort to create a group that would nominate the new organization's board of directors. Clumsily called the National Coalition of Independent Public Broadcasting Producers and itself lacking a structure to reproduce or govern itself, the coalition negotiated painfully with the Corporation for Public Broadcasting over the course of a year, helped along with some prompting from legislators rallied by Larry Hall, the Hill guru of the team. CPB finally acceded to the fundamental demand of the group: that filmmakers control the board nominations and steer the incorporation process. But nothing could make CPB like either the process or the entity. In fact, one reason why CPB finally capitulated to losing control over the board nomination process may have been because it expected filmmakers to fail at running the organization.

The bad blood between filmmakers and public broadcasters that set in motion the process to create ITVS marked the relationship during its first rocky years, but gradually ITVS—particularly after 2001 and the arrival of president Sally Jo Fifer, who retired in 2023—became the most efficient and prolific production entity producing for national distribution on public TV, and by far the most diverse. ITVS became the only television production entity that could claim a majority-diverse board and staff, coproducing with a majority-diverse population of producers featuring majority-diverse participants and stories.

Fifer, who also subscribed to a Deweyan vision of democratic agency, built bridges between ITVS and the organizations that needed to support it for distribution and continued support for its budget line item. (It was a true honor to discover, when I joined the ITVS board of directors, that she had found my essays and speeches helpful in shaping her worldview on the role of media in a democracy.) She was able to make the case to them that ITVS's stories, scrupulously vetted for accuracy, ethical integrity, and mission relevance, served an important function for public TV. Among other things, ITVS programs could demonstrate to Congress that public TV programming was reaching beyond coasts and elites to serve American publics. At the same time, Fifer and the ITVS team were able to offer filmmakers across the US coproduction services they were unable to get elsewhere. Eventually ITVS, which continued to offer "open call," or an open solicitation process where pitches were evaluated by reviewer teams of fellow filmmakers, came to be so much a default resort for independent filmmakers everywhere that its rejection rate was an astounding 98 percent. This was, among other things, a demonstration of the need for such a service, and an argument for greater funding—which never stopped being a struggle.

Certain realities about the commercial marketplace in which even public broadcasting inevitably participated endured, even as relationships were built. The concerns filmmakers wanted to dodge—the "ratings and numbers game"—were impossible to avoid, particularly since ITVS had no access to programming except good relationships with stations and PBS. Stories needed to find a way to be accessible to general audiences, while still holding on to their community-based realities. In fact, ITVS programs brought in viewers from communities not always well represented in public TV audiences; they drew the youngest and most diverse audiences on public TV. ITVS's coproductions with independent filmmakers also routinely collected more trophies and awards than any other public TV entity. Nonetheless, stations, PBS, and CPB all showed chronic reluctance to commit either to the programs of the ITVS series *Independent Lens* and of *POV*, which were often preempted at the station level, or to expanded financial support for ITVS. Quinn and Kartemquin nonetheless remained committed to the defense of ITVS as a space of documentary for democracy.

Kartemquin later spearheaded two campaigns that mobilized filmmakers to save *Independent Lens* and *POV,* the two anthology series most important to independent filmmaking, both part of PBS's standard prime-time package, from ratings death. In 2013 and again in 2015, both PBS and the lead producing station WNET wanted to shift the programs off the prime-time schedule, into ratings limbo. A coalition called Indie Caucus was formed overnight when the 2013 news hit on December 22, just before the winter holidays. Gordon Quinn and the Kartemquin communication director, Tim Horsburgh, were anchors of the coalition. Filmmakers mobilized nationally to protest, and to engage organizations that had partnered with them on their productions as well. By January 8, PBS and WNET had turned around and the programming was reinstated. When they tried again in 2015, the Indie Coalition, this time with some help from anonymous private foundation donors, and again with Quinn and Horsburgh in leadership, mobilized again. This time, it hosted national town-hall conversations in several key cities. Kartemquinites Dinesh Das Sabu and Rachel Dickson organized a town hall in the Chicago Cultural Center. Amazingly, during a blizzard the event was packed with Midwest producers, and public broadcast executives who had also made their way through the snow listened to them. American University also hosted a town hall, organized through my Center for Social Media (now Center for Media & Social Impact). Once again, as a result PBS and WNET changed course, and left the programs offered in a prime-time slot.

ITVS created new stakes in the relationship between public TV and independents, but the relationship between indies and public TV generally was always fraught. The Kartemquin vision continued to infuse the discussion. For instance, in 2005, the Center for Social Media hosted a meeting co-convened by the Ford Foundation at American University. Meeting minutes show that Quinn made two main points. First, public TV makes it too easy for independents to forget why public TV is important to them. "It's a unique resource, precisely because it gets government funds, which allows the public to make claims upon it," he said. "Whatever possibilities new technologies bring, indies must defend the notion that one of those public voices, which will be different from the others, *must be publicly funded* [italics in original]. One of the functions of public media is that it often keeps other voices honest." His second point was that the way forward was for indies to organize. "We can't expect public TV to sign on for a civil society agenda that showcases the value of indies; rather, organizing needs to demonstrate to public TV that they need to be as afraid of 'us' as of anyone else."

PUBLIC ACCESS TELEVISION

Another site of Kartemquin's activism, beginning in the 1980s, was public access television. Access channels were originally mandated by the Federal Communications Commission on all cable systems in 1969. They were to offer an opportunity for citizens to be able to make their own TV, viewably by anyone with a cable account. Once that requirement was found unconstitutional in 1972, Congress passed a law in 1978, giving the FCC permission to set rules for the use of utility poles by, among other actors, cable companies. Leveraging this opportunity, activists worked with and on localities to make access centers a requirement in local cable systems.

Public access channels are usually located at the bottom of the channel lineup—accessible to all—next to government access (usually dedicated to public meetings and government information services) and educational access (airing board of education meetings, trainings, and educational information). Public access centers provide, increasingly on a semi-curated basis, outlets for artistic experiment, sociality, social issue discussion, public affairs in non-English languages relevant to the community, and outright silliness. Particularly in a time of declining local news sources, they have become lifeline services for hyperlocal information.

Chicago's public access service, Chicago Access Network or CAN-TV, was established in 1983. The relatively late adoption of cable in Chicago, because of delays related to political corruption, benefited access activists, who were able to draw upon others' experience; Quinn in fact had made a trip to Boston to learn the issues. He saw cable not only as a possible access point for independent filmmakers, but another potential site for public formation, in a Deweyan sense. In building support for its creation, CCOM held public meetings, resulting in the Chicago Citizens Cable

Coalition (CCCC). The formation of the group to create Chicago Access Network was, in itself, a Deweyan act of public-forming. CCCC focused on the municipality's ordinances, eventually creating the access channels that continue today. Quinn brought Community Film Workshop's Margaret Caples into the group, which was originally only a handful of activists. It grew, he recalled, to hold meetings in churches and with organizations that wanted access to cable, with perhaps 150 organizational leaders attending at a time. Both Quinn and Caples were chosen for CAN's earliest boards of directors. "We saw CAN public access TV as a place where filmmakers could develop projects with involvement with communities, because it was public. The dream was not fully realized, but a lot of filmmakers did make some inroads at CAN-TV," recalled Caples.

The negotiations were sometimes confrontational. Both municipal government and cable companies have reason to dislike the power of publics; publics make demands that may be inconvenient. The cable companies attempted to whittle away at early wins, including insisting on placing the public channel in the attic of the cable menu, where it wouldn't easily be found. CCCC members pushed back not only on the cable companies but on corporate media members of the group, to say that the channel had to be placed on the most accessible rung of the programming ladder, along with other basic services. They won. CAN-TV continues today.

FAIR USE

Kartemquin's work as an institutional member of the filmmaking public evolved with the issues. In the twenty-first century, a growing area of film-citizen activism was on copyright, which was becoming more important for filmmakers. Kartemquin films such as *Trick Bag* and *Chicago Maternity Center Story* used entire popular songs as soundtrack. For its first decades, Kartemquin was in the mainstream in casually reusing copyrighted material without much thought. For instance, the early films by D. A. Pennebaker also featured extensive, unpermissioned use of copyrighted material, including music. Mostly, filmmakers did not know whether or not their uses were fair under copyright, or whether the work was even under copyright. There was a decent chance that something from a previous generation might not be, after all. Until 1978, when the vast rewrite of the Copyright Act in 1976 went into effect, companies had to renew their relatively short licenses in order to maintain copyright, and in an era where aftermarkets were rare, they often didn't. But most of the time, independent filmmakers simply didn't worry about copyright when employing third-party material.

The 1976 revision to the Copyright Act vastly extended copyright holders' monopoly rights, both in terms of copyright length and extent. The revisions abolished the need for renewal, and made copyright the default upon creation of a work. The metastasizing of copyright monopolies shrank the range of the public domain (the body of work that is outside copyright), and made heretofore little-considered exceptions, such as fair use, suddenly important.

Then the digital era brought a vastly increased ability to track uses, as well as a fundamental challenge to mass media companies' profit streams. Copyright vigilance became a primary tool with which media companies could shore up their aging business models. Not only were media companies increasingly litigious; they also increasingly employed technological measures to enforce their claims. They also conducted extensive "educational" campaigns to scare potential users with the threat of litigation, for any copying whatsoever. Filmmakers came to believe that licensing any copyrighted material, right down to phone ringtones that might go off during a scene, was the professional choice. Their lawyers reinforced this belief. It had profound effects on what kinds of expressive decisions, and even films, they thought they could make.

In 2004, at American University, legal scholar Peter Jaszi and I won funding from the Rockefeller Foundation to explore how documentary filmmakers coped with copyright problems, given their constant quoting of audiovisual materials. Along with others in the academic community, we suspected that this expansion of copyright monopoly and copyright enforcement had chilling effects on speech. We learned that filmmakers were avoiding major kinds of films and topics, because of the high cost of licensing. Copyright law actually permitted them to quote such material, in most cases, without licensing under the doctrine of fair use. Generally, under current judicial interpretation, use of copyrighted material of any kind (music, photographs, text, graphics, for example) needs no licensing or permission, if it is used for a different purpose than the material's market and using the appropriate amount for that purpose.

Ignorance of the law wasn't the only thing keeping filmmakers from using this material. But if they did know about the law and tried to use it, they faced new obstacles. Insurers for errors and omissions—crucial insurance for distribution—typically would not insure for fair uses. Lawyers warned filmmakers to avoid what they saw as a "gray area." Broadcasters only accepted fully permissioned work. "Everyone knew" that fair use was, functionally, unusable.

With funding from the MacArthur and Rockefeller Foundations, Peter Jaszi and I then worked with the field of documentary makers to establish best practices in employing fair use. Filmmakers were now alarmed by our report on the high creative cost of self-censorship. We then held convenings nationwide with national filmmaker associations, to discuss with filmmakers a responsible interpretation of the law. We asked them to put aside their convictions that they would never be permitted to employ it, and brainstorm within a "what if" world in which they could. We asked them to think about why they felt they should be able to reference this material without paying or getting permission, and what kinds of uses would exceed what they thought was acceptable. Once they had a consensus, we asked legal experts to review our synthesis of their conclusions. Kartemquin hosted several of these conversations, and when the Documentary Filmmakers Statement of Best Practices in Fair Use (cmsimpact.org / documentary) was issued in 2005, Kartemquin became an early adopter and proponent of it. The Documentary Filmmakers Statement was instrumental in changes in insurance policy the next year, as errors-and-omissions insurers all began to insure for fair use. That also meant that broadcasters and other distributors would accept it.

Gordon Quinn had immediately understood the free speech implications of being able to employ unpermissioned materials. Quinn had been working long enough to remember an era before the fully permissioned one. Fair use was a way to regain freedom of speech, to access a wider range of raw materials, and to discuss important issues without encountering the private censorship of permissions. "I connected it to Dewey," Quinn recalled. "In a digital, image-driven age, fair use was a critical part of the democratic process. If we could not tell stories of history, culture, politics, and social movements because the audiovisual record was owned by someone, this was crippling for public discourse. Fair use was necessary for a democracy in our modern communication age."

Quinn became an evangelist among documentary filmmakers, film professors, and even lawyers, many of whom feared changing longstanding practices and relationships. He spoke at numerous filmmaker gatherings, incorporated fair use into internship training, and trained others, such as rising Kartemquin filmmaker Dinesh Das Sabu, to speak out about it. (Sabu is now a film production professor, teaching fair use to future filmmakers.) These days, fair use training is part of all Kartemquin's internships, and part of its Diverse Voices in Documentary programs as well.

Kartemquin also became involved in related copyright activities. For instance, the Digital Millennium Copyright Act (DMCA) made decrypting encrypted media in order to copy it a criminal act, even for fair uses. But if a class of people can show that they cannot do their work without decryption, they can apply for an exemption. In 2008, Quinn and Kartemquin engineer Jim Morrissette traveled to Washington, DC, to present a forty-slide explanation of why they needed to break encryption to a Copyright Office tribunal. They were backstopped by the University of Southern California's legal clinic, led by attorney Jack Lerner.

In submissions before the session, industry lawyers had proposed that filmmakers were already able to copy work from a VHS tape, or even by shooting an image off a television screen. Quinn and Morrissette had to show why that wasn't possible. They split the presentation job. Quinn provided the conceptual argument that fair use was "an important part of a free and open society and a democratic society," and critically important to documentary work. Then Morrissette, the uber-geek, launched into an extended and technical breakdown of what it would take to get a clip from VHS tape into a broadcast-ready documentary. He noted that VCRs were no longer even being made. Then soberly and methodically, he went through steps to convert the material, referencing terms such as "Macrovision copy control," "timebase corrector," "black level," "head switch," "synch signal," and "blanking signal." The result, he noted, was often unacceptable to broadcasters, even after all that work. Then he took on scan conversion, or just taking a picture of what's on a screen. This led

Figure 12. Gordon Quinn and Jim Morrissette at the Library of Congress after their presentation to the Copyright Tribunal, which featured a highly technical slide presentation, one slide of which Morrissette displays. Source: Gordon Quinn.

him to discuss aspect ratios, limitations of the recording machinery, the clash between computer and television imagery and standards, and the difference in image between analog and digital. At the end of the process, he stressed, odds were also great that the product was still not acceptable for broadcast. When he finished, the hearing room was silent. People were stunned. Morrissette recalled the presentation later with a smile; he said he had found the proposals of the media company lawyers "hysterically funny," and he enjoyed showing them why their proposals were ridiculous. You would never have known this from Morrissette's nearly funereal demeanor in the presentation, though. (I enjoyed the whole performance from my seat four rows behind them in the Copyright Office.)

Kartemquin's presentation, along with the law clinic's good work, won the exemption for all documentary filmmakers, permitting them to break encryption to access short clips for fair uses. Filmmakers have done so every three years since (the process requires triannual renewal). What started out as a special waiver for documentary filmmakers now also applies to fiction filmmakers, to professors, and to film students. Others have also won such exemptions, including the blind, independent repair experts, K–12 teachers, and anyone making nonprofit videos, such as fan fiction creators do.

For Kartemquin, action to affect the institutions and power flows that affected their ability to work was as essential as filmmaking. It was part of the role they imagined for Kartemquin as a builder and enabler of publics. It was their way of practicing the citizen agency that Dewey talked about when he talked about forming publics. And it was guided by their understanding of how cultural production was enabled or limited by the forces of power structuring it. Generations of Kartemquin filmmakers have learned how to take that citizen action. Their work has expanded the range of voices on public broadcasting, made local community television available, expanded government benefits beyond the commercial fiction world to nonprofit and documentary production, and made access to the copyright doctrine of fair use available to filmmakers.[1]

7 Filmmakers Become Artists, Art Becomes Experience, and *Hoop Dreams* Changes Everything, 1985–1995

Kartemquin now turned to the challenge of making art for broad audiences. Its move away from collaborative, activist filmmaking with and for local groups and toward the never-inviting television business was enabled by success with grants and public TV. But as well, it was a personal choice of the Kartemquin's remainers. They were exhausted, dismayed at and depressed by the weaknesses and losses of the labor movement and social movements, and by the brutalities of Reagan-era neoliberalism. They shifted their self-perceptions from being cultural workers to being socially engaged artists. They dreamed of telling stories that matter to broader citizenries. But no one there anticipated the overwhelming national recognition from the little 30-minute film project that grew up to be *Hoop Dreams* by 1994. *Hoop Dreams* changed everything.

The long years of Republican rule between 1980 and 1993 locked in fundamental change to American politics. The political parties themselves changed. Republicans backbenched remaining "Rockefeller Republicans"; leaders embraced a harshly neoliberal, pro-business, anti-regulatory stance. The notion that government should provide basic services that the market does not or cannot provide to all, something that the New Deal had boldly asserted and normalized, was now being challenged by both major political parties. The principle that the federal government should return as much power as possible to the states—a position that favored regressive social policies, particularly in the American South and West—had become entrenched. Republicans zealously gerrymandered their districts while they held power to improve their electoral chances, with Democrats scrambling to do the same when they could in response. The Democratic Party, with Bill Clinton as chief evangelist, also embraced the pro-business, low-regulation positions of neoliberalism, in a pragmatic effort to regain territory on what had become Republican ground. Left-leaning liberals were now politically homeless in the two-party system. Under the neoliberal umbrella, international trade without protections for labor flourished to the detriment of workers' rights worldwide, unprecedented numbers of people entered the stock market, and the rich found capital easier to access with lowered taxes. Economic polarization accelerated. The entire world of broadcasting and telecommunications was restructured to favor concentration and re-monopolization in the name of freedom from government, a tendency locked into law in the 1996 Telecommunications Act.

For working and middle-class people, the gap between them and the investing class was ever-widening, the next step in the great hollowing out of the middle-class economy in America. Kartemquin's labor work had captured the crisis in decaying industrial areas, the beginning of a long spiral downward. Social movements for equality, justice, representation, and environmental sustainability multiplied without being able to build cross-issue coalitions. A Rainbow Coalition vision did not emerge. There were bright spots, though, such as the cross-race, cross-class coalition that put Harold Washington into office.

The digital economy, still nascent, was meanwhile building. The laptop computers that had become generally accessible by the mid-1980s were capable of interconnecting on the early internet, via what now seem unbearably slow and tedious modems requiring individual settings for each connection—but which then seemed miraculous. By 1993, the first graphical-interface app, the publicly funded Mosaic, made the World Wide Web suddenly friendly even to newbie users, and it enabled a vast array of new web-based businesses. Among other things, digitization and increased portability came to film production, even though innovation was uneven and formats sometimes nonstandard. The new digital economy would overheat into a "dot-com bubble" of wild-eyed investment, and then crash in 2000, before the digital economy restructured again. But the digital era's practical advances were fascinating to the ever-tech-curious Kartemquinites, especially engineer Jim Morrissette. They were constantly on the lookout for ways to do their jobs better. Computers were becoming basic office equipment. Kartemquin was an early adopter of it all. Its first computer was an Epson, running a proprietary prototype of text-editing programs, the slow and clumsy Valdocs on a CP/M operating system.

As Kartemquin tried out its capacity to produce television programming for broad audiences, it continued to survive on commercial work, particularly as a provider of crew and editing services for corporate films and videos. Worker training films for McDonald's and the union at United Airlines that ultimately restructured the company as worker-owned, as well as commercials for the large, independent commercial TV station WGN in Chicago, paid the bills. Kartemquin also rented out editing suites and equipment, and continued to pull in educational revenues. Educational sales, mostly to universities, were lucrative even though the market was small (about three hundred universities); 16mm film copies often sold for hundreds of dollars, and as video gradually supplanted film, university librarians continued to pay high prices. Kartemquin's earlier work with social movement groups and for nonprofits continued to do well in the educational market, through their efforts at New Day, the collective distribution nonprofit, and elsewhere.

Dedicated and aspiring young people continued to arrive, with combined dreams of making art and doing good, and they did crucially important support work. Jill (now Joey) Soloway, a Chicago-born graduate of University of Wisconsin Madison, was in charge of the commercial work in the late 1980s and worked on *Hoop Dreams*. Later, they became a noted Hollywood TV producer, including developing the popular TV series *Transparent*. Ed Scott, a Black, newly minted graduate of the School of the Art Institute of Chicago, had seen Kartemquin films including *Taylor Chain* and *The Last Pullman Car* in his classes. As soon as he graduated in 1989, he wangled an internship, which he paid for with a second job. His internship gradually became a paid job as facilities manager.

Scott dived into the substantial challenge of organizing the space of the rambling old house that housed Kartemquin. He sorted film cans and cleaned equipment, and took on the transition from film to video. He recalled getting his basic education in video, a cutting-edge new skill at the time, from Jim Morrissette. Most of all, he later remembered, he felt he had found a welcoming home: "I never really felt that I was seen differently at Kartemquin [because of his skin color]. I think they saw me as who I was, someone who had skills, and was willing to work long hours for not much money. I was being paid full-time, entrusted with duties I wouldn't get elsewhere in Chicago." He felt lucky.

Colorado-born and bred, Fenell Doremus in 1992 was a recent sociology graduate from the University of Wisconsin Madison, who had relocated to Chicago on a whim. She decided she wanted to become a documentary filmmaker after seeing *Eyes on the Prize*, the award-winning, pathbreaking, public TV civil-rights series in class. She had heard about Kartemquin from her mother's college friend Nell Cox, who herself had worked with cinema verité pioneer Al Maysles. Quinn also knew Cox, from his days working on editing *Festival* with her.

"Before I called, I went to hear Judy Hoffman speak at some event about women breaking into the film business. I fell in love with her at that moment," Doremus recalled. She considers Judy one of her mentors to this day. Ed Scott hired Doremus immediately for an unpaid internship. She soon filled a vacant admin position, turning to Scott for help when she was confused. "I felt like the luckiest person in the world," she recalled, although her job involved not only doing assistant editing work on *Hoop Dreams* but also taking out the trash. Soon she hired interns to do the routine admin work. She helped Quinn with grant proposals and pitches, assisted with budgets and bookkeeping, went on shoots as a production assistant, and even producing some work-for-hire projects. But she never stopped having to clean up the kitchen, where the men, and particularly the men who came together around *Hoop Dreams*, congregated but apparently never picked up after themselves. It also fell to her, as workplaces became more smoke-conscious, to tell Jerry Blumenthal—the last holdout—that he had to go outside to smoke. He resisted, she recalled, with his usual good-natured feistiness.

Scott also brought on Jim Fetterley, who ended up working on many productions. Fetterley was the child of a single mom who was a housecleaner and cocktail waitress. He had been raised in the working-class suburb of Loves Park (then known, Fetterley recalled, as "Loves Parkensaw"). He was still in school at the Art Institute of Chicago when in late 1991 he saw a posting for an unpaid internship at Kartemquin. Leveraging a state grant that subsidized unpaid internships, he applied, and was instantly charmed. "They greeted us like guests, it wasn't like an interview. I went to the kitchen, there was chips and salsa. I waited a few minutes, read the posters on the wall. I'd never been in such a fascinating place. A library! And it looked like someone's home? I thought, full on, I'll do whatever it takes to work here."

Fetterley had been struggling to make sense of the heated political atmosphere of the School of the Art Institute. Its dean, Carol Becker, who had a PhD in English and American Studies, was an active member of the leftist, feminist, and activist art world, and had also briefly been on staff at *In These Times*. She saw culture as a prime site of social conflict and social change, as two later books of hers articulated in depth—*The Subversive Imagination* (1994) and *Zones of Contention* (1996). She encouraged her students at SAIC, which had a history of activism (documented, among other things, by Kartemquin with *What the Fuck Are These Red Squares?*, filmed in 1968 and released in 1970), to execute politically engaged art projects.

The right wing also saw culture as a site of struggle. The late 1980s and early 1990s saw a well-funded, calculated attempt to position "political correctness" as a political problem. The SAIC became a site of conflict between the two poles. In 1988, white art student David K. Nelson Jr. exhibited a scandalizing portrait of recently deceased Mayor Harold Washington, dressed only in women's underwear. Chicago's first Black mayor had famously bucked a racist, corrupt, white city council and political process to succeed. His first term had been almost open warfare with the dominant white faction of the council. When he suddenly died of a heart attack after winning reelection, many—especially in Chicago's long-suffering Black population—were in mourning. Several Black councilmen indignantly seized the painting, and were forced by police to return it; the city ended up settling in 1994 with Nelson for almost $100,000 for violation of his civil rights, after extended publicity. As the court case churned, the student's work spurred many public conversations about the role of art in society, discussions made that much harder by the fact that many struggled to find purpose in the student's art. Jesse Jackson's Operation PUSH and Black activist Louis Farrakhan denounced the painting, and the SAIC president defended its right to exist but pronounced it in poor taste. Becker staunchly backed her student.

As this controversy rolled out, in 1989 another student, "Dread" Scott Tyler, who is Black, created an artwork that hinted at his future in participatory artwork that critiques racism in American society. He laid an American flag on the floor, and put a collage of images including flag-covered coffins and South Korean students protesting the US presence in Korea in front of it; viewers would have to step on the flag to see the images. He put a podium on it, with a notebook where viewers could record how the installation made them feel. In Chicago, military veterans professed themselves outraged. President George H. W. Bush inveighed against it, and Congress passed the Flag Protection Act. (Tyler joined others in burning a flag, and became part of a court case that the Supreme Court ultimately decided in favor of the protesters.)

This was the heady environment Fetterley was encountering at school, and he felt naïve and underequipped for the challenge. His social-justice inclinations, and particularly his sense of class inequalities coming from his own upbringing, seemed poorly matched with the loud, confusing, activist environment at SAIC. And besides, there was practical concern: "I needed to be employable. A semester of school was more than my mother's annual income. When I got to Kartemquin, I thought, Here's a path. They were so stimulating and they were so generous with their knowledge. It led to an interest in open-source [the movement to design software available without restriction for anyone to use] later in my life."

With Scott as his mentor, he soaked up the practical learning he'd been starved for at school. He volunteered for everything; paid for only two days a week, he regularly showed up on weekends. Even mail sorting (this was pre-internet) was thrilling to him—labor newsletters, the democratic socialist newspaper *In These Times*, the trade publication *The Independent*, all were windows into new realities. And seeing the Kartemquin films being developed opened his eyes to cinematic social inquiry, in a way that spoke to his intuitive sense of social justice. He treasured conversations with Gordon Quinn. "He told me about John Dewey. 'Who's John Dewey?'

I thought. Gordon spent time with interns, he took time to be interested in them, what it was that drew you there." When he learned about Kartemquin history, he particularly loved stories of the collective era's feminists: "I was raised around a bunch of hardworking, independent women." As he learned the practicalities of shooting and editing, practicing with Susanne Suffredin on work-for-hire jobs, he also picked up the practice of ethical filmmaking: "I would ask, 'How do you collaborate with your subjects?' Gordon or Jerry would say, 'Often, if someone feels uncomfortable, you're not treating them with respect.' It wasn't about manipulation."

The culture of the place continued to be porous, a sometimes-fractious but creatively communitarian family. Ed Scott recalled the "funky" atmosphere, the collegiality and idealism as well as the parlous finances. (He once wanted to go to the hardware store for nails, but discovered there wasn't enough credit to cover the cost.) His desk was next to Gordon Quinn's. "One minute he's working on proposals, then there's a meeting and discussions about films, and then you were fixing a Steenbeck with him," Scott remembered. "I liked sitting in the editing room with Jerry, too. He was very fast, very sharp, very funny. Sometimes, when he and Susanne Suffredin were editing, you could hear the expletives and know to stay away, but you also knew things were working. You could get down and dirty with the principals but also be cerebral and creative." The creative atmosphere was contagious. "One day Steve James would be working on *Hoop Dreams*, and some young Art Institute filmmakers would be in another room across the hall renting an edit suite, and Steve would say to them, 'Can you take a look at this and tell me what you think?,'" recalled Doremus. "We'd sit in the kitchen and have a long discussion about whatever projects people were working on at the time."

Kartemquinites loved to watch Quinn and Blumenthal bicker with each other over their opinion of movies neither of them had seen. They would call the recurring conversation "Gordon and Jerry, Not at the Movies." This referenced a TV show featuring the nationally known Chicago film critics Gene Siskel and Roger Ebert, *At the Movies* (1982–90). But Quinn and Blumenthal engaged in their spiky arguments without, apparently, even needing to see the films.

If it was a place where young people could learn, it also depended on them being willing to improvise, find their own spot, and work for less than market rates. "We were given a lot of opportunities, but we weren't always given the guidance to fulfill it and I, in particular, didn't know how to ask for it," said Doremus. "That said, everything I learned about filmmaking I learned from Jerry and Gordon trusting me enough to send me out to produce a work-for-hire project with very little practical experience—it was trial-by-fire filmmaking school." Gita Saedi, who ended up coordinating the huge *The New Americans* project, recalled, "Kartemquin changed my life. It changed how I see meaningful work. It also sucked. It was incredibly difficult." The precarity of projects, she recalled, was nerve-wracking, although the work was exhilarating. The low salary, supplemented by her outside work, was only possible because of her youth and lack of family obligations.

The logistical side of the operation was always embattled. Steve James was briefly the executive director, but by his own admission, a terrible one, focused mostly on his own filmmaking. Quinn and Blumenthal continued to be the anchors for mission, but Blumenthal always shrugged off the management issues. Strong, competent, and mission-driven women such as Marcy McCall, Stephanie Wertlake, and Fenell Doremus kept the place running.

Kartemquin's shift toward broadcast-oriented humanism did not happen abruptly. Throughout the period, Blumenthal, Morrissette, and Quinn also worked on short projects in coordination with other nonprofits and arts organizations. Kartemquin alumni continued to turn to the place to do nonprofit and collaborative work. But now, even work like that could see a broadcast possibility. One such example was *The End of the Nightstick* (1994).

Peter Kuttner returned to Kartemquin, taking a break from his work in the film industry as an active member of the powerful union IATSE, where he constantly recruited more diverse members. He wanted to work with Denise Zaccardi, a grassroots media activist in Chicago and friend of Kartemquin. She had won a MacArthur grant for a film about grassroots organizing, and Kuttner eagerly joined the effort. Zaccardi's vision, harking back to the collective's dream, was to assist an activist group in telling their story. She put out a call into the activist community. Quinn did site visits to inform the choice of the group to be funded. One group was working on police brutality, and the egregious case of one Chicago cop who had notoriously used torture, learned from training he had received in Vietnam. Drawing on his close study of Norman Fruchter's filmmaking in the Newsreel days, Kuttner developed a feature documentary at Kartemquin, along with Cyndi Moran and Eric Scholl, who he had met at the postproduction house Kartemquin worked with. He was co-owner of a Betacam at Kartemquin, which gave him easy access rights. Focusing on institutional racism in the police (a topic he had been all too familiar with as a young man at the hands of the Chicago police), *The End of the Nightstick* was completed in 1994. Although it had activist roots, it managed to find a place on the public TV series *POV.* (Ed Scott, who had left Kartemquin by then, shot some of the interviews.) "Knowing I had access to Kartemquin's facilities, that I was still something of a partner there, made it much easier for me," Kuttner recalled. He made no money on the project. "My payback was I could take time off from my work in Hollywood."

Several short projects ended up using Kartemquin's facilities. Jerry Blumenthal mentored Fenell Doremus and Jim Fetterley, as they made a little film for Blumenthal's ex-wife, to promote a local public school that served mostly Mexican American immigrants. The principal, competing with charter schools, needed a promotional film but had no budget; the Kartemquinites did it for free. "I really got to know Jerry and got to learn how to make a film," Doremus recalled. "I really came to so appreciate his mentorship, and value who he was as a creative storyteller. He was an amazing editor. This little film, he could really see it. He could see exactly what was wrong and how to fix it."

Jenny Rohrer drew on Kartemquin's staff and facilities to make *Science Held Hostage: RU486 and the Politics of Abortion* (1992). Like the *Gender Gap* film, this was a short contributing to a political debate. The Women's Issue Foundation in 1992 contracted with Kartemquin to make an advocacy film supporting legalization of the drug that can trigger a miscarriage. It told the story of three women, one of whom, Vicky Starr, had featured in *Union Maids,* and another of whom was a sportscaster, Jeannie Morris, who cofounded the Women's Issue Foundation. Actress Cybil Shepherd hosted. Shepherd screened the film on Capitol Hill, and the Turner Broadcasting Network aired it without commercials.

GOLUB (1988): PERMISSION TO BE ARTISTS

The film that launched Kartemquin's broadcast-first era, *Golub* (1988), demonstrated the evolution of Kartemquin's commitment to art as social inquiry as well as its reorienting to a primarily broadcast audience. It also was the first of several broadcast-oriented projects at Kartemquin that focused on artists, including *A Good Man* (2014), *Almost There* (2014), and *For the Left Hand* (2021). While still boldly socially engaged, its storytelling was designed for audiences in a broadcast environment. It featured a major Chicago-native painter then New York based, Leon Golub (with appearances from his equally well-known artist wife, Nancy Spero), at work creating art that makes sharp, leftist political commentary. It was a particularly important project for Blumenthal, the filmmaker whose self-image was that of an artist.

The project came about because a wealthy business owner, Jack Jaffe, a fan of the labor films, wanted to sponsor a Kartemquin film project on the arts. Jaffe himself was an amateur photographer. Peter Gilbert made the connection, because of his father's relationship with Jaffe; Gilbert's father was a photography collector. Quinn and Blumenthal had heard of a show of Golub's work at the Museum of Contemporary Art. Blumenthal's ex-wife Shirlee Jensen was also an artist, and she knew Golub and his reputation. They took Jaffe to the museum, and all of them were bowled over not only by the art but by the way viewers interacted with it. Making a film about Golub appealed to Jaffe.

It also appealed to the artist. Golub had heard of Kartemquin as a maker of labor-oriented work. He was as intrigued with Kartemquin's artistic process as they were with his. After one meeting in New York, the artists and filmmakers had committed to each other. "I think it was kind of love at first sight," Quinn recalled.

Jaffe provided a third of the budget up front, which made it possible to complete the film in about a year. The filmmakers fundraised throughout the process. Private foundations, especially Jaffe's Focus / Infinity Fund with $91,000, anchored the budget. A $30,000 National Endowment for the Humanities grant provided a majority of public funding, and the Illinois Arts Council contributed $12,000. Even so, the budget was limited. Sometimes the filmmakers could not travel to New York, where

Golub was located. But Golub accommodated them. He would put the painting they were chronicling aside and work on other paintings until the filmmakers could get there.

Judy Hoffman joined the project, as assistant camera to Quinn, archival researcher, and associate producer. Blumenthal took over the editing. The filmmakers needed news / documentary footage to illustrate the relationship of Golub's subject matter to the burning issues it referenced. They were able to get some from fellow independent filmmakers, such as Pamela Yates. But some was from mainstream TV, which they employed under fair use. They hired an emerging Chicago composer Hoffman recommended, Tom Sivak, for the musical score; much later, now well-established, he also worked on *'63 Boycott* (2017).

The filmmakers, with Blumenthal in the lead, followed the creation of a single piece of art, in a process that mirrored how Dewey talked about art as experience in production. Then they showcased how viewers perceived and talked about that piece of art, an example of art as experience in reception. Dewey saw art not only as cultural products (a film, a painting, a piece of music) but as a process, where the experience of ordinary people everywhere in a culture is synthesized and made boldly clear. Artists took the messy uncommented day-to-day reality, mixed it with imagination, and gave it new meaning. "Art throws off the covers that hide the expressiveness of experienced things; it quickens us from the slackness of routine and enables us to forget ourselves by finding ourselves in the delight of experiencing the world about us in its varied qualities and forms," Dewey wrote in *Art as Experience*. Art, he argued, lets people dream of more coherence and integrity in experience than they get in daily life. It releases possibility, aspiration, hope: "Art departs from what has been understood and ends in wonder."

Works of art emerged, Dewey argued, out of the thick texture of culture and provided to their users an intense experience, which is the key to culture-building. So the experience of the users of art was as much a part of the art as a particular thing. The interaction of, say, viewers of a painting, with the work of art gave the work itself meaning. Dewey judged modern industrial society woefully lacking in art as experience, because so much art was segmented off into elite platforms, such as opera houses, galleries, and museums. Capitalism had leveraged art for a status symbol, and

Figure 13. From left, Gordon Quinn, Leon Golub, Judy Hoffman, and Jerry Blumenthal relax after shooting an exhibition of Golub's work in Derry, Northern Ireland, for *Golub*. The exhibition included the painting Golub created over the course of the film. Source: Kartemquin Archives. Credit: Meg Gerken.

artists cut off from their audiences justified their aesthetic loneliness as Romantic creativity. Meanwhile, the life of working people was surrounded by brutal ugliness, and they were forced into equally alienating labor.

Given this framework, you could not find a better artist to look at than Leon Golub, a left-wing painter married to a left-wing, feminist painter. His large-scale paintings closely caught the gestures of modern barbarity. As a World War II veteran, he was obsessed with the horrors of war and the injustices of power. He was also dedicated to a Deweyan vision of art. Along with other members of what one critic called the "Monster Roster," he wanted to make art that referred to events, patterns, and issues the public needed to know and talk about. He had mobilized artists to protest the Vietnam War, and he came to focus on neo-imperialism as a theme. When Kartemquin came across him, he was in a phase where he was focusing on terrorism, state-sponsored and otherwise, including gender violence. The Iran-Contra scandal was in the headlines at the time. The US government was covertly backing opposition to the socialist Sandinista government in Nicaragua, the Contras, and funding it by secretly violating its own embargo on selling weapons to Iran. The Salvadoran civil war and Guatemalan dictatorship were also generating horrific headlines about torture, massacre, and rape. Golub's work referenced those tumultuous conflicts.

His technique involved studying news and other photographs (including, sometimes, sadomasochistic pornography) for gestures. He then sketched out his designs, and gradually began layering the canvas. Working the canvas multiple times with multiple media, he built up new surfaces. He then liquified the outer layers and scraped some off, creating textured surfaces featuring hugely looming figures of mercenaries, thugs, and torturers. As technology aficionados, Quinn and Blumenthal were fascinated by Golub's use of devices such as a meat cleaver, scraping canvas to sculpt textures, and studying photographs to capture gesture.

The film begins with the sight of museumgoers transfixed, with troubled gazes, at the monumental portraits. It then moves into Golub's studio, where he is studying files of photographs, and begins to create his painting. Golub in person is a funny, wry man with a quick but kind wit. His wife, Nancy Spero, drops over for critique, comment, and an occasional wisecrack. She is creating her own work, which features joyful, polycultural images of women. The painting process is practical—"Get a receipt," he reminds the assistant sent out to buy a toy gun—and, he says, the process is also "boring and slow." As he works on one figure, he says, "He's gonna be as pretty a fascist as you ever saw."

At the same time, Golub reflects on its purpose: "Art is a report on civilization—who has power and who's getting the stick." He wants to "make people feel uncomfortable." At the same time, he realizes how privileged he is. For instance, he says, he was able to turn down a trip to Brazil while it was under dictatorship, because his fellow artists there wouldn't be able to do what he does without being punished for it, and he didn't want to lord it over them. He describes painting Black men holding in their tense stances their desire for dignity and success in the face of racism. We then see intercut the wary faces of young Black people on the street, enacting that same stance. But we now see it anew, through the eyes of the artist.

Interspersed with the creative process are scenes from museums and galleries, focusing on viewer reactions. The painting is unveiled in Derry, Northern Ireland, in the midst of The Troubles, where soldiers who could have stepped out of Golub's paintings patrol the streets. Viewers are fascinated. "This guy," says one, pointing to a torture victim, "he's a victim, but these guys [pointing to the torturers] are too, but they don't realize it." It's a stunning observation, and one that Golub has been trying to evoke, we know from watching the process. In Montreal, where the curator faced criticism for displaying violence, viewers critique American imperialism, and comment on the human capacity for violence, on the instability of the world. So we see the painting we watched being made then hung on the walls of museums, and we watch the viewers engage with it. We watch art as experience.

Blumenthal's gifted editing brought film artistry to the storytelling about an artist. This was inspirational to a young editor who saw editing as an art form himself, David E. Simpson—soon to become a Kartemquin stalwart:

> *Golub* was special for me, because it was about art; the artistry of the film was central. There was a certain kind of fun and colorfulness and juice in the cutting Jerry did. It was aesthetically charged. I remember the moment when Golub comes back from Ireland. There's a music cue and a montage—first of soldiers, pedestrians, and conflict-centric graffiti in the streets of Derry during "the Troubles," then of Golub walking briskly to his studio in New York. The score, the cutting, and the graffiti tie the two locations together and represent the tension that runs through Golub's work. It's a strong, energetic moment. It's beautiful cinema.

Although Golub welcomed the filmmakers into his work process, he also had strong feelings about their portrayal of him. In fact, they tussled about the end of the film. The filmmakers had created an ending that emphasized the political urgency of his works and their ability to alarm and engage people. He wanted them to feature his newer work, going in a less obviously political direction. He wanted this not least because he knew that his New York community of fellow artists would read the ending Kartemquin wanted as pretentious and overclaiming. Blumenthal and Quinn resisted, because they believed their ending would bring home the point of the work viewers had seen created. But they worked with him at length, and ultimately modified the ending. "It was a great example of coming to terms with what you owe your audience and what you owe your subjects," Quinn later said.

Another filmmaker, Denis Mueller, who had been inspired by Kartemquin's social-inquiry approach, described *Golub* in Deweyan terms in his PhD dissertation:

> The view of the documentary film being part of an experience of the community, which becomes an overt action, is a participatory community-based experience. The modes of inquiry established by Dewey become a virtual blueprint for understanding the documentary film. We start with a problem, followed by initial inquiry that uses the camera as its research tool; this is followed by the adjustments made from the changes in the historical world, which result in an art based in experience. The filmmaker does not pretend to be neutral but has a political point of view grounded in the knowledge that they, and their subjects, have acquired. Both of them together seek to either bring light to a problem or to initiate action based on the faith in the intelligence of the public to solve its own problems without the guidance of elites. This is what democracy looks like in the Deweyan mode. The filmmaker is an engaged citizen in a democracy. This model seeks to establish involvement by the audience as well by making the audience part of this democratic expression.

Less explicitly, other reviewers recognized the refocusing away from the art world and toward art in society. The *Chicago Reader*'s noted critic Jonathan Rosenbaum referenced the Deweyan approach while calling the film "essential viewing": "One of the inspirations of this highly concentrated and kinetic documentary was to eliminate the critical discourse of the art world entirely; what we get instead are the comments and reactions of ordinary spectators, many of which are penetrating and perceptive." The team had indeed decided not to include the voice of critics, although they had done some interviews.

The film was shown on public TV's *POV*. PBS, which had approval rights because it carried the series on prime time, had no problem with the subject matter, but did want some curse words eliminated. Quinn insisted that they be bleeped audibly, to let the audiences know that they were watching censored material. *Golub* brought Kartemquin much-needed national visibility. It was *Golub* that finally won Kartemquin an invitation to join the annual Flaherty Seminar, founded in 1955 by the widow of the "father" of documentary, Robert Flaherty. The prestigious seminar, an annual summer gathering led by film curators and scholars, somehow had always looked past Kartemquin's work (and continued to do so thereafter); *Golub*, a film about an artist, was invited to its session in Riga, Latvia. Quinn later recalled making a friend there in Marlon Riggs, whose visual poem celebrating Black gay identity, *Tongues Untied*, left him thunderstruck. (Riggs was another filmmaker-activist who worked for the creation of ITVS.) Among the project's other long-range benefits to Kartemquin was that it brought Peter Gilbert deeper into the Kartemquin fold.

Later, in 2004, Kartemquin released an updated version: *Golub: Late Works Are the Catastrophes*. It was the 1988 film, with a followup interview with Golub and his wife, Nancy, on his "whimsically apocalyptic" approach to art at the end of his life (he died in 2004, just as the film came out on public TV). The film was done in Quinn and Blumenthal's spare time, with bare-bones funding. Blumenthal wanted to capture the artist's coming to terms with his mortality. Blumenthal was its champion and guiding light; this was his crowning achievement as a socially engaged film artist. He had stayed in contact with Golub, talking on the phone every few weeks.

Catastrophes provided a new life for the original film, with disturbing topicality in the referencing of new horrors, such as photos of prisoner abuse from the Abu Ghraib prison in Iraq, which the US had invaded. It also features a discussion by Golub and the filmmakers about what was wrong with the filmmakers' original ending to the first film, which is shown. It was first broadcast on the satellite-distributed LinkTV (available to TV viewers receiving their programming via satellite dish) in 2005, and then on a PBS series, *True Lives*, in 2006. It also had an active festival life, and educational sales.

HOOP DREAMS (1994)

In 1986, two recent college graduates in film from Southern Illinois University, Steve James and Fred (later Frederick) Marx, walked in the door. To them, Kartemquin was mecca. At the new, student-run Big Muddy Film Festival, Jerry Blumenthal had been an early presenter and judge, alongside experimental filmmaker James Benning and Jim Jarmusch. He had shown *Taylor Chain II* and *The Last Pullman Car*. "I remember watching *The Last Pullman Car* and feeling, 'Wow, this is *really* good!'" recalled James. "It lodged in my mind that Kartemquin was really interesting. And Jerry was very impressive—classic Jerry, thoughtful and funny and compelling."

So they made an appointment. Quinn met them, and looked at their proposal for a half-hour film about urban pickup basketball. He was impressed, not only with their passion and vision but with the fact that they had in hand a $2,000 Illinois Arts Council grant. "I could see that they understood how to write a proposal," he recalled. James later recalled that he was thrilled with Quinn's interest: "He said, 'Sure, we won't give you any money, but we'll give you guidance.' That was the Kartemquin way, then." Kartemquin also gave the young men a place to work and write their proposals.

James and Marx decided to use the entire grant to buy videotapes. That was a big decision, which everyone made reluctantly. James in particular was in love with film. But on a frayed shoestring of a budget, video was the only option. Morrissette was video's major champion, seeing its enormous possibilities and confident he could overcome the technical weaknesses of video. He convinced the team to use double-system sound—recording the sound separately—which permitted more flexibility. And his meticulous oversight limited degradation in the still-agonizing linear editing process. When the film eventually and unexpectedly became a huge hit, the team would also have to convert the tape to 16mm for the Sundance Film Festival, at a time when very few companies did that work; Peter Gilbert used his connections to find a place. Then, once the film won at Sundance, they had to blow it up to 35mm for theatrical release.

Now, the filmmakers needed to look for a cinematographer. They wanted someone who could shoot broadcast-quality video. In this, they directly confronted the fact that they were white men making a story about Black culture. This was territory James was uncomfortably familiar with. "I grew up in Virginia, in a racially fraught community," he said. "I heard the n-word and saw Confederate flags a lot, but I was also playing basketball with a mostly Black team. In the summers I would work for my dad, who had a flooring and tile business. He had a Black employee who I would help. I was his helper and also the boss's son. There was a lot to think about."

Looking back decades, James said:

> We couldn't make *Hoop Dreams* now the way we did, and that's all to the good. I also came to see the issue differently when I made *No Crossover*, about Allen Iverson. I thought I had had these basketball relationships with Black players; I also played one year as a college player. But they were never more than just teammates.... We had great rapport and camaraderie and talked trash and snapped towels at each other. But I was never in their home, they were never in my home. We didn't have a real friendship. Maybe what I was seeking to get at in *Hoop Dreams* was learning more about their lives than I could possibly get as their teammate.

Quinn suggested that they ask Margaret Caples, head of the most important Black film organization in the city, for suggestions for a Black team member; he hoped they would get a Black cinematographer. And she provided some names. But the matches didn't work, as Caples explained later: "We didn't have filmmakers who could just drop everything, get their camera and go. We [Black people] don't operate that way, because of the inequities and everything. You've got to have somebody backing you, and you've got to have that constant flow of income coming in." Furthermore, she said, people like to work with people they know and have things in common with. Emerging Black filmmakers looked at Kartemquin and saw a white business. And at that, it was a business that underpaid even its full-timers.

Steve James agreed with Caples's recollection. He had also reached out to a Black cameraman who worked at WTTW: "But it wasn't practical, because he was not going to shoot for free for these strange white guys, and we had nothing to offer him [in the way of money]. Because of the structural issues of racism in the industry, there were few people of color who had reached competency and success, and you couldn't ask those people to come work for nothing."

The lone Kartemquin staffer working on administrative tasks, Marcy McCall, had an idea. "You know who'd be perfect for you?" McCall said to

James. "Peter Gilbert." Gilbert, who now also owned his own Betacam as well as his 16mm camera, was also a basketball fanatic. She still treasures thinking of herself as the midwife of the team's birth. Gilbert had just finished working on *American Dream*, a crash course in verité production. In that production, "We were always asking, how can we turn this interview into a scene?" he later recalled. Also, he was, like James and Marx, a Chicagoan with a fanatical passion for basketball. "The first phone call Peter and I had," James recalled, "we didn't stop talking for three hours, and most of it was about basketball."

The new team shot for a week, thinking they would focus on one basketball court in Chicago, and track different characters—young, adult, older—who used the court for a half-hour film. Again, the team tried to incorporate Black members, a plan that foundered on finances again. "We hired a Black assistant cameraman—Brian Pitts—but we didn't really need one," recalled James. (Pitts went on to a career working on leading Hollywood films.) "He had been a player at Northwestern. We found out about him through Peter Kuttner. But not only did we not need him, but on projects where there's no money you gravitate toward people who are willing to work for nothing, and Peter also came with a video camera. We also hired a Black sound man for the first week too. But I could do that, and I'm free."

In the course of that week, the entire project changed. They had sought out Isiah Thomas's childhood court, and Thomas's high school coach Gene Pingatore pointed them to an African American friend and colleague, "Big Earl" Smith. Smith took the team to various playgrounds around Chicago. At one of them, Smith singled out Arthur Agee. "This kid's interesting," he said. When Agee heard about the film, he was, in his own words, "gung-ho," although he had trouble convincing his mother he wasn't making it all up. Smith made the introductions to the family, and talked to Agee's mother about enrolling him in Pingatore's summer camp, which featured Isiah Thomas. At the summer camp, they met another boy, William Gates, who Pingatore thought might be the next Isiah Thomas. Suddenly, the movie was taking another direction, following the boys and not the playground court action.

With their week's worth of shooting, the team crafted a sizzle reel, and began fundraising in earnest. They also began cultivating a relationship with the families. "It was a long process to build trust with the families," recalled Quinn. "The boys were there right away, but one of the mothers later said, 'It took about a year before we really trusted you and felt we could share what was really going on.'" A turning point came when Agee, whose family couldn't afford the school any more, left Pingatore's program at St. Joseph's. He was shocked to see the film team continue to follow him. The realization that the team was interested in him, not just his basketball success, solidified their relationship with the entire family.

They supported themselves with commercial work. James was also working as a production assistant on TV commercials, gradually becoming a production manager at Ebel Productions. His schedule was flexible enough to let him work on his own projects as well. In between paid jobs, the production team searched for grants fruitlessly for two years, working from a desk at Kartemquin. They turned to Quinn for advice, since Blumenthal was furiously finishing editing his passion project, *Golub*. Sometimes Quinn and Blumenthal threw them some Kartemquin work. "Kartemquin carried us," recalled James. "They sustained the film through thick and thin, but mostly thin and thin." The project was way ahead of its time; sports documentaries had yet to become hot items in the documentary film marketplace, although they had been a part of TV programming for decades. *Hoop Dreams* would ultimately break the sound barrier for the genre.

James also began to imbibe the Kartemquin mix of politics and aesthetics. While Quinn "waxed poetic," in James's words, about John Dewey, he couldn't get James to read Dewey's work. But James—someone who later became the face of Kartemquin's "democracy through documentary" claim—came to admire both Quinn and Blumenthal's approach intuitively:

> They're both guys whose politics are left, but they're not reductionist. They have a sense of humor, of the complexity of the world we live in. That's been infused in the films over the years. They're not doctrinaire, or just tools for social change. The social change is infused in the films, and often very much in the civic engagement and outreach. But the films themselves center on the complexity of human beings. Gordon in his role as exec producer pushes in that direction. He's not interested in simple answers. It's people, against the larger backdrop of the world we live in, and how they try to influence

that world. You think and you feel. And the films stay with you. They are not the fast food of cinema.

The Kartemquin connections finally began to work. The Minneapolis public TV station, KTCA, impressed with *Golub*, reached out to ask Kartemquin what they were working on. KTCA was also ahead of its time in imagining documentaries as not only entertaining but also lucrative. Soon, the team was in negotiations with KTCA for a contract. The producers were desperate, and KTCA's executives knew it. So KTCA drove a brutal bargain: 50 percent equity in the film in return for a $70,000 grant KTCA got from CPB. This would turn out to be an extraordinary windfall for KTCA. Quinn sat in meetings for two solid days arguing about the contract, and ultimately lost. But they had saved the project. The public TV money gave the project a financial foundation for the first time.

KTCA had more luck raising money for a documentary that it could pitch as purely educational: a stay-in-school documentary, *Higher Goals* (1992). It featured, among others, William Gates and another high schooler, Kim Williams (who later was a WNBA star), and basketball star Isiah Thomas. As well, *Saturday Night Live* comic Tim Meadows played a basketball-fanatic kid who needs to be talked into staying in school. Toyota Motor Sales provided $256,000 and the Minnesota Timberwolves, the pro basketball team, added $40,000. At half an hour, it was widely shown on public TV station, and predictably, it was embraced by public TV stations nationally. It wasn't made in the Deweyan mode; it was a classic uplift, bootstrapping, message film. It wouldn't disturb the comfort of public TV's privileged membership. *Higher Goals* may have been nothing like *Hoop Dreams*, but it was essential to keeping *Hoop Dreams* alive.

Another Kartemquin connection put *Hoop Dreams* over the top, at another crisis point. When the MacArthur Foundation was preparing to host a meeting of the private foundations' association, the Council on Foundations, Woodward "Woody" Wickham proposed that rather than a physical tour of funded projects, the foundation fund a locally produced film about them. He chose Kartemquin to make it.

Wickham is a legend among media funders. A Michigan doctor's son and Harvard graduate, he had a profound understanding of privilege. He had spent a sobering time in his early twenties in Mexico, absorbing an understanding of US imperial realities. In all his work, he unpretentiously leveraged his power and privilege to create opportunities for others. His sharp wit—he had been editor in chief of the *Harvard Lampoon*—was wrapped in generosity. At a time of network broadcast TV, he perceived commercial media as a cultural force maintaining inequality. Over the course of his tenure at the MacArthur Foundation, between 1990 and 2003, he fostered countless audiovisual projects to expand expression and capacity. He hired female programming officers who shared his vision, including Patricia Boero (a Latin American), Alyce Myatt (a Black American), and Elspeth Revere, an idealistic and public-minded white graduate of the University of Chicago. His projects included not only many documentaries but also funding to public broadcasting and funding to media arts centers across the nation, where young people got training in video expression. For years he and I served together on the ITVS board, where he became board chair. His wisdom on complex political problems in media was extraordinary.

Wickham approached Kartemquin to make *Grassroots Chicago* (1991), a half-hour film profiling several Chicago nonprofits in a verité style. Quinn gave the project to James, for a simple reason: "He had a family, he needed the money." Quinn shot the film, with help from Morrissette, and Blumenthal handled sound. James was director, writer, and coeditor with Susanne Suffredin.

James had a dream for leveraging *Grassroots Chicago*. "I told Peter and Fred, I have a master plan. I'm gonna do a great job on this film, and then get them interested in funding *Hoop Dreams*." It worked; Wickham found in James a rising star. "I went to breakfast with him and he asked if it would ever be in theaters," James recalled. "I said—it's funny now—'No, that'll never happen, it's on video.' But he loved the project. Later we got a call that was typical Woody. He says, 'I think I left my flannel shirt at Kartemquin,' and I said, 'OK, I think it's here.' 'Thanks,' he says. 'Oh and by the way one other thing, MacArthur has decided to award you a quarter of a million dollars for *Hoop Dreams*.'"

The film grew to be massive and unwieldy, and Fred Marx was losing his grip on the editing. James's and Marx's relationship was frayed to the breaking point. Finally Quinn stepped in, inviting them both over to his house, where he was down with the flu. Using the mentorship skills for

Figure 14. From left, Steve James, Peter Gilbert, and Fred Marx shooting for *Hoop Dreams*. Source: Kartemquin Archives.

which he became justly known, he worked with the two angry men to prioritize making the film. They finally came to an agreement. James would take over the editing of the project, and they would continue to share credit. James would continue to work with Bill Haugse, who had been a second editor, to reshape and cut the story. Quinn sat in the editing room with them. James credits Quinn with teaching him how to edit.

"It was like an ongoing master class in storytelling," James recalled. "One of his great strengths, even up to today, is thinking how you get into and out of scenes. He was good at internal structure. Quinn, for his part, said that James came with superb editing instincts. It was James who decided the last line of the film would be college athlete and devoted dad William talking to his little daughter: "People say to me, 'Don't forget me when you make it.' I want to say to them, 'Don't forget me if I don't.'"

They had their disagreements, though, which reflected Quinn's enduring concern for respect to subjects. "We got into a big argument," James remembered, "because he didn't want Arthur talking about how he hates school. Arthur says in the film, 'If it closed, I wouldn't be holding up a picket sign saying, Open the School.' I said, It's funny. But Gordon didn't want it in. He would bring it up again and again—he's a dogged guy. I think he was worried about reflecting badly on Arthur. I thought it was revealing of Arthur's personality." The scene stayed in.

The film's narrative throughline was the struggle of two Black American families to seize rare opportunities, to negotiate with an alien and often hostile white environment, and to find education and success in the process. It was a grassroots story of Black American agency in the face of systems that consistently deny it. The two boys Kartemquin followed, filming over five years, both managed to get higher-education opportunities through their sports prowess. One starts a family in high school, and neither ends up in professional sports. But they survive the everyday cruelties of American racism and poverty, and their families, who support them in myriad ways throughout, share their pride. Viewers have been invited into the intimate process of growing up Black in Chicago, hoping against hope that the improbable vehicle of basketball can become a way to counterbalance the disenfranchisement that fills frame after frame of the film. Viewers have also been invited into families that fight every day for their dignity and the chance for its next generation to negotiate a way into the ordinary dignity that white, middle-class kids take for granted.

Even before the film was finished, in 1993, Wickham worked to ensure that his promise to the MacArthur board—that this would be the most important film on public TV that year—would come true. He convened a meeting of PBS, CPB, KTCA, and nonprofits, as well as film distribution professionals, to brainstorm how they could help make this film more than a passing PBS special. Their planning meshed with the work of the producers' representatives Iltis & Sikich and a distributor, Fine Line Pictures. The big hurdle for public broadcasting was permitting the film to have a theatrical release first; that deal became an important example for later documentaries with public broadcasting funding. The film went to Sundance, and took the documentary audience award. John Iltis conducted a heated bidding war for the film, which raised its price dramatically. Lawyer John Sloss negotiated a "cash corridor" that benefited Kartemquin, and which James credited with saving the film financially. Quinn recalled the importance of the producers' reps: "If not for Iltis and Sikich, we would have been eaten alive. I had no experience with an environment like that. I'd have probably wanted to take the first offer with money." The film went on to make substantial revenues in theatrical release, very unusual for documentaries. Public broadcasters then leveraged that publicity for the broadcast.

Once the film was sold, Quinn recognized the need, as did the directors, to meet with the families and work out an unprecedented deal to profit-share. Sloss was aghast; it was unheard of. Furthermore, the number of people involved was huge. But ultimately, everyone who spoke in the film received a payment proportional to their screentime. William and Arthur, the two boys profiled, received payouts equal to the filmmakers. The filmmakers knew William and Arthur would face pressure to share their own money with family, so they also allocated a half-share of what the filmmakers and the boys got for each of the families. The participants or their descendants or estates were still receiving checks as of 2023.

Then came the struggle to hold on to the soul of the film during the marketing of it. Marketing professionals wanted to turn it into an uplift film, a bootstrapping story. The filmmakers fiercely resisted, pushing for marketing that maintained the social themes of the film, and they eventually won. The nearly three-hour theatrical version went to public TV, and it was shown around the world.

A great point of pride, both for the filmmakers and Quinn as executive producer, was that Black viewers embraced the film. "*Hoop Dreams* is the film that was embraced by and large by the African American community, including Spike Lee, who was very helpful," recalled Quinn. "I think the reason African Americans embraced it was because the film was saying something to the white community that they wanted said, and it was accessible to white people." At Kartemquin's fiftieth anniversary celebration, he pointed to the *Hoop Dreams* portrayal of Arthur Agee's mother: "We have seen her struggles, but more importantly we have seen her power as a mother, her resiliency, and her triumphs. That's why that film was so successful and still works today.... A democracy needs stories that help different parts of the population understand each other." Spike Lee, who went out of his way to lend his clout to the film's promotion, also consulted on the design of the related merchandise, and signed on as executive producer of a (never-made) fiction version of the film.

Reviews were adulatory. On the nationally syndicated, immensely popular TV show *Siskel & Ebert & the Movies* (aka *At the Movies*), the review show that Roger Ebert and Gene Siskel had started in 1975 on public TV and morphed into a mini-genre of its own, Ebert praised the film to the skies—and for the reasons the filmmakers had made it. This boost was another triumph for John Iltis, who got the film to the duo before it went to Sundance; unprecedentedly, they reviewed it at a time viewers couldn't see it. In fact, it was the duo's rave review that gave the film so much Sundance buzz. Although *Hoop Dreams* was widely described as a masterpiece, Kartemquin was rarely mentioned. Quinn asked James to explicitly mention it. And he tried, but still the Kartemquin name was routinely left out. "I remember saying to Gordon, the press doesn't care about the production company. Think about Barbara Kopple, who knows about Cabin Creek Films? I think I was wrong in the long term, because Kartemquin has built itself into a brand. But it was a source of tension."

When the Oscar nominations were released, press hovered at the Kartemquin's door, and filmmakers inside waited. The film received, unprecedentedly, a nomination for its editing. But it was not nominated in the documentary category, to national critical outcry. The *New York Times* reported, "The omission of *Hoop Dreams* prompted not only bewilderment but also questions about how documentaries are selected." The *Chicago Tribune* used the phrase "a kick in the teeth." On NBC News, anchor Tom Brokaw called it "for many of us, a big disappointment." Within the Academy of Motion Pictures Arts and Sciences, a restructuring of the way documentaries are selected was put in process as a result. In the Kartemquin bathroom, someone mounted a framed copy of a *New Yorker* cartoon, by Nurit Karlin, showing a basketball player shooting over the head of an Oscar statuette.

At the same time, some critics entirely missed the film's framing of the story as one of Black American agency in fighting against enormous systemic odds. Black American feminist scholar and activist bell hooks, contributing a contrarian voice at a moment when *Hoop Dreams* was at the height of its popularity among majority-white audiences, distrusted it as a film with a white perspective on Black culture. hooks loved its positive portrayals of Black people, especially Black mothers, calling it a "compelling and moving real-life drama" that exposed sports exploitation. But she also argued that Arthur and Williams's NBA dream "is presented as though it is no more than a positive American dream," providing a "con-

Figure 15. A *New Yorker* cartoon by Nurit Karlin, showing a basketball player shooting over the head of an Oscar statuette, is on display above the toilet in a Kartemquin bathroom. Source and credit: Mar Garvey.

servative vision of the conditions for 'making it' in the United States." She believed the film's treatment of Arthur's dad's drug addiction confirmed stereotypes rather than contextualizing it. Much later, in 2022, Jill Godmilow, who had brought a film to Kartemquin way back in 1976, wrote a manifesto, *Kill the Documentary*, which echoed some of hooks's charges. Godmilow, an ardent proponent of sharp-elbowed radical and experimental filmmaking, attacked *Hoop Dreams* as an uplift story rather than a systemic investigation of oppression.

But this viewpoint was unusual, including among Black critics. Many pointed to the way the boys' determined struggle was set in a context of brokenness, to the families' clear-eyed recognition of the costs and odds, and to the ethnographic richness of the storytelling. Ten years later, novelist John Edgar Wideman, who himself had leveraged basketball for opportunities, heralded the film as "one of the most insightful, accurate, affecting, least sentimental, least propagandized treatments of Afro-American family life" he had ever seen, in an essay included on the Blu-Ray version of *Hoop Dreams*. The essay echoed the Deweyan spirit that drove the Kartemquinites:

> At its best, *Hoop Dreams*, in the manner of African-American folklore, works through indirection and signifying, transforming mundane, concrete details of everyday life into haunting, daunting metaphor. *Hoop Dreams* doesn't appropriate, exploit, or pretend to explain the complex inner reality of the two young men whose lives it follows over the course of five years. By doggedly, expansively, scrupulously recording the outer reality of images and voices surrounding them, the documentary authenticates the secret heart-place taking shape inside its protagonists. Viewers are positioned less to judge this private process than to identify with its excitement and pain.

Wideman noted, "A sense of gradual, dramatic revelation, of complicity in lives unpredictably unfolding, is achieved, in spite not because of the camera's intervention." From specifics, the film told a larger story of "what happens in the lived space between any reality and any dream, examining the minute-by-minute choices, trials, the step-by-step grind or dance or crawl or flight over burning coals that constitutes anybody's journey toward a dream's ever-receding, mythical shore." And it told a larger reality: "The film exposes a network of deeply rooted prejudice, hypocrisy, and lies that makes coming of age in an economically deprived urban environment a kind of inherited incarceration with very few means of escape."

Kartemquin was fundamentally changed by *Hoop Dreams*. It wasn't just the extraordinary success of the film. It was also that Kartemquin was now associated with a particular style, which James both described ("you think and you feel") and personified. That style aligned in a profound sense with the core philosophy of the organization. Kartemquin had begun as a semi-academic project to conduct social inquiry via cinema verité. It then became, almost overnight in the 1970s, a political-activist collective, producing films for and with local radical political organizations. After the collective's collapse, the work on *Golub* gave permission for Blumenthal and Quinn to perceive themselves as artists. With the arrival of Steve James, whose personal style centered on character-driven storytelling, and Peter Gilbert, who combined his compassionate storytelling with knowledge of and connections in commercial broadcast/cable, a new identity was taking shape within the same philosophical framework.

The success of *Hoop Dreams* acquainted Kartemquin staffers with the business of independent documentary for the entertainment (broadcast and cable) market. It also gave them access to funding. MacArthur's imprimatur also opened doors to other funders, and *Golub*'s success under the patronage of a rich donor opened doors there too. The pathway to funding for future films ran through character-driven, social-issue documentary.

THE UNMADE PROJECTS

In this pivotal time, several highly ambitious projects failed to get off the ground. All of them were high-concept, and none featured a character-driven approach, which would become key to Kartemquin's future. They all asked questions about systems and human agency in political change.

"When Art Makes a Difference" was to consider art controversies in context. The team's proposal to ITVS opened with a quote from John Dewey about the underappreciated role of the arts in shaping society. The project's purpose was clearly tied to Kartemquin's mission: "By starting outside the U. S. with the emerging Czech democracy and looking back at ourselves, we hope to get beyond current controversies to the essential, but often unnoticed, way art functions in the democratic process."

The project grew out of personal experience. Quinn had contacts with Czech artists through his colleague and friend Chuck Olin, who had made a film in Czechoslovakia the year before (Jim Morrissette on camera) about the Universal Declaration of Human Rights. Artists, including the poet Václav Havel (who would become the country's president), had stood up to the Communist government during the Velvet Revolution, as well as artists who had worked for the Communist regime. Post-Communism, Czech artists typically resisted any connection between art and democracy, after their bitter experience with government-driven arts. Meanwhile, in the US, conservatives charging "political correctness" and decrying critical art as un-American were eagerly looking for examples to feed the media. Art students provided plenty of material, as the scandals at the School of the Art Institute of Chicago showed.

Another proposal imagined a television series focused on the role of volunteering, civic activism, nonprofit organizations and unions, and unpaid labor in contributing to the American democratic culture—the so-called "independent sector," or nonprofit and nonmarketplace work. Two pilots were developed (I was involved, as a writer) and pitched to public TV; ITVS funded the development process, but the proposed series never got production funding.

Yet another project, "Looking for Democracy," failed to get funding from public TV in various iterations. Originally, the Kartemquin team, led by Quinn, James, and Blumenthal, imagined a series focused on how grassroots and community organizations relate to politicians and electoral campaigns. The early version of the proposal argued that the place to find democracy in action was at ground level, John Dewey style:

> It is by looking at how these organizations actively engage in electoral process that we can best see an alternative to the hermetically closed triangle of the individual, the TV, and the voting booth that defines much of our political landscape. Though grassroots organizations are not the most powerful players on the current political scene, they are a good place to look for new ways to re-involve citizens in the democratic process.

Later, the proposal evolved into a set of tag-team vignettes, in which working people would choose someone in their lives to talk with about where they find democratic participation in their daily lives—perhaps a church group, family, union, or community organizations. That person would then choose the next interviewee, ending in a talk show featuring all the interviewees. None of the versions, however, caught fire.

Quinn, with his friend Michelle Citron, who was teaching film at Northwestern, and another Northwestern colleague, Michael Hall, launched an ambitious project on the human cost of industrialized healthcare, with a massive proposal to the National Endowment for the Humanities. However, after winning small development grants, it failed to win NEH support in a highly competitive environment.

Toward the end of this era, Doremus worked with Quinn and Blumenthal on a project, "Sweet Dreams," to follow the crisis of the Brach's candy company and the Chicago candy industry. Brach's was closing, and labor organizations were trying to organize their workers to make it an employee-owned company. The team imagined a film that could contribute to the argument that the candy industry, with Brach's as a primary player, was important to Chicago; it followed the work of an industry association, the Candy Institute, which worked with companies, unions and government. The project was mostly self-funded with a little development money, but the effort to save Brach's fell though, and with it the project.

These proposals demonstrate that Kartemquin continued to have appetite for a more issue-oriented direction, when it was fundable. It was exploring Deweyan questions of public formation actively. The projects also articulate themes that animated more character-driven approaches, which often built out the public-formation work in outreach and engagement.

END OF AN ERA

As always, some Kartemquin personnel moved on, without ever really severing ties. While working at Kartemquin, Ed Scott began working part-time in 1990 with Community Film Workshop, where he became a teacher. When he left, he recommended Jim Fetterley take over his position, and Fetterley leaped at the chance. In 1987, Marcy McCall left her Crate & Barrel job and the business side of Kartemquin for graduate film school and work in the Hollywood studio system. She had never gotten a chance to practice the art of filmmaking at Kartemquin.

CHAPTER 7

Kartemquin would henceforth become the place in the Midwest where people with a social conscience went to tell humanistic, character-driven stories that could move people and, with luck, motivate them to become more active in a democratic process. It was a larger shift than might have first appeared. Kartemquin had historically been a contestatory site of inquiry about the terms of the status quo. Its first film asked pointed questions about how we treat old people, and why. Its collective-era films boldly aligned with social-justice organizations to make vividly clear the human cost of structural inequality. Its labor films not only provided a workers' point of view but also a systemic understanding of labor's role within capitalism.

The narrative direction in which *Hoop Dreams* sent Kartemquin departed significantly from this focus on structural sources of inequality. This character-driven narrative style put individual stories in the forefront, with structural issues the context. It fit well into the niche that public TV created, and it appealed to public TV's demographic of relatively upscale viewers. It implicitly promised those largely white viewers a safely guided experience beyond their culturally cloistered world. This was what Barry Dornfeld, in analyzing this trend in public television, called "televisual humanism," which "appeals to a sense of equality and empathy by seeing universalism within difference," within familiar broadcast expectations. That humanism could serve a useful function, within public television, as a way to avoid never-ending conservative assaults by sidling up to rather than aggressively dissecting hot topics. The genre could also build audience; neoliberal congressional representatives always wanted ratings. Some of Kartemquin's earlier-era stalwarts, such as Judy Hoffman and Susanne Davenport, saw this shift with alarm and dismay, as betraying a social-justice mission. And certainly this style could become simple uplift, or sensationalism, or the turning of an oddball into a celebrity. Kartemquin, however, anchored that approach in the Deweyan concept of art as experience, making stories that could bring viewers beyond what they take for granted, and toward the hope for something better. That model kept the humanism of the films true to the characters' situation, and honest with the audience.[1]

8 Making Broadcast and Cable Stories with Integrity, 1995–2008

With *Hoop Dreams*, Kartemquin had suddenly become the new darling for television distributors and programmers, a group that had gotten much bigger over the previous decade with cable. But few TV programmers knew the organization's anchoring philosophy, and the Kartemquin's values did not necessarily mesh with their priorities. "I could get a meeting with almost anyone," recalled Quinn, "but once we started talking, there was no common ground, except at public TV and for a few of Steve's projects." In this period, Kartemquin established crucial relationships with private foundations, some cable companies, and public TV. It became a place to produce storytelling with integrity and democratic mission for an entertainment-oriented marketplace. But Kartemquin never lost sight of its goal of storytelling for democracy, or its interest in off-broadcast work focused on specific social-change objectives.

The world of television was changing dramatically. In the early 1980s, satellites for the first time made cheap distribution of programming possible over local cable systems across the nation. Regulators let cable companies control both their hardware and their programming, breaking the long-standing rule that transport companies couldn't also own the stuff carried on that transport ("common carriage"). They quickly became

179

corporate behemoths. National channels burgeoned, and documentary became a popular format, since it was comparatively inexpensive to make and acquire. Channels such as Discovery, Arts & Entertainment (A&E), History Channel, Bravo, National Geographic, and CNN began to create more opportunities to watch documentaries. At the outset, these channels often mimicked the look of public TV, partly to gain legitimacy and partly because product was available, given public TV's small window for independent documentaries. They quickly morphed into brands with highly formulaic looks and feels. The templating of formats also lowered costs and ramped up output, while excluding indies—except for the occasional documentary the companies thought might win an award. Another aspect of commercialization was the development of branded content (documentaries funded by sponsors, carrying sponsors' messages) and routine product placement. Public TV began searching for ways to distinguish itself in an ever-more-crowded factual marketplace.

Cable programming also inevitably fractured the broadcast audience. Manufacturers of television sets enhanced the threat to broadcasters by making the cable connection a default, forcing viewers to flip a switch to get broadcast signals. In 1997, broadcasters finally won a Supreme Court decision that forced cablecasters to include broadcast programming on the cable lineup. But by 1990, broadcasters had already seen their peak audience ratings and would henceforth settle for smaller parts of the viewership pie. These changes brought both new opportunities and new challenges for Kartemquin Films.

It was also a time of sea change in technology, an area in which Kartemquin had always been a leader. The group had leapt into computers early; now, Kartemquin moved early to nonlinear editing, purchasing an Avid. As the technical resources manager until 1999, Jim Fetterley became Kartemquin's learn-on-the-job IT guru, mastering fast-changing formats and innovations.

Documentary outreach and engagement work adapted quickly to new technological affordances. The digital video disc (DVD) and the digital video recorder (DVR) arrived in the late 1990s. Websites became first possible and then affordable, and soon every film project had one. As the humanistic, character-driven social documentary form was appearing on more programming venues on television, following the example of *Hoop*

Dreams's popular success, so was the idea of a companion campaign to be conducted with related materials, including modules drawn from the film's materials but not merely excerpted from the film itself. This notion had been used in advocacy work of all kinds, including for *American Revolution 2* and *The Murder of Fred Hampton*. It was now moving into the mainstream, and DVDs and the internet could multiply possibilities. In doing so, Kartemquin could draw on its deep experience of engagement in all its films.

A subfield of outreach / impact producers was developing, to serve the burgeoning after / beside-broadcast market. The 1993 National Advocacy Video conference in Washington, DC, organized by the Benton Foundation and its president, Larry Kirkman, showcased the power of video for left and liberal social change. (I worked with Kirkman on the event.) By 1999, public TV established a National Center for Outreach, which coordinated and shared strategies with public TV filmmakers for about a decade. Small businesses coordinating outreach, such as Active Voice and Roundtable Media, sprang up. Kartemquin would use these outreach strategies, which today are known as impact campaigns, on its biggest new series of this era, *The New Americans*. In fact, ever since Active Voice led the engagement work *The New Americans*, Gordon Quinn served on its advisory board.

As public funding came under ever greater conservative scrutiny, investment by private funders proliferated. The Council on Foundations held a film festival, starting in the mid-1990s, at its annual conference, showcasing work funded by its members; I curated it and wrote the catalog for a decade. The goal of the festival was to encourage more funders to think of funding film. This development both created more opportunities for Kartemquin and a need to expand its funding strategies.

The association of documentary with social impact and activism for funders created a sea change in funder styles. The "gray ladies" of private funding for documentary—the Ford, Rockefeller, and MacArthur Foundations—all funded with profits from the industrial era—had long since established a genteel, humanistic approach to their missions. Their boards and leadership strove to avoid charges of political or social activism. At the same time, they espoused such general values as democratic participation, human rights, and conservation / environmental sustainability, and their program officers were likely to support work aligned with equity, justice, and representation. They were Deweyan in their understanding of political agency in the public. For them, the character-driven, humanistic documentary was ideal. The new technological tools in the outreach toolkit made it easier for them to fulfill mission with such stories.

MacArthur in particular became a stalwart of Kartemquin funding. Wickham's program-officer team—Patricia Boero, Alyce Myatt, and Elspeth Revere—trusted Kartemquin's values as responsive to theirs. They knew as well that Kartemquin reliably finished the films they started, and that, as Revere later recalled, "They respected the filmmaker's vision and they were respectful of the subjects. They made the kind of film that led the viewer to their own conclusions; they weren't advocacy filmmakers." MacArthur could be confident that a filmmaker they funded, working with Kartemquin, would both finish the film and it would be the film the filmmaker wanted to make. At the same time, they could trust, in this new era of documentary-friendly programming opportunities, that the film would reach wide audiences.

For other funders, particularly foundations whose wealth derived from the growth of digital technology and high-tech industry, the turn to impact strategy fit well with their corporate culture and sometimes with founder predilections. For these foundations, a targeted advocacy mission, clear metrics for effects, and close accountability of makers to funders all fit their objectives. Sometimes, as with the Skoll Foundation (created out of eBay money), the backer of Participant Media (2004–2024), the funders openly aspired to the "double bottom line," doing good while also being commercially successful. Sometimes, as with the Gates Foundation's focus on public health, they were funded and evaluated with metrics that aligned with specified real-world outcomes. These foundations designed campaigns around strategic communication, with a persuasion objective. Kartemquin's approach was not always aligned with this kind of funder, since the Deweyan objective of public formation through communication was a long-term political project, not a targeted persuasion campaign. But as time went on, Participant in particular came to be associated with Steve James's work such as the more recent *America to Me, City So Real,* and *A Compassionate Spy* (2022). The leadership of the late Diane Weyermann there, whose vision of documentary did align with

Kartemquin's, was critical to that relationship. James's films always could be counted on to have a wide audience, and also to have substance and respect for and of their participants.

There was also a third kind of documentary funder: the right-wing foundation. At the turn of the twenty-first century, this kind of documentary funder was still rare, as right-wing foundations (e.g., Scaife, Koch, Mercer) spent their money on elite-oriented activities such as think tanks, which generated policymaker-oriented reports, and on pressuring mainstream media, including public TV. But the rising popularity of documentary film also made these foundations more interested in funding right-wing documentaries, such as those produced by Michael Pack (later a Trump appointee) and by Citizens United. These funders also cultivated conservatives who looked for ways to affect and enter public television. For instance, Kenneth Tomlinson, a *Reader's Digest* editor who oversaw the entity overseeing Voice of America and other state media in the Reagan administration, was appointed during the George W. Bush administration to chair the Corporation for Public Broadcasting. He brought in, among others, Pack and Tucker Carlson, before being fired for corruption in 2005. Right-wing interest in documentary signaled, among other things, the rising reputation of documentary and its commercial viability. It also signaled a new level of right-wing investment in attempts to either thwart or redirect media designed for democratic purposes.

Kartemquin now experienced the disjunction between its ideals and the business of TV directly. For instance, HBO's Sheila Nevins, a towering figure in the documentary business, met with James and Gilbert soon after the debut of *Hoop Dreams*. Nevins was trying to make HBO Documentaries a place filmmakers could trust, and she always wanted award-winning documentaries to balance out more sensationalist fare. Gilbert recalled her asking if they could make "a real inner-city film" this time, something whose conflicts and tensions could capture an audience that, say, had just watched a *Rambo* film (a Sylvester Stallone franchise about a heroic military veteran). James recalled that she gave as an example a film about rival Black and Latino gangs in a local high school. They didn't need to think much before declining. Some Kartemquin-related filmmakers started calling themselves "associates," while they also formed their own companies for work that did not align with Kartemquin's mission. Steve James and Peter Gilbert formed a little company, Longshot Films, to generate work with a first-look deal from Disney.

RUNNING IT LIKE A BUSINESS

The work-for-hire and equipment rental were still revenue streams, but now Kartemquin tried to build its workload and business around new broadcast / cable projects, and new opportunities in sales to the consumer market. For that, Kartemquin needed a level of organization it had never had. Women played a large role in keeping Kartemquin afloat, and steering it toward a new future. They helped to redefine Kartemquin as a media arts center, proudly identified with documentary for democracy.

Fenell Doremus introduced a lifeline to Kartemquin: Karen Larson. Larson, after receiving a degree from the University of Kansas in accounting, had returned to Chicago, where Kartemquin was for her a legendary institution. Then she met Doremus at a yoga class and saw she was wearing a Kartemquin T-shirt. The connection was made. Larson brought her superb organizational and financial skills to an organization perennially short on both. She created for the first time a cash flow structure, obtained health insurance for employees, and instituted the first human relations policy. She arranged all of the royalty payouts for Steve James's new film, *Stevie* (2002). Finally, Kartemquin could plan. But to achieve these accomplishments involved a learning curve. She had dived into her work, loving being a "behind the scenes person," but imposing order onto financial chaos with stern Midwestern rigor ruffled feathers.

Soon Steve James took her to what she recalled as "an expensive lunch," where he explained that she was essential to the place, and she also had to learn not to lead with "no." Heeding his advice, she later said, she learned to brainstorm with different production groups about how to share resources, time their uses of equipment and the editing room, and explain why budget juggling had to happen. She learned collaboration, and she applied those lessons to the rest of her life. Indeed, she said it helped her be a better parent. And she also learned how to join the heated ethics debates in the kitchen.

Karen Larson was Quinn's hope for a new executive director, a role he was desperate to shed, until she decided to start a family and left the work

Figure 16. Steve James talks with editor Susanne Suffredin in the kitchen, the center of Kartemquin's socializing. Source: Kartemquin Archives.

that featured unpredictable hours and subpar salaries. As had been true with Marcy McCall and others, she found that the pace and stress of work at Kartemquin was not compatible with family obligations. She quietly resigned. "I have worked very different jobs after that, but Kartemquin is fundamentally a part of me," she said. "It fundamentally changed how I view art and documentary."

Becky Stocchetti, who came in as an intern on a cable project, *At the Death House Door* (2008), and transcribed most versions of the film, also brought precious organizational skills that Kartemquin desperately needed. But she had a different experience. She had learned about Kartemquin from Judy Hoffman while studying at the University of Chicago, and idolized the organization. She continued, working as an impact producer for Joanna Rudnick's film *In the Family* (2008). To pay the bills, she did a host of other jobs, from working at a farmers' market to hospital night shifts in pediatric neurology. While she treasured working with seasoned Kartemquinites such as editor Aaron Wickenden, she smarted from the meager rewards and the sense that she was dispensable labor.

Two women who came into Kartemquin as Larson was leaving, Joanna Rudnick and Justine Nagan, had a profound effect on the organization, and they fundamentally restructured Kartemquin financially and organizationally. Joanna Rudnick arrived in 2004 and became director of development, while she worked on her own film. Rudnick, who had worked with the *American Masters* public TV series in New York, had moved back to Chicago to be closer to family. She had found she was a carrier of the BRCA gene, predisposing her to both breast and ovarian cancer. Editor Leslie Simmer worked on editing her film on this subject, *In the Family*, while Zak Piper held down both production and postproduction operations. As head of development, Rudnick was squarely in the center of Kartemquin's endless financial drama. She saw that the organization needed to solicit operating funds, not only project funds. It needed to define itself publicly as what it was already: A media arts organization that nurtured new voices in service of a stronger democracy.

Justine Nagan had learned about Kartemquin in college. During a master's program at University of Chicago, she was thrilled when her professor Judy Hoffman used Kartemquin films in teaching. She had worked at Madison's Wisconsin Public Television, a powerhouse station regionally. In 2004, she showed up at Kartemquin's door ready to do anything, including volunteering with Joanna Rudnick. She joined productions and learned a lot. Nagan rapidly moved into a temporary catch-all position, and then in 2005 designed a role for herself as "director of marketing and distribution." Her top priority was building a Kartemquin brand. "Everyone knew *Hoop Dreams*, and nobody outside Chicago knew Kartemquin," she recalled. She set about creating and marketing DVDs, selling merch, building out the website, and strategically placing Kartemquin in national and regional events.

Blumenthal bowed out of the discussion, as he had never been interested in the logistics part of the organization, and he was allergic to a branding discussion. He was also feeling his age, and increasingly felt alienated from the environment, which gradually was losing that small-family feel. Quinn, however, embraced the challenge. He knew how precarious the finances of Kartemquin were. After the biggest project of this era, *The New Americans*, wrapped, leaving Kartemquin without stopgap projects to cover the planning time to the next big thing, Quinn took to calling it Kartemquin's "special period," sardonically invoking Cuban officials' term for brutal austerity after the 1989 collapse of the Soviet Union and loss of its subsidies. "We were bankrupt several times," he later recalled, "but we didn't know it, so we just kept on going." At one point

Figure 17. Joanne Rudnick (left) and Justine Nagan brought new management and fundraising skills, as well as filmmaking ambition, into Kartemquin. Source: Kartemquin Archives.

Quinn suggested to editor Leslie Simmer and to Zak Piper, who was already working as both postproduction manager and production manager, that maybe the two of them could take over the billing. It was so clearly an idea born of desperation that Simmer later recalled weeping on Piper's shoulder, unsure whether Kartemquin could keep its doors open. Piper, obviously flailing, suggested that this was an opportunity for Kartemquin to get stronger. Simmer was not consoled.

Undaunted, for years Rudnick, Nagan, and Doremus pushed the organization to both plan for and raise funds for a more stable financial future. Rudnick and Nagan brought in a nonprofit consultant to help them do management planning. Meanwhile, Quinn and Finitzo began meeting with Ford Foundation program officers. His program officer, Orlando Bagwell—himself a documentarian who came up with the *Eyes on the Prize* series, and a funder of documentaries (he was also a major funder of my center)—encouraged him to propose an institutional development grant. Having been given the hope of a multimillion-dollar grant, Quinn, Rudnick, and others developed an elaborate plan for restructuring. They developed a mission statement, proposed a real board of directors with fiscal responsibility, and imagined new programs. By 2007, the project of imagining a future beyond the founders had begun.

FUNDED FILMMAKING

Cable programmers' appetites for award-winning films led to some opportunities for post *Hoop Dreams* Kartemquin. They could now make films that had upfront funding and a guaranteed outlet, although they would not own rights to those films. Its first such project was *Vietnam, Long Time Coming* (1998), Kartemquin's second feature in the emerging sports documentary genre. The nonprofit World T. E. A. M. (The Exceptional Athlete Matters) Sports, with participation from *Sports Illustrated*, brought the concept. World T. E. A. M. Sports, a nonprofit, had been founded in 1993 to promote the capacities of disabled athletes; it coordinated events to showcase them. Steve Whisnant of World T. E. A. M. Sports was impressed with *Hoop Dreams*'s sports story with a difference. He already knew Gilbert, and approached Quinn, Blumenthal, and Gilbert with the idea of covering a disabled veterans' bike ride through Vietnam. The disabled vets were to travel 1,100 miles, through both North and South Vietnam, on adaptive bicycles, joined by disabled Vietnamese vets, celebrities such as cyclist Greg LeMond and swimmer Diana Nyad, and politician John Kerry (who as a Vietnam Vet worked tirelessly in the antiwar movement).

The film uses experiential, extended scenes and character-focused editing to capture the evolution of the participants into a group, the dynamics of interchanges between Americans and Vietnamese, and ultimately the power of human interchange to address inner turmoil from unfinished business. It was directed by Blumenthal, Gilbert, and Quinn.

Gilbert chose to bring the film to Kartemquin, rather than to his and James's own little production house that had a Disney first-look deal. He knew that the Kartemquinites had contacts in the military veteran community, partly through the Agent Orange scandal, which Quinn had wanted to make a film about. Vietnam War vets, like the Vietnamese, suffered long-term effects from the military's use of napalm during the war, and organized to demand healthcare for themselves and their affected relatives.

Taking on the project was controversial within Kartemquin, because it was sponsored. But it was also mission-aligned. This was a rare hybrid in their world, where for-hire and on-mission work were usually different, although for-hire work never contradicted mission. It was accomplished within a year, and on deadline, because all the funding had come up front. To meet the deadline, Blumenthal as producer-director drew on the talents of, among others, Sharon Karp from the collective days, and David E. Simpson, soon to be a Kartemquin regular.

David E. Simpson had admired Kartemquin as an MFA student at the Art Institute, where he was fascinated by the magic of editing in making experimental film. After a brief internship, he had gone to Minneapolis, where he worked with the legendary Polish filmmaker Marian Marzyński. He later reconnected with Kartemquin when Quinn and Blumenthal were impressed with the film he took to Sundance in 1995, *When Billy Broke His Head*. The two thought his storytelling belonged at Kartemquin, and brought him into *Vietnam*. His slow, solo editing style faced the challenges of collaboration:

> I had never managed a project like this. I was used to going slowly and deliberately, having everything my own way. The first time I did a screening of something I'd been working on for, say, three weeks, it was way too fat, too long, and I remember Jerry walking out, muttering, "If we don't finish this fucking film soon, I'm gonna slit my fucking wrists." Quintessential Jerry—unafraid, hard edged, foul-mouthed, and what I needed to hear.

The film required thoughtful work in trust-building and negotiating difference. The Kartemquin team was balancing precariously between military veterans who distrusted these left-liberal filmmakers who had been antiwar, a powerful funder, and the censorship of the Vietnamese government. The first challenge was the veterans themselves. Quinn remembered,

> We were clear that not only were we not vets, we had all been antiwar. There's a scene early in the film that we wanted to film, showing tensions between the vets and the people putting on the tour. They were going to

meet with the vets only on the bus, and I wanted to be on the bus to shoot. I explained why I thought it was important, and they ended up taking a vote and let us on the bus. I think our transparency helped build the trust to do that.

The welcome funding brought its own issues, too. The executive at World T. E. A. M. Sports who funded it also had final cut. His cofounder, Steve Whisnant, worked productively with the Kartemquin team to negotiate many sticking points. Only one decision still rankled in Quinn's mind, three decades later:

> We had a scene where one of the African American guys, constructively but using the word "racism," addresses the whole group about the low representation of soldiers of color. He says, "I don't see on this trip the brothers I fought with in Vietnam." It was great, and he was great. But one of the trip's backers starts arguing with him—he thinks it reflects badly on the group. They got into a huge argument, and Peter Gilbert filmed it all. In the edit, we didn't use the argument, just the vet's presentation. Later in the film, it really pays off, because he's excited about what the trip has meant, and on his bike, he says right to the camera, "This has been a great healing journey, and we really need a ride across America to heal the racial divide."

But in an all-too-predictable display of white fragility, the funder hated that comment just as much the second time, and demanded they remove it. Several cuts later, they thought they had assuaged his concern. But finally, he insisted on taking it all out. Simpson recalled, "That was one of the first examples for me of Gordon not being afraid to push the conversation, wanting to be provocative, say the hard truths with our films. Sometimes that butted up against someone else's desire to not say it."

Dealing with the Vietnamese censors was also not easy. The entire trip was shepherded by two minders, one strict and the other more relaxed. The stricter one was also a karaoke star, as the filmmakers saw when they went with her to bars where she would perform as a celebrity. The personal openness of the Kartemquinites humanized the relationships and smoothed over problems, but problems were also often solved by the Vietnamese themselves. Quinn had hired a Vietnamese cameraman, Tran Le Tien, without approval, but when it turned out that the strict handler and he had gone to college together, "my problems went away," Quinn said. The importance of having a Vietnamese cameraman was evident in My Lai, when he captured a scene with a Vietnamese vet about his enduring anger about the massacre; "the American crew could never have gotten that," said Quinn.

At another point, they were shooting as they passed an old US Air Force base, now a Vietnamese military camp. Quinn recalled:

> I saw a big sign, so I said to the handler, "What does that say?" and she says, "That says, 'No Pictures.'" Then a soldier with a rifle waves us over, they can't find the right commander to deal with us, we're there for a couple of hours. She starts crying, she thinks her life is ruined, she should have stopped us. The commander finally shows up, and he's clearly not that upset. I say, "OK, I'll erase this part of the tape but I'd like to keep the other part of it." He agrees. By the time we left, he and Jerry were showing each other pictures of their kids. We never told the other, tougher minder about it.

The film aired nationally on NBC, in a sports slot, at a time when military topics were popular. (*Saving Private Ryan* [1998] was topping the box office.) It was the first time Kartemquin had gotten anything on national commercial networks. The NBC reps were reluctant to share the news that it had been moved out of primetime, to an afternoon sports slot. But the directors were overjoyed. "We realized that for our audience, veterans, this is a great time. They also were offering to do extra stuff, because of removing it from primetime. We were happy with that," recalled Quinn. The film also won the Directors Guild best-documentary award and two Emmys, as well as some festival awards. The fact that it was a sponsored project, though, kept it out of some festivals. (For festivalgoers in the 2020s, when branded and sponsored films dot the typical festival lineup, this may be hard to imagine.)

For Peter Gilbert, the film was the moment he finally "arrived" at Kartemquin, being treated at last as a professional equal by Quinn and Blumenthal. "It's the most joy I've ever had working on a film," he recalled. He relished getting so close to the process, watching Quinn and Blumenthal interact as the work-siblings they were. *Vietnam, Long Time Coming* also marked the Kartemquin debut of Leslie Simmer, the extraordinary editor on staff who remained part of the core culture of Kartemquin for more than two decades. Simmer had learned editing at Columbia College, while she

Figure 18. An American and Vietnamese war veteran, both disabled, found a shared moment, in *Vietnam, Long Time Coming*. Source: Kartemquin Archives.

was working at the Great Books Foundation (where she said she sharpened her critical thinking skills). She joined Kartemquin as a freelance assistant editor, only taking the step-down, assistant-level job because "it was Kartemquin." She stayed to do postproduction management, angling for the editorial position she eventually got. Simmer, whose emotional empathy is part of Kartemquin lore, became an integral part of the "family."

AT THE DEATH HOUSE DOOR (2008)

Steve James and Peter Gilbert returned to Kartemquin later, in 2006, with another fully funded project, on the death penalty. The *Chicago Tribune* was researching the case of a Texas prisoner who protested his innocence up until his execution. A *Tribune* editor contacted Kartemquin with the prospect of making a film about the prisoner's case. Quinn and James decided instead that the focus should be Reverend Carroll Pickett, a minister who had been at dozens of executions. Pickett had recorded his doubts and concerns after each one into a home tape recorder, and had become an activist against the death penalty. (He had published a memoir in 2002.) James contacted Gilbert, who had already made a film on the topic. Together, they put together a pitch, and cable channel IFC bought the project. With Quinn as executive producer, they made *At the Death House Door*, which released in 2008.

The topic was current and controversial. Anti death penalty protest shifted its rhetoric in this time period. Opposition traditionally was a moral objection, deeply rooted in organized religion. The death penalty had been abolished by a Supreme Court ruling by 1976. That ruling reflected the heft of the civil rights movement, which shone a bright light on racial inequities in the criminal justice system. The NAACP and the ACLU had led the effort and arguments, grounding them in a civil rights based constitutional argument about racial injustice. White backlash, evident in the electoral process as well, shifted public discourse. Public mobilization had ebbed by the time another Supreme Court decision turned around the policy.

As neoliberal governments, especially at the state level, vastly expanded criminal punishments and prison populations, the moral argument failed to mobilize people. The political right portrayed it as racially biased. Major organizations such as Amnesty International began to shy away from invoking racial arguments, for fear of antagonizing possible supporters. Anti death penalty advocates increasingly sought out pragmatic arguments against the death penalty, including high costs, proven ineffectiveness in deterrence, and known cases of executions of innocent people of all races. Black death-penalty opponents often saw in this pragmatic fear a more general resistance among white liberals to discussing race.

At the Death House Door has a double focus, on both the moral and pragmatic issues, each represented in a participant. Pickett's story is one of conversion, from a moralistic death-penalty supporter to someone who opposes it pragmatically—because it's ineffective, and the criminal justice system is imperfect. He is reserved and guarded. His cultural world is bounded by whiteness. Rose Rhoton, the other main protagonist, is the warm-hearted sister of an innocent, executed man, Carlos De Luna, whose story was featured in the *Tribune*. Her Latina family had never trusted the police or the criminal justice system, and her brother had been caught in a spiral of poverty. Her attempts to save him were fruitless, but they were part of an inspiration for her to struggle against stacked odds toward stability and community. As well, Pickett's story is personal, and hers is systemic, as critic Cynthia Fuchs noted. Both are moving stories of grief and transformation, which implicitly as well as explicitly raise critiques of the death penalty, without veering into advocacy. The two stories speak to politically different audiences, within the same potentially public-making space.

The film also avoids the true-crime genre, as it does not relitigate the De Luna trial. This also means that the known failures—indeed, possible crimes—of the prosecution also go unexplored. This was the filmmakers' choice, partly because the *Tribune* eight-part series had done that work. "[The reporters] allowed us to, in essence, stand on their shoulders and use their credibility and hard work so that we would not have to get into all the details of Carlos's case. We were conscious of not wanting that part of the story to turn into a *Dateline* or *20/20* crime report," James told *Documentary* magazine.

Reflecting on the making of the film, Peter Gilbert noted how rare this kind of work is in the commercial environment. He had worked as director of photography on various Hollywood productions, thanks to the entrée that Peter Kuttner gave him. He had produced with other production houses. But his experience with Barbara Kopple, James, Quinn, and Blumenthal, while all were distinctive voices, shared some precious characteristics: "They all have this intense sense of empathy; they say to their protagonists, I care about telling your story correctly, I want you to have a voice and talk to us. Making friends with your participants, having a point of view, and also being a good human being. I've never seen that kind of empathy at work elsewhere."

At the Death House Door's production terms reveal how organic and unstructured participation in Kartemquin's filmmaking was at the time, and how people won opportunities. The film was a big break for Zak Piper. He learned of Kartemquin in film school at Columbia College and thought, "This is the place I want to be. It's politics, it's filmmaking, it's social issues, this is all the things I'm interested in and care about." From an intern, he had become a Kartemquin staffer and editor. At the time, he was only learning sound, and was eager to join the production. But it began inauspiciously. On a shoot in Texas, the crew hurriedly set off after lunch. Only after they reached an eight-lane highway did he remember two wireless receivers he had left on top of the car. By the time they found them, the receivers had been flattened. He recalled thinking, "'Oh my god—not only am I screwed, but I just destroyed thousands of dollars of equipment.' But Peter Gilbert was great. He said, 'It's just gear. Just use the cables. We're OK. It'll suck but it's OK.'" When he returned, Piper confessed to Quinn, and suggested Kartemquin garnish his wages. "Gordon said, 'No, we have insurance, and I want you to investigate how to replace everything. Just don't do it again.'"

As Piper got more comfortable with the production, he approached James and Quinn with the idea of taking on a producer role. They had been thinking the same thing. He moved up to a decision-maker in the production. "I would come in impromptu for meetings, cuts, scenes," he recalled. "Aaron Wickenden was cutting [editing] on it, and Steve and Peter and Aaron and I would sit down and talk and watch things. The door was always wide open. Karen Larson was office manager and finance person, but she was also weighing in on things all the time."

After a successful festival debut, and getting short-listed for the Oscars, the film showed on IFC. James and Gilbert had high hopes of an IFC investment in outreach, which did not work out. IFC put its money instead behind a physical "toolkit," a boxful of trinketry, not human resources or strategy. With the ACLU, the filmmakers did arrange screenings and discussions around the death penalty at sites throughout the country. And Kartemquin had at least negotiated control of rights to the DVD. Thanks to entrepreneurially minded Justine Nagan, that DVD provided a steady revenue stream to Kartemquin for years.

STEVIE (2002)

Meanwhile, Kartemquin was still an anchor for the impossibly uncommercial humanist documentary. After *Hoop Dreams*, Steve James had returned to Kartemquin with his heart's-dream project. Encouraged by his wife, a social worker, James had been in a Big Brother program, mentoring a troubled white youth mired in poverty. Bothered by the limitations of mentoring across class lines, and for such a short time, in 1995 James returned to his mentee, Stevie Fielding, to explore that relationship. He found an angry, even more troubled young man. He followed Stevie over four years, during which Stevie was arrested on pedophilia charges. There is no happy ending. The film raises hard questions about class differences, poverty, prison, and sexual deviance and treatment.

Funders hated the idea, even at the start. (The exception was MacArthur's Wickham, who was supportive, but couldn't fund it.) They wanted an inspirational *Hoop Dreams* follow-up. They conveniently missed the fact that *Hoop Dreams* itself was unfundable for years, and was also a sobering look at the failures of the American dream, as well as a celebration of the creativity of Black families in seizing what opportunities they could. But this film was a true affair of the heart for James. Quinn, James, and Singer decided to each throw in $10,000 to purchase film stock, a medium they all preferred, in order to make a short film. James and Quinn decided to coproduce it. Peter Gilbert did shooting until he got pulled away by other work; Adam Singer stepped into producing. Quinn and Dana Kupper did the lion's share of the shooting. Eventually, after getting a little funding from the BBC and CBC, their lawyer John Sloss

Figure 19. Director Steve James (center, standing, with Gordon Quinn and Adam Singer) wrestled with the ethics of making a film about his one-time mentee in *Stevie*. Source: Kartemquin Archives.

crucially connected them to a wealthy entrepreneur, Robert May. After selling his personal security business, May wanted to enter the film world.

The film posed huge ethical challenges, which precipitated many conversations in the field and at Kartemquin. Stevie loved the attention, and simply wanted to hang out with Steve, and he signed releases. But it wasn't clear that he did or even could understand the implications of being filmed. This made James so uneasy that he decided to drop the project. Above all, he feared exploiting an already vulnerable man. In the end, he decided to proceed and, encouraged by Quinn and Adam Singer, to do something he had been hoping to avoid: Putting himself on camera, mulling the ethical challenges. Viewers could make up their own minds. "When people said later that they disliked Steve in the film, feeling he had exploited Stevie, our response was, 'We put that in the film so you could see it,'" Quinn said. "Much of Steve's voiceover was taken from his journals of the time."

The film, designed for discomfort and spurned by so many funders, brought surprising positive attention. Quinn, Kupper, and Gilbert shared

Sundance's first cinematography award. *Stevie* was short-listed for an Oscar, and won the grand jury prize at the International Documentary Festival at Amsterdam, the largest documentary festival in the world. Steve James shared the film's successes with the whole team. For instance, the film won a cash award at the Yamagata Film Festival in Japan. James used the proceeds for the main subjects in the film, including the family of Stevie's victim. Zak Piper never forgot it: "They [Kartemquin leaders] were modeling the character, the commitment—I thought, these are really good people." *Stevie* is recognized today as one of James's great films.

Stevie was only one of the Kartemquin projects in the budding years of its television orientation that succeeded in spite of lacking the easy elevator pitch. Others also showed the dexterity with which Kartemquin filmmakers navigated films with Deweyan values and goals onto television sets nationwide.

5 *GIRLS* (2001)

Maria Finitzo's first big Kartemquin project was a film to reframe public perception of teen girls, toward an awareness of their agency in the world. She ultimately found support for that vision at public television. Finitzo had worked on TV commercials and Chicago TV host Bill Kurtis's documentary series *The New Explorer*. It was her goal to become a Kartemquin filmmaker. "They were the only place in Chicago that was making docs that were the art form of doc films, not commercial—actual stories that should be told. The presence of the filmmaker mattered in those stories," she said. Finitzo had always supported herself with commercial work, but she knew becoming an independent producer was risky. She was lucky to have a husband willing to support her financially.

She wanted to show teen girls like her own daughter as emerging strong women. "I wanted to change how young girls saw themselves," Finitzo said. "I was inspired to make the film when I read Carol Gilligan's *In a Different Voice*." The 1982 book, by a feminist psychologist, argued that women's moral evolution prioritized relationships, and it stressed an ethic of care. "I came to understand that growing up, as a young girl, I censored my voice all the time," Finitzo recalled.

While facing rejection after rejection for her proposals, she got steady feedback and contact information from Quinn and Blumenthal. "Neither had anything to gain," she recalled. "I was a nobody in the film world. But they helped me. Gordon cares about the craft of doc filmmaking so much, and he believes very strongly in the power of doc to change people's thinking, to change the world for the greater good." That was Finitzo's goal, too.

Finitzo followed five teens for two years, searching for funding. The success of *Hoop Dreams* opened the door; shortly after it launched, the Corporation for Public Broadcasting gave Finitzo a $350,000 grant to make *5 Girls* (2001). The film eventually cost about $500,000, some of which ended up being sweat equity among the veteran Kartemquinites. It debuted on *POV* as the season opener in 2001.

The film follows a diverse group: Two white girls, one of whom is lesbian; two Black girls; and one Vietnamese American girl. "Kartemquin would never have let me make a film with just white girls," Finitzo said. "In 1998 when I began the film, I knew I needed a diverse group of subjects. I had to search for representation. And I knew that would be central to the film's success." Fenell Doremus became associate producer. In the process, she also learned sound from Jim Morrissette and Jim Fetterley, so Kartemquin could field an all-female crew.

5 Girls was designed from the start not only for broadcast but with extensive outreach. To develop what would now be called an "impact campaign," Finitzo worked with Active Voice, as she planned for the film's release on public TV's indie strand *POV*. They developed a website and a toolkit. The filmmakers and Active Voice had summits across the country in 2001, among organizations concerned with issues affecting adolescent girls, including girls of color. The outreach also had an added benefit: The film has stayed valuable as a discussion tool in academic communities.

After her success with *5 Girls*, Finitzo, who gravitated to big issues and women subjects, chose as her next project the controversy over stem cell research, with the help of Justine Nagan. Her subject was a paralyzed college student, whose father was a neurologist. Both father and daughter are charismatic, strong characters, and passionately articulate. The father is outraged about limits imposed on stem cell research for political reasons, when the research might help his daughter walk again. The daughter, at nineteen exploring her options at Harvard, good-naturedly resents being

Figure 20. Maria Finitzo came to Kartemquin to tell stories that could not be told elsewhere. Source: Maria Finitzo.

portrayed as a victim whose plight is driving her father's work. *Mapping Stem Cell Research: Terra Incognita* (2007) won the George Foster Peabody award. The film is both grounded in science and a humanist exploration of the implications for real people directly affected by antiscience policies. In accepting the Peabody award, Finitzo quoted John Dewey: "The real purveyors of the news are the artists, who infuse fact with emotion." The film received funding from the MacArthur Foundation and aired on the ITVS series *Independent Lens*. Finitzo savored the fact that ITVS was an organization Quinn had fought to bring into existence.

Finitzo was lucky, she thought in retrospect, to have been able to participate in the era when documentaries were funded by public TV and private funders committed to social purpose. As she was making the film, "nobody had an opinion about *5 Girls* and *Terra Incognita* except people whose opinion I trusted."

IN THE FAMILY (2008)

Another notable film by a Kartemquin filmmaker was *In the Family*, Joanna Rudnick's first film, about the challenging choices women carrying the BRCA gene face. Given the high chances of ovarian and breast cancer, these women are counseled to have their ovaries and breasts removed before they are forty years old. Rudnick brought her own background as a science journalist to keep the science rigorous, and she brought her own experience as a BRCA carrier to the challenge of telling an intimate story. Public TV became the home for her project.

The film intertwines Rudnick's own story with others. She is a twenty-seven-year-old Jewish American woman wanting a family, trying to assess the risk of postponing surgery while in the first phases of a romantic relationship. She turns to Black poet and breast cancer activist Martha Haley, noting the many ways structural racism leads to higher mortality rates for Black women. She addresses how cancer challenges women's female identity with Linda Pedraza, who is living with metastatic cancer. We watch as three daughters in a family get the news together that two of them have the BRCA gene. The filmmaker's emotional quest concludes with Rudnick's flagging of policy issues around DNA testing—patent overreach, health insurance, surveillance, and the lurking potential of discrimination against diagnosed patients.

She benefited throughout from Quinn's consistent mentoring, from Blumenthal's witty presence and frank feedback, from Leslie Simmer's patient editing, and from critique discussions with the entire staff during Kartemquin's rough-cut screenings of her own work and others'. She thought, looking back, her experience didn't just help her make a film but gave her entrée into a lasting set of professional friendships:

So many studios and shops are about one filmmaker doing films and bringing other people in to make them. But at Kartemquin, I saw the lifting up of voices of each filmmaker, having it be their face and story. Gordon could have made successful film after successful film. But he was so delighted and interested in helping other people tell their story. Some of my favorite moments ever were being in the editing room and being able to go head-to-head with him. I realized, 'I just gained so much confidence in this moment, this will take me to the end of this film.'

I was blessed to get to work with Jerry closely. He was an amazing heart and one of the best editors I've ever seen in my life. He knew how to bring an audience along through many emotional states. He and Gordon both shared the political element, seeing injustice and wanting to use film as a way to foment discussion and potentially change. Jerry made me laugh so hard. And Gordon and Jerry's friendship and partnership was unique.

The film was shown on public TV's series *POV*, and there it faced a new challenge: station squeamishness. The film showed female breasts and breast reconstruction. Applying the lessons of integrity and transparency she had learned at Kartemquin, and with the help of *POV*'s head Simon Kilmurry, she wrote a letter circulated to all stations explaining the importance of showing these body parts, to address a terrifying medical reality. It worked; no station preempted the film. The film also had a festival life, was shown broadly internationally, and is used in many educational venues today, including medical schools. A *Journal of Bioethical Inquiry* review called it a "must-see" for its utility in biological sciences.

Kartemquin in this period also attracted outsiders, including nonfilmmakers who came in with projects and potential funders, and wanted Kartemquin's vision and filmmaking expertise.

REFRIGERATOR MOTHERS (2002)

Refrigerator Mothers centered the collaboration between filmmaker and advocate, and also demonstrated, like *Terra Incognita*, the double goal of broadcast and outreach. JJ Hanley came into Kartemquin's orbit as an outraged mother. The parent of an autistic child, she was horrified at psychologist Bruno Bettelheim's claim, in *The Empty Fortress*, that autism was caused by unfeeling, or "refrigerator" mothers. Bettelheim's interpretation was still extant when her child received the diagnosis. She used her skills as a local journalist to research the issue thoroughly, and had become an activist. The site she eventually created to connect businesses to people with disabilities, JJ's List, continues today. She wanted to make a film, but came with no filmmaking skills. Gordon Quinn encouraged her to partner with David E. Simpson.

Simpson had experience working with novices. He had taught filmmaking, and had encountered an angry young man weathering disabilities from a motorcycle accident, Billy Golfus. With him, Simpson made the memoir film *When Billy Broke His Head* (1995), pioneering for its refusal to espouse uplift and its insistence on full acceptance of and accommodations for disabled people. His codirector and coproducer, Billy Golfus, refused sympathy and patronizing; his anger was a driving force of the film. Simpson had negotiated an extraordinarily challenging relationship with the highly temperamental Billy, some of it shown on-screen. This was an early example in broadcast TV of filmmakers working intimately with participants in production and giving them authorial credit, variously called personal essay, memoir, and assisted storytelling. The film had been funded by ITVS, gone to Sundance, won a dozen awards, and been shown on public TV.

Working with JJ Hanley was infinitely easier, but Simpson drew on core learnings from *Billy:* "To get authentic access and acceptance from the subjects required that it be someone from their community talking to them." Hanley made connections with a variety of women, seven of whom were profiled in the film, in context of the accusations made by the medical establishment against mothers of autistic children.

The film needed Simpson's editing expertise. As director and coproducer, he linked together the stories of seven very different mothers, one Black and one Puerto Rican, all of whom reminisce about their autistic child's childhood and diagnosis, and the cruelty of the treatment they themselves received. It shows them all as loving mothers to their adult children. Interwoven with this are medical experts who debunk Bettelheim's theory, and context-providing clips from media of the era, including from popular movies. The women lead and carry the story, which is one of love overcoming disastrously wrong medical expertise, without slighting the gargantuan problems of care for autistic people.

Quinn played multiple roles in the film—camera, coproduction, executive production. He realized that "[JJ Hanley] had exactly the right idea [for Kartemquin]. This is a story about the mothers who were victims of injustice. I was always interested in experts and their accountability to the public, and this was a story of experts doing real damage." Bettelheim's institute was still running when Quinn was a University of Chicago student. He also shot some of the film, and he mediated predictable differences between the makers. Simpson recalled, "I remember when we sat down to make a contract for the production, I coined the term, 'Rabbi Quinn.' We made Gordon the decision maker if we couldn't see eye to eye. I trusted his ethics and common sense, and his wanting to do the right thing by people you want to portray."

Quinn put in motion the extended Kartemquin network, building on Hanley's research to help find the right participants. The team wanted diverse mothers in the story. Quinn turned to Sue Davenport, who had gone back into education and who knew a Black mother of an autistic child. Davenport's contact, Dorothy Groomer, ended up in the film, and had one of its more vivid moments. Bettelheim's theory argued that overeducated, alienated mothers—typically white—did not love their children; medical professionals often assumed Black children couldn't be autistic. "According to my doctors, my son could not be autistic," Groomer says in the film. "I was not white, and it was assumed that I was not educated. And therefore, he was labeled 'emotionally disturbed.' Here your child has a disability that you recognize. And they said, 'No, you can't be that. You can't even be a refrigerator mother.' The irony of it all."

Quinn also led the management of rights issues. Even before the creation of the Documentary Filmmakers' Statement of Best Practices in Fair Use, as we saw in *Women's Voices: The Gender Gap*, he knew the value of the copyright doctrine that permits some unlicensed use. *Refrigerator Mothers* was loaded with copyrighted material, used among other things to show how Bettelheim's idea was congruent with popular ideas about psychology. All of the uses were transformative; they were not used the way the original work was designed for. The team licensed some of that material, but fairly used other parts of it. Public TV accepted their fair uses. Later, Kartemquin broke down all the uses, to help other filmmakers understand their logic and how to apply fair use, a resource still available online at the Center for Media & Social Impact.

Refrigerator Mothers made use of the evolving funding environment. It benefited from ITVS's funding and coproduction, as well as National Endowment for the Arts and Illinois Humanities Council funding—all now becoming staple resources for Kartemquin. As well, it received funding from a variety of family foundations, smaller foundations and individual funders. This funding reflected JJ Hanley's activist network, and the engagement she had envisioned from the start for the film. The film had an extensive festival tour, showed on public TV series *POV,* and had an outreach campaign associated with the broadcast, coordinated by Active Voice. Parents of autistic children would call in to talk shows and join discussions, grateful for the recognition. Autism-related nonprofits also used it.

MILKING THE RHINO (2008)

The Kartemquin name brought in another match between a committed activist and Kartemquin associates. Jeannie McGill, a white woman who had conducted some educational safari tours in East Africa, was concerned about how conservation discourse often excluded the people who live there. She was intrigued by ecotourism as a way to support local economies.

Quinn paired her as well with David E. Simpson, who loved her idea, not to mention the prospect of visiting sites in Africa. The film became *Milking the Rhino*, and it featured local citizens discussing how best to develop a sustainable local economy. Simpson recalled: "It was about the kind of thing Kartemquin often focuses on, but in an international setting. It was about communities under a lot of pressure and transition, communities not dealt into the game and trying to be more enfranchised, but in a completely different setting." Quinn saw that connection as well; he thought the issues resonated with local controversies about gentrification. And he geeked out on the meetings under a tree, which he thought were "the heart of democracy." MacArthur's Elspeth Revere, who had taken over from Wickham, funded the film.

Partnering with, among others, award-winning independent South African filmmaker Rehad Desai, who had met Quinn at IDFA, Simpson tracked two projects: a Maasai-run tourist lodge in Kenya dealing with drought and white neighbors; and a grass-roots Namibian NGO helping a community-run conservancy navigate its growing pains. The film won praise as "brilliant" in *American Anthropologist,* because "Simpson structures the film around a primary protagonist for each conservation area, drawing on interviews with residents, development workers, conservation officials, and others as well as excerpts from community meetings, archival footage, and other visual materials with minimal narrative voiceover to present the context and challenges of the projects as they have developed, changed, and been challenged over time."

THE NEW AMERICANS (2003)

One project almost engulfed Kartemquin as it was learning how to make multiple productions, by filmmakers both inside and outside the organization: *The New Americans,* its first broadcast miniseries.

This gargantuan project developed over eight years, and had a long life in educational and nonprofit settings. It vastly increased Kartemquin's size. It innovated in the cinema verité series genre, interweaving multiple stories into each episode. It featured a diverse cast of directors. The project also jeopardized its future, as it sucked in all Kartemquin's resources.

The series began with a project that Steve James and Peter Gilbert incubated independently after *Hoop Dreams* launched, through their Longshot Films. James had the notion of following immigrants' journey to the US, starting in their home countries, and tracking their progress from visa application through arrival and settling in. The project was in research and development for more than a year before it came to Kartemquin, although both Blumenthal and Quinn were brainstorming from the start; it took eight years to make. It is still being used by teachers and social workers.

In 1996, James and Peter Gilbert needed more talent for their new company, Long Shot Films. They brought on board Adam Singer and a young producer, Gita Saedi. Saedi, an Iranian American from an immigrant family, had learned filmmaking by working in Ireland after college, and then in New York, working for CPB and PBS on long-form documentaries for four years. Upon return to her native Chicago, she had worked with another independent production firm, Nomadic Pictures, and she was friends with Fenell Doremus.

She had written her own proposal for a PBS series on immigration. But when James explained their project, she said, "I remember thinking, 'This is such a better idea!'" She wanted to work on it, for personal as well as professional reasons: "Coming from an immigrant family, always being 'the other' in the communities I lived in, that experience was at the heart of why I thought documentary film was so important. The mainstream doesn't hear these stories, and the result is ignorance and xenophobia. A human story can change the hearts and minds of a community."

James and Gilbert self-funded the R&D process. Disney money paid Saedi's salary for the first eighteen months. The series proposal eventually attracted funding from two crucial sources: ITVS, which found the series concept appealing at a time that PBS was prioritizing series, and the MacArthur Foundation. Saedi became series producer of the entire project, which involved five teams of producers—two from Kartemquin and three from outside. Those teams were majority diverse. Quinn, James, and she oversaw the entire project. She and James, who was the primary creator on the project, found the directors and refined with them the stories to follow. Originally the list included luminaries such as Barbara Kopple and Charles Burnett, but they ended up dropping out during its difficult eight-year climb.

The group focused on five stories, showing a range of reasons for immigration. Blumenthal, Quinn, and Doremus undertook the story of a Palestinian immigrant, who was marrying her Palestinian American fiancé. She arrived, with aspirations to live the American dream, just in time to experience anti-Muslim sentiment after September 11, 2001. Susana Aiken and Carlos Aparicio told the story of two young Dominican men who hoped to make it in major-league baseball. Steve James, with Gita Saedi and, until he was pulled away, Peter Gilbert, led the team for the story of two Nigerian families fleeing political persecution and death threats. Indu Krishnan followed an Indian couple who found each other through online matchmaking and moved to Silicon Valley during the dot-com boom, staying for the dot-com bust. Renee Tajima-Peña and Evangeline Griego followed the family of a Mexican man working as a meatpacker in rural Kansas, as they struggled to make a home there, but finally turned to migrant farmwork in California. Their family was worse off in many ways there, but they had more community. A Vietnamese story led by Renee Tajima-Peña, which had begun outside the project, was mostly shot when PBS cut the available hours from eight to seven, and it had to be sacrificed, since it was the least complete segment.

Each story was interwoven with others, in each episode. The arc of the seven-part series is chronological, beginning with meeting the hopeful immigrants in the homes and communities they will be leaving. Thus, the viewer meets them first in their cultural context of origin, and spends enough time with them to get a sense of what they are leaving behind. The verité camerawork then follows them through their first days, months, and finally years. Viewers experience the migrants' trepidation, confusion, and confrontation with their own expectations. They face the challenges of poverty in a consumer society, different mores, intergenerational conflict. Finally they become new Americans, but not without real grief for the life they left and lost.

The different people we meet are vividly delineated, portrayed as they negotiate complex personal crises. When Naima marries Hatem, she expects to leave a tragic past behind on the West Bank. Her brother had paid for his pro-Palestinian activism with his life. She never thought her Chicago husband would become the kind of activist that her brother had been. José, a Dominican baseball star, has the chance of a lifetime after being recruited by the Dodgers. But as we watch him kiss his third girlfriend goodbye in Santo Domingo, we already know that he is not a guy who is only going to stick to baseball. And he doesn't, with consequences. Nigerian mom Barine's twin teenage girls look ominously to her like rebellious American girls, in danger of losing their Nigerian heritage. On the school bus, though, Nina and Zina chafe at teasing about their foreign accents and clothes.

The ultimately hugely successful, monumental seven-part series took eight years because the funding didn't cover all the bills. At one point, the whole project went on hiatus for eight months. Throughout, the makers were taking other work. Among other things, James made two narrative features—a biopic for cable channel TNT, *Passing Glory* (1999), and

Figure 21. The *New Americans* team at the Wellington storefront doorway: From left, Gordon Quinn, Carlos Aparicio, Evangeline Griego, Fenell Doremus, Jerry Blumenthal, Susana Aikin, Steve James, Renée Tajima-Peña, Gita Saedi, and Indu Krishnan. Source: Kartemquin Archives.

another, *Joe and Max* (2002), for the cable channel STARZ. Saedi took on multiple side jobs, including with James on the TNT film. She routinely edited small segments for WTTW's *Artbeat*, and took occasional freelance jobs with visiting productions. Quinn pieced together a salary from a cluster of small-budget projects for which he was executive producer, and by working with Blumenthal on other producers' industrials and commercials.

What also kept the project going was passion and dedication. Quinn recalled a moment when the project had no funds available, and when the Mexican family was getting ready to leave for the US. Without capturing that moment, the Mexican story was in jeopardy. The segment producer-director, Renee Tajima-Peña, producer Evangeline Griego, and Quinn as cinematographer all went there unpaid. When Quinn showed up, he asked, "Who's doing sound?" Tajima-Peña and Griego looked at each other and him, helplessly. So he gave them an instant tutorial on the boom and on audio recording. The shoot captured one of the iconic scenes in the film, when grade-schooler Pedrito has to say goodbye to his classmates, and his teacher warmly wishes him well. He turns away, despondent, his shoulders slumped in grief. The moment he shuffles sadly out of his classroom and his old life still brings tears to viewers' eyes, even when shown as a stand-alone clip. To Quinn, it was about something essential in *The New Americans:* "We wanted American audiences to see that these people are leaving so much of value, and they're leaving it all behind forever."

The challenge of weaving all the stories together was gargantuan, given that the group decided each episode should carry forward a moment in the immigrants' transition, including all their stories. They were experimenting with a storytelling mode Kartemquin would go on to do with distinction in later series such as *Hard Earned, America to Me,* and *City So Real.* David E. Simpson recalled it as a hair-raising, roller-coaster experience:

> The first concept was that each of the five codirectors would do a rough cut of their story. Then at some point, the producers decided this wasn't working, so they hired me to edit with Steve. I love editing with Steve. He cares, he's a perfectionist, and he has this attitude: schedule and budget be damned, we'll make this the film or series it wants to be. We probably turned Gita's hair gray. This kind of project embodies the crazy, dysfunctional dynamic of KTQ in those years, which I found beautiful. The organization was wanting to get a little more buttoned down in a way that could earn respect and funding, but it still had this chaotic, perfectionist, doing-it-for-the-love-of-film ethos.

"There's no way we could have made it, if not for so many people on the team who cared so deeply," recalled Saedi. "As series producer, it was a great opportunity for me, but also overwhelming. I would have quit if Gordon or Steve [as executive producers] weren't pushing it to the next stage. We wouldn't have made it to the end without the perseverance of an institution like Kartemquin." The experience also acquainted her with how to strive for, and operationalize, power-sharing in storytelling: "It opened my eyes to the right way of storytelling. We weren't telling somebody else's story. We were finding a way to have somebody tell their story, and helping them tell it. Kartemquin was where I learned about collaboration, community, and accountability."

The broadcast of *The New Americans* on *Independent Lens,* ITVS's series with PBS, received rave reviews, and it was also shown on BBC's prestigious *Storyville* series. But its success was in much more than the marketplace. *The New Americans* continued the Deweyan vision of engaging viewers as active citizens in an open society. It addressed a topic rife with confusion and misinformation in the media—immigration. It invited viewers into the lives of the families it followed. It showed viewers what they irrevocably lost in deciding to leave their cultures and countries behind; the hard work, loneliness, and alienation of attempting to find their footing in a new world; the generational conflict that inevitably ensued; and the wealth of talent, skill, and stories the immigrants brought with them. It did not just give the viewers human faces to associate with an issue. The human stories behind those faces gave viewers ways to understand immigration problems in a far more nuanced and experiential way, from the viewpoint of the people who took this life-changing gamble. *The New Americans* asked viewers to reimagine what they thought the reality of immigration was, and what was possible to solve the problems that came along with it.

This work was done not only in the broadcasts but, crucially, in Kartemquin's most elaborate outreach effort since the collective days. Outreach funding from the Annie E. Casey Foundation made it possible. For two years before release, Kartemquin worked with outreach organization Active Voice to create both assets and events focused on three themes: education, civic engagement, and interethnic dialogue. Each was chosen after deliberations with social-service professionals who work with immigrants. Kartemquin created modules drawn from the raw material of the series, but tailored to key concerns and needs of the constituencies for each topic, with feedback from focus groups held by Active Voice. Active Voice founder Ellen Schneider summarized the results of the discussions for the filmmakers, who were excluded from them because she wanted potential users to speak with total frankness about what they needed and what would not help for their goals. The module *Supporting Families* was designed for teachers of immigrant students. *Building Bridges* addressed the challenges of building understanding between older and newer members of a community. *Finding Community* targeted immigrants themselves, as active members of a democratic society. Active Voice created discussion guides and offered training to relevant organizations in how to use the modules, which had an entirely different look and feel from the series.

Steve James, in materials distributed to community users, said that the series allowed "larger concerns for issues [to] grow" out of the individual stories told. The broadcast series was aimed at an audience whose majority was white, middle-class television viewers. One of the filmmakers said on a panel, "If a film is too hard-hitting and does not leave any wiggle room, you will make people too uncomfortable and you will lose them." The modules, on the other hand, could be tailored to specific learning concerns of specific constituencies.

The New Americans showed public television executives and funders that Kartemquin could work at scale in a broadcast environment, and appeal to a range of audiences. It was a huge step forward professionally. But it had also sapped the resources of the organization. The effort to finish it required so much focus from all staff and filmmakers that no projects were in the works when it aired. That led to economic crisis, and the hard work of restructuring that was to come.

CLUBHOUSE AND COMMUNITY

One anchor, in all the change and turmoil, was the Kartemquin kitchen, the center of the old, creaky house. "There were fantastic late-night conversations in the kitchen—me, Jerry, Gordon, and Peter Gilbert," David E. Simpson recalled. "I was getting introduced to the Kartemquin dynamic of arguing and hashing it out. It was much like my extended Jewish family around the kitchen table. It was wonderful." Peter Gilbert recalled in particular his love and gratitude for the Gordon/Jerry team: "Jerry was the go-to person on the editing side. He was like an older brother to me. If you did something he liked, he'd say, 'Kid, I'm proud of you.' He was more emotional than Gordon, but intellectually they were great foils for each other. It was fun to watch." At the same time, Fenell Doremus moved on to become a freelancer without breaking ties with Kartemquin. She remembered that she, Ed Scott, and other people in support positions had to clean up the dishes from the late-night conversations, move the smokers outdoors, and improvise to cover up the fact that they didn't always know how to do what needed to be done.[1]

9 Becoming a Media Arts Organization, 2008–2022

With the awarding of a major grant for reorganization in 2007, Kartemquin launched a new era, as a board-run media arts organization, inheriting a stellar reputation and a shaky business model. Within a decade, Kartemquin became a national media arts center, where diverse filmmakers could find support, and a place to come with a film with integrity, destined for TV and theaters. Both its programs—including diversity, mentorship, and interning—and its projects multiplied.

The Ford Foundation's "big bet" promise of a million-dollar institutional grant turned out to be a mirage, although finally Ford granted Kartemquin about $100,000. But as that hope faded, the MacArthur Foundation announced a new project. MacArthur was shifting from funding individual films to funding institutions. Kartemquin dusted off its Ford proposal, and MacArthur responded with a $600,000 grant. The purpose was to avoid "founder syndrome," to prepare Kartemquin to survive a leadership transition. In issuing the grant, MacArthur celebrated Kartemquin because "besides creating films that galvanize popular attention and civic action, Kartemquin sees itself as a home for independent filmmakers."

As a media arts center, Kartemquin had kinship with other such institutions. Some had existed since the 1970s, but others bloomed as documentary became more accessible and popular. The youth media programs that Denise Zaccardi had pioneered in Chicago were a movement throughout the US, some growing out of cable access centers and the media arts institutional funding that the MacArthur Foundation had maintained throughout the 1990s. Scribe Video Center in Philadelphia, which began in 1982 as a loose-knit group of minoritized artists interested in documentary, by 2004 under Louis Massiah's guidance was showcasing community history projects. Gordon Quinn would drop by Scribe when he was in town, to catch up with Massiah. Arts Engine in New York, run by social activist filmmaker Katy Chevigny and which she originally founded in 1997 with Julia Pimsleur, was conceived as a media arts organization for the digital era. Arts Engine filmmakers and Kartemquin filmmakers often worked on each other's projects. (Arts Engine eventually collapsed in the mid-2010s, a victim of the endemic precarity of socially committed media.) Firelight Media in New York transformed from a Black-led production house to a media arts organization with multiple projects, including an incubator for projects by filmmakers of color at all levels in their careers. Quinn, Nagan, and Tim Horsburgh met with Firelight's Marcia Smith to brainstorm shared projects at one point, and some graduates of Kartemquin's diversity program, including Dinesh Das Sabu, would take projects there.

In the Midwest, Brad Lichtenstein's Milwaukee-based 371 Productions, launched in 2003, both ran programs, including diversity programs, and produced films. Kartemquin has often been a partner on his productions. In Chicago, the Media Process Group began in 1985, worked on a model similar to Kartemquin's, and often collaborated with it. The Kindling Group, another sometime Kartemquin partner, founded at the turn of the twenty-first century, focused on cross-platform, social-change films and digitally enabled impact work. In 2014, Chicago Black filmmaker Yvonne Welbon, who had long been in the larger Kartemquin orbit, launched Sisters in Cinema, which celebrates Black women filmmakers with film productions and programs. Some of its productions held screenings at what would become Kartemquin Labs.

More commercially oriented documentary studios with ambitious agendas also developed with commercial appetite for documentary. For instance, Alex Gibney's Jigsaw Productions in New York, with a well-earned reputation for hard-hitting, journalistic documentaries, vastly increased its scope, and in Los Angeles, Davis Guggenheim launched Concordia Films as a high-end production house.

The expansion of mission-driven production houses into media arts organizations and mini-studios was a small bay in the ocean that the documentary film market was becoming, though. Cable brands used new prestige-documentary lines to boost their reputations: CNN Films (2012), ESPN's *30 for 30* (2011), HBO Documentaries (HBO had documentaries from 1979, but it consolidated and invested heavily in award-winners after 2004). National Geographic and Discovery Channels became rivals in thrills-every-second unscripted adventure. Public TV now faced serious competition both for its audiences and for filmmakers.

Streamers became serious rivals to cable and broadcast, and documentaries were unsuspectedly popular. In 2007, Netflix began streaming as well as mailing DVDs, and by 2011 it had competition from other streamers. The DVD market peaked in 2008 and then declined rapidly, partly because of the recession and partly because of the rise of streaming video on demand. The emerging streaming market threatened the traditional way independent filmmakers made long-term money, especially through educational sales to schools and higher education. In 2016 and 2017, Netflix vacuumed up documentaries at Sundance Film Festival; by 2018, it was producing its own. Other streamers followed its lead. Streamers began airing limited documentary series. Equity investors, following the early lead of Impact Partners, discovered the documentary.

As the money poured into the sector, so did scandal and blurring of categories. *Tiger King* (2020), a Netflix documentary series, was watched by more people than watched Disney+'s *The Mandalorian*. But some faulted *Tiger King* for exploiting its characters and implicitly sanctioning abuse of the large cats in private zoos. *Roadrunner* (2021), about food commentator Anthony Bourdain, controversially used artificial intelligence surreptitiously to replicate his voice. *Making a Murderer,* a highly popular Netflix series, was found to have manipulated footage to slant the story in favor of the convicted murderers. (I'm featured in a TV series that recounts and analyzes this ethical failure, Shawn Rech's *Convicting a Murderer* [2023]; that film also had a Kartemquin Labs screening.) Mike Rowe's *Six Degrees* on Discovery+ was openly funded by fossil fuel corporate interests, reflected in his constant plugs for fossil fuel. These controversies, only a few among many, were emblematic of a still-muffled conversation about ethics that was building in the field.

The growing popularity of documentary also led to formulas, even in social-issue filmmaking. Scholar Joshua Glick noted the Netflix style, which was influential throughout the streaming environment:

> Films tended to address a social issue relevant to our contemporary moment ... The subject was then emplotted in a narrative that involved elements of classical Hollywood storytelling as well as television journalism. From the former, the films drew on charismatic characters or small groups of individuals confronting some kind of central challenge or set of extraordinary circumstances. From the latter, they borrowed a steady flow of expository devices (voice-over, onscreen monologues, title cards, interviews) to guide the viewer through a subject.

Kartemquin was both in and apart from this overheated documentary moment. In an ethics-challenged field, Kartemquinites were guided by a vision that always highly valued relationships with participants. They steered in the opposite direction from charismatic pseudo-solutions or sensationalism, instead distilling the experience of creative problem-solving within contexts rife with unfairness. In a cookie-cutter production environment, Kartemquin films took what time they needed, particularly in editing. In a top-down production environment, Kartemquin facilitated the distinctive vision of the filmmaker who brought in the project. At the same time, Kartemquin had to play in the new financing and distribution environment.

RESTRUCTURING THE ORGANIZATION

The challenge of a transition from a founder-run organization was also a challenge to construct a formal management structure. There was only a paper board of directors; Kartemquin's formal channels of leadership were unclear. It was sporadically producing films by associates, without standard terms. Filmmakers from all corners of the US came to Kartemquin and particularly Quinn for advice and mentoring, but there was no way to monetize this service or even budget his time. It was also the beginning of a conversation about the building, which had out-of-date wiring and plumbing and no disabled access.

Rudnick, Nagan, and Beth Iams had revamped the Ford proposal into an institutional proposal at MacArthur's invitation, and they implemented it. Nagan and Quinn built a board, their top priority for its first iteration being trust in the mission and character of the organization. Later boards included members who could bring funding and connections for fundraising. The founding board was composed of people with demonstrated ideological and institutional commitments to the organization. Members included familiar names: Peter Gilbert; Margaret Caples from Community Film Workshop; nonprofit executive Steve Whisnant, who had been an executive producer on *Vietnam, Long Time Coming;* Susan Gzesh, head of a human rights program at University of Chicago; and me. Our job: Expand Kartemquin's brand visibility, find greater financial stability, and find an executive director.

No one wanted to lose what worked, but there were tensions. Peter Gilbert remembered his frustrations, as he saw the rapid transformation of the business—the multiplying venues, the pivot to video in what had been print journalism, the rise of Netflix (still then a DVD-rental company). He wanted Kartemquin to develop a capacity to engage more with commercial production, as they had with *Vietnam, Long Time Coming* and would with their next big project, *Hard Earned.* Gilbert was one of the Kartemquin associates who routinely got contracts with cable channels. He wanted Kartemquin to be in the running with other production houses that, say, an HBO would think about when approaching a topic. Above all, he wanted some kind of consistency and sustainability. Others looked for more sustainability in Kartemquin's nurturing of budding filmmakers, in providing services to productions in progress.

The search for an executive director proved arduous, given the fragility of the organization and the reality that coastal candidates would not want to move. So it was restricted to the Midwest, where there was heavy competition for nonprofit leaders. Quinn approached Nagan about applying for the position, but she demurred. She was working on her first film, *Typeface* (2009), an exploration of the past and future of typeface. She felt she was too young and inexperienced. But after looking at the resumés submitted, she reconsidered and decided to apply. "I'm fully invested in this organization and would have a lot to offer, as well as knowing where all the bodies are buried," she remembers thinking. Quinn backed her, the board agreed, and in 2008 she became executive director.

The longer-range question was who would eventually replace Gordon Quinn as artistic director. Quinn was ready to mentor a successor. But he was unique; a former intern, Rebecca Parrish, who worked on *America to Me*, called him "documentary Buddha." Later, in late 2017, Kartemquin tried a mentorship/shared leadership model. Quinn brought on Maggie Bowman, who had been a producer with Kartemquin, as associate artistic director for a six-month stint. She reveled in the opportunity to work closely with him and learned much, she later said, as they teamed up to provide creative guidance. But she was also playing a leadership role in other field organizations, as well as believing strongly the next artistic director should be a person of color. But as Kartemquin's new, more formal structure was emerging, Quinn was focused on the executive director.

Building a new Kartemquin that could incorporate the old was for Nagan a job of storytelling. "We would read 'Cinematic Social Inquiry,' and share it with the interns. We'd talk about *Home for Life* and the work of documentary. It was about getting people excited about being part of the story. I learned all of it from Gordon," Nagan remembered.

A new mission statement emerged from many sessions of board work. It bore the traces of the organization's origins, and incorporated key elements of the organization's evolution into a policy-relevant, collaborative, social-justice-focused media arts organization:

> Kartemquin Films is a home for independent filmmakers developing documentary as a vehicle to deepen our understanding of society through everyday human drama. Focusing on people whose lives are most directly affected by social and political change and who are often overlooked or misrepresented by the media, Kartemquin's films open up a dialogue, both in communities and between the general public and policymakers.
>
> Kartemquin documentaries are supported by civic engagement strategies that are developed with local and national partners to foster understanding, change thinking, and build support for social change. As a locally- and nationally-recognized media arts organization, Kartemquin acts as a trusted bridge between communities and the media, fosters the growth of emerging filmmaking voices passionate about social issues

Figure 22. The team expanded during Justine Nagan's tenure. From left, first row: Matthew Eckford, unidentified, Robby Sexton; second row: Jerry Blumenthal, Maria Finitzo, Gordon Quinn, Joanna Rudnick, Dinesh Sabu; third row: Aaron Wickenden, Zak Piper, Leslie Simmer, Kelley Moseley, Justine Nagan, Jennie Gambach, Martin Perdoux. Source: Kartemquin Archives.

and media policy, and encourages staff and stakeholders to play a role in advocating for a strong public media.

But change was challenging. When Nagan promoted better branding, some board members and filmmakers bristled at corporate language; others, including Peter Gilbert and me, welcomed the conversation. When the organization held a fundraising gala, Gordon Quinn and others wanted to give away so many of the tickets that it would defeat the purpose. New policies, such as having a default percentage take for Kartemquin of new productions, ran up against long-standing, more casual practices. Furthermore, setting some defaults was hard when each project was so different. As well, Nagan's decision to organize staff roles across films, with a focus on making sure institutional needs were met, was controversial in an organization where historically someone might be a staffer and also on a filmmaking team.

The aged building and casual maintenance continued to plague the work process. In one staff feedback form from this period, now nestled in the archives, Leslie Simmer noted with exasperation:

> I need to understand that there is some plan in place that will ensure that my office will not be inundated again, placing whatever project I'm working on in peril. Right now as it was left I am in charge of making sure that David's [Simpson] storm window is closed so that rain doesn't enter the building again. This is not a feasible program to deter incipient water damage. If David leaves after I do or comes in on the weekend and leaves his window open, I can't be responsible for coming in every night to check on the window's status.

She also noted that she had been promised a new phone for years, needed a window shade, and had an antique laptop.

Diversifying the organization's revenue stream, including the laborious and personal process of cultivating wealthy supporters, was a core priority for Nagan. Kartemquin continued to supplement income with work-for-hire projects, including for local government and the Newberry Library, an internationally renowned private research library in Chicago that is open to all. But everyone wanted to be able to grow the signature production revenue stream. Over time, more people who brought financial and expertise assets to Kartemquin from throughout the Chicago business community joined the board. Among them was Adrianne Furniss, the head of the Benton Foundation and a member of a well-known publishing family in Chicago. Her grandfather had owned the Encyclopedia Britannica, which had provided so much work to Kartemquin and other local film firms, and her father had a business distributing films to the educational market. The whole Benton family celebrated the importance of communication in the public interest. As someone who understood Kartemquin's vision, the media world, and well-connected Chicago, Furniss was an important bridge to the future.

Nagan also formalized and grew the internship, now with a stipend. Her goal was to increase the pool and provide them with a guarantee of value. She designed a training program, which formalized and documented Kartemquin's expertise. New intern cohorts got a biweekly workshop with one of the departments. Quinn or his mentee Dinesh Das Sabu would provide a fair use workshop, and Quinn hosted an extended lunch for them as they ended their terms. The internships became extremely competitive, with a 90 percent rejection rate.

Nagan initiated Kartemquin Labs as well. The labs formalized the long-standing process of providing feedback to filmmakers. A free service, it made available the Kartemquin "brain trust" for a screening, followed by group critique. The screening sessions were open to all Kartemquinites, and anyone anywhere could ask to screen. It was designed as community outreach, a service to regional filmmakers. People soon began coming in from the coasts for the opportunity.

And then Nagan won a million-dollar grant for Kartemquin in 2015 from the MacArthur and Sage Foundations to provide development grants to filmmakers. The problem she had identified at the start was finally addressed with a grant that changed, finally, what Kartemquin could offer to aspiring filmmakers.

But back in 2008, the question of how to monetize relationships with filmmakers who wanted to associate with Kartemquin for a project was huge. Everyone wanted the mentorship of Quinn and Blumenthal, and many benefited from skills and equipment from Kartemquin, but what was the right business model for that? They tried rationing mentorship until a partnership agreement could be made. The partnership split initially was for 25 percent of a film's budget to stay at Kartemquin but having the filmmaker choose the services to be used. Kartemquin would also take 50 percent of the back end. It solved some problems, Nagan recalled, and created others, and it needed to be adapted to different circumstances for each filmmaker. Many variations have been tried since.

One of her first hires, in 2009, was Tim Horsburgh, a young British import who had followed his wife to Chicago, and who was profoundly in love with "how movies make you feel, more than the act of making them." He reverentially admired Kartemquin films, and had been "knocked out" by *At the Death House Door*. He arrived as office manager and communications manager, and quickly developed a portfolio as communication strategist, logistics coordinator, and distribution expert. He built the marketing plans for several films in his first year: *Prisoner of Her Past* (2010), *Typeface*, and then Kartemquin's latest Steve James big-ticket film, *The Interrupters* (2011). He understood the mission of the new-era hires:

"Gordon and Jerry won't be here forever, but we have something special in this house, and it's time to take it out into the world. We're really good at telling people how to make their films better, especially in editing. We're really good at building community around the film. Let's make it much bigger." He wanted Kartemquin to be known as "a place you can have a sustainable career without giving up your principles." Horsburgh developed sophisticated social-media strategies tailored to each Kartemquin film, and became the distribution guru. As the DVD era ended and the streaming one began, he positioned Kartemquin in a good place to take advantage of the best in both. Kartemquin staff, especially Nagan, started going to film festivals, to promote the new Kartemquin brand.

Beckie Stocchetti, with her extraordinary organizing skills, took over Horsburgh's work on programs. She expanded and deepened the Diverse Voices in Documentary (DVID) program Horsburgh and Nagan had started. As the MacArthur Foundation shifted its funding focus, the programs Stocchetti worked on became ever more important to Kartemquin's bottom line. Within a decade, Kartemquin programs would have five hundred alumni.

The revamped internship program continued to attract budding filmmakers inspired by Kartemquin's reputation and work. One of them was Ryan Gleeson. He had grown up in a languishing blue-collar town near Cincinnati, embracing punk culture. In the film program at Columbia College, he met Quinn, Blumenthal, and Peter Kuttner, and began to imagine making films about people like the folks in his small forgotten town. By 2012, he had taken an internship, and soon he was on staff, becoming what he called "the office's Swiss Army knife," and eventually postproduction manager. He loved the community that he sometimes referred to as "Gordon's Island of Misfit Toys." (The Island of Misfit Toys features in a 1964 TV special, *Rudolph the Red-Nosed Reindeer*.)

He felt especially close to Jerry Blumenthal. "Jerry was legendarily mean at feedback screenings, but there's so much love under that abrasiveness," he recalled. "Some people couldn't read it, but I could. I come from a loud Italian family. His love and abrasiveness is there in the movies too. Jerry was punk before punk existed. He's the first person that ever gave me confidence in myself. When he lifted you up, he lifted you like no one else."

One symbolic illustration of the transition was Jerry Blumenthal's desk. Blumenthal had placed it at the most charming part of the creaky old building: the turret. Although he had effectively retired, Quinn convinced him to come back to edit *Prisoner of Her Past* (2010). Howard Reich, a *Chicago Tribune* journalist and book author, brought the story—about his investigation of his own mother's early life—to Kartemquin, and Rudnick and Quinn embraced it. She was a Holocaust survivor unknowingly haunted by trauma suffered in her early childhood.

But once that project was wrapped, Blumenthal increasingly worked from home, and then—never the businessman—gradually didn't work at all. His desk stayed, even as space became precious with the expanding staff. New members wanted to make the turret area a meeting space, and Kartemquin veterans dreaded bringing it up with Blumenthal. Finally Justine Nagan did have that conversation, and the desk was replaced with a round table. The transition was complete.

Jerry's departure left an emotional hole in Kartemquin. (He passed on in 2014.) Adam Singer, one of the enduring associates, noted, "Gordon wants and needs a creative collaborator, someone who's intellectually on his level and has a dynamic with him." He believed that their contrasting affects—Jerry's warmth, Gordon's phlegmatic analysis—had uniquely balanced each other.

Jerry's relationship with his mentees is evident in a story Zak Piper shared. He got the news that his mother had suddenly and tragically died while the team was working on *Prisoner of Her Past*. When he got the phone call, Piper was in disbelief. "He heard me walk past his door, and when I told him, he teared up, and was so kind." Later, they held a feedback screening in the Kartemquin storefront. The film, featuring the producer's mother, evoked unbearable memories of his own mother for Piper; he fled the screening, shuddering with emotion. As he sat in his office,

> I heard his finger tapping on the door, and he said in the softest voice, "Zaak, Zaaak . . . . " And I said, "I think about my own mom," and his eyes were filled with the biggest tears listening to me. He had been working his butt off editing the film and of course he wants to be in that screening, and yet he chose to come and sit with me, and showed that I matter to him more than the film or the feedback. He was so patient, he was just there. Jerry never mentioned it again.

The revamped Kartemquin produced more work than ever before, although sometimes by trial and error on the business side. Public television continued to be Kartemquin's staunchest ally, but cable and the new world of streaming also made some projects possible.

THE KARTEMQUIN-BASED FILMMAKERS

As Kartemquin evolved under Nagan's leadership, its veteran filmmakers undertook ambitious films that managed to win funding, distribution, and engagement for challenging topics. Their work showcased the wide range of styles and issues generated under the tent of Deweyan cinematic social inquiry. Topics included race, public education, and mental illness; styles ranged from experiential to interview to essayistic. A throughline was the role of art as experience in a society's ability to understand itself.

Gordon Quinn made several films, both broadcast-bound and activism-focused; as always, his secret was collaboration. *A Good Man* (2011) brought him back together with familiar colleagues, Bob Hercules and Keith Walker, the coprincipals of Media Process Group. It was a project that combined politics and art: A profile of Bill T. Jones, the Black choreographer, developing a project reflecting on Abraham Lincoln and race in America. Walker, who is Black, was director of photography. Joanna Rudnick, a particularly gifted fundraiser, became producer on the project. David E. Simpson became editor, integrated completely into the process.

The production began sunnily, with the Ravinia music festival in the Chicago suburbs approaching Kartemquin to make a documentary on Bill T. Jones's Ravinia performance of a dance about Abraham Lincoln's legacy. But Ravinia's money for the project fell through. Joanna Rudnick as producer wangled a deal with PBS's *American Masters,* where she had once worked. The team, now deeply committed to the film, was running out of money when a miracle happened: ITVS had funds from a previous film deal with *American Masters* that had fallen apart, and wanted to work on this one. The project was on.

A Good Man allowed the filmmakers to explore the Deweyan questions about the role of art in a democracy, as well as the issues Jones wrestles with in the film—How does a Black artist, descended from enslaved people, assess Lincoln? Can we say he was, "a good man"? "We knew that Bill was going to have to grapple with democracy, the big questins about America," recalled Quinn. And coming face to face with Lincoln meant confronting the meaning and legacy of racism in America.

Early on, they decided the film would be about the process of making the work, rather than just film the performance; they would look at art as experience, as they had in *Golub*. They went monthly to New York to film Jones and his dancers in their rehearsal space. They followed dancers home, they followed Jones into speaking engagements, and they tracked the evolution of choreography from first practice to final performance. Jones embraced the film from the start, although not shy with sharp and useful suggestions in fine-cut stage.

The film invites viewers into the complex artistic process; the film both chronicles art as experience and invites viewers into the same challenge. But how to end the film? They didn't want to tie the film up with a bow; the issues were too big. Finally, they ended upon a scene of Jones quoting Lincoln, "Fondly do we hope, fervently do we pray . . ." before asking himself, "Pray for what, Bill?" We leave him in partial shadow, in reflection. Viewers have to face the same question.

The film had a robust festival run, and debuted on-air, on *American Masters*, one of the most prestigious strands on public TV. Quinn recalled one of his favorite festival moments, at the premiere at FullFrame Documentary Film Festival. Coincidentally, the ballet company was performing nearby, and they all attended. Bill T. Jones, impromptu, danced onto the stage for Q&A, to roaring applause.

Quinn also codirected, with Leslie Simmer, *For the Left Hand* (2020). Like *Prisoner of Her Past*, this was a project that started with a *Chicago Tribune* article by Howard Reich, who became producer and writer on the project. Reich had written about Norman Malone, a seventy-eight-year-old, Black, retired music teacher and choral director. Reich had been a music major; indeed, on the team, including Diane Quon as producer, everyone but Quinn had played classical piano. Reich loved Malone's story. At the age of nine, Malone had been attacked and left for dead by his mentally ill father, and was left with a paralyzed right hand. But he got a musical education in spite of the odds and discouragement, and became a beloved music teacher in Chicago public schools.

The great storytelling challenge, Quinn recalled, was to avoid an inspirational, uplift overtone, which patronizes and objectifies the person being so portrayed. The film instead tells the story of Malone working toward the moment when he plays a famed Ravel concerto for the left hand, which he had worked on for five decades, with a full orchestra. A small moment in the film revealed the Kartemquin ethos of accuracy. When Malone describes his family history to Reich, the journalist says he needs to verify it, and then does so. "It's in the movie because it's important that people understand about fact-checking," Quinn recalled. "That credibility is incredibly important."

The film had a warm reception at film festivals, and continues to be shown in schools, especially music institutions. Norman Malone was so gracious that the Kartemquin team finally worked with him to prioritize. "We had to protect him from all the demands," Quinn recalled. The team developed a study guide, for long-term educational use. It also issued a DVD, although the format was fading, because disabled people turned to that format for audio description and captions. At one screening, Quinn recalled, Howard Reich opened up the question of whether it was appropriate for white filmmakers to make this film about a Black artist. A lively discussion ensued, in which Black audience members expressed views on both sides, in a conversation that remained open-ended. Malone himself was supportive of the filmmakers, who stood aside from the discussion. It was a moment that exemplified the public-making process that filmmaking could facilitate.

Steve James, most of whose prolific production in this period is discussed in the next chapter, had one of his biggest successes in *Life Itself* (2018), not only putting Kartemquin in the spotlight but bringing in desperately needed revenue. As Kartemquin was rebuilding in 2013, one of its strongest supporters was dying. Nationally recognized, Chicago-based critic Roger Ebert had been a staunch champion of Kartemquin from early days, and was critically important in promoting the visibility of *Hoop Dreams*, on air and in print. He was also a critic whose humanist values, sturdy recognition of injustice and inequality, and love of art resonated with Kartemquin's work and vision. In 2002, Ebert was diagnosed with salivary-gland and thyroid cancer, and in 2006 had part of his jaw removed. After his memoir *Life Itself* was published, he also worked with Steve James to start a film about his life. CNN Films came in as a backer. Martin Scorsese came on as an executive producer. Kartemquin associates—Zak Piper, David E. Simpson, Gordon Quinn, Dana Kupper, Emily Hart—dotted the credits.

Life Itself featured not only a wealth of (sometimes fairly used) archival material but also interviews, mostly in the hospital, that showcased enormous courage not only from Ebert but from his indomitable wife, Chaz. The film, like the memoir, does not avoid the failures and challenges of Ebert's life, including his early alcoholism and his prickly relationship with Siskel. It also doesn't step around the fearsome damage done by the disease, which killed Ebert five months into filming. It starts with the gruesome and intimate sight of Ebert enduring a suction process to clear his airways, a process that also exposes the disfigurement of his jaw surgery. Ebert wanted the scene in from the start; after the shoot he wrote on his pad to Steve, "So glad you got that." Chaz opposed it originally, but came to embrace it as a way of introducing us to the realities Ebert copes with, while he savors the life he has. The film's arc was the celebration of a film critic whose own work was in the same spirit as the filmmaker's. James's and Kartemquin's collaborative approach with participants is on-screen, as Roger and Chaz Ebert openly discuss the film process. The *New York Times* called it "a wake where the departed is still present."

This was, finally, the Steve James film that had to overcome no barriers to find critical adulation. It debuted at the most prestigious venue for documentaries, Sundance Film Festival. It won best documentary awards from myriad film critic associations and garnered attention at many film festivals, including Cannes. It was short-listed for the Academy Awards, the fifth time since *Hoop Dreams* was discussed more informally as a potential candidate in pre-short-list days. (The others were *Stevie, At the Death House Door,* and *The Interrupters.*) Again, there was an industry stir when it was not nominated. It won an Emmy editing award, and reached a national audience on CNN, after a theatrical run. It also had an impact campaign, including by leveraging the online tools of Influence Film Club, one of the companies that had sprung up to serve the film-engagement market.

Almost There (2014) is not only a profile of an artist but a look at the ethical challenges in making it. Kartemquin editor Aaron Wickenden and his friend and colleague Dan Rybicky, a Columbia College professor, knew an aging, hoarding artist living in a rotting home and utterly resistant to suggestion. The film follows their attempt to uncover and celebrate Peter Anton's "outsider art," while also trying to help him find a safer way to live. They, like others before, get drawn into a relationship with him that disturbingly enables his own dysfunction. They also discover upsetting news about his past, raising yet another ethical challenge in an entire thicket of them. Their process of ethical confrontation is as much a part of the film as Anton's peculiar artistic approach.

Joanna Rudnick revived her Kartemquin affiliation to work on the half-hour short *On Beauty* (2014), about a fashion photographer's quest to shake up the industry's beauty conventions. It had a robust festival run, and continues to have an engagement life. Maria Finitzo completed her 2015 film *In the Game*, with foundation and government arts funding. Featuring Latina girls from a Chicago high school aspiring to soccer success, it showed how combinations of race, class, and gender affect opportunity. "I thought it would be about how the boys get everything and the girls don't," Finitzo remembered:

> Then I saw that it was a story about class. The boys didn't have anything either. The boys' skill was better but none of the kids had anything. It was a big public high school in Chicago, which was my neighborhood growing up. I went there thinking it would be a terrible place, and I didn't find that at all. The kids loved the school, the teachers were committed, the school anchored the neighborhood. All my preconceived notions of what story I was going to tell went out the window. These young women appreciated their coach and had challenges in their lives because they were girls of color and had no money.

In the middle of filming, the Chicago school board drastically cut funding to the school, which Finitzo was able to document because she was already inside. The film's story ended up centering on a familiar Kartemquin theme: The importance of public education, for all the reasons John Dewey celebrated. "What I know about John Dewey is what I read because Gordon kept talking about it. When I was making *In the*

Game I read a lot of John Dewey about the importance of public education," she recalled. "That became part of my argument about making the film. It became part of my identity." Kartemquin stalwarts editor Liz Kaar, Peter Gilbert, Leslie Simmer, and Jim Morrissette were all involved.

The film showed at many festivals, and was broadcast on the public TV series *America Reframed*. One of the immediate consequences of screening the film—in fact, at its debut in Chicago—was more support for the girls at the high school. A representative of the David and Reva Logan Family Foundation pledged support at the opening. His donation created a college fund at the school, as well as support for first-generation girls experiencing challenges in college. The three main participants in the film got college scholarships.

Then, in *Dilemma of Desire* (2020), Finitzo took on an impossible challenge: To make a film accessible to everyone about the clitoris. In the end, she did it, but faced so much resistance in the marketplace that she said she might never make another film. Like others of Finitzo's films, it is less emotionally warm and more feisty than the signature Kartemquin films. But it also makes the case for feisty. The film confronts the lies women are told about their own anatomy. She shows how the medical establishment, the entertainment business, and education team up to do that. The film also spends delightful time with an artist who celebrates the clitoris, in spite of constant challenges, including getting blocked from distribution for the artwork she creates.

The same problem the artist encountered also afflicted Finitzo. Initially, she could not get commercial distribution, outside of educational, for the film. She thought she knew why: "My film says women need to be empowered by their sexuality. If you don't allow women to have knowledge of their own body and how it works, then what other rights can you take from them? We aren't comfortable with women as people, with the same agency over their bodies that heterosexual cisgendered men do." Ultimately, Utopia Media purchased the film in 2021 and sold it to Showtime, after a festival run that started in 2020 with a South by Southwest (SXSW) premiere (virtual, because of Covid-19). It also showed at more than eighty festivals worldwide. Finitzo gets requests for the film constantly, including from a feminist group in China and a group in New Zealand wanting to show the film to high school girls.

COMMISSIONED MINISERIES: *HARD EARNED* (2015)

Kartemquin's biggest project of the era, the multipart series *Hard Earned*, came in over the phone. Tim Horsburgh got a call one morning from Al Jazeera America (AJA), a new cable channel that was fighting to establish its credibility and its autonomy from its corporate parent in Qatar. Al Jazeera wanted a series about work in America. They were ready to pay $300,000 an episode, to own the contents outright. Horsburgh and Justine Nagan were both delighted, and Nagan quickly built a relationship with AJA. It was the kind of deal Kartemquin had done before, in both *Vietnam, Long Time Coming* and *At the Death House Door*. Kartemquin now had experience in producing a miniseries, after *The New Americans*.

Since its earliest days, Kartemquin members wanted to tell ordinary working people's stories about the real terms of their lives. After the labor films of the 1980s, Kartemquin had launched proposal after proposal for films and series dealing with the terms of work in America, without luck. Finally, Kartemquin would be paid to do just that. They pitched the idea of focusing on low-wage work, and for Al Jazeera America, Carrie Lozano executive-produced the series and oversaw the production. She had been producer on an earlier film by a Kartemquin associate, *The Weather Underground* (2004), and she later went on join the Kartemquin board and work for International Documentary Association and the Sundance Institute before becoming the chief executive officer of ITVS.

Maggie Bowman joined as series producer. She came from a big Chicago family, with deep union roots, but one that lived paycheck-to-paycheck. She had just returned to Chicago after working at Big Mouth Productions, part of the New York media arts center Arts Engine. She had Kartemquin on her radar since getting editing advice from Quinn and Rudnick on the Big Mouth film that became *Election Day* (2006). During screenings at the Kartemquin Lab, she had developed friendships with Nagan, Rudnick, and Gilbert.

For Bowman, the series was notable for its wealth of ethical challenges, which they addressed collectively:

> Every day there was an ethical quandary because of the power dynamic between the filmmaker and the working people being filmed. Who's paying for the manicure we're filming? How do we deal with responses to the fine

cut we show the participants? How do we navigate the public release of the film with those participants? There were disagreements, arguments, opposing points of view. But ultimately we had shared values. Through the conflict over those situations came something better than any of us could have done individually, and all with Gordon's ethical compass guiding us.

Looking back, Bowman also saw more clearly the ways these conversations were limited by the creative team's lack of diversity. Some people working on the film were BIPOC, but the executive producers—Quinn, Nagan, and James—and the lead creative team were all white. The executive producers prioritized supporting existing Kartemquin filmmakers, to support them as they fundraised for other projects. "We were a mostly white team. How on earth in 2013 did we not make a bigger effort to hire beyond our existing Rolodexes?" Bowman reflected. "It would have made for a stronger and more representative series. When I look at that, I think, 'I have to do better on every project I work on in the future.'"

The six-part series featured five diverse families both at work and at home—making family budgets, struggling with schedules, debt, and schooling. The stories of all five are interwoven, as was in *The New Americans*. We learn the names of their family members, their bank balances, their health worries, their job stresses. The precarity of hard-working people's lives in the world's wealthiest nation and the family relations they both treasure and need to survive are on display. A sixty-five-year-old woman with bad knees must take retirement, but then looks for a part-time job to keep her home out of foreclosure. A Walgreen's worker gets a great job as a union staffer, but to keep it he needs a car and has no savings. His girlfriend commutes on public transport an hour home from her job, tightly holding on to her preschoolers. She desperately needs to see a doctor, but can't get a day off work to see one. A clerical worker needs just one math class to be able to get his associate's degree and higher wages, but he struggles mightily, and guiltily, with it. Waitresses, vets, admins, janitors, cashiers, counselors—people whose stories are routinely ignored in American media invite the filmmakers and viewers into their daily dramas. What is striking is how much they have in common across circumstances, how little they complain, and how they maintain their quiet dignity. The film is both a celebration of their creativity and community, and an indictment of a society whose wealth does not return to those whose work builds it.

As always, Kartemquin showed participants how they were represented in the film in advance. As always, although participants had signed releases early on, they also were consulted about their portrayal, and the team made every effort to accommodate concerns. In one case, a woman was worried that her portrayal would threaten her job; at first, she wanted to back out of the production altogether. Bowman and Quinn worked with her to address her concerns, cutting some elements, until she was comfortable.

The series accounted for fully half the organization's income for the fifteen months budgeted for the film. Maria Finitzo, one of the directors, loved the experience: "*Hard Earned* matched the values of the organization, and it was fast and furious. I thought it could be a model for how to keep us employed." But the working conditions were hard, there was too little space, the process took three months longer than budgeted, and the aged building didn't cooperate, either. A sewage pipe broke in freezing weather, flooding the basement and leaving a lingering smell. Then the repaired pipe backed up during a polar vortex. In the subzero weather, staffers could choose between using a portable toilet on the sidewalk or hiking down to a local bar to use their bathroom. To bridge the budget gap, some staff donated time. Bowman worked unpaid for months to finish the project; she later recalled that she used up the savings she had proudly built up doing commercial work, and that she didn't come back from the financial hit she took until seven years later.

The upfront funding also came at a heavy price in distribution. Al Jazeera America owned all the rights. The newbie cable channel had no experience, budget, or interest in any kind of impact work or outreach. And then it closed down, not long after the series first aired in 2015. As a result, *Hard Earned* missed out on repeat programming and hardly got any reviews. It did win a DuPont-Columbia award in 2016, as well as being nominated for best limited series at the International Documentary Awards. It is available educationally.

PARTNERING FOR PRODUCTIVITY

A goal of Nagan's vision for Kartemquin was to facilitate partnerships and increase the volume of work, so that revenue could flow more evenly.

Kartemquin's promise to filmmakers was to shepherd work within Kartemquin's vision of documentary for democracy. This vision would be the value that the streamer Hulu later invested in when it began a partnership with Kartemquin in 2018 to incubate diverse projects there. At the same time, Kartemquin pledged to honor the individual filmmaker's voice and choice. Often with support from public TV, and with a lot of experimentation and tailoring, these partnerships produced notable and distinctive work. The range of topics was stunning: neoliberal anti-unionism, rural poverty, exploitative tourism, civil rights, endangered archeology. The storytelling made viewers care, think, and talk.

Brad Lichtenstein, whose 371 Productions was based nearby in Milwaukee, opted to make his alarming and prescient film *As Goes Janesville* (2012) with Kartemquin. Lichtenstein, an Atlantan by origin, had Kartemquin on his radar ever since he watched *Hoop Dreams* on its debut. As an ally for racial justice, he had been a campaign volunteer for John Lewis, and worked for the civil rights organization Southern Regional Council. Through SRC, he met the legendary filmmaker George Stoney, and began to imagine a career in documentary. He eventually joined the social-issue production house Lumiere in New York, among other works making, with David Van Taylor, *With God on Our Side* (1996), about the political clout of right-wing evangelicals. When his wife got a job in Milwaukee, he called up Gordon Quinn. They discovered they shared political perspectives and film styles.

As Goes Janesville dives into the economic and political realities of a Wisconsin town that housed a General Motors plant until it closed a year after the 2008 financial crisis devastated the country. It provides an experiential, close-up look at families and politicians grappling with economic crisis. The once-unionized factory workers struggle to replace a living wage, and union members accept relocations that require long commutes or a move far from family. Meanwhile, ambitious right-wing governor Scott Walker passes a union-destroying agenda designed to win employers to the state at any cost—including a living wage. Leslie Simmer edited it at Kartemquin. Funded in part by ITVS, it was shown on public TV and was nominated for an Emmy.

The Trials of Muhammad Ali (2013) was Bill Siegel's second film for ITVS. After he codirected the 2004 *Weather Underground*, Siegel had begun working with Kartemquin as a researcher, and continued to make films around his full-time job at Britannica's Great Books Foundation (where Leslie Simmer had also worked). For this film, he worked with Aaron Wickenden, who edited the film at Kartemquin. The film focuses not on Ali's sports career but his values and integrity. His choice to join the Nation of Islam; his fierce opposition to the Vietnam War and refusal to be drafted; his career as an antiwar activist and later global ambassador for peace; his grace in coping with Parkinson's disease—all are elements of a story about a man who challenged racism, economic injustice, and imperialism, and paid a heavy price.

When Siegel fell ill in postproduction, Kartemquin filmmakers worked together to finish the film. In a call from his treatment center, Siegel asked Quinn about the film's ending, about which they had disagreed. "Bill, we're making the film you wanted. It's your film, it's your ending," Quinn told him. Kartemquin was committed to executing the filmmaker's vision. The film debuted at Tribeca Film Festival, showed on national PBS, won an Emmy and was nominated for another. It was nominated for an NAACP Image Award as well. (Siegel died in 2018.) It's now available on Netflix.

In taking on *Saving Mes Aynak* (2014), Kartemquin turned a broadcast news style project into an emotionally rich short film. Brent Huffman, a journalism professor at Northwestern who teaches documentary filmmaking and has deep experience in broadcast journalism, wanted to get feedback on a project. Mes Aynak is a magnificent, sprawling site of an ancient Buddhist city in Afghanistan. At the time, it was threatened by a Chinese mining company. (It is now threatened by political turmoil generally.) He asked to have a Kartemquin Labs session, which gave him the confidence that he had a film; it also changed the nature of the project to a character-driven story. Quinn remembers long hours in the editing room: "He had a great central character. We were good at finding the story, and we said, 'This guy is your central character.'" Huffman was able to get private foundation funding for the film, including $100,000 from the MacArthur Foundation, and it debuted at IDFA, the largest documentary film festival in the world. There it also screened off-festival to Afghan refugee community members in Amsterdam. The film has won more than twenty major awards and has been broadcast on television in over fifty countries.

Minneapolis-based filmmaker Sergio Rapu, the son of an archeologist who was also former governor of Easter Island / Rapa Nui, made *Eating Up Easter* (2018). It looks at the high cost of international tourism to the island. He came to Kartemquin with some public TV funding and plenty of experience with cable TV productions. He got in touch with Tim Horsburgh, who he knew through mutual friends, and Horsburgh directed him to editor Liz Kaar. She encouraged him to think about making his film a Kartemquin coproduction. There, he appreciated the support and Horsburgh's superb grasp of the economic landscape of distribution. And he got the benefit of mission-driven insights from Matt Taylor, Leslie Simmer, Maggie Bowman, and of course Gordon Quinn.

"Gordon and Maggie gave really great notes, which were challenging at times, and also they went against what we were hearing from other people," Rapu recalled. "At one point, I was struggling with how much to dumb this down. That was my experience producing for other audiences. Gordon said, basically, It's OK to trust in your audience, to believe your audience is interested and engaged. It was such a relief, not to have that additional filter." *Eating Up Easter* was broadcast on PBS's *Independent Lens*, and was sold extensively overseas as well.

Margaret Byrne, already an experienced filmmaker, came to Kartemquin to produce *Raising Bertie* (2016). The film is a closely observed, unflinchingly documented season in the lives of Black North Carolina high schoolers, facing the multiple challenges and dysfunctions arising from rural poverty. Byrne had been cinematographer for *American Promise* (2013), a film about two Black children enrolled in an elite New York school. This was to be a complementary story, for rural America. North Carolina rapper J. Cole, who had grown up nearby, volunteered to come on as an executive producer. She followed the schoolkids for six years; she showed them cuts as the film evolved. What had started out as a story of hard-won success changed when the alternative school they all attended was closed down. The film shows how many people help to sustain life under brutal poverty. But it also shows that even with all that, the three young men face daunting odds, because the system, the way society works, is stacked against them and their community.

Byrne, the child of a pharmacist and a nurse, had learned about Kartemquin in her film program at University of Illinois Chicago; one of her professors was Jim Morrissette. When she returned to Chicago after establishing herself in New York, she found in him someone who had even more faith in her vision for the film than she did: "He really thought this would be an important story to tell." The film struggled to raise money until Byrne got a grant from the MacArthur Foundation, and then an ITVS coproduction contract. Kartemquin's commitment was crucial to the project, as the participants' school lives got harder and their futures ever more fraught with risk. Leslie Simmer came on as in-house editor, and Ian Kibbie, who started as an intern, became a producer. Byrne's relationship with Kartemquin was later made turbulent when she was caught in accounting confusion (discussed later). She also chafed at the rigid financial arrangement in place when she arrived—a 50/50 revenue split with filmmakers. But Byrne's objective was solidly within the goal of the post *Hoop Dreams* Kartemquin mission. "Our biggest hope is that this film creates the space and empathy needed to have harder and more nuanced conversations," she told *Huffington Post*. It showed on PBS's *POV* after a robust festival run and rave reviews. Its engagement campaign was carefully organized and executed.

Other work with shared commitment to public-making through documentary percolated through Kartemquin, demonstrating its expanded capacity to handle multiple projects. Fenell Doremus produced *Cooked* (2019), Judith Helfand's long-delayed project about the poverty- and racism-driven death rate in Chicago during a 1995 heat wave, with a MacArthur grant. Laura Checkoway's poignant short film *Edith + Eddie* (2017), about elder abuse by corrupt guardians, was nearly done when she came to Kartemquin, mostly for advice. Quinn fell in love with the film, because the topic was "exactly where a documentary can start a conversation." Karen Weinberg, an editor for *Hard Earned* and for cable TV, returned to Kartemquin for her feature documentary *Keep Talking* (2017), joined by several Native producers. The film tells the story of four Alaska Native women who work to revive Kodiak Alutiiq, which only a few dozen Native Elders still speak fluently. Lance and Brandon Kramer, who had benefited from Gordon Quinn's extensive mentoring for their earlier *City of Trees* (2015), worked with Quinn and with Leslie Simmer as editor for their profile of the controversial Van Jones and the politics of criminal justice reform, *The First Step* (2021). The range of topics and voices was wildly diverse, but the stories were all guided by the same philosophy.

PARTNERING FOR IMPACT: *THE HOMESTRETCH* (2014)

The Homestretch demonstrates in one film several threads typifying this moment for Kartemquin. It was an experiment in partnership; it was a long-term project with engagement at the center; it combined powerful storytelling and policy goals. Two white New York based film and theater directors, Ann de Mare and Kirsten Kelly, spent five years tracking several homeless Chicago high school students trying to graduate. Their production took five years to make, and ultimately received ITVS support, as well as funding from the MacArthur Foundation, the Sundance Institute, Chicken & Egg Pictures, the Chicago Community Trust, Polk Bros. Foundation, and Pierce Family Foundation, among others.

After working with seven homeless teens, they focused on three who they and the interviewees felt would be helped, or at least not hurt, by their interaction—an undocumented immigrant, Roque; a Black lesbian girl whose family has rejected her, Kasey; and Anthony, a Black high schooler with a six-month-old in foster care, who needs a GED to get a job. The teens film themselves as well as being interviewed by the filmmakers, and the filmmakers also visit with school counselors, social workers, and religious organizations serving the homeless. The film also includes the subjective experience of providers, and it provides context with damning statistics about the overwhelming scope of the problem: most schools nationwide have a homeless liaison, because homeless kids are everywhere; a substantial minority are LGBT+ and homeless because their families rejected them; many homeless students have been abused at home, and they are likely to be abused on the street. *The Homestretch* rejects the triumph-of-the-human-spirit model. It shows how humanistic caring and support, although essential for the constantly imperiled students we meet, cannot substitute for a functioning social safety net. It also invests viewers in the homeless kids fighting for their lives, and the school and social-work staff fighting for and alongside them.

Kartemquin was essential to the production for the novice filmmakers, both New York based social-action theater artists. Kelly had lived in Chicago, and even from New York she had helped to create a Chicago schools-based Shakespeare project. It was there that she learned about student homelessness. They thought about Kartemquin as a natural fit for a Chicago story; they knew it mostly because of *Hoop Dreams*. Kartemquinites met with them over months, unsure about their level of commitment. But when the two decided to spend months in Chicago, Kartemquin took them on as a coproduction, one of their first. The filmmakers and Kartemquin each had 40 percent participation and ITVS had 20 percent. Remarkably, all participants eventually chose to reinvest any profits in the outreach campaign, including paying the filmmakers for their time.

Although the Kartemquin name opened doors for them, the filmmakers did all their own fundraising. The greatest value, the two said in 2022, was ongoing professional support. They had an in-house editor, Leslie Simmer; even when they didn't have funding, they could depend on her. They benefited throughout from Quinn's coaching and mentoring, always in support of their own vision. Horsburgh gave them endless advice on distribution. "They had such faith in us and the project," Kelly remembered. The Kartemquin Labs experience was crucial for them, because of its generous sense of community. "There was very little ego in that room," Kelly said. "People were excited to help that film. The film and the story were at the center of that process. I've never experienced that anywhere else. There was a trust in that room." De Mare added, "And we were having people in the kitchen a week later saying, 'I keep thinking about that scene.'"

Leslie Simmer found this project challenging to work on, because of the excruciatingly sad subject matter: "So many interviews didn't end up in the film. I'd watch them, then I'd go away and sob, and then come back and work again." She even asked herself whether she should be helping homeless kids directly, rather than editing a movie. "But Kartemquin is a place where you can ask yourself questions like that."

The filmmakers believed that the fact that they were two white filmmakers telling the stories of marginalized young people gave them a particular duty to stay in touch with the caregivers who did have the kids' trust, and who could hold the filmmakers accountable. The filmmakers and their mentors both were hyper-aware of their participants' vulnerability. The filmmakers made sure the teen participants had an adult to check in with outside the film team, whether therapist, counselor, or teacher, and the team checked in with those adults. "We didn't want to push them to tell a story they didn't want to tell," said Kelly. De Mare recalled a teen whose mental health problems surfaced in preproduction. "We pulled back, because we couldn't be sure that the process would be good for her. I'm still haunted by her."

The filmmakers were frustrated by the combination of privilege and precarity that precluded collaborating with filmmakers whose life experience was closer to the story. They could handle the high cost of doing the project themselves, although it was a sacrifice, but they couldn't engage others with even fewer options to do the same. "The fact that Kirsten and I have been able to create work without getting paid for vast periods of time is an indication of privilege," De Mare said. She noted that while the documentary business is lucrative, the money isn't flowing to the people to make the films. "As we look at how to have a nonextractive form of production, that discussion is happening within a nonsustainable industry." Even a restructured Kartemquin could not solve that problem, which was systemic.

The Homestretch showed on public TV, was a festival darling, and won an Emmy. It also had an engagement long tail, partly in conjunction with ITVS. Although the filmmakers were able to raise money to pay participants for their work, they were unable to cover costs for themselves. The toll was brutal, but the engagement piece was central to their commitment from the start. The directors' goal had been to awaken awareness about the problem, to break common stereotypes about who homeless teens are, and for people with that new understanding to improve the support systems. Effects were immediate and long-ranging. Six years after the film was released, organizations concerned with youth, schooling, and homelessness were all actively using the film, as the film's website showed.

They focused on advocates and policymakers. They worked with the federal Department of Health and Human Services, bringing department heads from five agencies together to talk. Those department heads learned they had to shift their understanding, and thus their strategies, from homelessness as primarily related to mental illness and veterans and toward families and young people. The filmmakers also worked with a nonprofit, Washington, DC based Civic Enterprises, focused on lowering the high-school dropout rate. When its leaders attended a Capitol Hill screening, they realized they needed to include homelessness in their work, and they changed their approach. A Center for Media & Social

Impact study demonstrated the power of storytelling to affect providers. The film was shown via ITVS's OVEE online platform, which permitted real-time reactions, to 322 professionals working in federal, state, and local government agencies that deal with education and teen homelessness throughout the nation. They overwhelmingly found it worth their time, and were most engaged by the personal stories, not the hard data. Almost all rated it a useful tool to engage policy discussion, and 88 percent planned to use it in their own work. Also important to them was finding validation of their hard daily work.

THE SPIRIT OF THE COLLECTIVE

Several activist efforts brought the spirit of the collective era back to Kartemquin, but now in a world with screens everywhere.

In 2014, *The School Project* launched. Mayor Rahm Emanuel had proposed to close dozens of schools, accelerating what had become an annual ritual of school closures over the previous decade. Parents and community members rallied. Bob Hercules of Media Process Group and Daniel (Danny) Alpert of Kindling Group came to Kartemquin with the idea to produce a miniseries of short films to address the human issues that this financial decision affected. They were joined by Free Spirit Media, Siskel/Jacobs Productions, producer Rachel Dickson, and editor Melissa Sterne, as well as media partners: the *Chicago Reporter*, an investigative web-based journalistic outlet; one of Chicago's two daily papers, the *Chicago Sun-Times*; and public TV station WTTW. Kindling Group created a website, and journalistic entities drove traffic to it. It was also used by community groups rallying against the budget cuts.

The episode directed and produced by Gordon Quinn and Rachel Dickson was the longest, and also dedicated the most time to experience inside the classroom. They followed a class of students using civil rights leader and educator Bob Moses's peer learning model to improve skills in algebra. We watch the kids work out problems, the teachers directing the class, and the teachers conferring with each other about progress. The film cultivates our respect for and interest in both the kids and the teachers, and we learn about the impressive success rate of the program. Still, the program was only in five of the city's eighty-two schools. And at the end we learn that four of the program's teachers, including one profiled in the film, were fired because of budget cuts. While the film is nondirective, it also dramatically illustrates what is at stake. By focusing on at-risk children who achieve success, it turns around preconceptions without turning theirs into an uplift story.

Stranded by the State (2016), a miniseries of topical shorts, was created by then Kartemquin editor Liz Kaar. Experienced in editing, she was casting about for experience in directing. The headlines provided a perfect topic. The Republican governor of Illinois, Bruce Raumer, a wealthy private equity firm CEO, had taken office in 2015, and openly battled the Democratic legislature to a standstill. He cut labor union fees out of government employees' salaries and demanded drastic budget cuts. This stymied efforts to create a state budget over two years, while social services, public transit, higher education, and many other state functions of government went unfunded and undelivered. The state's bond rating tanked.

Kaar won a small grant from Chicago Filmmakers, and began a project that far outstripped the budget. Her friend and roommate, the publisher of *In These Times*, thought that *In These Times* could cocreate with Kartemquin short, online films that showed how this political faceoff affected ordinary people. The series of eight films, each 8–10 minutes long, looked at public higher education, at-risk youth, homelessness, meals on wheels, adult education, home visits for young mothers, and childcare assistance. It also looked at the effect on municipal and state budgets and ordinary people of predatory lending leading to the 2008 financial crash. The episodes featured a mix of expert explainers, social work providers, community activists, and users of government services. Among the programs suffering from the budget impasse was CeaseFire, the featured organization from Steve James's *The Interrupters* (discussed ahead).

Quinn leveraged connections with the Peoria public TV station, to package it for TV. The series ran throughout the state as two 30-minute TV episodes, and continues to live on the *In These Times* website, as strandedbythestate.com. Quinn believed that stations throughout Illinois picked it up because it had been launched at a regional station, Peoria, rather than the Chicago powerhouse station, WTTW (although WTTW also ran it).

We Are Witnesses: Chicago 2019 (2019) was commissioned by the Marshall Project, as a follow-on to their New York version. Stacy Robinson, a well-established, Black cable doc filmmaker, and Maggie Bowman worked together as codirectors. Short webisodes feature interviews with people involved with the criminal justice system—a former prison inmate, a judge, a crime victim. The webisodes were used in public events, where citizens discussed the issues surfaced in the films. For Bowman, "It was a great experience, a profound experience in doing something very local—even at the micro level, connecting with people at screenings at the Chicago Public Library over fifteen months." It showed the value of mission-matched commissioned projects, as *Hard Earned* had: "They came because they want the Kartemquin-ness of what we do in their brand. And in both, the relationship with the commissioner was enough for me to feel we had agency to fight for what was important to us."

But because it was commissioned, Kartemquin also lost control of the material. Chicago public radio station WBEZ used the interviews to create two half-hour programs, which went to other Midwest stations as well, but participants were not shown that version. "We were very concerned about what we owed our subjects, especially on the criminal justice topic," Quinn said.

'63 Boycott (2017) brought Quinn back to his roots. At half an hour—designed to fit nicely into classroom schedules—it was a bookend work to material that he shot when he was still a student, with Jerry Temaner, Stan Karter, and Mike Shea. Quinn and his producer Rachel Dickson contacted people from the original footage who were involved in the one-day boycott—at the time the largest civil rights demonstration yet in the North. They also used some of Dickson's material from her own film project on school closings in Chicago. Tracye Matthews, a Black academic historian (now at the University of Chicago), conducted the interviews, researched the history, and became a producer. The team found interviewees who had appeared in the fifty-year-old footage in a two-step process. First, they built a simple website featuring five hundred stills from the footage, which let visitors tag anyone in the footage, and publicized it on social media. Then, as leads dwindled, teachers helped them by sending postcards home with schoolkids. The postcards asked the kids to bring their elders to the website, and help them identify people in the photos.

Figure 23. A rough cut of *'63 Boycott* debuted at the DuSable Black History Museum and Education Center in Chicago, on the fiftieth anniversary of the boycott. Historian Tracye Matthews introduced the film to a packed house, before the screening and panel discussion with film participants. Source: Kartemquin Archives. Credit: Rachel Dickson.

The filmmakers wove their interviews into the original footage of the march, and drew parallels with today's parent and student protests for equal rights in Chicago public schools.

'63 Boycott also involved another intersection with Bernie Sanders. The website included footage of a scene from a demonstration leading up to the day of the boycott. Several people were able to identify the action, and one sent Kartemquin a news clipping about six University of Chicago students being arrested. It named Sanders, who at the time was running for president. Kartemquin sent the clip to his campaign, which both confirmed it and licensed the footage for a commercial.

Both students and parents used it in their organizing for better schools. It was also short-listed for an Oscar. The film also offered an opportunity to reunite with Quinn's old sociologist friend, Howard Becker, when the team went to Paris for a screening Matthews had arranged.

For Quinn, it was also a chance to look back at how his own work had evolved. He was proud that he had finally learned not to make it "too long," so teachers could use it effectively. "Our core idea worked; people got a complicated story that's told from different perspectives," Quinn said. It showed, he thought, how their initial concept of documentary for democracy had evolved: "With *Home for Life*, we were overly purist. We hadn't yet evolved into a collective, where our style changed." *'63 Boycott*, while short, was also emotionally rich, respectful of the demonstrators' experiences, and had an analysis that linked long-ago and present-day social protest. "It's been a dialectical relationship between the films we're making and the consequences we were trying to have in the world," Quinn said.

BIG CHANGES

By 2015, Kartemquin was a transformed organization. Nagan was proud of the work she had done, but she also felt ready for new challenges. She had brought ambitious ideas, charisma, an entrepreneurial attitude, and an ability to manage complex projects and develop a strategic plan to Kartemquin. In doing so, she had to take on entrenched and prestigious filmmakers. While she got extraordinary access to Quinn, he sometimes did not protect her from criticism for executing decisions they had previously agreed on together. "He got to stay the good guy," Nagan noted wryly.

When Simon Kilmurry left his job at PBS's independent film strand *POV* and invited her to apply in 2015, she welcomed the opportunity to move. At the same point, Elspeth Revere, who had inherited the media portfolio from Woody Wickham in 2010, stepped down and onto Kartemquin's board, and then became essential to the transition. Nagan left behind a transformed Kartemquin, with multiple new programs, grant funding from previously untapped foundations, and an organizational chart. By the time she left, the organization's annual budget had grown from $800,000 to $3.5 million, the staff from five to fifteen, and film releases from one or two to three or four a year. Before Nagan left, she also put in place two processes that would ensure Kartemquin's legacy: the creation of Kartemquin's archives, and the plans for Kartemquin's fiftieth birthday party.

ARCHIVES

Creating an archive meant preserving institutional memory. Quinn's own packrat tendencies were legendary. And Kartemquin had also kept raw footage, assemblies, and rough cuts of its films going back to its first efforts. But like many film production houses, Kartemquin had no preservation policy. Nagan and Quinn both realized its importance, however. And there was someone else who had been itching for the challenge for some time.

In 2004, Carolyn Faber had asked Judy Hoffman to set up a meeting with Quinn, to talk about archiving. Faber was a professional archivist who worked with various film archival organizations, including the WPA Film Library (a stock library in Orland Park), the Chicago Film Archive, and Media Burn. Media Burn was launched in 2006, to house and document the history of the guerrilla television movement. It has since become a major repository for noncommercial video work, the majority based in Chicago.

Faber knew Kartemquin, starting from her time at Ithaca College, where Patricia Zimmermann taught her classes about Kartemquin films. At their first meeting, Faber suggested that Kartemquin apply for a National Film Preservation Foundation grant, for *Home for Life*. Nagan seized on the opportunity, and Kartemquin won that grant in 2006. Zak Piper became a champion of the archiving project. Eventually they received funds from, among others, the National Endowment for the Humanities, the Chicago-based Donnelly Foundation, and Logan Family Foundation. Faber conducted an assessment for Kartemquin in 2008, and inventorying took place between 2011 and 2014, cataloging 18,000 objects. Interns and staffers rotated through Kartemquin's downstairs screening room / library / storage area and surveyed four storage units.

The archive project became an important piece of Kartemquin's work. Nora Gully created the archive associate position later held by Nancy

Figure 24. By the time Kartemquin's archives were catalogued for transfer to Washington University in St. Louis, several storage units were overflowing with shelves full of boxes. Source: Kartemquin Archives.

McDonald and then by Ingrid Roettgen. Roettgen, a communications graduate who went from intern to staffer, had originally sought out Kartemquin after an internship at Brad Lichtenstein's 371 Productions in Milwaukee, because it answered a question for her. She had never been able to embrace journalistic objectivity; and Kartemquin's commitment to storytelling as social justice, as much as its collaborative style, was exactly what she was looking for. Her work on the project, when she wasn't working as a production associate, contributed to the smoothness of the archive's eventual handoff. Eventually, Kartemquin hired Elise Schierbeek full-time to work on the archives.

The biggest stumbling block for the organization and for Quinn was recognizing the need to partner with an outside organization to store and manage the collection. This realization, Faber recalled, took a full decade to resolve, but by 2016 Quinn took the lead in looking for appropriate Midwest partners. No Chicago-based institution, including the University of Chicago, had the capacity. Indiana University and Washington University of St. Louis became the final contenders. Washington University, which also had the Blackside collection (the company that made *Eyes on the Prize* and other historical series), eventually was chosen. By 2020, Kartemquin's history was now part of a major academic library collection.

THE FIFTIETH ANNIVERSARY

Nagan saw the fiftieth anniversary as a huge branding opportunity, a chance to solidify Kartemquin's profile as a media arts center, and to chart the future. Before she left, she developed an elaborate set of partnerships to make it happen. The year-long celebration put Kartemquin in the spotlight both as a Chicago and a national arts institution. The new executive director, Betsy Steinberg, entered the organization just as the fiftieth anniversary year was about to start, and tackled the enormous job of running and fundraising for a year-long event, while still learning the names of her new employees.

Kartemquin retrospectives were hosted in New York, at the Museum of the Moving Image, and Los Angeles, at the UCLA Film and Television Archives (in conjunction with the International Documentary

Association), as well as Chicago. Festivals honored Kartemquin: Hot Docs; St. Louis International Film Festival; Ashland International Film Festival; Dallas Videofest; Chicago International Music and Movies Festival (CIMMfest); Peace on Earth Film Festival; Chicago Latino Film Festival; University of Chicago Doc Films; University of Chicago Center for Human Rights; Northwestern's Block Cinema; Chicago Filmmakers; and Black Cinema House. The International Documentary Association gave Gordon Quinn its career achievement award in December 2015, and featured Kartemquin at its biannual conference Getting Real 2016. Kartemquin hosted a three-day festival to show work exclusively of graduates from Kartemquin Labs and DVID, culminating with Dinesh Das Sabu's *Unbroken Glass* (2016).

An exhibit opened at the museum space Expo 72 in Chicago, across from the Cultural Center; it featured Quinn's dog-eared copy of Dewey's *The Public and Its Problems.* This quote (also featured in many grant proposals) was highlighted on the wall: "Artists have always been the real purveyors of the news, for it is not the outward happening in itself which is new, but the kindling by it of emotion, perception and appreciation."

WTTW aired films from the Kartemquin archive monthly throughout the year, each preceded by introductions from Justine Nagan and the filmmakers. Turner Classic Movies paid homage as well. Kartemquin, in a prescient move led by Horsburgh, created its own streaming platform, running a different Kartemquin film for a week at a time throughout the year. As well, thanks to work by Nagan and Horsburgh, Kartemquin self-published a small book summarizing its history, *Kartemquin Films: Democracy through Documentary,* and a weekly newsletter throughout the year.

The culminating moment was a huge gala, downtown by Lake Michigan, for a thousand people, coordinated by Steinberg, following through on Justine Nagan's preparations. (Quinn praised Steinberg's negotiating for the location as a strategic cost-saving move.) Every single credited person on any Kartemquin film was invited. Muhammad Ali's widow was flown in; a photo of her with Chaz Ebert and Ameena Matthews marked the occasion. Quinn welcomed the group with a succinct vision statement: "Our mission is supporting filmmakers and ensuring the documentaries they make are part of the democratic process. We also engage with other media makers, community organizations, broadcasters and

Figure 25. Kartemquin's fiftieth anniversary year included an International Documentary Association career achievement award for Gordon Quinn; it prompted unusual sartorial splendor. The picture is displayed prominently in the Kartemquin kitchen. From left, Liz Stanton, Hillary Bachelder, Maggie Bowman, Elspeth Revere, Betsy Steinberg, Justine Nagan, Gordon Quinn, Tim Horsburgh, Liz Kaar, Ruth Leitman, Brad Lichtenstein. Source: Gordon Quinn.

distributors, challenging our field to live up to its democratic promise." Kartemquin looked different now from 1966, he said, but "our core values remain intact." He said, "We try to find the balance between respecting our subjects and the issues affecting their lives, and the needs of the audience to understand and empathize with the diverse people in front of our cameras, the people they are living alongside in our democracy."

"The anniversary year put us on the same map of Chicago artistic institutions as Second City and Steppenwolf," Horsburgh recalled. For Elspeth Revere, who was by then on the Kartemquin board, it was deeply moving. "I was so touched to see how many film participants were there. That's our community and it's so different from the community of other film places. They came."

But the legacy guaranteed nothing for the future.[1]

10 Crisis to Crisis

Kartemquin's evolution as a postfounder, board-led media arts center faced formidable challenges in the second decade of the twenty-first century. The two most important leadership roles, executive director and artistic director, were hard to fill. The programs that brilliantly launched the new era, particularly the diversity program, both opened up possibilities and raised new questions about how Kartemquin as an institution would incorporate diversity into its daily work. And then the Covid-19 pandemic added to the challenges.

How Kartemquin addressed those challenges is a story about the commitment of its staff and filmmakers to the institution's unique place in the documentary ecology, and what it meant to the people who worked with, on, and through those problems. It is also a story about the frailty of mission-driven institutions that must depend on commitment to overcome resource deficits. And finally it is a story about the challenge of producing documentary for democracy at a time when democracy itself is imperiled.

MANAGEMENT CRISES

When Justine Nagan left in 2015, the Kartemquin board, now populated in part by wealthy local businessmen who were not necessarily familiar with film, selected Betsy Steinberg as the new executive director. She was a trusted part of the friendship network of some board members, and she was in a related area. Steinberg had been managing director of the Illinois Film Office, where her job was attracting films, television shows, and commercials to be produced in the state. She had also succeeded in expanding the film tax credit so projects could realize more savings. She helped guide many documentarians, including at Kartemquin, through the process, which made a huge difference in getting the films made. Before that, she had been a writer, producer, and eventually VP for business development at Towers Productions, which produced documentaries for the basic cable market. She had served on nonprofit boards, though this was her first time running one herself.

She inherited big problems—a discontented staff, a business model that demanded a pipeline of new productions and one still experimenting with its terms, endless building maintenance problems. Then new problems appeared. The organization's accounting had always changed with each new director of finances, recalled Yvonne Afable, who over the years had served as a part-time accountant before serving on the board. Accounting was inevitably complex in an organization where each film project had its own budget, and only more so as new projects proliferated. A new finance director, a close friend of some board members who had coding skills, designed a new, bespoke system. The results were catastrophic; simple logistics failed to work. At one point, a $50,000 check got lost on the finance director's desk for months, several filmmakers recalled. Several filmmakers interviewed recalled facing intractable accounting snarls. When staff tried to bring to Steinberg, and then to the board, the disastrous state of Kartemquin's accounting, the problem was not addressed. Years later, Steinberg, when asked about financial issues, recalled that while some filmmakers were at odds with the accounting department, she believed they were all working in good faith through complicated circumstances, and that all three finance heads of her era had the "highest ethical standards."

CHAPTER 10

Steinberg also faced uneasiness toward existing policies perceived as jeopardizing the Kartemquin ethos. "It had turned into a marketplace," Dinesh Das Sabu recalled. "It was less of a community and more like, we'll bet on twenty films, and maybe five at any time will be successful. It'll be a cycle." This was the model of equity investors like Impact Partners or Chicago Media Project. But it did not fit Kartemquin. Most Kartemquin films, by their subject matter alone, would never be blockbusters, although *Hoop Dreams* was always there to remind people that the improbable happens. It was also a problem of scale. Kartemquin simply did not have the cash to gamble on which films would hit big. It had always depended on revenue from commercial work and equipment and expertise rental to pay the bills.

The entire staff participated in long, whither-Kartemquin discussions, Ingrid Roettgen recalled. There were thorny issues. Some of Kartemquin's staple funding sources—renting out the edit bay and services of people like editor Leslie Simmer, as well as equipment rental—were less in demand as production processes changed. "We had so many meetings about what direction to take the company in," she said. "Where to focus the resources? Some people wanted us to focus on awards, Oscar nominations, big-name filmmakers, and grants. Others wanted to do emerging filmmaker mentor programs. Some said, Do as much work-for-hire as we can. And so many filmmakers wanted so many services from us."

Kartemquin began hemorrhaging staff. Maggie Bowman became frustrated with Steinberg's management and left. Hillary Bachelder—who had become director of production, worked on a dozen Kartemquin productions, and whose *Represent* (2020), about Midwest women who challenge the establishment to run for office, would win awards—threw in the towel. Ryan Gleeson, Kartemquin's "Swiss Army knife," had entered clubhouse Kartemquin, with its long conversations in the kitchen. He just wanted to work on movies, not solve big logistical and administrative challenges, particularly under Steinberg's direction. He quit in 2018, but continued to work on Kartemquin productions. "Kartemquin isn't the company," he said. "Ultimately, it's the community and our collective attitude. It's an idea." Beckie Stocchetti began planning her leave-taking once Steinberg came in; she believed there was a skills mismatch in Steinberg's hiring, and that smarted even more because she had harbored dreams of applying for executive director herself, which Kartemquin leaders had discouraged her from doing. She took a job with the City of Chicago organizing all its film programs; there, she arranged for a screening of a restored version of *Inquiring Nuns*.

By 2018, Betsy Steinberg too left Kartemquin once her three-year contract was concluded; she recalled later this was largely for personal reasons. She had recently been through a serious illness and wanted more time to devote to her health and her family. The organization was in a catastrophic financial situation. Elspeth Revere stepped in as interim director and led a rigorous search process for executive director. The board selected Jolene Pinder, who had attended the University of Florida Documentary Institute (the institute is now at Wake Forest University), and who there had met Peter Gilbert, a teacher in the program. She also had worked at Arts Engine in New York, when cofounder Katy Chevigny was working with Gordon Quinn on a project. She had produced films, and had heard impassioned conversations about public media and arts policy. She had gone on in 2011 to run the New Orleans Film Society, building the organization's supports for Southern storytellers, and then to a grantmaking and mentoring organization, #CreateLouisiana. Kartemquin was, it seemed, her dream job. It looked like a solid organization, with an impressive staff size. Pinder loved the prospect of fundraising for the organization. When she got a moving allowance, she recalled, "I thought, 'Finally! Stability!'"

But right behind the curtain, the reality was horrifying. "There were years of tough decisions that hadn't been made," she said. Pinder unflinchingly addressed the financial catastrophe. She brought in a human relations firm, accepted the finance director's resignation, and laid off a third of the staff—carefully waiting until after the Christmas holidays to do so. Among those fired was Jim Morrissette, a much-beloved staff member who had been there since Kartemquin's earliest days. She had consulted with Quinn, who heart-brokenly agreed it had to be done. "It was the hardest thing I've ever done," she recalled. "It was a place that is such a family and a mass layoff sent ripples of harm throughout the entire community." The layoffs shattered morale. "It wasn't fun," said Ingrid Roettgen in a masterpiece of understatement. She was also let go. Pinder cut her own salary, not once but twice. She also arranged for a meeting with the larger arts community, led by board chair Pamela Sherrod Anderson, Quinn, and herself. The financial problems were addressed, and within a year the loan from the reserve fund that had kept the organization afloat was repaid.

But then came the pandemic. One of the first victims was Gordon Quinn, who contracted Covid-19 in March 2020 and almost died. He had just returned from Australia, where Covid-19 had also broken out. At seventy-eight and with a well-managed but still very real case of chronic lymphocytic leukemia, and at the pandemic's outset when little was known about Covid-19, he was not a good candidate for survival. But amazingly, after two weeks on a ventilator, he moved to a rehab center, where he spent time viewing films and providing notes. He returned home three weeks later, to an only slightly relaxed schedule. (The day he left rehab, he instantly responded to an email check-in from me, telling me he was booked for the next couple of days but could chat later in the week.)

Among other things, his profound illness shook Kartemquin to the core, as people finally confronted the possibility of a Gordon-less future. Meanwhile, Pinder shut down the physical office in the second week of March, and coordinated a work-from-home scenario, including bringing equipment home. She successfully applied for federal relief funds, through the Paycheck Protection Program, which functioned, she recalled later, as an "oxygen mask" for Kartemquin for a year.

The pandemic offered a chance for reflection, as well, especially with the PPP funds floating the opportunity. Because so many people worked from home, it also postponed the discussion about whether to find new space. Pinder could clearly see the organization's core assets: "Gordon's story guidance, Tim's distribution knowledge and network, and the diverse community of storytellers thoughtfully supported through KTQ's programs and program staff."

The fact that both Quinn and Horsburgh were white men was a problem for an organization whose staff now aspired to be BIPOC-forward. She brought in two consultants, to help launch an internal process of reflection toward action in racial reckoning. She also initiated an ongoing, all-staff conversation about the future of Kartemquin, and particularly about its institutional relationship to race and racism.

As the Covid-19 pandemic settled in, the whither-Kartemquin conversation at work continued without resolution, finances continued to be precarious, and Pinder ultimately decided to return home to New Orleans, to resume teaching and producing. Elspeth Revere stepped in as interim executive director. A year later, Chicago nonprofit activist Betsy Leonard was hired. She relaunched and formalized the process of recruiting an artistic director, with a priority on hiring a person of color. She too faced the harsh realities of an unstable business, and a roiling internal conversation about the organization's future.

Along with the business challenges, which ultimately lay with the executive director, was the question that had put the entire restructuring in motion in 2007. Who would ultimately replace Gordon Quinn as artistic director? Who would uphold the vision of documentary for democracy? The organization had been looking, first informally and then formally, for an artistic director for years. In 2017, Kartemquin briefly established an artistic fellowship. The only recipient was Maggie Bowman, who shared the title and work with Quinn until financial disaster struck down plans for other fellows. She came to believe that the next artistic director should be a person of color. The search continued, while Quinn continued to advise informally.

RACE AND DIVERSITY AT KARTEMQUIN

Kartemquin's long internal debate about its future was centered on questions of racial justice. The national discourse about race evolved from 2012 to become known, in shorthand, as a racial reckoning for the nation. The deaths of young Black men such as Trayvon Martin in Florida in 2012 and Mike Brown in Missouri in 2014 attracted national attention, with protests that swelled into the Black Lives Matter movement. This issue was particularly front-and-center for Chicagoans; police had publicly and notoriously been consistently brutal to Black and brown populations for many decades. There, the deaths of Rekia Boyd in 2012 and Laquan McDonald in 2014 had mobilized massive protests, and Kartemquinites were part of those protests. A *New York Times* series, *1619*, repositioned American history with race in the center, leveraging and popularizing rich historical work done by American historians, some of whom *In These Times* had featured since its founding. "Diversity, equity, and inclusion" had become a new corporate buzzword. And predictably, there was a growing right-wing backlash, with claims that teaching of "critical race theory," or anything about inequality and its history, was making young white children feel bad about themselves, and that "woke" behaviors were the new "political correctness," impairing freedom of speech.

The urgency about racial injustice that pervaded the atmosphere was reflected nationally in the documentary field as well. When Jigsaw Productions announced a documentary about Tiger Woods with an all-white production team, the field began debating who should make a film about BIPOC people. This grew into a larger conversation about duty of care more generally—toward participants, makers, and audiences. The Documentary Accountability Working Group, in which I participate, developed a set of values to guide thinking, at docaccountability.org. Film festivals showcased panels and workshops on the topic.

The racial reckoning conversation was grounded in a historical reality: the slavery-fueled colonialism that fueled capitalism, and the Jim Crow and immigration policies that followed slavery, had created a culture that poisonously and systemically used racism to justify brutal exploitation. The challenge for all organizations was how to incorporate this reality into their own actions and systems. The Rainbow Coalition proposed by Fred Hampton had provided insights for action in Kartemquin's collective era. The faith John Dewey had placed in people coming together around common problems had sustained a commitment to storytelling that built democratic practices into process itself. But in this era, in which identity politics provided the political framework and a billionaire-bankrolled right-wing was seizing its every opportunity, the next steps were not obvious. It was a problem as big as the entire society, but individuals, organizations, and sometimes budding social movements were wrestling with it in different ways.

The next steps for one fragile arts organization were particularly unclear. There was film production by Kartemquin's veterans, mostly white, who typically raised their own money and depended on existing relationships with mostly white colleagues to do their work. Did their whiteness exclude them preemptively? If not, what was their role in the future? And what would Kartemquin do without the money they brought in? Also, the programs launched in 2011 to nurture more diverse filmmaking talent showed that there was an abundance of talent, but a lack of resources to keep them working once they had been through a program.

Could Kartemquin offer these people more than a one-time opportunity? And if so, with what resources?

Kartemquin filmmakers had never shied away from understanding their positionality, including as white professionals. Positionality was central to the job, in fact, as endless "Structure and Identity" sessions during the collective era revealed. As it evolved into a production house noted for its humanist storytelling designed to enhance agency in a democracy, race continued to be a strategic issue, interwoven and intersecting with labor conditions, disability rights, women's rights, and veterans' issues.

At the same time, addressing positionality hadn't created lasting opportunities for many people of color at Kartemquin. As Kartemquin's films oriented increasingly to a broadcast, cablecast, and streaming audience, they also increasingly spoke to broad sectors of viewership. In that environment, a Kartemquin film had to ring true to a white viewer (the largest subsector of television viewers for broadcast and cable) first encountering the human reality of a disenfranchised experience, as well as to the typically disenfranchised people in the film and others living that experience. *Hoop Dreams*, which launched the Kartemquin era oriented to broad television programming, succeeded in doing that. At the same time, *Hoop Dreams* was made with an all-white team, in spite of good-faith efforts to diversify; an unfunded production could not support diverse professionals, who typically needed more income stability.

In the ensuing years, Kartemquin was a place for people making films about and with people with disabilities; brown, Black, and Native communities; international communities facing threats; and women. In the second decade of the twenty-first century, Kartemquin's productions also featured more diverse filmmakers, some because of long-standing ties (for instance, Keith Walker), and some because of talent nurtured within Kartemquin (former interns Bing Liu and Rubin Daniels Jr.). At the same time, there were also familiar white faces in directors' roles.

STEVE JAMES AND STORYTELLING ABOUT RACE

At Kartemquin, Steve James was the pastmaster at telling stories of disenfranchised people and helping others to do it. He was the biggest name among Kartemquin filmmakers. Now, he also engaged openly with the question of his role in the struggle for greater diversity in documentary production. His work in this period is a microcosm of the issues raised.

Steve James brought his most challenging work to Kartemquin, and the films he made there post-2008 were superb examples of his mature style. He has called himself a "humanist filmmaker," who like David Simon "tells the stories of people within that system, good people who are trying to do right and who are worth remembering," or telling "personal stories that usually have larger social implications." He avoids the label of social activist, although he has worked for and raised funds for impact campaigns around his films. After 2008 and the restructuring at Kartemquin, most of his work put race in the center of the stories about American culture. In so doing, he directly confronted the racial realities of his own experience, and often built them into his storytelling.

When offered a commission from sports channel ESPN for its *30 for 30* series, James decided to focus on the community reaction to an incident that put controversial basketball star Allen Iverson behind bars as a seventeen-year-old. James and Iverson grew up in the same town, where the incident was big news. *No Crossover: The Trial of Allen Iverson* (2010) is centrally about race in America. As a high schooler, Iverson went to jail for an interracial brawl; the community was and remains divided in its understanding of what happened, based on race. White locals usually believe Iverson was justly punished for a crime, and Black locals usually see racialized injustice.

James's strategy for demonstrating the gap in the cultural realities across racial lines features his own experience, as someone who discovers the limits of his own perception. He reflects in *No Crossover* that he thought, in making *Hoop Dreams*, he could tell that story because he had played basketball with Black players in high school, in the same town Iverson grew up in. (Hampton, Virginia, is also the first place where enslaved Africans landed in America, he also points out.) But, he says, that didn't mean they were friends. James leaned on the presence of his Black cameraman, Keith Walker from Media Process Group, to give confidence to Black people he interviewed generally. Walker regularly challenged him, and some of that ended up in the film, too. "I was telling a story about hearing people use the 'n' word as a young person," James recalled, "and he said, 'Why didn't you confront them?' That's in the film. When I talked about my Black teammates, he said, 'Did you ever wish you were Black?' I said, I don't think so, but I wished I could play like that. And I asked him, 'Did you wish you were white?' And Keith said, 'Sometimes, absolutely.' That went in the film, too." James recalled his struggle to get on camera a Black teacher who had led the effort to help Iverson. "She'd talk to me, but she kept saying no to being filmed. I kept asking, Why? She said, 'You don't get it. You're a white guy from here, you grew up in this poisoned culture as a white person. I don't trust that you can tell this story.' Somehow I finally convinced her to be interviewed, and to say that on camera. It was important." *No Crossover* as a result is both the story of the conflict that interrupted the career of a basketball superstar, and a story about the deeply fissured and racialized communities we all live in. It argues that you can't understand what happened to Iverson without understanding both stories.

His next Kartemquin project, *The Interrupters* (2011), also featured Black participants and organizations. James's old friend Alex Kotlowitz had written a major *New York Times* article about efforts to mitigate street violence in Black Chicago, and before that a notable and heart-wrenching book, *There Are No Children Here*, about life in the Chicago housing projects. The filmmakers, including Zak Piper, followed the work of the organization Kotlowitz had profiled, CeaseFire, which works on the streets of Chicago to intervene in potentially violent situations.

The filmmakers followed several of the organization's streetwise agents, themselves veterans of gangs and prison life, for a year. The most charismatic is Ameena Mathews, daughter of an imprisoned gang and community leader. Temaner and Quinn had actually met with her father about making a film, in Kartemquin's first few years. Mathews was now a convert to Islam after her hard-partying, drug-dealing adolescence. The interventions, followed experientially, sometimes work and sometimes don't. One particularly truculent case is Flamo, who rejects the group's best attempts to get him to calm down, while also courting their attention. He ultimately backs down from retaliation, with their help. A young man recently released from prison returns to the barbershop he robbed, and he painfully tries to make amends to the owner and customers he threatened. Ameena struggles to connect with her mentee Caprysha, who ricochets across the emotional spectrum before disappearing.

The film is an appreciation of CeaseFire without being a hagiography. Even the viewer who would never dream of entering the kinds of neighborhoods the film's participants live in becomes familiar enough with the people in the film and their circumstances to share in the CeaseFire activists' frustrations and victories. It's also clear how profoundly scarring and even maddening the experience of poverty, racism, and dehumanization is for young and old alike, and what a superhuman struggle it is to try to address these problems from within them, no matter how extraordinary the people who try are. The people in CeaseFire are good at their jobs, and impressively hopeful in dire situations. They show that people can change, and that sustained care, attention, and provision of opportunities makes all the difference. But this isn't a solutions film. The argument of CeaseFire's founder, epidemiologist Gary Slutkin—that violence is a public health problem that can be addressed as a disease—is neither proven nor disproven by what the Interrupters themselves do. But their work is one way of revealing the larger truth, which calls for a true public health solution that addresses poverty. This was a reason the film received strong support from the people the filmmakers worked with, while they were making it and after the film came out.

The film was a festival favorite, won a variety of "best documentary" awards, and took away an Emmy and a Dupont-Columbia award. In 2012, it aired on PBS's *Frontline*, the premier investigative journalism series. It was also designed with outreach and activism in mind from the start. In-house, Zak Piper led the outreach effort, which involved several consultants and staff members. Sonya Childress, who had trained at Active Voice, brought formidable skills and strategy to the task. The effort was primarily self-funded; Kartemquin charged, where possible, for screening events, largely at universities, and sold DVDs in tandem. Those funds were then redeployed to fund events and activities for organizations (including some universities) that could not pay. The funding was enough to keep one person employed, almost full-time, on *The Interrupters* alone. One of the biggest achievements, Piper later thought, was connecting CeaseFire with similar organizations in many other American cities.

James positioned himself carefully as ally and outsider, and he believed he could contribute to addressing the profound cruelties of racial and other injustices with it. He explained to *Cinéaste* in 2011:

Figure 26. Ameena Mathews, a lead participant in *The Interrupters*, with filmmakers Steve James, Alex Kotlowitz, and Zak Piper. Source: Steve James.

For me, coming into these situations requires patience and the building of trust between filmmakers and subjects. I've been amazed and heartened over the years by how accepting people in these neighborhoods have been. A key is openness and honesty about our intentions, which include trying to understand and explain, rather than judge and condemn. Still, I am not naïve. I know that I am always an outsider and that—despite my commitment to the films being largely in the voice of the subjects—the perspective of the film will still be that of an outsider. An insider filmmaker has obvious strengths: immediate rapport and relatable experience being just two. But being an outsider isn't necessarily a bad thing. Sometimes the outsider sees things that the insider has long become immune to, or stopped questioning. And really, isn't what inspires people to make documentaries—a desire to come to know and understand the world beyond their own neighborhood or class or ethnic group? To find common ground and universal truths that transcend our differences?

Furthermore, James said the presence of that outsider filmmaker, if empathetic, can be helpful to the people being filmed: "I love trying to get into the heads of subjects and have them ruminate on their lives. I think what making a documentary has to offer subjects, beyond some possible fleeting fame or notoriety, is that it can be a therapeutic experience for them, a chance for them to examine their own life while they live it."

In *Abacus: Small Enough to Jail* (2016), James told a story about anti-Asian racial discrimination and governmental abuse in economic crisis. In the wake of the 2008 financial crisis, a New York bank catering to Chinese immigrants had been prosecuted for fraud. The 2008 financial crisis had been set off by speculation in the financialization of mortgages. The private market in rebundling mortgages got far out of control in the 2000s, enabled by deregulation of the financial sector. Shaky towers of unbacked assets were constructed, each new financial product built on a previous and similarly unbacked assets. Then, insurance companies started selling insurance on these assets and openly corrupt bankers bought both insurance and shaky assets, sometimes from the same company. By late 2006, those towers were trembling, and by 2007, they started tumbling down. The entire international economy hung in the balance for a few weeks until European and US taxpayers bailed out most of the banks and the insurance companies. That didn't keep families across the US from being foreclosed upon, or losing their jobs and businesses in the Great Recession. The banks were "too big to fail"; but the little guys were not.

No investment banker ever went to jail. But several members of the small, family-owned Abacus Federal Savings Bank, which the Sung family founded for Chinese immigrants who faced discrimination from other banks, were accused of mortgage fraud. Abacus wasn't even an investment bank, the kind that caused all the problems. They had not only done nothing wrong; they had bent over backwards to do the right thing, both legally and ethically, when they caught an employee taking bribes. Ultimately, the Sung family was found innocent. James came in as they were about to go to trial. He wanted to tell their story, as a grassroots tale of misplaced governmental postcrash vigilance. He also saw a story of an immigrant business serving its community.

Abacus: Small Enough to Jail features retrospective storytelling, interviews, and warm, intimate cinema verité material of the family, three of whose four daughters work for the bank. The film also sharply draws parallels between the family and one of their favorite movies, *It's a Wonderful Life* (1946), in which the protagonist, who runs a savings and loan, helps the whole community. Finally, it shows what Manhattan district attorney Cyrus Vance Jr. will not say out loud: That his office focused on a small community lender to get an easy win, and to duck charges of being soft on banks at a time when public outrage was sky-high.

In this project, James depended on the Kartemquin old guard, all white. The film got ITVS funding, and it showed on public TV's *Frontline*. But first it debuted at the Toronto International Film Festival, one of the top festivals in the world, to begin a whirlwind festival run. It also notably had a successful theatrical run as well—a great rarity for a social-issue documentary. The film won an Academy Award nomination, a Peabody award, three Critics' Choice awards, and an Emmy.

Then, building upon the learnings from *The New Americans* and *Hard Earned*, James began making miniseries. This suited the binge-happy distribution environment, and it gave James the room he loved to develop stories. He quickly adapted his storytelling techniques to encourage bingeing. But he continued to take up challenging, complex issues at the heart of America's racial divide. He didn't have to bring these projects through Kartemquin, but he did, and they aligned perfectly with Kartemquin's mission. "Steve has a lot of gratitude for Kartemquin, and what it offered him," recalled Jolene Pinder. "He has given back. In the absence of a robust, sustainable business model, Steve's projects provide the most steady income."

Increasingly, James was working with more diverse teams and diverse segment directors. And, as a result of conversations at Kartemquin about representation, James was asking himself more questions as a result of active engagement at Kartemquin and with his colleagues in the field. For *The Interrupters*, for example, "Both Alex and I had put in time on the streets of Chicago. We thought that was enough and I didn't question it then," he said. "When I look back it now, though, we would never do that film now that way."

The result of that engagement was evident in hiring on the next, gigantic project, with backing from Participant Productions, a ten-part miniseries: *America to Me* (2018). For this project, the segment directors were diverse, and took leadership. James hired two nonwhite Kartemquinites— Bing Liu and Kevin Shaw—and a woman, Rebecca Parrish, to direct segments. Parrish, who is lesbian, was tracking a high schooler who was coming out. Rubin Daniels Jr. was associate editor; Simmer and Simpson edited. James tried to give Liu, Shaw, and Parrish story-director credits, and take his own credit only as series director. When the Directors Guild would not approve that, they all received segment-director credits. The segment directors had autonomy over their segments, and they also joined all press interviews.

The title comes from the famous poem by Harlem Renaissance poet Langston Hughes. This poem was particularly apt for a film that considered injustice intersectionally. The poem is pointedly anticapitalist in tone, calling out systemic injustice, for instance:

I am the poor white, fooled and pushed apart,
I am the Negro bearing slavery's scars.
I am the red man driven from the land,
I am the immigrant clutching the hope I seek—
And finding only the same old stupid plan
Of dog eat dog, of mighty crush the weak.

The film's title references the passage, "America never was America to me / And yet I swear this oath— / America will be!"

The timing was right. Racial-reckoning conversations had come to television, although white backlash was growing on the right at the same time. *Queen Sugar*, Ava DuVernay's series about a Black family farm in Louisiana's racist sugar-cane agriculture, came out in 2016. *Dear White People*, about Black and brown students in an Ivy League college, debuted in 2017. *Get Out*, a horror film about white oppression, was a 2017 hit in theaters, then on TV, and won an Oscar. *Watchmen* (2019), from the graphic novel that wove Jim Crow violence and ongoing racism into a science fiction story, was in production.

America to Me follows ten Black and brown and two white students, their parents, and their teachers both Black and white. (Many white students and parents were reluctant to get involved in the film.) These participants navigate a high school in Oak Park, where white people pushed back against white flight in the 1960s, welcoming Black residents. But racism persisted. The students and parents encounter both blatant discrimination and the daily acts of minimization and erasure that stem from systemic racism, poverty, and unequal access. The onscreen cluelessness of white colleagues and teachers is a truth-telling mirror held up to white fragility. The resilience of the students and their families is as evident as the scandal of needing it.

The reviews were raves. The *New York Times* called it "an invaluable look at where inequity begins." *The Atlantic* review's closing line—"the thoughtfulness and nuance James and his team bring to the subject offer at least a small bit of hope about what a truly honest confrontation with race might spark"—was an inadvertent nod to the Deweyan promise behind such Kartemquin work, to spur more productive conversations about shared problems. The RogerEbert.com site called it a "momentous achievement." Black NPR critic Eric Deggans called it "one of the best documentaries on TV this season."

The series debuted at Sundance, by which time it already had four offers. It had a festival run, picking up several award nominations and a Cinema Eye award. It was sold to Starz for $5 million, the highest price a Kartemquin film had ever sold for, and became the third-highest-rated new TV show of the year. Its outreach was extensive, coordinated by Participant. High schools, colleges, and parent groups all used engagement materials on Participant's website; follow-up surveys showed change in attitudes, skill acquisition, and intent to take action. The series was used at a national conference for high school principals, who broke into smaller groups to brainstorm lessons for their schools.

James was wrapping up production on *America to Me* while he undertook another miniseries: The four-part *City So Real* (2020), in which Chicago electoral mayoral politics is an X-ray of the intertwining of race, class, and gender in entrenching inequality. Again, Participant was a partner. Kartemquin came in only for the accounting. Black filmmakers on the project included cinematographer Kevin Shaw (a mentee at Kartemquin soon to make his own film, *Let the Little Light Shine* [2022]) and field producers Sylvetta Christmas and Janea Smith. Quinn continued to provide occasional notes. Zak Piper coproduced it with James. David E. Simpson and James coedited, with Ruben Daniels Jr. providing additional editing. This series too debuted at Sundance, just after Joe Biden's presidential win.

The series was another eye-popping exploration of the politics of race in the lived dramas of the election. That white people so frankly express their racism during the trial of the police officer who murdered Laquan MacDonald is as impressive a revelation on camera as is the close-in look at underdog candidates trying to cut through garden-variety Chicago electoral corruption. It received two Emmy nominations and multiple other awards, and after National Geographic aired it commercial-free, its corporate sibling Hulu took it. (The festival run was curtailed by the pandemic.) *Rolling Stone* called it James's "crowning achievement." *Variety* called it "a quietly radical act of service."

Steve James's work in these years took head-on how race structures perception and action, and these projects proposed different realities to many viewers than the ones they came with. His projects incorporated some of the more diverse talent being nurtured at Kartemquin, while still depending on relationships that had matured over decades with the white filmmakers there. He built teams to support his vision, which was one of a more truly diverse and truly democratic nation. And of course, they contributed essential revenue streams to an always edgy financial reality at Kartemquin.

During Kartemquin's grappling with the racial reckoning, Steve James openly asked himself how and why he had consistently made films about, as well as increasingly with, people of color. He undertook a months-long round of conversations with peers and a listening tour among colleagues. He looked for ways that he could modify and leverage his leadership role, while still telling his stories:

> A number of my Black filmmaking colleagues want this change [at Kartemquin, toward leadership by people of color] to happen so that people are empowered to tell their own stories in their own communities, and they also want the power to tell stories beyond their communities too. It's an essential part of the artistic endeavor. Filmmakers tend to venture beyond their borders to tell their stories. The moment we're living in, there's a huge corrective that needs to happen. I'm down with the pendulum swinging because it's important. My hope for all filmmakers is that once there's more equity and it's felt more universally, we'll get beyond reductionist arguments about skin color and storytelling.
>
> I'm doing a film on Bill Walton now, a white basketball player, but I have a diverse team both shooting and editing. I feel more obligation to have a diverse team no matter what the story than I used to. It's more important to hire people of color. I'm making more of a commitment to mentorship, if

Black filmmakers want it. Middle-class filmmakers, including filmmakers of color, often have enormous learning curves once they're out shooting in a besieged neighborhood that's very different from where they grew up. But at the same time, an inexperienced Black, middle-class filmmaker in a poor Chicago neighborhood is still inherently better positioned to tell that story than a similarly experienced white counterpart.

Kartemquin's legacy projects were increasingly, as Steve James's work evidenced, incorporating diverse talent nurtured in and around Kartemquin. James, like other Kartemquin directors, was raising his own money to make these films. The next challenge was how to feature the visions and voices of diverse and marginalized people whose talent had been encouraged there. These filmmakers would need more and continuing financial and professional support. The Kartemquin programs that Nagan and Stocchetti had put in motion became a place to test out how to take up that challenge.

PRIORITIZING DIVERSITY WITH DVID

When Kartemquin was restructured in 2007, with unprecedented access to foundation resources not just for films but for the organization itself, people knew where they wanted to focus: On the obstacles that disenfranchisement put in the way of Black and brown aspiring filmmakers who saw a promise in Kartemquin's vision. Nagan, Quinn, and the new board had decided, among other things, to leverage the MacArthur grant and raise more money for fundable projects, most importantly one to address Kartemquin's chronic diversity problem. Kartemquin launched a diversity fellowship, to fund one filmmaker for a year, working on the project of their choice. Chicago-based Black filmmaker Yvonne Welbon was hired as the consultant to research and develop the initiative. Margaret Caples of Community Film Workshop was a partner in the project from the start.

The winner of the first round was Usama Alshaibi, an immigrant, who wanted to make a film about his post-911 experience of racism as an Arab American. Alshaibi was not an experienced producer, and like many newbie makers, even after two years and $100,000 he did not have a viable piece of work and still needed to raise more money. Kartemquin ended up supporting the production to keep it going. The eventual result, an hour-long, uncompromising film, *American Arab* (2013), is a memoir of his rocky adjustment as an immigrant to a racist America. Finished in 2013, it was shown broadly at festivals both domestically and internationally. It had a broadcast life on American, Canadian, Norwegian, and Japanese public channels.

Kartemquin regrouped after that first round of diversity funding, and revised its expectations. Rather than use all its annual funding for one filmmaker, it would provide guidance and partial funding to incubate projects, through fellowships to a cohort. Margaret Caples helped design the project, and she insisted that the appeal be to people of color generally, not only Black Americans. The project would now be housed at Community Film Workshop, on Chicago's South Side, which has a majority-Black demographic, to ensure that Kartemquin's location in a now-upscale neighborhood wasn't creating discomfort. Each cohort would get both training and mentorship, and have regular work-in-progress meetings. This way, Kartemquin could best leverage its talents' own expertise and access to nurture new, diverse voices. Nagan came to realize that providing development grants was the *sine qua non* to success. Launching Diverse Voices in Documentary (DVID), Kartemquin's diversity initiative, in 2011 took an extensive fundraising campaign across institutional funders and individuals.

By 2015, DVID had run for four seasons, and some of the alums were also producing films at Kartemquin. Kartemquin's decision to prioritize diversity in selecting and paying interns also bore fruit. The films were as diverse as the makers. The Kartemquin DVID program was becoming a hallmark program of its kind, and its filmmakers launched careers with it.

In 2016, Anuradha (Anu) Rana, who had been a DVID cohort member in 2014, returned to Kartemquin and took on the job of DVID coordinator. She had moved from India to Chicago to take an MA in documentary at Columbia College. There, she learned about Kartemquin from classmates working as interns, and from visits by Steve James and other Kartemquin filmmakers. After graduate school, she taught, made films, and became cochair of the documentary department at DePaul University. Rana brought DVID from an ancillary program to the center of Kartemquin activities, drawing upon her educational experience.

Figure 27. Kartemquin's programs burgeoned post-2008. The 2018 Diverse Voices in Documentary cohort with Pamela Sherrod Anderson (far left), a graduate of the first cohort and later head of Kartemquin's board of directors; cofounder of DVID Margaret Caples (center front); and to her right, in order: DVID director Anu Rana (right of Caples); executive director Betsy Steinberg; head of programs Laura Gomez-Mesquita; and Gordon Quinn. Source: Kartemquin Archives. Credit: Andrea Raby.

"When I came in, even though Kartemquin had made a commitment to issues of race, there was still a sense of DVID being 'over here,' and Kartemquin is 'over there' with mainstream films," she said. "We've learned that it isn't enough to have a program for makers of color. You have to invite them to the table, and actually listen. That's taken a lot of work, but it shows a different kind of commitment."

This reorientation was hard work, she said. The DVID effort and the work to expand opportunities for those who entered the program took strategic planning. Some Kartemquinites found change uncomfortable. But the shift was embraced, and there was consistent progress. Rana expanded the time DVID filmmakers met, from once a month to day-long sessions twice a month. The emphasis was on developing the filmmaker's voice, and building community in ways that give filmmakers an entrée into the business, she recalled: "What Kartemquin is strong at is helping people to ask themselves what story they want to tell." That inquiry is always rooted in the Deweyan promise of artists bringing imagination to the challenges of democracy. DVID also experimented with expanding mentorship capacity, eventually paying, then raising the pay rate, of mentors and diversifying the mentor pool.

Among the interns was Rubin Daniels Jr., a Black film student who while completing a graduate degree at DePaul saw an announcement about Kartemquin internships. He had never heard of the company, but he liked the films he watched to get a flavor of their work. His first jobs were entry-level, such as transcription. He was captivated, though, by the Kartemquin Labs experience, where he was encouraged to give his opinions. He soaked up marketing and distribution knowledge from Horsburgh, and editing mentoring and skills from Quinn and Leslie Simmer. He worked as assistant editor on a couple of projects, and people saw his unusual talent. He soon got an offer from Steve James to work on *America to Me*. Daniels rose from assistant editor to associate editor on that project. He also apprenticed to Quinn in his artistic director functions. "I tried to be the junior Gordon," he recalled.

DVID AND DIVERSE FILMS

Three of the debut films by diverse makers were personal memoirs, emerging from the first-time filmmakers' confrontation with their own pasts as they searched for topics for their projects. In 2016 came Dinesh Das Sabu's *Unbroken Glass*. It had been nurtured in clubhouse-Kartemquin, with Leslie Simmer encouraging Sabu about his story arc, while Sabu was also working as Gordon Quinn's travel booker. David E. Simpson would drop by to work on a project, and then consult with Sabu on the side. Matt Lauterbach, who had been postproduction manager, did editing; he had a deep interest in disability issues, a theme of the film. Sabu made the film over eight years, piecing together grants and surviving on for-hire work, using the office for free. He only paid himself a small stipend in the last year. "A film like mine, made that way, with that modest funding, couldn't exist in the current iteration of Kartemquin," he recalled.

The film tracked Sabu's journey to discover his own past. At six years old, the youngest of five children, he lost his irascible father to stomach cancer. A month later, his schizophrenic mother died. His older sisters kept the family together. His journey to recover the past takes him back to his parents' families in India, and into his own anguished subjectivity as he worries that the mental illness that destroyed his mother might reappear in the next generation. It's a low-key and reflective film, without gotcha reveals, and at an hour was perfectly sized for broadcast. It showed on public TV's *America Reframed* series on WGBH's (now GBH's) World Channel. It also had a solid festival run at ethnic and regional / city film festivals.

Sabu also took the film to fifty community screenings, including at a Hindu temple, mental health organization meetings, and universities. "That's the Kartemquin idea, bring the films to the people," Sabu said. "Those labor films they made weren't playing at the Berlin Film Festival, but at a bar, to show what's at stake in organizing. It was exhilarating for me to understand that process, and to see the potential of documentary."

Bing Liu was a young cinematographer, who had been mentored by veteran cinematographer Tom Ciciura. Ciciura helped him become a union cameraman, working on studio and TV productions in Chicago. As camera assistant on a Hyundai commercial, Liu stumbled upon the DVID internship information. His 2014 DVID internship was door-opening in many senses. He had known nothing about documentaries, and Kartemquin not only offered history and skills but a perspective:

> That specific Kartemquin school of filmmaking has a lot to do with ethics, which doesn't parallel with the larger doc industry's concerns. It's instilled early on in that you should think about power, ethics, morality, as someone who tells stories about real people and real people's lives. I wanted to impact the world, have tangible, practical social impact. I learned there's different ways of doing that, that Kartemquin was formed to do that, and has been doing that. That instilled a lot of fire in me.

He had a little project. It was about young men who reminded him of his childhood friends, who had fled abusive homes for the thrill of transgressive skateboarding with each other in down-at-heels, postindustrial Rockford, Illinois. He had been filming them for some time already. As he went through DVID, it was clear the project had immense potential.

Figure 28. Minding the Gap director Bing Liu (center) worked with old friends to tell his own story; here, he stands with Kiere Johnson (left) and Zack Mulligan (right), two of the film's participants. Source: Bing Liu.

When Tim Horsburgh saw his demo reel as a submission for the Diverse Voices in Docs program, he flagged the project as a possibility for Kartemquin coproduction. As soon as Liu finished the program, Justine Nagan and Gordon Quinn offered a simple production agreement and Liu, without a lawyer, happily signed. He teamed up with Diane Quon as a producer. Quon, who had worked on Maria Finitzo's *In the Game*, volunteered for the position, explaining to Quinn that she wanted to help an emerging Asian American filmmaker.

As what became *Minding the Gap (2018)* evolved, Nagan moved over to *POV* and offered Liu's film a slot on the broadcast series. That kindled ITVS's interest, and suddenly his project was funded. Meanwhile, Steve James hired him on *America to Me*, which James was acutely aware needed more BIPOC people on the team.

The film developed quickly, with both Kartemquin and ITVS providing production assistance and feedback. It morphed, with Kartemquin's feedback, from a film about skateboarders in various places to a combination memoir and focus on his Rockford friendship group. It incorporates earlier footage into his close observation of a skateboarding friendship group in the same town, as they lurch into turbulent adulthoods. Each has a history of family abuse and poverty; they are all aging out of the period when skateboarding could be an ecstatic release from ground-level misery and an alternative world of achievement. They're struggling with jobs, and one has a child in the course of the film. We learn about their painful relationships with parents. Near film's end, Liu finally sits down with his mother to talk frankly about her failure to protect him from his stepfather's violence. The portrait of directionless young men, trying hard to find their footing on and off the skateboard, is a loving but frank mini-portrait relevant to exurban, rural, and postindustrial America.

Liu went to the Sundance Film Festival with not one but two films: his own *Minding the Gap*, and Steve James's *America to Me* series. The two films were the talk of the festival. *Minding the Gap* participants came; Diane Quon hired Maggie Bowman to work with them. Participants saw the film in advance (some had seen it in rough cut), and the team used the advice of experts on domestic violence and child abuse to help them meet participants' needs. Each participant was paired with someone from the film team during Sundance, to alleviate stress. *Minding the Gap* won a jury award for breakthrough filmmaking. It won a host of other festival awards before being nominated for an Academy Award.

Tim Horsburgh succeeded in negotiating through what Liu called a distribution "three-dimensional chess puzzle." He struck a deal between Hulu, which initially wanted to claim all rights, and PBS, ITVS, and *POV*. The public TV entities had first dibs on release, via public broadcasting, after providing the majority of production funding, and they had wanted to hang on to postbroadcast distribution. To make this three-dimensional chess happen, Justine Nagan at *POV* was crucial; in addition to her belief in the power of public media, she understood that the Hulu visibility could benefit public broadcasting. Horsburgh, Quinn, Nagan, and Hulu's Belisa Balaban—along with lawyers and colleagues from all sides—worked out an arrangement. Hulu could brand the film as a "Hulu Original" and release it six months before PBS aired it, and Hulu would then let the film be used for *POV*'s impact/engagement campaigns, and allow it to be

Figure 29. Gordon Quinn and Tim Horsburgh in unaccustomed tuxedos (Quinn's was assembled from thrift shops) at the Academy Award ceremony, when *Minding the Gap* was nominated for Best Documentary. Source: Kartemquin Archives.

released on home video (in a separate deal Horsburgh made with the Criterion Collection). ITVS and PBS agreed to limit the broadcast and streaming and worked out a deal around awards.

The film got rave reviews everywhere, but one critic summed up the way in which the film reflected Kartemquin's core, Deweyan values. Critic Matt Stoller Seitz at Roger Ebert's website wrote: "Liu's generosity as a filmmaker refuses to consign any character to either / other categories. They're always both / and. You like them, you want them to succeed, you understand why they are the way they are, and yet at the same time you're allowed to be frustrated with their inability to see themselves clearly and change their lives."

Liu took a position with Guggenheim's Concordia Studios in Los Angeles, but he remained immensely grateful for Kartemquin's launch of his career: "I entered Kartemquin through a diversity program, I really appreciated that. Kartemquin always tried. That doesn't mean they always succeeded, but I think Diverse Voices is doing a good job. Every year that program gets better and better, with more funding support."

At the same time, Liu recognized he benefited from the last moments of a previous era: "The tumultuous times started when I started producing, from 2015–2018. It taught me a lot about nonprofit organizations and the existential dilemma of the documentary industrial complex. Kartemquin can always be that collective if enough filmmakers want to do it, but I don't know if there's enough drive." Also, he noted, the indie filmmaking scene has shifted from a mission of media for social change to a focus on the culture of creators, fostered by many support programs from arts / film organizations specific to the creators. "It's hard to exist in that culture and also have Kartemquin thrive," he said.

Pamela Sherrod Anderson and Kelly Richmond Pope were in the first DVID cohort. Both are Black, and both made films. Anderson came with filmmaking experience, and through her experience in DVID made a moving film, *G Force*, about grandparents raising their grandchildren. Also a professor at DePaul University, she became the chair of the Kartemquin board.

Pope was a full professor at DePaul University, and an expert in forensic accounting. She already had created an educational case-study film to use in classes, and saw a local scandal as another potential educational tool. Rita Crundwell, city comptroller for Dixon, Illinois, had been found guilty of defrauding her town of $53 million over twenty years. While she built an empire in quarter-horse breeding, city services and infrastructure languished.

Like Anderson, Pope took the DVID training to professionalize her filmmaking skills, and then developed her film, leaning heavily on Gordon Quinn's feedback. She funded the film over five and a half years with donations from corporate connections she already had. "This business doesn't provide a return, so you have to beg," she reflected wryly. "And money for the arts is a very niche market. You're competing for that money with people who have real, immediate problems—hunger, housing."

All the Queen's Horses (2017) does not look like other Kartemquin films. It isn't a character-driven documentary; rather, the fraud itself is the central character. Combining expert interviews, man-on-the-street comments, archival news footage, and explanatory animations, the film walks us through what she did, how she did it, what the consequences were, and how it fits into a broader pattern of embezzlement of governmental coffers worldwide. It is a superbly crafted tutorial on forensic accounting, as well as an eye-opening crime story that takes us past the headlines. It is also about holding government to account. It achieves what Quinn told the director was her challenge: "to make accounting interesting."

Pope wanted to make a feature film with a long-tail educational market, but also wanted it to get media coverage as a Kartemquin film. And she really wanted an Emmy. She only got some of what she wanted. Kartemquin's services, including Horsburgh's distribution chops, didn't align well with her project, which had an educational function. The film didn't fit into an authorial festival model, either; she was rejected from sixty-two of the seventy-five film festivals she applied to. Her business partner, not Kartemquin, was the one to connect at Sundance with Gravitas Ventures, which released the film on digital platforms and secured a one-year licensing deal with Netflix. Kartemquin helped with negotiations and in launching a multi-city theatrical run. The film continues to be shown. It aired on public TV throughout Illinois when Rita Crundwell was let out of prison because of the Covid-19 pandemic.

Quinn, who consulted extensively with Pope and her editor, believed she came in with a clear image of what the film should be and do, and that the point of his mentoring was to help her fulfill her vision of it: "Kelly is very ambitious. She's a well-known person, she's a professor, and now her profile is a lot higher because of that film." *All the Queen's Horses* was a good example of the way in which Kartemquin could permit a filmmaker to make the film in the style and for the purpose that they imagined, without forcing it into a set of aesthetic expectations.

Ashley O'Shay, a Black filmmaker from a working-class family in Indianapolis, had Kartemquin on her radar since she took a class at Northwestern University and learned about their films. She took an internship, and then entered the DVID program. Her idea, to follow Black women within the Movement for Black Lives, won her a $10,000 grant from Kartemquin, via its Sage Foundation funding. As she raised small amounts to keep on making the film, including through crowdfunding,

Figure 30. Unapologetic participant Ambrell Gambrell electrifies her audiences. Source: Kartemquin Archives. Credit: Chan C. Smith.

she paid the rent by freelancing and a part-time job at the Siskel Film Center. Eventually, she signed a coproduction agreement with Kartemquin.

Unapologetic, produced by Morgan Elise Johnson and edited by Ruben Daniels Jr., debuted during the pandemic, in 2020, in the midst of a racial reckoning. The film follows two very different women, both Black and queer, as they become leaders in Black Lives Matter. Janaé Bonsu, an aspiring PhD student in social work, gets caught up in the movement. She struggles with academic imposter syndrome and the sometimes-personal growing-pains politics of movement organizations. Ambrell Gambrell, an electrifying, gamine-faced presence, is a performative organizer, galvanizing action with rap. The film tracks their engagement with each other, the police board, city hall, and fellow protesters. The film had a robust festival round. It then aired on public TV's *POV*, before going the next day to Amazon Prime and other streaming venues.

Finding Yingying (2020) resulted from a Kartemquin grant out of Sage funding for Jiayan "Jenny" Shi, who was a DVID alumna. Yingying Zhang, an upbeat, bright, twenty-six-year-old Chinese student, went missing six weeks after she started graduate work at the University of Illinois. Shi, attending Northwestern at the time, almost immediately began filming, as she joined other Chinese students looking for her and became a support for Yingying's distraught and desperate parents once they arrived from China. The film follows their frustrating search amid the bafflement of negotiating a foreign country, the horrifying news of Yingying's murder, and the parents' anger-filled grief and self-destructive misery back in China. The film interweaves verité with excerpts from Yingying's diary. It is less true crime (it never dwells on the killer) than a chronicle of loss. The search reveals who Yingying was to her family, boyfriend, friends, and even people at the university she so briefly attended. The film debuted at SXSW, won a special jury award, and got rave reviews. It found a home at MTV Documentaries, where Sheila Nevins had just moved in after decades at HBO Documentaries.

Another Kartemquin project that featured nonwhite makers and participants, *Wuhan* (2021), came in as a partnership, "in association with" Kartemquin, during the pandemic. Directed by Chinese Canadian director Yung Chang, whose first feature *Up the Yangtze* (2007) was a hit on US public TV, it was an inside look at how Wuhan residents rallied to confront the pandemic. Diane Quon, who had produced *Minding the Gap*, brought it in. The film won rave reviews and went to Netflix.

The films made by diverse filmmakers resulted from Kartemquin programs to nurture new diverse talent. They showcased new perspectives, voices, and aesthetic range. They also depended on legacy Kartemquin expertise and relationships.

STRUGGLING WITH THE CONVERSATION

By 2018, the staff was half BIPOC but also white-led. The DVID project was flourishing, but the mentees in the project didn't stay at Kartemquin, which had no way to fund their projects. After Steinberg left, the staff began strategic planning conversations for an operating grant. The process extended well past a year, with sometimes painful group discussions. As in so many other organizations at this time, members of color with long-suppressed opinions were openly conversing, sometimes contentiously, with white members who had recognized but perhaps not reckoned with privilege. The Kartemquin Labs, which had been a safe space for frank but supportive feedback, now sometimes became platforms for prickly conversations about diversity and inclusion.

Among those tasked with leading the conversations was Laura Gomez-Mesquita, who had first learned about Kartemquin in my own film classes at American University. After moving to Chicago, she had worked at Free Spirit Media, a media program for Black and brown young people. Kartemquinites, including Gordon Quinn, would come to her students' final screenings. She became manager and eventually director of programs at Kartemquin. Gomez-Mesquita came in a champion of addressing fundamental power imbalances at work. She also arrived just as Kartemquin discovered the depth of the organization's financial mismanagement.

The financial and diversity conversations were intertwined. For instance, mentoring had informally been a feature of Kartemquin, but now Kartemquin wanted to formalize the process and include more BIPOC mentors, with hopes of a mentors-of-color-only rule. They also hoped to provide training and set expectations for mentors. But finding time to pull together curriculum and meet was always a challenge, and mentors—all working filmmakers—were not always available either. Nor were they paid.

When the pandemic hit in 2020, DVID was suspended for a year, and the staff took that time to interview some sixty DVID alumni, as part of the soul-searching process to build a stronger, BIPOC-forward Kartemquin. Some alumni were delighted, but some provided dismaying feedback. They were grateful for the opportunity, but they didn't necessarily have that family-like experience earlier generations had. The kitchen conversation was gone; the clubhouse had evaporated. Some of them felt the experience was transactional, without enough to transact with; a few felt they were diversity tokens. The end of the fellowship was "like falling off a cliff." There was no money to fund their projects, and some projects were abandoned. Often, they had arrived hoping to join Kartemquin, and found out that they couldn't because it wasn't even structured that way. "It still feels like a closed system to them," Gomez-Mesquita said. "Some of it is racial, and some of it is experience. Kartemquin has been historically an organic community. A lot of the same people get the gigs and build that experience." Anu Rana also thought that building community and opening doors was the hardest challenge for DVID. "What people need is access to the field," she said. "We're still on the learning boat for that." DVID project completion rate was at 25–30 percent.

Some diverse alums had positive experiences. Bing Liu's career, which had a rocket-like trajectory, was launched at Kartemquin, and he was grateful. Rubin Daniels Jr., who had learned enough in a short time to set up his own editing business, was in constant touch. "I want to continue to build the relationship," he said. "Kartemquin is about collaboration and community, with a mission. As a person of color, you can sometimes be in a place where white men can take up the space, and I've never felt that at Kartemquin." Ashley O'Shay, whose *Unapologetic* fell afoul of the accounting problems, said,

> I had a very positive experience with them. They were the reason why I started *Unapologetic*. I've had my moments, I've struggled with their capacity, the agreements took months to get aligned, I've been frustrated. But they are an institution that's constantly looking to change and improve. They advocate especially for emerging filmmakers. A lot of other institutions in the industry don't put trust in emerging filmmakers.

The staff, now separated entirely from the filmmaking process, had their own issues. Some BIPOC staffers thought some of the white legacy filmmakers were struggling with the new era. Gomez-Mesquita saw that legacy filmmakers "were white folks doing work on social justice, at a time when that was considered woke and progressive. And the shift to what it would mean not to just give people a one-off opportunity but invest in them, that feels to some white folks here like we're taking away the power of what was done before. It's as if we're saying Kartemquin never did it right."

Gordon Quinn was fully behind a move toward more inclusion at Kartemquin. As he noted at a Kartemquin retrospective at University of California, Los Angeles, when asked about the Trump presidency, this was a viciously enduring problem: "The real issue is that no one ever dealt with white supremacy after Reconstruction, and it's always available for people like [the Trump base] to mobilize around."

Peter Kuttner reflected on his decision to retire as a Kartemquin mentor. Kuttner had been a Kartemquinite in the collective era, part of the Rainbow Coalition, and focused on work with white, working-class organizations. "This is different from the time we came up, when people were building in their own communities," he said.

> Kartemquin is going through a needed phase. I mentored for a long time, and I enjoyed the relationship I was able to develop with staff, with interns, and finally with Diverse Voices in Documentary. But the role of a white, older male as a mentor doesn't work like it used to, particularly in a project that's talking to a diverse group of people. I think it's reasonable. The concept of the white savior is very uncomfortable to me. They can always get to me later. There's a time to step back. I'm able to send people on to jobs, help them into unions. I still want to be part of the Kartemquin community, even though my own part is small.

Adam Singer, who increasingly took commercial work outside of Kartemquin, continued on the board of directors. But there, he found himself publicly uncomfortable with endorsing a reparations framework that did not also explicitly prioritize creativity, although he came to see the importance of making this new framework a priority for the organization: "In addition to [a mission statement about] equity and reparations, I want Kartemquin to continue to emphasize creativity. We all want to see Kartemquin doing what it does best—making compelling, challenging, emotional films."

Tim Horsburgh also embraced the dream of a truly diverse Kartemquin. The work ahead, for Horsburgh, was to move from having a diversity program to building a truly inclusive institution. Kartemquin's latest wave of successes had established it as a success in the marketplace—after all, it sent two films to the Oscars in one year, one of them made by a filmmaker who came up through DVID. But if it was not to sell its soul, it also needed to assert its mission. At the same time, Horsburgh thought that the sometimes-tense discussions at Kartemquin could lose sight of Kartemquin's achievements. "You might not make *Hoop Dreams* the same way now," he said, "but that doesn't make it any less of a great film. It's a mistake to dismiss the care and craft and love in that film, even though the filmmakers were white. Proximity is not a guarantee of quality. Trust is a guarantee of quality in documentary."

In 2021, Horsburgh decided that he was no longer playing a productive role in Kartemquin's evolution, in part because he was a white man interested in leadership. He had imagined a role for himself as head of production, with an executive director running the organization. As Kartemquin staff debated its future, Horsburgh could see that his vision would not prevail. He became a sought-after consultant, and then took an executive position with National Geographic Documentary Films.

STRUGGLING WITH THE CULTURE

Could Kartemquin survive if you changed the culture? If you took out the parts of Kartemquin that let people work long hours for less—the kitchen conversations, the chance to tag along on a film project, knowing that somebody cared about you like family—could it still work? Could you build a truly diverse new "family" at all in a nation that for centuries had segregated not just people but entire cultures? Could people really work together across the fault lines of privilege and power? Kartemquin had been a family—sometimes a dysfunctional one, but a family nonetheless. The kitchen had been the beating heart of social life, in what associates had called a clubhouse. It had mostly been a white family, composed of people who came from working-class or striving middle-class families, from anonymous suburbs and exurbs and tough corners of Midwestern cities, who were fed up with injustice and who had stubbornly imagined themselves into the role of engaged artists. Now, after years of creative reimagining, Kartemquin was a media arts center, with programs that required constant grant application processes, desks, and job descriptions. It had staff over here, and it had talent over there. It was a business. Perhaps not a viable business, but a business nonetheless.

The difference was already clear to Fenell Doremus, by the time she returned to Kartemquin in 2013 with the project *Cooked*. "Tim Horsburgh worked at the desk I had sat at, front and center. I'd sometimes resort to my former, casual demeanor around Kartemquin, and then I would realize how it's different. If you wanted to talk to Tim, you emailed him. Everybody had their lane. People would say, 'I don't feel welcome at Kartemquin anymore, I miss the days when I could hang out in the kitchen.' But they were also running a much better organized institution and turning out multiple films a year."

The shift seemed to some like moving from an artisan's workshop to a small factory. "It was like a punk record label that only signs local acts for forty years and then reaches out anywhere it can," Gleeson said. He missed what he called the "fuck the world, we're gonna do this our way" spirit of the organization he'd joined: "We had to double the size of the postproduction department, because it was the only department that can make money. Overnight we doubled the capacity of the whole thing, without really understanding the most efficient ways to do that." The building, with its aged wiring, posed its own challenges in the expansion, he recalled. The cultural shift was a big reason for him to leave.

Once workflows and work status were locked, different kinds of conflicts emerged. For instance, Zak Piper had been working, on call day and night, on Steve James's ambitious film *The Interrupters* (2011), and yet was still struggling to pay his bills. But he could not get a raise. As well, he also partially lost a battle for profit participation in *The Interrupters*. The producers supported his claim, but Nagan didn't agree. (Kotlowitz and James finally split their combined profit participation evenly with him.) He decided to move on, although he continued to work for Kartemquin as a freelancer.

Beckie Stocchetti, Horsburgh's right-hand person for outreach and education, developed programs, raised money, and led impact campaigns, but never could get Nagan to agree to give her the title of program director, or to include her in the leadership council; she was also working for subpar wages. She could not get filmmaking experience, either. She had good friends there, especially the producer Adam Singer, the editing wizard Aaron Wickenden, the director Maria Finitzo, and Horsburgh, but she felt she was treated as "cheap labor" rather than the arts administrator she aspired to be: "I wanted what Gita and Judy had. I wanted a sense of family, a purpose in the world, and I would have worked for free if I'd been given that. But it was just a company."

STRUGGLING WITH THE BUSINESS MODEL

Kartemquin wasn't a functional place for some filmmakers. Its equipment room was a mess after Morrissette was let go. Little start-up money was available. There was no fundraising staff left to help the filmmakers raise money themselves. The old building was inaccessible to disabled people and dispiriting to some. Fundraising in a racial-reckoning moment could be difficult, especially because private foundations wanted to fund BIPOC-led organizations. But could even a well-organized Kartemquin, monetizing its most valuable single asset of mentoring, really be financially stable? Fenell Doremus noted that focusing on incubating the talents of first-time filmmakers was expensive, especially because most of them used Kartemquin to launch, but then left to build their new careers: "It wasn't financially viable for them to come back."

Tim Horsburgh noted that in some ways, Kartemquin had returned to the spirit of the collective era. With its staff-wide conversations and open brainstorming about strategic planning, it was also modeling community practice and shared responsibility. This time around, though, Kartemquin was not only committed to social action but also to fueling filmmaking careers—an unproven and improbable financial model. "Kartemquin's door was always open, and that was a valuable reason for existing for many years," Horsburgh said. "But now it has to also embrace the fact that it's an institution."

Laura Gomez-Mesquita saw the structural problems. She thought that bringing in more BIPOC filmmakers also meant providing much more support for them and that Kartemquin couldn't deliver that: "We can't pay everyone who walks in the door $25,000 to do their project." Overburdened staff couldn't be asked to take on even more responsibilities, or to work overtime without pay. But she also wanted the group to think creatively. Could group insurance lower healthcare costs? Could there be babysitting swaps?

Gomez-Mesquita was optimistic: "Kartemquin is trying to grapple with decolonizing docs, with questions of ownership, no story about us without us. Who are the leaders, what do we codify as our values? And those are really interesting problems. It's a privilege to show up every day and talk about documentaries." She also saw great possibilities, because of the kind of people attracted to Kartemquin: "We are as strong as the people who come here to get their work done." But she too left.

A mid-pandemic search for sponsored and commissioned projects to pay the bills and get filmmakers experience proved difficult. As had happened before, clients didn't particularly want newbies on their projects. And one project, for Walmart—on efforts the company was making to rebuild relationships on Chicago's Black South Side—was challenging because, it seemed to Kartemquinites, of internal conflicts at Walmart. Communication breakdowns sucked time and energy out of Kartemquin, all for a work-for-hire project.

Bing Liu said that he would love to return to Kartemquin to do a project of the heart. He noted, "It's both admirable and scary that Kartemquin doesn't abide by the imperatives of capitalist culture. Where they excel is in nurturing filmmakers who tell personal stories about communities they have a relationship with." Margaret Byrne agreed: "The strength of Kartemquin and the culture is that they have built community in the city. The biggest thing I learned from Kartemquin, from Gordon especially, is how powerful and great it is to support other storytellers. It's as wonderful as being able to tell stories. How do we work collectively? Either at Kartemquin or because we're part of the same community." Byrne's second film, *Any Given Day* (2021), which follows three people who, like her, suffer from mental illness, was not produced at Kartemquin. But the film drew on the talents of people who had gotten their start there.

Steve James commented on the brutal realities of Kartemquin's business model:

> Kartemquin has been a threadbare operation. It's always been a dance. The arts organization model has been successful in many ways. It helped put Kartemquin on the map, more filmmakers seek Kartemquin out, and it's led to creating the various programs they have there, many of which serve filmmakers of color. Unfortunately they also had to staff up considerably, so even though they don't pay people enough money, they still have a largish payroll.
>
> Kartemquin used to provide things you couldn't get, like the edit room and equipment. Since 2008, I edit at home. Nowadays, when I do a project, I buy a camera. Then I donate the camera to Kartemquin. If I need to use it, they don't charge me for it. When the project is of a certain size, then that's where Kartemquin can also be of tremendous value, having the structure of payroll, equipment, edit rooms. Where Kartemquin gets more in trouble is the smaller films.
>
> I have two projects, one through Kartemquin and one through my own LLC. For the Kartemquin project, the budget is in place and the work that's

necessary is such that I'm not worried about pulling it off with Kartemquin involved. And I also feel a duty and obligation to bring work through Kartemquin. Leslie Simmer works on projects where they bill at a more market rate for her time when she works on someone else's film. On *America to Me*, we paid market rate for her services, and Kartemquin paid her about half that. But she gets insurance and a salary, too. Am I getting my money's worth? Probably not. Gordon watches the stuff I make now, but he only occasionally plays any role in the films I make since *The New Americans*.

Leslie Simmer wondered if any artistic director could fully replace Gordon Quinn, her constant interlocutor for twenty-five years. And she also didn't know if new staff understood or appreciated her own depth of production knowledge:

> What is Kartemquin now? How do we ensure that we can keep helping the filmmakers who need us most? Once I came here, I never found another place I wanted to go to. Most editors are freelancers. I'm grateful; it's provided me with community, security and continuity. I stayed through Betsy Steinberg, and Jolene, and I kept thinking it was important to have someone with institutional knowledge. I don't want corporate, period. I'm one of the income streams for Kartemquin; I could make more money freelancing. Why am I here? Because it's given me my identity. I learned how to be myself when I came here, I can authentically be myself. It's my tribe. Although that was possible for me, I know, because I'm white.

But eventually, a heartbroken Simmer left Kartemquin to set up her own business, although she planned to keep working with Kartemquin projects.

For David E. Simpson, the choice of the artistic director would be key to Kartemquin's future: "Gordon's spirit and his presence are the heart of Kartemquin. It's crucial and important that we think smartly about succession, but to be absolutely honest I don't know if the version of Kartemquin that survives Gordon will be something I want to continue to be involved in. I hope so." Simpson was concerned about the way that young people, including Hillary Bachelder and Ryan Gleeson, had left the organization during the Steinberg era, and about the organization's inability to hold on to Maggie Bowman. He was looking for someone who knew the tradition to carry on the vision that Quinn and Blumenthal had incarnated for so many years, and he couldn't see them.

Figure 31. Gordon Quinn's farewell roast, hosted by local TV news anchor Robin Robinson (far left), drew the Kartemquin community together; to Robinson's right, Steve James, Bing Liu, Gordon Quinn, Bob Hercules, Judy Hoffman, and Jenny Rohrer. Source: Kartemquin Archives.

Elspeth Revere faced the possibility that replacement might be impossible, and Kartemquin might finally close its doors: "But organizations live and die. If Kartemquin were to no longer exist, it will have left an incredible legacy, a really important archive, films that influenced other films, filmmakers who influenced other filmmakers. And Gordon's advocacy has had an impact."

Kartemquin's continuing struggle to find a way forward together was an extraordinary act of faith in democratic process at the organizational level. It unrolled in a time of polarizing turmoil, in which not just that vision but the rickety frame of an increasingly eroded democratic process was being tested to its limits. But the very nature of what the Kartemquin filmmakers and staffers were struggling about also bespoke the deep vitality of demands for justice, agency, and hope in communities everywhere that the Deweyan vision embodies, and to a commitment to a democracy responsible to society, not beholden to the bottom line.

The organization, amazingly, entered the postpandemic (or endemic) era with renewed hope. Betsy Leonard and the Kartemquin staff concluded its self-assessment, and begun planning for the future. Gordon Quinn continued to consult and advise from his half-time position, while the search continued for a diverse artistic director, after film curator Amir George took the position for a few months.

In December 2022, the organization held a roast that officially honored the work and legacy of Gordon Quinn, now eighty, as he passed the torch to the new team. Hundreds attended, and funds were raised, a statement about the confidence of leading Midwest cultural supporters and funders in the organization. Kartemquin would continue, at least for now, to be the improbable experiment in documentary for democracy that had started in 1966.[1]

11   Documentary for Democracy?

How, over six decades, has Kartemquin's guiding philosophy of a documentary practice in service to the construction of more robust publics held up?

It certainly succeeded by providing decades of Kartemquinites a reason to wrestle with never-friendly terms for independent makers with a social conscience. It evolved a distinctive style of humanist storytelling, in collaboration with participants, that shows how people cope with and strategize around often-inhumane systems and circumstances. Kartemquin filmmakers told powerfully character-driven stories about struggle and challenge, specifically avoiding the sentimental and the falsely inspirational. The heart of a Kartemquin film was experiential, but experience carefully chosen for its insights into how we invent possibility within our contexts. That throughline held over six decades, partly through consistent mentoring; through the way that like-minded people were drawn into the Kartemquin community; and by a vision explicitly rooted in Deweyan philosophy.

Kartemquin projects benefited from the existence of public policies such as public television, the copyright exception of fair use, tax exemptions, government cultural grants, and the private foundation grant and individual donations enabled by charitable tax policy. They leveraged the interest of commercial providers, whether broadcast, cable, or streaming, in prestigious productions that might win those distributors awards. They found commercial freelance work that did not violate their principles, and used it to fund their dreams. Kartemquinites both identified such opportunities and collaborated to build or support them, within a filmmaker-public.

The organization's vision was always more expansive than the resources to put it into practice. It always depended on sweat equity and love, and people offered that up, for an organization that allowed them to make media for the public good in a workplace where, by and large, they felt respected. The Kartemquin community, imagined from the start as a mini-public itself, was remarkably porous, and structure was flexible. At the same time, the Kartemquin family was also one where people often had to leave to support themselves and where the intellectual framework of democratic socialism also occurred within a culture that was largely white.

Kartemquin's challenges in the era of racial reckoning were a microcosm of the challenges faced in film and arts institutions across the United States. Any real confrontation with the racism, misogyny, and the brutal contempt of elites for working people that affects every aspect of the wider culture and film business was bound ultimately to go to the deepest structures of any institution. Confrontation with those realities now meant centering Black and brown experience, both on-screen and behind the camera. That challenge then confronted the harsh terms under which work had been accomplished at Kartemquin in the previous decades.

With Kartemquin's commitment and against the odds, Black and brown people became directors of films that were distributed, shown at festivals, and won awards. Their styles were as different as the cinema verité approach of *Unapologetic* and the forensic walkthrough of *All the Queen's Horses*. But they all shared in the storytelling goals articulated in the original vision of cinematic social inquiry.

The pandemic was also a stress test of American society's provisions for its citizens. The country failed that test on virtually every front. Among those it failed were creatives, and especially filmmakers. Any pandemic funding directed in the general vicinity of filmmakers usually routed around them; the Corporation for Public Broadcasting, for instance, which received ample relief funds, distributed it to stations, without a penny going to organizations such as the National Media Alliance and ITVS, which serve filmmakers. Jolene Pinder's ability to secure Paycheck Protection Plan funding to keep the organization afloat was a testament to her dedication and the organization's capacity.

The expanding and intensifying larger political crisis posed whole new challenges. The vision that Gordon Quinn, Jerry Temaner, and Jerry Blumenthal infused Kartemquin with at the start was an optimistic one for a better, more participatory, more just, inclusive, and resilient democracy. The Deweyan democratic philosophy depended on the ability of people oppressed by either corporate or government interests to mobilize for democratic change, through mutual understanding of a common problem. Ultimately, an engaged public is all that keeps democracies democratic, in Deweyan thinking. Kartemquin filmmakers and staffers had always shared a belief that telling powerful stories to illuminate such mutual understanding could fuel such democratic mobilization. Kartemquin's filmmakers' fate was inevitably linked to the possibility of social movements demanding more genuinely democratic government, then to the capacity of media systems to transmit those stories, and to some extent, to democratic governmental structures' ability to respond appropriately.

The racial reckoning also provided plenty of fodder for white nationalist organizing, as the Trump presidency brought home. Deep cynicism on the left and in disenfranchised communities about the capacity of democratic institutions to address injustice was joined by cynicism about democracy on the part of libertarian elites. Those elites were happy to mobilize white nationalists, evangelical Christians, and fearful white suburbanites for culture wars. In between was an increasingly disaffected working population that had already been ingrained with neoliberal disrespect for government and was plagued by social dysfunction: addiction, deaths of despair, housing instability. A decade of highly public Black and brown protest against open police brutality had led to increased resources to police and continued police murder and maiming, a horrifying statement about the capacity of government to respond to citizenry. Was democracy broken?

And yet people in and around the organization found the optimism to continue. Kartemquin had, throughout its decades, not only created films but communities of people who shared pragmatic idealism. That work would continue, whether or not Kartemquin did. The evidence for that is in the afterlives of the people who worked at Kartemquin. Alumni and alumnae often continued to stay in touch, but they also struck out and started new careers and initiatives, often in the same spirit. Altruism, a spirit of service, and compassion infused their professionalism. The legacy of Kartemquin was not only in its films but in the nurturing of professionals with a commitment to democratic engagement and discourse. A few of their stories are here.

Some stayed in the orbit of the labor movement, without abandoning filmmaking. Alphonse Blumenthal became a proud International Alliance of Theatrical Stage Employees member, carrying his values into commercial productions. (He died in 2000.) Peter Kuttner became a lifelong IATSE activist, bringing more diverse members into the union. Betsy Martens worked as a community organizer in the Logan Square neighborhood in Chicago, and as a union typesetter, and also became an environmental advocate. Maggie Bowman worked with several unions on media-industry-related issues, while also active in the documentary film environment.

Some stayed in the nonprofit sector. After working on *The Last Pullman Car*, Greg LeRoy took a job with the Midwest Center for Labor Research and in 1998 founded Good Jobs First, a nonprofit still thriving in 2023 that promotes corporate and government accountability in economic development. Vicki Cooper's career focused on workplace safety and health, and she became director of the environmental tech program at Wilbur Wright College (where Meg Gerken taught photography for thirty years), one of the community colleges offered by the city of Chicago and the only one with an environmental studies degree in Illinois. She also led the Chicagoland Green Collar Jobs initiative. Sue Davenport returned to education, and was active in the school reform movement. Jim Fetterley ended up combining his fascination with art, his social conscience, and his passion for open access to knowledge. He was an early remixer; Video Data Bank's attention gave him national recognition, commissions, and teaching posts in art schools. Fetterley eventually became the technical director at UCLA's contemporary art and culture museum, The Hammer Museum, where he addressed open-access and open-source questions, initiating the Hammer Channel to help remixers. In 2016, he convinced The Hammer to host a mini-retrospective of Kartemquin work.

Many kept their hand in filmmaking, often with Kartemquin, and some combined nonprofit work and filmmaking. Tim Horsburgh's leap into National Geographic was well-primed at Kartemquin. Editor Matt Lauterbach maintained his commitment to accessibility issues, as codirector of Chicago's biennial ReelAbilities Disability Film Festival, and producer of Beyond Blind: A Guide for the Sighted, a web resource. Susan Delson went on to work at the Museum of Modern Art in New York as a programmer in education, and as a magazine editor; she authored books, and was producer-director of an award-winning video on Japanese art. She also worked on *Far from Poland* (1984) with Jill Godmilow, and *Cause and Effect* (1989), produced by Todd Haynes and Christine Vachon. Fenell Doremus became a freelance producer, drawing upon the Kartemquin network. She joined the Kartemquin board in 2017, becoming one of its most hard-working members. Sharon Karp became a freelance film editor, pioneering nonlinear editing. She started a video production and postproduction company, working on many socially relevant films, and in 2014 directed a documentary about her own family's flight from the Nazis, *A Song for You*. She consulted with Quinn on the production. Justine Nagan left *POV* in 2020, relocating for family reasons to San Francisco, where she joined the production house Actual Films. Leslie Simmer planned her departure from Kartemquin knowing she would continue to edit its films. Ex-Kartemquinites such as Zak Piper, Ryan Gleeson, and Rubin Daniels Jr. continued to pop into projects. Editor Liz Kaar became a sought-after editor in Los Angeles, and then returned to her home base in Chicago. Ashley O'Shay, Ingrid Roettgen, and other more recent Kartemquinites circulated in the Chicago film production scene.

Morgan Elise Johnson, who had produced *Unapologetic*, went on to cofound The Triibe, a burgeoning web-based journalism and documentary platform dedicated to "reshaping the narrative of Black Chicago and giving ownership back to the people." Marcy McCall went to UCLA to earn her MFA, then entered a brutally misogynist Hollywood decades before the #MeToo movement would give that abuse a name. She gravitated to independent production houses like Orion Pictures, and to independent artists like George Romero. "There were things I couldn't stand, because

Kartemquin had given me a compass," she said. "It was about being ethical, especially with the story and subject matter." When she left Hollywood to focus on her family, she organized around disability rights in education, originally because of her own child. She recalled, "It was almost like a Kartemquin movie. I drew on the example of organizing and fighting the power in Kartemquin films. If I had not had that example, I wouldn't have known about that or thought of myself as having that role." She particularly remembered learning from Jenny Rohrer.

Judy Hoffman, a path-breaking IATSE member, after a busy career working with nonprofits, community organizations, and producing documentaries and TV programs, became a professor of practice at the University of Chicago. Her most memorable work, she believes, was with 'Namgis people of the Kwakwaka'wakw nation, in British Columbia, a contact she got through Chuck Olin, for whom Kartemquinites had often crewed. Throughout the 1980s, she helped the Native group learn video techniques to record their own culture and stories for themselves.

Jenny Rohrer settled for years in Washington, DC, where she leveraged Kartemquin connections to work with labor unions for their film needs. (In DC, our families shared meals and outings, and I sometimes joined her on labor work.) She later moved to Missoula, Montana, and thanks to Quinn, connected with Gita Saedi Kiely, who had moved there with her husband. Rohrer and Kiely became filmmaking partners, and Rohrer continued to freelance producing work for nonprofit organizations nationally, including unions, and local arts organizations. She became a leader, with Kiely, in developing the Big Sky Documentary Film Festival. Eventually, Gita Saedi Kiely took a job with Internews' FilmAid program. We serve together on the ITVS board of directors. Kartemquin was formative, she said, in shaping the rest of her career, both in terms of craft and networks: "It's the first place I learned that what you're doing has everything to do with making the world a better place and not very much to do with you getting ahead. But the work I did at Kartemquin and with Steve James on other projects actually made my career. I feel very lucky. I'm always trying to build or find other communities that make me feel the way I did at Kartemquin."

Richard Schmiechen moved to New York and then Los Angeles. His *The Times of Harvey Milk* (1984), the story of San Francisco's first gay mayor, tragically assassinated, won an Oscar. He continued to produce award-winning documentaries, including, with his partner David Haugland, *Changing Our Minds: The Story of Evelyn Hooker* (1992), about the scientist whose pioneering research showed that homosexuality was not an illness. An LGBT+ rights leader, he died in 1993, at the height of the AIDS epidemic.

For Ed Scott, Kartemquin was a bridge to Community Film Workshop, where he began to teach and found a passion for it. He also worked as a VISTA volunteer. He met Denise Zaccardi through Kartemquin, and worked with Community TV Network, including with Judy Hoffman. He taught at Antioch College, Columbia College, Street Level Youth Media in Chicago, and American University in Washington, DC, and worked as a freelancer news producer. He eventually worked in video at the United Nations.

As the lives of Kartemquin alumni showed, the work of Kartemquin has not just been filmmaking, and not just involved contributing to the media spaces and policies that make it possible. It has also, and crucially, been the work of building grounded hope among media makers that they could contribute to more vital communities and a stronger democracy.

Acknowledgments

I owe a debt to research assistants, including Mariana Sanchez Santos, Atika Alkhallouf, Kim Anastácio, and Emily O'Connell, for extensive literature reviews and compilation of reviews. Marissa Woods, once a graduate assistant and afterward a colleague, has been invaluable at many stages, and graciously helped me in the complex process of preparing the manuscript for submission. I also am grateful to American University for sabbatical time to work on this project. I thank Andy Uhrich at Washington University of St. Louis for extraordinary care in giving me access to Kartemquin's archives there, even though for him it meant working through still-uncatalogued boxes. My editor at University of California Press, Raina Polivka, was supportive, thoughtful, and critical, always in service of both reader and writer. My readers, Patricia R. Zimmermann, Angela Aguayo, Richard Herskowitz, Steve Schwartzman, and Larry Sapadin, among others, were helpfully critical; their insights all strengthened my work. Kartemquinites were exceptionally generous with their time. I owe a special debt to Elise Schierbeek, who was my liaison for archival material and personal contact information for years, and who helped me find the pictures for this book. None of this would have happened without Gordon Quinn's endless and endlessly patient insights, connections, and resources. He let me talk to him over three years, read several versions of the manuscript, and scrupulously avoided telling me what interpretations he disagreed with. All the interviewees saw their quotes and surrounding material in advance, in order to offer a chance to correct information, which they all kindly did. No relevant factual information had to be sacrificed in the process.

I was able to do this because of the terms of my employment at American University, where research makes up 40 percent of my time, sabbaticals happen every seven years, and tenure permits intellectual risk. I marvel at my luck, and at the courage of Sanford Ungar, the dean who went out of his way in 1988 to hire me, in whose debt I remain forever. These terms of work, over decades in which they got ever rarer even within academia, enabled this and many other cultural projects (some with Kartemquin) for a more just society. Thanks to secure employment, I could also afford a project with no significant revenue prospects and thousands of dollars of out-of-pocket costs, including indexing fees, travel to archives, and purchase of book copies for all interviewees.

I was supported in many collaborations discussed in this book, although not this particular project, by private foundations. They include the Rockefeller, Ford, MacArthur, Annie E. Casey, and Sloan and Mellon Foundations. I am unendingly grateful for the trust those program officers demonstrated in my work.

My family, anchored by my partner, Steve Schwartzman, has been an enduring and ever-evolving place of joy, respect, and mutual recognition. I am honored to know them all, and I love them very much.

Appendix: Interviews

For my interview subjects, I of course selected people who had made films with Kartemquin. I also depended on longtime leaders such as Gordon Quinn, Justine Nagan, and Tim Horsburgh to suggest names of staffers who might not appear on a credits list. Finally, I also depended on snowball sampling—asking people I interviewed who else was important to talk with. I did not ask for Institutional Review Board permission, since this was not a replicable study. However, as I have done on some IRB-approved studies where interviewees may talk about issues that affect their reputations, I briefed interviewees before proceeding on the project; I asked their permission to record only for my own note-taking; and I promised to delete the interviews once the manuscript was submitted, which I did. I also promised to show the interviewees all their quotes in the manuscript before final drafting, which I also did. I incorporated their feedback, none of which violated factual accuracy. I took these precautions in order to assure the interviewees that they were free to be frank, given that they would be talking about their colleagues, friends, and mentors, in a remarkably small world where reputation is crucial to getting work.

With all interviewees, I asked them about their family backgrounds, how they first heard of Kartemquin, how they got involved in the organization, what their work experience was, and what they had done since. Further questions depended on the person's experience. Interviews were conducted on the telephone or via Zoom on the following dates with the following people:

APPENDIX

Yvonne Afable: October 31, 2023
Maggie Bowman: July 13, 2021
Margaret Caples: April 12, 2021
Sara Chapman: August 24, 2021
Rubin Daniels Jr.: June 22, 2021
Suzanne Davenport: October 18, 2021
Fenell Doremus: May 6, 2021
Carolyn Faber: July 13, 2021
Jim Fetterley: July 12, 2021
Maria Finitzo: May 4, 2021
Peter Gilbert: May 11 and 17, 2022
Ryan Gleeson: June 11, 2021
Laura Gomez-Mesquita: July 13, 2021
Judy Hoffman: June 24, 2021
Tim Horsburgh: April 23, 2021
Steve James: June 16, 2021
Gita Saedi Kiely: June 17, 2021
Peter Kuttner: May 11, 2021
Karen Larson: December 9, 2022
Greg LeRoy: December 13, 2022
Brad Lichtenstein: February 4, 2022
Bing Liu: August 26, 2021
Marcy McCall: June 16, 2021
Nancy Meyer: April 19, 2022
Jim Morrissette: December 13, 2022
Justine Nagan: August 26, 2021
Ashley O'Shay: September 28, 2021
Jolene Pinder: August 4, 2022
Zak Piper: July 14, 2021
Kelly Richmond Pope: September 10, 2021
Gordon Quinn: Repeated interviews throughout 2020–2023
Anuradha Rana: August 3, 2022
Sergio Rapu: September 10, 2021
Elspeth Revere: June 7, 2021
Ingrid Roettgen: June 25, 2021
Jenny Rohrer: April 27, 2021
Joanna Rudnick: October 4, 2021
Dinesh Das Sabu: July 13, 2021
Ed Scott: June 30, 2021
Leslie Simmer: June 9, 2021

David E. Simpson: June 1, 2021
Adam Singer: July 2, 2021
Betsy Steinberg: November 1, 2023
Beckie Stocchetti: August 3, 2022
Marc Weiss: August 24, 2021

Notes

CHAPTER 1. KARTEMQUIN FILMS: A SHARED STORY

1. I have consolidated and minimized endnotes, in order to facilitate reading. Furthermore, the endnotes contain only partial references for works listed in Further Reading at the end of the book. In developing the brief overview of documentary's recent history, I drew on my own half-century of academic and journalistic research, and on public broadcasting, media policy, copyright policy, the history of documentary, and the documentary genre generally. Some of it has been published in book form, more in academic journals, and the Center for Media & Social Impact as well as American University's open-access institutional repository houses many of my (often coauthored) reports. A synthetic overview is available in *Documentary Film: A Very Short Introduction*. As I note in that book, all documentary scholars owe a huge conceptual debt to Erik Barnouw, whose book *Documentary* continues to be essential. If you want to delve into more recent scholarship, several anthologies are very helpful: Christie Milliken and Steve F. Anderson's *Reclaiming Popular Documentary*, Brian Winston's *The Documentary Film Book*, Jonathan Kahana's *The Documentary Film Reader*, and Joshua Glick's and my *Oxford Handbook of American Documentary Film*.

On business trends in documentary, historical and current, I depended on reporting in trade outlets such as *Deadline* and *Indiewire*, as well as research firms such as Peter Hamilton's Documentary Business, Ampere Analysis, Nash

Information Services, and ComScore. As well, I benefited from independent polling services such as by Gallup and Pew for trends, and of course on works mentioned in Further Reading.

The Documentary Accountability Working Group's guidance on values to inform documentary filmmaking with vulnerable participants resides at docaccountability.org.

Books referenced in this chapter and not in Further Reading include Michael Chanan, *The Politics of Documentary* (London: British Film Institute, 2007), and Jack C. Ellis and Betsy A. McLane, *A New History of Documentary Film* (New York: Continuum, 2005).

2. *In These Times* continues to publish, although now as a website and a monthly magazine, and it remains true to the democratic socialism of its founder, James Weinstein, and as a major national voice on labor issues. *In These Times*'s archive is on its site, and Weinstein's inaugural essay is available in the August-September 2023 issue, p. 48. The books of historians James Weinstein and Martin Sklar (another *In These Times* editor and mentor when I was there), as well as of other writers such as political analyst John Judis (yet another *In These Times* editor and mentor), and of academic historians such as Larry Ceplair, Leon Litwack, Eric Foner, and Roy Rosensweig (all writers for *In These Times* at some point), are all in the tradition of critical American history and historiography. The rigorous research of these and other historians about the history of the American left, labor movements, and social movements informed the choices of *In These Times* editors, including me, in the newspaper's coverage. It informed my own espousal of the kind of democratic socialism that has always been expressed in the left wing of the Democratic Party and with independents such as Bernie Sanders. I describe the challenges of being cultural editor of a left-wing newspaper in my collected essays, *The Daily Planet: A Critic on the Capitalist Culture Beat*.

3. The role of the University of Chicago and Robert Maynard Hutchins is the topic of much good scholarship on education, but a place to put it in context is Christopher Lucas, *Crisis in the Academy*.

CHAPTER 2. HOW KARTEMQUIN THINKS

1. This section is informed by reading in three general areas. Within documentary studies, among the works I turned to were those of Angela Aguayo, Patricia Zimmermann, B. J. Bullert, Chris Holmlund, Cynthia Fuchs, Lorna Roth, and Chris Robé, although each very different from the others. Media industry scholars, particularly on television, such as Joshua Glick, Anna McCarthy, Thomas Doherty, Tom Mascaro, Michael Curtin, Amanda Lotz, Kevin Sanson, and Ramon Lobato, have informed my understanding throughout this book. Although his body of work has focused on Australia, the example of Stuart Cun-

ningham's media industries work has been important in my understanding of how to chart Bourdieuian power flows.

Within cultural studies and to track the debates of cultural Marxism, the names and titles mentioned in this chapter can guide you to some of the most important resources in shaping this work's questions. Extremely helpful to me has been Robert Westbrook's *John Dewey and American Democracy*, a deeply insightful intellectual biography, with meticulous summaries of Dewey's work that are much more readable than Dewey himself. One of Dewey's great inheritors, in the communication field, was James Carey, an academic mentor of mine and whose entire body of work carries Dewey's imprint. To begin exploring the work of thinkers discussed here, the Routledge Critical Thinkers series can provide helpful introductions. The works of cultural studies eminences Cary Nelson and Lawrence Grossberg, including their coedited *Marxism and the Interpretation of Culture*, are reliably useful. James Baldwin's Cambridge speech is archived, among other places, at the American Archive of Public Broadcasting, at https://americanarchive.org/catalog/cpb-aacip_151-sn00z71m54.

2. For an understanding of evolution of the term cinema verité, Geoffrey Newell-Smith's *Making Waves: New Cinemas of the 1960s* (at 82–96) is masterful in putting this movement and other simultaneous movements in context. Peter Wintonick's slyly ironic documentary film *Cinéma Vérité: Defining the Moment* (1999), available from the National Film Board of Canada's website, is a delightful introduction not only to the diversity of styles within the genre but to the people who imagined them into existence. There is also a concise overview in my *Documentary Film: A Very Short Introduction*, drawn from many sources. The manifestos referenced, including Julio García Espinosa's "For an Imperfect Cinema" and Fernando Solanas's and Octavio Getina's "Toward a Third Cinema," can be found in Scott MacKenzie's fascinating anthology, *Film Manifestos and Global Cinema Cultures: A Critical Anthology*. Roy Armes's venerable *Third World Film Making and the West* remains essential for understanding the "new cinema" movements, and Robert Stam and Ella Shohat's *Unthinking Eurocentrism* can deepen that understanding. For insight into the film theories of the era, Robert Stam and Toby Miller's *Film and Theory: An Anthology* (Malden: Blackwell, 2000) is a rich resource.

There is a wealth of good literature on the network era of TV, but of particular use to me were Erik Barnouw's *Tube of Plenty* (his discussion of the "great wasteland" speech is wonderful), the cultural histories of Anna McCarthy, Thomas Doherty's *Cold War, Cool Medium*, Tom Mascaro's *Into the Fray: How NBC's Washington Documentary Unit Reinvented the News* (Washington, DC: Potomac Books, 2012), and Joshua Glick's *Los Angeles Documentary and the Production of Public History, 1958–1977*. Other historians whose work gave me a wider context include Susan Douglas, Robert McChesney, Robert Horwitz, Richard John, and Paul Starr.

3. I was able to read Gordon Quinn's thesis thanks to a copy he loaned me. Quinn and Temaner's essay is cited in Further Reading. For an understanding of Chicago's history, I benefited from Isabel Wilkerson's masterful *The Warmth of Other Suns* on the Great Migration. Adam Cohen and Elizabeth Taylor's *American Pharaoh* provided me with a detailed map of Mayor Daley's political structuring of Chicago, and his response to social movements of the 1960s and 1970s. The brochure from which I took Scharres's remarks was provided as a photocopy by Kartemquin, and has been sent to Washington University of St. Louis archives for cataloguing.

CHAPTER 3. CINEMATIC SOCIAL INQUIRY, 1962-1970

1. I drew on both highly specific and general resources for this chapter, as well as on interviews (see Further Reading for full references). I quoted from John Dewey's *Art as Experience* (at 70). On Chicago Black parents' organizing for better school options, Dionne Danns's graduate thesis, "Something Better for Our Children: Black Organizing in the Chicago Public Schools, 1963-1971," recovers important history. Eddie Rice Cole's *The Campus Color Line: College Presidents and the 1960s Struggle for Black Freedom* puts the University of Chicago unrest in context. On the Chicago politics of the era, including around the convention, resources include Adam Cohen and Elizabeth Taylor's *American Pharoah* and Jakobi Williams's *From the Bullet to the Ballot*. For polarization on the American left within the context of American Cold War repression, sociologist Todd Gitlin's *The Sixties* remains essential reading. (Gitlin himself was a cofounder of Students for a Democratic Society.) Bill Nichols, a leading scholar of documentary, wrote his first book (and graduate thesis) on Newsreel (*Newsreel: Documentary Filmmaking on the American Left* [New York: Arno Press, 1980]), and it includes discussion of radical film collectives more generally. Amid the wealth of material on FBI suppression of left protest, Ward Churchill and Jim Vander Wall's collection of documents, *The COINTELPRO Papers*, is appropriately jaw-dropping; David Cunningham's *There's Something Happening Here: The New Left, the Klan, and FBI Counterintelligence* (Berkeley: University of California Press, 2004) provides context. On the history of La Leche, Jule DeJager Ward's book in conjunction with the league, *The La Leche League*, provides background.

For context about the development of collaborative / participatory filmmaking, among the many resources are the websites of Doc Society and Center for Media & Social Impact, and among monographs, Patricia Zimmermann and Helen De Michiel's *Open Space New Media Documentary*, Katerina Cizek and William Uricchio's *Collective Wisdom*, and the entire body of work of Caty Borum (Chattoo). To understand the ferment in the National Film Board of Canada at the time, Zoë Druick's *Projecting Canada* and Thomas Waugh et al.'s edited anthology *Challenge for Change* make great reading.

Jerry Blumenthal's thesis can be found at the Kartemquin archives at Washington University of St. Louis. Morgan Elise Johnson's short *Kartemquin's First Camera* is available at https://www.youtube.com/watch?v = x75ZByoCDmA.

CHAPTER 4. FEMINIST VOICES AND REVOLUTIONARY CINEMA, 1970–1978

1. For background on the media and movements of the era, Erik Barnouw's *Tube of Plenty*, Peter Biskind's *Easy Riders, Raging Bulls*, Roy Armes's *Third World Film Making and the West*, Alan Rosenthal's *The Documentary Conscience* (in which the interview with Jerry Blumenthal and Jenny Rohrer appears), Angela Aguayo's *Documentary Resistance*, Ruby Rich's *Chick Flicks*, and Chris Robé's *Breaking the Spell* were all useful in this chapter. Specifically for video and for community television movements, Deirdre Boyle's *Subject to Change*, Kevin Howley's *Understanding Community Media*, and DeeDee Halleck's memoir-by-document anthology, *Hand-Held Visions*, were among the resources I drew on. To understand Jean Rouch's body of work and perspective, which was so important to Judy Hoffman, Steven Feld's collection of Rouch's writing, *Ciné-Ethnography: Jean Rouch*, is excellent. The ateliersvaran.com website continues to serve grassroots storytellers worldwide.

For background on the era and its social movements, among the many sources are, for second-wave feminism, Sara Evans's *Personal Politics*; Benjamin Kline's synoptic overview of the growth of the US environmental movement, *First along the River*; Eric Marcus's *Making Gay History*; Jennifer Nelson's history of feminist health movements, *More Than Medicine*; and of course Todd Gitlin's *The Sixties*. Christina Pappas's article on the CWLU provides context within second-wave feminism. For labor issues, the entire body of Staughton and Alice Lynd's work was important here, both for their knowledge and their role in Chicago labor history. Robert Cherny, William Issel, and Kieran Walsh Taylor's *American Labor and the Cold War: Grassroots Politics and Postwar Political Culture* provided good context. Jo Freeman's "Tyranny of Structurelessness" circulated widely after her delivery of the first iteration of the work in a 1970 speech; its evolution and a text is available at https://www.jofreeman.com/joreen/tyranny.htm, and it was republished many times since. Julia LeSage's interview with Kartemquin is at "Filming for the City: An Interview with the Kartemquin Collective," *Cinéaste* 7, no. 1 (1975): 26–30.

The Bard conference was reported in Chuck Kleinhans, Ellen Seiter, and Peter Steven's "Alternative Cinema Conference: Struggling for Unity," *Jump / Cut: A Review of Contemporary Media* 21 (November 1979): 35–37. My profile of

Julia Reichert, containing her recollections of *Union Maids*, is at "Julia Reichert and the Work of Telling Working-Class Stories," *Film Quarterly* 73, no. 2 (2019): 9–22, https://doi.org/10.1525/fq.2019.73.2.9.

Bill Nichols's analysis of Newsreel is at *Newsreel: Documentary Filmmaking on the American Left* (New York: Arno Press, 1980). Ron Howrigon's "A Brief History of Healthcare and Insurance in America," *Journal of Medical Practice Management* 34, no. 3 (2018): 139–41, was helpful in locating the role of insurance in healthcare at the time.

Books on labor referenced in this chapter include: Richard Owen Boyer and Herbert M. Morais, *Labor's Untold Story* (New York: Cameron Associates, 1955); Jeremy Brecher, *Strike!* (San Francisco: Straight Arrow Books, 1972); and Studs Terkel, *Working: People Talk about What They Do All Day and How They Feel about What They Do* (New York: Pantheon Books, 1974).

CHAPTER 5. CONFRONTING NEOLIBERALISM WITH WORKERS' AND WOMEN'S STORIES, 1978–1985

1. Regarding sourcing for public broadcasting issues: The relationship between independent filmmakers and public broadcasting has been a beat of mine as a journalist since 1978, when Gordon Quinn and other filmmakers in the area who were building a pressure campaign on CPB visited me at *In These Times* to make the case for covering the campaign. I strongly believed that public broadcasting was an important site of public knowledge and action, and saw the story as valuable for our readers. My coverage of these issues appeared regularly in *The Independent*, a publication of the now-defunct Association of Independent Video and Filmmakers and *In These Times*, and has been published in both journalistic and academic venues, including several chapters in my *The Daily Planet: A Critic on the Capitalist Culture Beat*. Much of the knowledge here and elsewhere in the book on this topic comes from that research, and some of it is in Further Reading. Greg Grandin's *Empire's Workshop* (in Further Reading) is a good place to turn to for, among other things, the Reagan administration's struggle to control content on public broadcasting at the time; this is also discussed in my chapter, "U. S. Public Broadcasting: A Bulwark against Disinformation?" in Lance Bennett and Stephen Livingston's *The Disinformation Age: Politics, Technology, and Disruptive Communication in the United States* (New York: Cambridge University Press, 2021), 213–37.

The geographer David Harvey's work overall provides both theory and context for the globalization and deindustrialization process, including his *The Enigma of Capital and the Crises of Capitalism*. For situated discussions of deindustrialization and recession at the time, Steven Dandaneau's *A Town Abandoned: Flint, Michigan, Confronts Deindustrialization* and David Bensman and

Roberta Lynch's *Rusted Dreams: Hard Times in a Steel Community* are useful as well. Doug Rossinow's *The Reagan Era: A History of the 1980s* provides concise political context.

I quote reviews from Staughton Lynd's "The Last Pullman Car," *Journal of American History* 73, no. 3 (1986): 841–42; and Bernard Beck's "Kartemquin Films: 'The Last Pullman Car, 1984,'" *Contemporary Sociology* 15, no. 2 (1986): 212. Judy Branfman's "Eyes on Labor: Documentaries on Work in the Neoliberal Era," *UCLA: Institute for Research on Labor and Employment Research and Policy Brief,* No. 20 (2015), provides a succinct overview.

Tom Zaniello's work, including *Working Stiffs: Union Maids, Reds, and Riffraff: An Expanded Guide to Films about Labor* (Ithaca, NY: Cornell University Press, 2018) and *The Cinema of Globalization: A Guide to Films about the New Economic Order* (Ithaca, NY: Cornell University Press, 2007), provides access to documentary and fiction work touching on labor issues.

CHAPTER 6. KARTEMQUIN IN THE FILMMAKER PUBLIC:
MAKING NOT JUST MEDIA BUT THE MEDIA LANDSCAPE

1. I have drawn extensively on my own involvement in the movements I describe here, and noted where my own involvement overlaps with Kartemquin's. In addition to notes in the preceding chapter on public broadcasting, data for diversity on public broadcasting can be seen at Caty Borum Chattoo, Patricia Aufderheide, Kenneth Merrill, and Modupeola Oyebolu, "Diversity on U. S. Public and Commercial TV in Authorial and Executive-Produced Social-Issue Documentaries," *Journal of Broadcasting & Electronic Media* 62, no. 3 (2018): 495–513. Articles of mine on public access television and on public TV are anthologized in *The Daily Planet: A Critic on the Capitalist Culture Beat;* some of these present the arguments that Sally Jo Fifer found helpful in framing her understanding of the role of ITVS. The anthology also includes research on the public importance of public access channels that I originally filed as an affidavit in a Supreme Court case, which repealed a section of the Cable Act of 1990 that threatened the existence of access cable. My own research on the public value of public access has continued, and I recently published work on the continuing vitality of public access: Antoine Haywood, Patricia Aufderheide, and Mariana Sanchez Santos, "Community Media in a Pandemic: Facilitating Local Communication, Collective Resilience and Transitions to Virtual Public Life in the U. S.," *Javnost* 28, no. 3 (2021): 256–72. The story of documentary filmmakers and fair use is told in my and Peter Jaszi's *Reclaiming Fair Use: How to Put Balance Back in Copyright.* The second edition details the profound changes in documentary filmmaking because of employment of fair use.

For the DMCA waiver hearings at the Copyright Tribunal, there is both a transcript and an audio recording:
https://www.copyright.gov/1201/hearings/2009/*transcripts*/1201-5-7-09.txt and
https://www.copyright.gov/1201/hearings/2009/*transcripts*/5709am1.mp3.

Archival materials were shared with me by Elise Schierbeek, then archivist at Kartemquin, before the materials were transferred to Washington University at St. Louis, where they now reside. When I consulted work there, they were still in temporary storage, awaiting definitive indexing.

CHAPTER 7. FILMMAKERS BECOME ARTISTS, ART BECOMES EXPERIENCE, AND *HOOP DREAMS* CHANGES EVERYTHING, 1985–1995

1. For the neoliberal trends in communications policy leading to the 1996 Telecommunications Act, consult my *Communications Policy and the Public Interest: The Telecommunications Act of 1996*. For a flavor of the "political correctness" controversies of the time, there is my 1992 anthology of contemporary writing on the topic, *Beyond PC: Toward a Politics of Understanding*.

The quotes from John Dewey's *Art as Experience* (New York: Minton, Balch, 1934) are from pp. 110 and 274. They are also quoted in Robert Westbrook's *John Dewey and American Democracy*, 290, 402; I used Westbrook's analysis of this book in my own summary.

The quotes from Barry Dornfeld's *Producing Public Television, Producing Public Culture* (Princeton, NJ: Princeton University Press) are both from p. 32.

Denis Mueller's 2007 PhD thesis, "John Dewey and Documentary Narrative," at Bowling Green State University, is available from ProQuest Dissertations. bell hooks's article was published as "Dreams of Conquest," *Sight and Sound* 5, no. 24 (April 1995): 22–23. The controversies at the School of the Art Institute of Chicago were widely covered not only by the Chicago newspapers but by others, including the *New York Times*. Juchuan Wang's "The American Flag as Art and Controversy: A Case Study of the 1989 Chicago 'Flag-on-the-Floor' Controversy" (PhD diss., Texas A&M University, 2001), provides background on the controversies.

Carol Becker's books include *The Subversive Imagination: Artists, Society, and Social* (New York: Routledge, 1994) and *Zones of Contention: Essays on Art, Institutions, Gender, and Anxiety* (Albany: State University of New York Press, 1996). Jill Godmilow's manifesto is *Kill the Documentary: A Letter to Filmmakers, Students, and Scholars* (New York: Columbia University Press, 2022).

John Edgar Wideman's essay, "*Hoop Dreams:* Serious Game," originally appearing on the Extras of the Blu-Ray version of *Hoop Dreams*, is now available at the Criterion website at https://www.criterion.com/current/posts/366-hoop-dreams-serious-game.

CHAPTER 8. MAKING BROADCAST AND CABLE STORIES WITH INTEGRITY, 1995–2008

1. In terms of tracking technological and industry changes, I have depended here as elsewhere on decades of teaching communication courses, using texts by, among others, Joseph Turow and Richard Maxwell. As well, I relied on my decades of reporting on communication policy, including the work that resulted in my *Communications Policy and the Public Interest*. On changes in private foundation funding, during which time I was a contract employee for Council on Foundations and a consultant to various projects, some information was generated by the organizations themselves. The Benton Foundation, which Larry Kirkman (who eventually was my dean at American University) headed for a generation, published *Making Television Matter,* and the Council on Foundations published *Why Fund Media,* available on the fundfilm.org website. In terms of changing landscape for documentary, my report to the Ford Foundation, *In the Battle for Reality,* is accessible at the Center for Media & Social Impact website. I quote from Alicia Kemmit's "Documentary Stories for Change: Viewing and Producing Immigrant Narratives as Social Documents," *Velvet Light Trap* 60, no. 1 (September 2007): 25–36. On Agent Orange, the Congressional Research Service produced a comprehensive 2014 report, *Veterans Exposed to Agent Orange: Legislative History, Litigation, and Current Issues*, available at https://sgp.fas.org/crs/misc/R43790.pdf. Ariff Moolla's review of *In the Family*, which I quote, is available at *Journal of Bioethical Inquiry* 8, no. 3 (June 2011): 303–4. Kathleen Fairweather's interview with Steve James is available on the documentary.org website. The breakdown of fair uses in *Refrigerator Mothers* is available at cmsimpact.org/resource/2553. I quote as well from Dorothy Hodgson's film review "Milking the Rhino: The Promise of Community-Based Conservation in Africa by David E. Simpson," *American Anthropologist* 113, no. 2 (May 2011): 352. Bruno Bettelheim's book is *The Empty Fortress: Infantile Autism and the Birth of the Self* (New York: Free Press, 1967).

CHAPTER 9. BECOMING A MEDIA ARTS ORGANIZATION, 2008–2022

1. *The Homestretch*'s website is http://www.homestretchdoc.com/.
The study on the response of professionals to *The Homestretch* is Caty Borum Chattoo and Casey Freeman Howe, *Connecting Audiences with OVEE, an Online*

Screening Platform: An Assessment of the Homestretch PBS Documentary (Washington, DC: School of Communication Center for Media & Social Impact, American University, Fall 2016).

Joshua Glick's "Platform Politics: Netflix, the Media Industries, and the Value of Reality," *World Records Journal* 5, no. 1 (June 2021), is accessible at the worldrecordsjournal.org website.

Gordon Quinn's entire speech is contained in Kartemquin's gala book, *Kartemquin Films: Democracy through Documentary*, available at Kartemquin Films.

CHAPTER 10. CRISIS TO CRISIS

1. On the economic context of the 2008 financial crash, Bethany McLean and Joe Nocera's "All the Devils Are Here: The Hidden History of the Financial Crisis," *Economic Affairs* 32, no. 1 (2012): 85–86, is a great place to start, and Adam Tooze's *Crashed: How a Decade of Financial Crises Changed the World* (New York: Penguin Random House, 2018), gives global context.

Steve James's interview with Jason Gorber is at "The POV Interview: Steve James on 'City So Real'," *POV*, June 4, 2020; the *Cineaste* interview with James is at Cobe Williams, Dennis West, and Joan M. West, "Interrupting Violence: An Interview with Steve James and Cobe Williams," *Cinéaste* 36, no. 4 (2011): 20–25.

Alex Kotlowitz's *There Are No Children Here: The Story of Two Boys Growing Up in the Other America* (New York: Doubleday, 1991) is an example of his body of work on the realities of the lives of the working poor in urban America. His "Blocking the Transmission of Violence," *New York Times*, May 4, 2008, https://www.nytimes.com/2008/05/04/magazine/04health-t.html, was the basis for *The Interrupters*.

Further Reading

DOCUMENTARY FILMMAKING

Aguayo, Angela J. *Documentary Resistance: Social Change and Participatory Media.* New York: Oxford University Press, 2019.
Armes, Roy. *Third World Film Making and the West.* Berkeley: University of California Press, 1987.
Barnouw, Erik. *Documentary: A History of the Non-Fiction Film.* 2nd rev. ed. New York: Oxford University Press, 1993.
Borum Chattoo, Caty. *Story Movements: How Documentaries Empower People and Inspire Social Change.* New York: Oxford University Press, 2020.
Boyle, Deirdre. *Subject to Change: Guerrilla Television Revisited.* New York: Oxford University Press, 1997.
Bullert, B. J. *Public Television: Politics and the Battle over Documentary Film.* New Brunswick, NJ: Rutgers University Press, 1997.
Cizek, Kat, and William Uricchio. *Collective Wisdom: Co-Creating Media for Equity and Justice.* Cambridge, MA: MIT Press, 2022.
Druick, Zoë. *Projecting Canada Government Policy and Documentary Film at the National Film Board of Canada.* Arts Insights. Montreal: McGill-Queen's University Press, 2007.
Glick, Joshua. *Los Angeles Documentary and the Production of Public History, 1958-1977.* Oakland: University of California Press, 2018.

Glick, Joshua, and Patricia Aufderheide. *The Oxford Handbook of American Documentary Film.* New York: Oxford University Press, forthcoming.

Halleck, DeeDee. *Hand-Held Visions: The Impossible Possibilities of Community Media.* 1st ed. New York: Fordham University Press, 2002.

Howley, Kevin. *Understanding Community Media.* Los Angeles: Sage, 2010.

Kahana, Jonathan. *The Documentary Film Reader: History, Theory, Criticism.* Oxford: Oxford University Press, 2016.

MacKenzie, Scott. *Film Manifestos and Global Cinema Cultures: A Critical Anthology.* Berkeley: University of California Press, 2014.

Milliken, Christie, and Steve F. Anderson. *Reclaiming Popular Documentary.* Bloomington: Indiana University Press, 2021.

Mueller, Denis. "John Dewey and Documentary Narrative." PhD diss., Bowling Green State University, ProQuest Dissertations, 2007.

Newell-Smith, Geoffrey. *Making Waves: New Cinemas of the 1960s.* London: Bloomsbury Academic, 2013.

Quinn, Gordon, and Gerald Temaner. "Cinematic Social Inquiry." In *Principles of Visual Anthropology*, edited by Paul Hockings, 53–64. The Hague, Neth.: Mouton, 1974.

Rich, B. Ruby. *Chick Flicks: Theories and Memories of the Feminist Film Movement.* Durham, NC: Duke University Press, 1998.

Robé, Chris. *Breaking the Spell: A History of Anarchist Filmmakers, Videotape Guerrillas, and Digital Ninjas.* Oakland: PM Press, 2017.

———. *Left of Hollywood: Cinema, Modernism, and the Emergence of U.S. Radical Film Culture.* Austin: University of Texas Press, 2010.

Rosenthal, Alan. *The Documentary Conscience: A Casebook in Film Making.* Berkeley: University of California Press, 1980.

———. *New Challenges for Documentary.* Berkeley: University of California Press, 1988.

Rouch, Jean, and Steven Feld. *Ciné-Ethnography.* Minneapolis: University of Minnesota Press, 2003.

Shohat, Ella, and Robert Stam. *Unthinking Eurocentrism: Multiculturalism and the Media.* Sightlines. London: Routledge, 1994.

Waugh, Thomas, Ezra Winton, and Michael Brendan Baker. *Challenge for Change: Activist Documentary at the National Film Board of Canada.* Montréal: McGill-Queen's University Press, 2010.

Winston, Brian. *Claiming the Real: The Griersonian Documentary and Its Legitimations.* London: British Film Institute, 1995.

———. *The Documentary Film Book.* Houndmills, UK: Palgrave Macmillan on behalf of the British Film Institute, 2013.

Zimmermann, Patricia Rodden. *Documentary across Platforms: Reverse Engineering Media, Place, and Politics.* Bloomington: Indiana University Press, 2019.

———. *States of Emergency: Documentaries, Wars, Democracies*. Visible Evidence. Minneapolis: University of Minnesota Press, 2000.

———, and Helen De Michiel. *Open Space New Media Documentary: A Toolkit for Theory and Practice*. New York: Routledge, 2018.

MEDIA INDUSTRIES

Barnouw, Erik. *The Sponsor: Notes on Modern Potentates*. Classics in Communication and Mass Culture Series. New Brunswick, NJ: Transaction, 2004.

———. *Tube of Plenty: The Evolution of American Television*. 2nd rev. ed. Oxford: Oxford University Press, 1990.

Biskind, Peter. *Easy Riders, Raging Bulls: How the Sex-Drugs-and-Rock-'N'-Roll Generation Saved Hollywood*. New York: Simon and Schuster, 1998.

Curtin, Michael, and Kevin Sanson, eds. *Precarious Creativity Global Media, Local Labor*. Oakland: University of California Press, 2016.

Curtin, Michael, and Jane Shattuc. *The American Television*. International Screen Industries. Houndmills, UK: Palgrave Macmillan, 2009.

Doherty, Thomas Patrick. *Cold War, Cool Medium: Television, McCarthyism, and American Culture*. Film and Culture. New York: Columbia University Press, 2003.

Lobato, Ramon. *Netflix Nations: The Geography of Digital Distribution*. Critical Cultural Communication Series. New York: New York University Press, 2019.

Lotz, Amanda D., and Ramon Lobato. *Streaming Video: Storytelling across Borders*. Critical Cultural Communication Series. 1st ed. Cambridge: New York University Press, 2023.

McCarthy, Anna. *The Citizen Machine: Governing by Television in 1950s America*. New York: New Press, 2010.

Starr, Paul. *The Creation of the Media: Political Origins of Modern Communications*. New York: Basic Books, 2004.

POLITICAL AND CULTURAL CONTEXT

Alinsky, Saul David. *Rules for Radicals; a Practical Primer for Realistic Radicals*. 1st ed. New York: Random House, 1971.

Bensman, David, and Roberta Lynch. *Rusted Dreams: Hard Times in a Steel Community*. New York: McGraw-Hill, 1987.

Boston Women's Health Book Collective. *Our Bodies, Ourselves: A Book by and for Women*. New York: Simon and Schuster, 1973.

Carnegie Commission on Educational Television. *Public Television, a Program for Action: The Report and Recommendations of the Carnegie Commission on Educational Television.* New York: Harper and Row, 1967.

Cherny, Robert W., William Issel, and Kieran Walsh Taylor. *American Labor and the Cold War: Grassroots Politics and Postwar Political Culture.* New Brunswick, NJ: Rutgers University Press, 2004.

Churchill, Ward, and Jim Vander Wall. *The COINTELPRO Papers: Documents from the FBI's Secret Wars against Domestic Dissent.* Boston: South End Press, 1990.

Cohen, Adam, and Elizabeth Taylor. *American Pharaoh: Mayor Richard J. Daley—His Battle for Chicago and the Nation.* Boston: Little, Brown, 2000.

Cole, Eddie Rice. *The Campus Color Line: College Presidents and the 1960s Struggle for Black Freedom.* Princeton, NJ: Princeton University Press, 2020.

Dandaneau, Steven P. *A Town Abandoned: Flint, Michigan, Confronts Deindustrialization.* Albany: State University of New York Press, 1996.

Danns, Dionne A. "Something Better for Our Children: Black Organizing in the Chicago Public Schools, 1963–1971." PhD diss., Indiana University, ProQuest Dissertations, 2001.

Ehrenreich, Barbara, and Deirdre English. *Witches, Midwives, and Nurses: A History of Women Healers.* Old Westbury, NY: Feminist Press, 1973.

Evans, Sara M. *Personal Politics: The Roots of Women's Liberation in the Civil Rights Movement and the New Left.* 1st ed. New York: Knopf, distributed by Random House, 1979.

Freeman, Jo. "The Tyranny of Structurelessness." *Women's Studies Quarterly* 41, no. 3 / 4 (2013): 231–46.

Gilligan, Carol. *In a Different Voice : Psychological Theory and Women's Development.* Cambridge, MA: Harvard University Press, 2003.

Gitlin, Todd. *The Sixties: Years of Hope, Days of Rage.* Toronto: Bantam Books, 1987.

Grandin, Greg. *Empire's Workshop: Latin America, the United States, and the Rise of the New Imperialism.* New York: Owl Books, 2007.

Harvey, David. *The Enigma of Capital and the Crises of Capitalism.* Oxford: Oxford University Press, 2010.

Holmlund, Chris, and Cynthia Fuchs. *Between the Sheets, in the Streets: Queer, Lesbian, and Gay Documentary.* Minneapolis: University of Minnesota Press, 1997.

Horwitz, Robert B. "Broadcast Reform Revisited: Reverend Everett C. Parker and the 'Standing' Case (Office of Communication of the United Church of Christ v. Federal Communications Commission)." *Communication Review* 2, no. 3 (1997): 311–48.

———. *The Irony of Regulatory Reform: The Deregulation of American Telecommunications.* New York: Oxford University Press, 1989.

John, Richard R. *Spreading the News: The American Postal System from Franklin to Morse.* Cambridge, MA: Harvard University Press, 1995.

Kline, Benjamin. *First along the River: A Brief History of the U.S. Environmental Movement.* 4th ed. Lanham, MD: Rowman & Littlefield, 2011.

Lewis, Carolyn Herbst. "At Home, You're the Most Important Thing: The Chicago Maternity Center and Medical Home Birth, 1932–1973." *Journal of Women's History* 30, no. 4 (2018): 35–59.

Lucas, Christopher J. *Crisis in the Academy: Rethinking Higher Education in America.* 1st ed. New York: St. Martin's Press, 1996.

Lynd, Alice, and Staughton Lynd. *Rank and File: Personal Histories by Working-Class Organizers.* Princeton, NJ: Princeton University Press, 1981.

———. *Stepping Stones: Memoir of a Life Together.* Lanham, MD: Lexington Books, 2009.

Marcus, Eric. *Making Gay History: The Half-Century Fight for Lesbian and Gay Equal Rights.* New York: Perennial, 2002.

McLean, Bethany., and Joseph Nocera. *All the Devils Are Here: The Hidden History of the Financial Crisis.* New York: Portfolio/Penguin, 2011

Nelson, Jennifer. *More Than Medicine: A History of the Feminist Women's Health Movement.* New York: New York University Press, 2015.

Pappas, Christina. "Second Wave Feminism and the Chicago Women's Liberation Union." PhD diss., Roosevelt University, ProQuest Dissertations, 2008.

Rossinow, Doug. *The Reagan Era: A History of the 1980s.* New York: Columbia University Press, 2015.

Schutz, Aaron, and Mike Miller. *People Power: The Community Organizing Tradition of Saul Alinsky.* Nashville, TN: Vanderbilt University Press, 2015.

Sklar, Martin J. *The Corporate Reconstruction of American Capitalism, 1890–1916: The Market, the Law, and Politics.* Cambridge: Cambridge University Press, 1988.

———. *The United States as a Developing Country: Studies in U.S. History in the Progressive Era and the 1920s.* Cambridge: Cambridge University Press, 1992.

Ward, Jule DeJager. *La Leche League: At the Crossroads of Medicine, Feminism, and Religion.* Chapel Hill: University of North Carolina Press, 2000.

Weinstein, James. *The Long Detour: The History and Future of the American Left.* Boulder, CO: Westview Press, 2003.

Wilkerson, Isabel. *The Warmth of Other Suns: The Epic Story of America's Great Migration.* 1st ed. New York: Random House, 2010.

Williams, Jakobi. *From the Bullet to the Ballot: The Illinois Chapter of the Black Panther Party and Racial Coalition Politics in Chicago.* John Hope Franklin Series in African American History and Culture. Chapel Hill: University of North Carolina Press, 2013.

MY RELEVANT WRITING

Aufderheide, Pat. "Public Television's Prime-Time Politics." *American Film (Archive: 1975-1992)* 6, no. 8 (1983): 53.

Aufderheide, Patricia. *Beyond PC: Toward a Politics of Understanding.* Saint Paul, MN: Graywolf Press, 1992.

———. *Communications Policy and the Public Interest: The Telecommunications Act of 1996.* Guilford Communication Series. New York: Guilford Press, 1999.

———. *The Daily Planet: A Critic on the Capitalist Culture Beat.* Minneapolis: University of Minnesota Press, 2000.

———. *Documentary Film: A Very Short Introduction.* Very Short Introductions. Oxford: Oxford University Press, 2007.

———. "Documentary Film since 1999." In *Blackwells Dictionary of Film*, edited by Cynthia Lucia. London: Blackwells, 2012.

———. "Documentary Filmmaking and US Public TVs Independent Television Service, 1989-2017." *Journal of Film and Video* 71, no. 4 (2019): 3-14.

———. "Leval, Pierre N. Toward a Fair Use Standard, 103 Harv. L. Rev. 1105 (1990)." *Communication Law and Policy* 25, no. 3 (2020): 412-17. https://doi.org/10.1080/10811680.2020.1767419.

———. "Perceived Ethical Conflicts in US Documentary Filmmaking: A Field Report." *New Review of Film and Television Studies* 10, no. 3 (2012): 362-86.

Aufderheide, Patricia, Caty Borum Chattoo, and Tijana Milosevic. *Diversity in Documentary TV Programming in the United States: Comparing Public TV and Cable Networks.* Center for Media & Social Impact, School of Communication, American University, September 2014.

Aufderheide, Patricia, and Jessica Clark. *The Future of Public Media FAQ.* Center for Social Media, American University, April 2008. http://cmsimpact.org/resource/1924/.

———. *Public Broadcasting & Public Affairs: Opportunities and Challenges for Public Broadcasting's Role in Provisioning the Public with News and Public Affairs.* Berkman Center on Internet & Society, Harvard University, 2008. http://cyber.law.harvard.edu/sites/cyber.law.harvard.edu/files/Public%20 Broadcasting%20and%20Public%20Affairs_MR.pdf.

Aufderheide, Patricia, and Peter Jaszi. *Reclaiming Fair Use: How to Put Balance Back in Copyright.* 2nd ed. Chicago: University of Chicago Press, 2018.

Aufderheide, Patricia, Peter Jaszi, and Mridu Chandra. *Honest Truths: Documentary Filmmakers on Ethical Challenges in Their Work.* Center for Social Media, School of Communication Center for Social Media, American University, September 2009. http://www.centerforsocialmedia.org/making-your-media-matter/documents/best-practices/honest-truths-documentary-filmmakers-ethical-chall.

Aufderheide, Patricia, and Echo Xie. *Public Television Viewers and Public-Purpose Programming: Viewer Reactions to PBS Schedule Changes That Reduce Access to Independent Documentary*. Center for Media & Social Impact, American University, April 2012. http://cmsimpact.org/resource/public-television-viewers-and-public-purpose-programming-viewer-reactions-to-pbs-schedule-changes-that-reduce-access-to-independent-documentary/.

Bello, Bryan, and Patricia Aufderheide. "The Public Interest and the Information Superhighway: The Digital Future Coalition (1996–2002) and the Afterlife of the Digital Millennium Copyright Act." *Information & Culture* 56, no. 1 (2021): 49–89. https://doi.org/10.7560/IC56103.

Denny, Garry, Sharon La Cruise, and Patricia Aufderheide. *Stories for a Stronger Nation: Building a Resilient American Public with Diverse Documentary Filmmakers and Public Television*. Center for Media & Social Impact, American University, September 2021. https://cmsimpact.org/wp-content/uploads/2021/07/Stories-for-a-Stronger-Nation.pdf.

Haywood, Antoine, Patricia Aufderheide, and Mariana Sanchez Santos. "Community Media in a Pandemic: Facilitating Local Communication, Collective Resilience and Transitions to Virtual Public Life in the U. S." *Javnost* 28, no. 3 (2021): 256–72.

THEORY AND PHILOSOPHY

Bourdieu, Pierre. *Distinction: A Social Critique of the Judgement of Taste*. Cambridge, MA: Harvard University Press, 1984.

Carey, James W. *Communication as Culture: Essays on Media and Society*. Media and Popular Culture. Boston: Unwin Hyman, 1989.

Dewey, John. *Art as Experience*. New York: Minton, 1934.

———. *The Public and Its Problems*. New York: Henry Holt, 1927.

———, and Reginald D. Archambault. *John Dewey on Education: Selected Writings*. Edited and with an Introduction by Reginald D. Archambault. Chicago: University of Chicago Press, 1974.

Gramsci, Antonio, and David Forgacs. *The Gramsci Reader: Selected Writings, 1916–1935*. New York: New York University Press, 2000.

Grossberg, Lawrence, and Cary Nelson. *Marxism and the Interpretation of Culture*. Urbana: University of Illinois Press, 1988.

Hall, Stuart. *Culture, Media, Language: Working Papers in Cultural Studies, 1972–79*. London: Centre for Contemporary Cultural Studies, University of Birmingham, 1980.

———. *Policing the Crisis: Mugging, the State, and Law and Order*. New York: Holmes & Meier, 1978.

———, David Morley, and Kuan-Hsing Chen. *Stuart Hall: Critical Dialogues in Cultural Studies*. Comedia. London: Routledge, 1996.

Jackson, Philip W. *John Dewey and the Lessons of Art*. New Haven, CT: Yale University Press, 1998.

Jones, Steve. *Antonio Gramsci*. Routledge Critical Thinkers. London: Routledge, 2006.

Procter, James. *Stuart Hall*. Routledge Critical Thinkers. London: Routledge, 2004.

Westbrook, Robert B. *John Dewey and American Democracy*. Ithaca, NY: Cornell University Press, 1991.

Williams, Raymond. *Culture and Society, 1780–1950*. New York: Columbia University Press, 1983.

Filmography

The Kartemquin Films website has streaming availability information for its films, as well as awards and festival information on individual films. DVDs of *The Kartemquin Films Collection: The Early Years*, in four volumes, are available on Amazon.com; extras include interviews with participants in films such as *Inquiring Nuns, Marco, Taylor Chain II, Now We Live on Clifton*, and others years or decades later.

Film	Release Year	Directors
A Compassionate Spy	2022	Steve James
A Miracle on 19th Street	2021	Mark Mitten
Ants & the Grasshopper, The	2021	Zak Piper, Raj Patel
For the Left Hand	2021	Leslie Simmer, Gordon Quinn
First Step, The	2021	Brandon Kramer
Wuhan Wuhan	2021	Yung Chang
A Mystery To Me	2020	Ben Strang
Finding Yingying	2020	Jenny Shi
City So Real	2020	Steve James
Unapologetic	2020	Ashley O'Shay
Represent	2020	Hillary Bachelder

(continued)

Film	Release Year	Directors
Dilemma of Desire, The	2020	Maria Finitzo
We Are Witnesses	2019	Maggie Bowman, Stacy Robinson
Eating Up Easter	2018	Sergio Rapu, Elena Rapu
America To Me	2018	Steve James
Minding the Gap	2018	Bing Liu
Cooked: Survival by Zip Code	2018	Judith Helfand
Edith+Eddie	2017	Laura Checkoway
All The Queen's Horses	2017	Kelly Richmond Pope
Keep Talking	2017	Karen Weinberg
'63 Boycott	2017	Rachel Dickson, Tracye Matthews, Gordon Quinn
Stranded by the State	2016	Liz Kaar
Abacus: Small Enough to Jail	2016	Steve James
Raising Bertie	2016	Margaret Byrne
Unbroken Glass	2016	Dinesh Das Sabu
Hard Earned	2015	Liz Kaar, David Simpson
In the Game	2015	Maria Finitzo
Almost There	2014	Aaron Wickenden, Dan Rybicky
On Beauty	2014	Joanna Rudnick
Saving Mes Aynak	2014	Brent Huffman
The School Project	2014	Jon Siskel, Greg Jacobs, Jeff McCarter
Life Itself	2014	Steve James
Homestretch, The	2014	Anne de Mare, Kirsten Kelly
American Arab	2013	Usama Alshaibi
Trials of Muhammad Ali, The	2013	Bill Siegel
As Goes Janesville	2012	Brad Lichtenstein, Leslie Simmer (Co-Writer)
The Interrupters	2011	Steve James, Zak Piper
A Good Man	2011	Bob Hercules, Gordon Quinn
Sacred Transformations	2010	Justine Nagan
No Crossover: The Trial of Allen Iverson	2010	Steve James
Prisoner of Her Past	2010	Gordon Quinn, Howard Reich (Writer)
Typeface	2009	Justine Nagan
At the Death House Door	2008	Steve James, Peter Gilbert
In the Family	2008	Joanna Rudnick
Milking the Rhino	2008	David E. Simpson, Jeannie R. Magill

Mapping Stem Cell Research: Terra Incognita	2007	Maria Finitzo
Golub: Late Works Are the Catastrophes	2004	Gordon Quinn, Jerry Blumenthal
The New Americans	2003	Steve James, Gita Saedi, Gordon Quinn
Refrigerator Mothers	2002	David Simpson
Stevie	2002	Steve James
5 Girls	2001	Maria Finitzo
Vietnam, Long Time Coming	1998	Gordon Quinn, Jerry Blumenthal, Peter Gilbert
When Billy Broke His Head	1995	David E. Simpson, Billy Golfus
Hoop Dreams	1994	Steve James
Chicago Crossings: Bridges and Boundaries	1994	Gordon Quinn, Jerry Blumenthal
Higher Goals	1992	Steve James
Grassroots Chicago	1991	Steve James
Golub	1988	Gordon Quinn, Jerry Blumenthal
Women's Voices: The Gender Gap	1984	Jenny Rohrer
The Last Pullman Car	1983	Gordon Quinn, Jerry Blumenthal
Taylor Chain II: A Story of Collective Bargaining	1983	Gordon Quinn, Jerry Blumenthal
Taylor Chain I: A Story in a Union Local	1980	Gordon Quinn, Jerry Blumenthal
The Chicago Maternity Center Story	1976	Jerry Blumenthal, Suzanne Davenport, Sharon Karp, Gordon Quinn, Jenny Rohrer
Where's I. W. Abel?	1975	Gordon Quinn
HSA Strike '75	1975	Judy Hoffman
UE/Wells	1975	Jerry Blumenthal, Gordon Quinn, Guillermo Brzostowski
What's Happening at Local 70?	1975	Judy Hoffman
Trick Bag	1974	Peter Kuttner, Kartemquin Films, Rising Up Angry, Columbia College
Viva la Causa	1974	Teena Webb
Winnie Wright, Age 11	1974	Kartemquin Collective
Now We Live on Clifton	1974	Kartemquin Collective
Sports-Action Pro-Files	1972	Jeffrey Pill
Anonymous Artists of America	1970	Gordon Quinn, Jerry Temaner
Marco	1970	Gordon Quinn, Jerry Temaner

(continued)

Film	Release Year	Directors
What the Fuck Are These Red Squares?	1970	Gordon Quinn, Jerry Blumenthal
Hum 255	1970	Jerry Blumenthal, Peter Kuttner (Newsreel), Jason Litvin, Gordon Quinn, Jerry Temaner, Anthony Thomas (Newsreel)
Inquiring Nuns	1968	Gordon Quinn, Jerry Temaner
Thumbs Down	1968	Gordon Quinn, Jerry Temaner
Parents	1968	Gordon Quinn, Jerry Temaner
Home For Life	1966	Gordon Quinn, Jerry Temaner

Index

Abacus: Small Enough to Jail (2016) (James), 262–63, 322
ABC network: Happy Mother's Day (1963) (Chopra and Leacock) and, 37; independent filmmakers and, 33; Pennebaker and, 33, 40
Abel, I. W., 79, 96, 97
Academy Awards of Merit (Oscar awards): Abacus and, 263; At the Death House Door and, 195, 198; Get Out and, 264; Harlan County, U. S. A. and, 114; Hoop Dreams and, 2, 3, 172–73, 281; Kartemquin and, 1, 172–73, 252, 281; Life Itself and, 227; Minding the Gap and, 273, 274fig.; short-list, 195, 198, 227, 243; '63 Boycott and, 243; Stevie and, 198; The Times of Harvey Milk and, 294–95; Wexler and, 50
accessibility: of documentaries, 8; Lauterbach and issues of, 293. See also disabilities; public access cable
accountability: Documentary Accountability Working Group, 256; in economic development, 292; of experts, 204; of filmmakers, 238, 256; of funders, 182; Good Jobs First, 292; Kartemquin and, 210; of media, 126; of organizations, 110; public demands for, 25–26

Active Voice, 181, 199, 205, 211, 260
activism: 1960s US documentary filmmaking, 8; activist era, 126; Black community activism, 49; CCOM and, 128; CeaseFire, 241, 259, 260; Chevigny and, 214; civil rights movement, 21, 107, 128, 152; Community Film Workshop, 82, 177, 217, 267, 268, 295; death penalty activism, 193; Democratic Party, 121; disabilities activism, 202–5; The End of the Nightstick and, 154, 155; fair use, 141–46; feminist activism, 64–65, 75, 132, 172, 174, 201; funders and, 181; IATSE, 154, 292, 294; independent filmmakers and, 136; The Interrupters and, 260; ITVS's creation, 4, 162; Kartemquin and, 4, 24, 67, 68, 74, 75, 103, 121, 127, 131, 133, 147, 175, 224, 240; labor activism, 79, 128, 132; left-wing activists, 8, 62, 83, 105, 120, 135–36; LGBT activism, 84, 132; Milking the Rhino and, 205–6; New American Movement (NAM), 63; over healthcare, 88; public access/public TV and, 31, 33–34, 82, 127, 133, 140–41; Rainbow Coalition, 12, 62–63, 148, 256, 280; SAIC and, 151, 152; social activist video, 78; student activists, 11; unmade project on,

325

INDEX

activism *(continued)* 176; of Wexler, 50. *See also* antiwar movement; Dewey, John; *In These Times* (periodical); media reform movement; New Left; student movements

addiction, 51, 52, 174, 291

advocacy: anti-death penalty advocates, 194; birthing advocacy, 56–58; disability rights advocates, 63; DVD technology and, 180–81; environmental advocacy, 292; feminist advocacy, 77; funders and, 182; *The Homestretch* and, 239–40; Kartemquin and, 9, 15, 280, 287; labor films and, 102, 113; La Leche League, 57; new technology and, 181; public interest advocates, 127–28; for public media, 219; *Refrigerator Mothers* and, 202–5; *Union Maids* and, 155; United Church of Christ and, 15. *See also* disabilities

aesthetics, 17, 23, 35, 124, 158, 160, 166, 276, 278

Afable, Yvonne, 251

Afghanistan, 105, 234

African cinema, 13, 29, 31, 64–65, 68, 135, 205–6

Agee, Arthur, 165–66, 169–70, 171, 172, 174

agreements: collective's agreement, 74; coproduction agreements, 277, 280; Kartemquin's original agreement, 45; labor agreements, 96; partnership agreements, 221; production agreements, 272

Aguayo, Angela, 5

AIDS epidemic, 295

Aiken, Susana, 207, 209*fig.*

Ali, Muhammad, 233–34, 248

Alinsky, Saul, 11, 77, 95

Al Jazeera America (AJA), 230, 232

Alk, Howard, 39–40, 45, 48, 51–52, 131

Alk, Joan, 40, 51, 52

Allen, Paul, 60

All in the Family (TV series), 64, 92, 94*fig.*

All the Queen's Horses (2017) (Pope), 275–76, 290, 322

Almost There (2014) (Wickenden and Rybicky), 156, 228, 322

Alpert, Daniel (Danny), 240

Alshaibi, Usama, 267–68, 322

Alternative Cinema Conference (Bard College), 83, 84, 105, 134, 135

alumni. *See* Kartemquinites

Amazon Prime (streaming platform), 277

American Arab (2013) (Alshaibi), 267–68, 322

American Dream (Kopple), 106, 110

American Film Institute, 128

American Masters, 186, 224, 225

American Playhouse, 106

American pragmatic philosophy. *See* pragmatic philosophy, American

American Promise (2013), 235

American Revolution 2 (1969), 51, 108, 181

American University, 15, 139, 142, 279, 295, 303n1

America Reframed series, 229, 271

America to Me (2018 miniseries) (James), 3, 61, 182, 210, 218, 263–65, 270, 272, 273, 286, 322

Anarchism in America (1983), 83

Anderson, Pamela Sherrod, 253, 269*fig.*, 275

And This Is Free (1965) (Shea), 38–39, 131

Anka, Paul, 37

Annie E. Casey Foundation, 211

Anonymous Artists of America (1970) (Quinn and Temaner), 323

anticolonialism, 8, 28, 29, 65, 90, 256

anticommunist politics, 8, 28, 96

antiwar movement: Catholic films and, 53–55; Democratic Convention of 1968, 48; draft-age people in, 68; experience gained from, 95; films for, 55; Kartemquin and, 62–63; left-leaning filmmakers and, 36; Muhammad Ali and, 234; sectarianism and, 14; splintering of, 14; student protests, 12, 34, 102; Students for a Democratic Society, 11, 63; support for RFK, 49; veterans and, 77, 188–90

Anton, Peter, 228

Antonio, Emile de, 31

The Ants & the Grasshopper (Piper and Patel), 321

Any Given Day (2021) (Byrne), 285

Aparicio, Carlos, 207, 209*fig.*

Appalachia, 48, 53

Appalshop, 109–10, 128–29

Aquinas, Thomas, 57

archives project, 18, 59, 245–47, 248, 287

Argentina, 29, 64, 101

Art as Experience (Dewey), 30, 157–58, 178

Artbeat, 209

Art Institute of Chicago, 13, 14, 65, 149, 151, 176

artistic director(s): Daniels as apprentice to, 270; George as, 288; as leadership role, 250; as person of color, 218, 255, 288; Quinn as, 218, 255, 286; search for, 218, 255, 286, 288

INDEX 327

artistic fellowship, 255
artistic filmmakers era: art for broad audiences, 147–55; end of the era, 177–78; *Golub* and, 156–62, 225; *A Good Man* and, 224; *Hoop Dreams* and, 162–75, 178; unmade projects, 175–77
Arts & Entertainment (A&E), 180
Arts Engine, 214, 230, 253
As Goes Janesville (2012) (Lichtenstein and Simmer), 233, 322
Asian American filmmakers: Choy, Christine, 110; Liu, Bing, 257, 263–64, 271–75, 280, 285, 287*fig.*, 322; Shi, Jiayan "Jenny," 277
Association of Independent Video and Filmmakers (AIVF), 84, 132, 136, 308n1
Ateliers Varan, 80
At the Death House Door (2008) (James and Gilbert), 185, 193–96, 221, 227, 230, 322
audiences: age range of, 90; anchor programs and, 106; audience awards, 2, 170; Black audiences, 226; broad audiences, 147, 149, 182, 183, 212, 257; broadcast audiences, 84, 156, 180, 257; cablecast audiences, 257; character-driven narratives and, 178; cinema-verité and, 46; diverse audiences, 138, 194, 256; for documentaries in 1960s, 8–9, 33, 34; general audiences, 131, 138; involvement of, 161; minoritized audiences, 133; New Latin American Cinema and, 64; public TV and, 215; Quinn on, 98, 161, 235, 249; regional and national audiences, 129, 227; streaming audiences, 257; target audiences, 9, 118; as treated with respect, 9; trusting the, 235; veterans as, 191; white viewership, 172, 212, 257; working-class audiences, 6, 133
Auerbach, Paul, 38, 41, 59
authority: filmmakers resistance to, 8, 28; formal authority, 75; informal authority, 75
autism, 202–5
awards: *Abacus* and, 263; *America to Me* and, 265; cable programmers and, 188; *Changing Our Minds* and, 295; Cinema Eye award, 265; *City So Real* and, 266; Critics' Choice awards, 263; Directors Guild award, 191; distributors awards, 290; documentaries and competition for, 7; Dupont-Columbia award, 232, 260; *Eyes on the Prize* series, 150; *Finding Yingying* and, 278; focus on, 252; *Hard Earned* and, 232; HBO and, 183, 215;

Home for Life and, 44; *Hoop Dreams* and, 170; information on, 321; International Documentary Awards, 232, 248, 249*fig.*; *The Interrupters* and, 252, 260; ITVS and, 138; *Life Itself* and, 227; *Minding the Gap* and, 273; NAACP Image Award, 232; Peabody Awards, 2, 200, 263; *Saving Mes Aynak* and, 234; SXSW jury award, 278; *Terra Incognita* and, 200; *When Billy Broke His Head* and, 203; Yamagata Film Festival, 198. *See also* Academy Awards of Merit (Oscar awards); Critics' Choice awards; Emmys; Peabody Awards; Sundance Film Festival

Bachelder, Hillary, 249*fig.*, 252, 286, 321
Bagwell, Orlando, 187
Balaban, Belisa, 273
Baldwin, James, 21, 23
Bals, Huub, 89
Bard Conference, 83, 84, 105, 134, 135
Barnouw, Erik, 6, 118, 303n1
Barrett, Elizabeth, 109–10
BBC (British Broadcasting Corporation), 130, 196, 210–11
Beck, Bernard, 118
Becker, Carol, 151, 152
Becker, Howard, 118, 151, 244
Benning, James, 163
Bensman, David, 118
Benton Foundation, 181, 220
Bergman, Ingmar, 32
Bettleheim, Bruno, 202–3, 204
Beyond Blind (web resource), 293
Bezalel, Ronit, 134
Bierman, Jack, 110–12
Big Mouth Productions, 230
Big Muddy Film Festival, 163
Big Sky Documentary Film Festival, 294
BIPOC issues: consultants for, 254; debates over, 256, 278; making films about and with BIPOC people, 228–29, 231, 236, 257, 272. *See also* Black people; people of color
Black Chicago narrative, 293
Black Journal, 64, 132
Black Lives Matter movement, 255
Black Panther Party, 11, 48, 50, 51, 52, 61, 72, 89, 102
Black people: African American folklore, 174; arrest of Black activists, 49; Black filmmakers, 82, 171, 214, 224, 242, 266–67, 275, 276–77; centering of

Black people *(continued)*
  experiences of, 290; as directors, 290; Firelight Media, 214; Free Spirit Media, 279; *The Negro Family* report, 53; in postwar Chicago, 11. *See also* BIPOC issues; people of color; Rainbow Coalition
Blackstone Rangers, 49, 60
Black theology, 53
Bloomfield, Mike, 13, 39
Blumenthal, Alphonse, 69, 292
Blumenthal, Jerry: Big Muddy Film Festival and, 163; branding discussion and, 186; *Chicago Crossings* and, 323; *The Chicago Maternity Center Story* and, 9, 46, 76, 84–90, 116, 117, 132–33, 141, 323; cinema verité and, 27; as collective member, 69; Doc Films, 100; *5 Girls* and, 199; Gleeson and, 222; *Golub* and, 156, 157, 159, 160, 166, 175, 323; *Golub: Late Works Are the Catastrophes* and, 162, 323; *Grassroots Chicago* and, 168; *Hum 255* and, 324; Jewish culture of, 46; joining Kartemquin, 46; Kuttner and, 195; *The Last Pullman Car* and, 9, 114–19, 121, 149, 163, 292, 323; mentoring, 155, 212, 221, 223; *The New Americans* and, 206, 207, 209*fig.*; photos, 158*fig.*, 219*fig.*; Rudnick and, 201–2; as second father/family/friend, 5; *Taylor Chain I* and, 99, 110, 111, 112, 118, 149, 323; *Taylor Chain II* and, 99, 110–13, 118, 124, 131, 163, 323; television and, 33; *UE/Wells* and, 101–2, 323; at University of Chicago, 34; *Vietnam, Long Time Coming* and, 323; vision of, 47, 286, 291; *What the Fuck Are These Red Squares?* and, 67–68, 82, 151, 324; Whisnant and, 188
Blumenthal, Lyn, 78
board of Kartemquin: Anderson as chair, 253, 269*fig.*, 275; businessmen on, 251; founding of, 16, 217; mission statement, 188, 217, 218–19, 281; nomination process, 137; proposal for, 188; Revere on, 244, 249; Singer on, 281
Boero, Patricia, 168, 182
Boggs, Grace Lee, 21, 26
Bognar, Steve, 110
Bonsu, Janaé, 277
Booth, Heather, 11
Booth, Paul, 11
Bourdain, Anthony, 215
Bourdieu, Pierre, 20, 22, 23
Bourne, St. Clair, 83, 84

Bowman, John, 116–17
Bowman, Maggie: on artistic director role, 255; departure of, 252, 286; *Hard Earned* and, 230–32; joining Kartemquin, 218; labor movements and, 292; *Minding the Gap* and, 273; photo, 249*fig.*; Rapu and, 235; *We Are Witnesses* and, 242, 322
Boyte, Harry, 14
Brach candy company, 177
branding: Blumenthal and, 186; cable channels and, 180, 215; expanding visibility of, 217; fiftieth anniversary and, 247; lack of, 6, 172; Nagan and, 186, 217, 219, 222, 247
Bravo, 180
Brightman, Carol, 37, 38
British Columbia, 294
British documentaries in 1930s, 7–8
broadcast and cable era: *5 Girls* (2001), 198–201; about, 179–84; audiences, 257; business priorities, 184–88; clubhouse and community, 212; *At the Death House Door* and, 193–96; *In the Family* and, 201–2; funded filmmaking, 188–93; *Golub* and, 156–62, 225; *Milking the Rhino* and, 205–6; *The New Americans* and, 206–12; partnerships, 4; *Refrigerator Mothers* and, 202–5; *Stevie* and, 196–98; streaming as competition, 215
Brotherhood of Sleeping Car Porters, 114
Brzostowski, Guillermo, 101–2, 102, 323
Buba, Tony, 110
Buckman, Larry, 33
Burnett, Charles, 207
Bush administration, George W., 183
Byrne, Margaret, 235–36, 285, 322

Cable Act of 1990, 309n1
cable channels, 7, 217, 230, 232; access centers, 140; audiences, 257; audiences for, 180; distribution of, 179–80; funding and, 188–93; national channels, 180; prestige-documentary lines and, 215; streaming as rival to, 215; Tower Productions, 251
California Newsreel, 136
Canadian Broadcasting Company, 130
Candid Eye, 28, 31
Cannes film festival, 227
capitalism: art and, 157–58; Kartemquin and, 70, 285; Marxists on, 20; systems of oppression and, 17

INDEX

Caples, Margaret, 128, 129, 141, 164, 217, 267, 268, 269*fig.*
Caprysha, 259
Carey, James, 19, 21, 305n1
Carlson, Tucker, 183
Carmichael, Stokely, 92
Carnegie Commission Report, 129, 130
Cassavetes, John, 92
Catholic Adult Education Center (CAEC), 53–58
Catholic films: *Inquiring Nuns*, 55–56, 58, 107, 253, 324; *Marco*, 56–58, 323; *Thumbs Down*, 53–55, 324
Cause and Effect (1989), 293
CBC, 196
CeaseFire, 241, 259, 260
censorship, 143, 161, 189–90, 198
Center for Media & Social Impact study, 139, 239–40
Center for New Television, 80, 82
Ceplair, Larry, 304n2
Cesar, Jaime, 134
challenges: from COVID-19 pandemic, 250, 254; diversity incorporation, 250; as media arts center, 224. *See also* crises
Chanan, Michael, 6
Chang, Yung, 278, 321
Changing Our Minds (1992) (Schmeichen and Haugland), 295
character-driven narratives: about struggle and challenge, 289; in broadcast-ready work, 9; pioneering of, 4; *Saving Mes Aynak* as, 234
charitable tax policy, 289. *See also* private foundation grants
Checkoway, Laura, 236, 322
Chester, Jeffrey, 136
Chevigny, Katy, 214, 253
Chicago: Art Institute of Chicago, 13, 14, 65, 149, 151, 176; arts and entertainment sector, 12–13; Black culture in, 12–13, 259; CeaseFire, 241, 259, 260; Chicago Access Network (CAN-TV), 140–41; Chicago Filmmakers, 13, 241; consumer base in, 13; corporate film, 13; creative professionals, 13; DePaul University, 91, 268, 270, 275; ethnic enclaves of, 11, 13–14; gentrification in, 13, 65, 91, 205, 268; industrial culture of, 13; Kartemquinites in, 293; Kindling Group, 214; Media Process Group, 214, 224, 240, 258; music scene, 12–13; patronage for government jobs in, 11; as production hub, 11; progressive organizing in 1960s in, 11; public school system, 38, 60–61, 155, 225, 243; riots in, 48; Second City, 13, 39, 249; Sisters in Cinema, 214; Street Level Youth Media, 295; theatrical scene, 13; *In These Times* in, 10; University of Chicago, 12–13, 186, 217, 243, 294; Wilbur Wright College, 292; working-class population of, 11
Chicago Access Network (CAN-TV), 82, 140–41
Chicago Citizens Cable Coalition (CCCC), 140–41
Chicago Community Trust, 237
Chicago Crossings (1994) (Quinn and Blumenthal), 323
Chicago Editing Center, 80
Chicago Film Archive, 245
Chicago Filmmakers, 13, 241
Chicagoland Green Collar Jobs initiative, 292
Chicago Maternity Center (CMC), 85–86
The Chicago Maternity Center Story (1976) (Blumenthal, Davenport, Karp, Quinn, and Rohrer), 9, 46, 76, 84–90, 91–92, 116, 117, 132–33, 141, 323
Chicago Media Project, 252
Chicago Newsreel, 74, 77, 80, 92
Chicago Public Broadcasting (CPB), 167
Chicago Reporter, 240
Chicago Sun-Times, 240
Chicago Women's Liberation Union (CWLU), 72, 73, 77–78, 85, 89, 103
Chicken & Egg Pictures, 237
Childress, Sonya, 260
The China Syndrome (1979), 50
Chopra, Joyce, 37
Choy, Christine, 110
Christmas, Sylvetta, 265
Chronique d'un été (*Chronicle of a Summer*) (1960) (Rouch and Morin), 31, 55, 56*fig.*
Chuck Olin Association, 108
Ciciura, Tom, 271
"Cinema as a Gun" exhibition, 29, 64
Cinema Eye award, 265
cinematic social inquiry: as business model, 32; Catholic films, 53–58; Fetterley and, 152–53; forming Kartemquin team, 45–48; founding of Kartemquin and, 29–30, 36–40, 119; *Home for Life* and, 40–45, 53, 218, 244, 324; Kartemquin-based filmmakers and, 224–29; as

cinematic social inquiry *(continued)*
mission, 27, 30–35, 290; nonprofit projects, 58–61; political polarization, 48–53; sectarianism and, 52–53; Temaner and, 38. *See also* Deweyan philosophy
"Cinematic Social Inquiry" (Quinn and Temaner), 79, 218
cinema verité genre: Canadian, 37, 81; classics of, 37, 55; commercials in, 66; defined, 27; democratic publics and, 30–31; equipment for, 66; *Grassroots Chicago* and, 168; within Kartemquin's philosophy, 27–30, 58, 82, 86, 175; Kuttner and, 81; legendary filmmakers of, 79, 81; Maysles and, 150; movement development, 8, 305n2; pioneers of, 33, 36, 41, 150; political films and, 67–68; purity of Kartemquinites, 58; Quinn and, 30, 37, 58, 86, 108; series genre, 206; styles of, 108, 110, 115, 116, 262, 290, 305; technical tinkering and, 41, 47; Temaner and, 40; term usage, 8, 28–29; *Unapologetic* as, 290. *See also Abacus* (2016) (James); *The Chicago Maternity Center Story*; *The Fight for Life* (1939) (Lorentz); *Happy Mother's Day* (1963) (Chopra and Leacock); *Home for Life* (1966); *Inquiring Nuns* (1968) (Quinn and Temaner); *Lonely Boy* (1963); *Marco* (1970); *The New Americans* (2003); *Taylor Chain II*; *Unapologetic* (2020) (O'Shay); *Warrendale* (1967); *What the Fuck Are These Red Squares?*
Cintron, Ralph, 91–92
Citizen Action Program, 11
Citizens Committee on the Media (CCOM), 128, 140
Citizens United, 183
Citron, Michelle, 177
City of Trees (2015) (Kramer and Kramer), 236
City So Real (2020 miniseries) (James), 3, 182, 210, 265, 321
Civic Enterprises, 239
civil rights movement, 8, 21, 63, 102, 107, 128, 150. *See also* Black Panther Party; Rainbow Coalition
Clasky, Ron, 66
CMC (Chicago Maternity Center). *See* Chicago Maternity Center (CMC)
CNN/CNN Films, 85–86, 180, 215, 227
Coalmining Women (1982) (Barrett), 110

Cointelpro program, 50
Cole, J., 235
collective era of Kartemquin: *The Chicago Maternity Center Story* and, 9, 46, 76, 84–90, 116, 117, 132–33, 141, 323; collapse of, 102–3, 104, 132, 175; collective structure, 69–77; creation of, 62–67, 175; feminists of, 153, 189; film and politics, 67–69; grassroots labor, 95–102; Hoffman and, 78–80; information on, 6, 18; Kuttner and, 80–81, 280–81; labor connections, 109, 178; media connections, 128, 131–32; members during, 69; *Now We Live on Clifton* and, 91–92, 323; outreach, 211; positionality and, 257; producing with organizations, 82–94; Rainbow Coalition and, 256, 280; Rohrer and, 77–78; social-justice organizations and, 178; social movements and, 16; spirit of, 240–44, 252, 275, 284; *Sports-Action Pro-files* and, 66, 323; Structure and Identity sessions during, 257; *Taylor Chain I* and, 99, 99–101, 110, 111, 112, 118, 149, 323; *Trick Bag* and, 9, 92–93; UE/Wells and, 101–2, 323; *Viva La Causa* and, 93–94; *What's Happening at Local 70?* and, 98, 323; *Where's I. W. Abel?* and, 79, 96–97, 323; *Where's Joe?* and, 96–97; white, working-class organizations in, 280–81; *Winnie Wright, Age 11* and, 91–92, 323; working-class groups, 90–95; Zaccardi and, 154
The College (1964), 38
A Comedy in Six Unnatural Acts (1975), 133
commercial productions: Blumenthal, Alphonse, 292; capacity for, 217; chroniclers of documentaries, 6; dependence on revenue from, 7, 252; documentary studios, 214; leveraging of, 289–90. *See also* broadcasters; cable channels; streaming
commissioned work: *Hard Earned* as, 230–32, 242; realities of, 61; *We Are Witnesses* as, 242. *See also* work-for-hire
Communist Party: Chinese Cultural Revolution, 63, 76; in Czechoslovakia, 176; disillusionment and, 10; left-wing activist documentaries and, 8; Revolutionary Communist Party, 52, 63, 73; UE and, 101; in US, 63
Community Film Workshop, 82, 128, 141, 177, 217, 267, 268, 295
community foundations: Crossroads Fund, 114, 120; funding from, 85

INDEX 331

community of Kartemquin: collective attitude of, 252, 284, 289; democratic socialism and, 290; generosity of, 238; Gleeson on, 222; Kuttner on, 281; as porous and flexible, 290; pragmatic idealism of, 291–92; racial challenges, 290; white culture of, 290
Community TV Network, 109, 295
A Compassionate Spy (2022) (James), 182, 321
Concordia Films, 215
Congress of Industrial Organizations (CIO), 101–2
Convicting a Murderer (2023 TV series) (Rech), 215
Cooked: Survival by Zip Code (2018) (Helfand), 2, 236, 282, 322
Cooper, Vicki, 69, 70, 72, 78, 95, 99, 292
Coppola, Francis Ford, 64
coproduction(s): *Eating Up Easter* and, 235; *The Homestretch* and, 238; ITVS and, 138, 205, 236; *Minding the Gap* and, 272; Quinn and, 204; *Unapologetic* and, 277
copyright policy issues: Copyright Act, 123, 142; copyright doctrine, 204; fair use and, 141–46; working on, 24. *See also* fair use
Copyright Tribunal presentation, 144–45
Corporation for Public Broadcasting (CPB): COVID-19 relief funds, 290–91; Finitzo and, 199; funding and, 113–14; funding of, 129; hostility from Reagan administration, 105; independent filmmakers and, 105, 135; interconnection ban, 131; *Matters of Life and Death . . . and Other Matters* on, 101; National Coalition of Independent Public Broadcasting Producers and, 137; PBS and, 106; pressure campaign on, 308n1; Tomlinson and, 183; TV Lab, 106, 115, 132. *See also POV* (TV documentary series)
Cottle, Bill, 48
Council on Foundations, 167, 181
COVID-19 pandemic: challenges from, 250, 254, 284–85; *City So Real* and, 266; DVID and, 279; filmmakers and, 290–91; SXSW and, 229
Cox, Nell, 150
#CreateLouisiana, 253
criminal justice reform, 193, 193–94, 236, 242
crises: addressing challenges, 250, 290; diverse films, 270–78; Diverse Voices in Documentary (DVID), 267–70; management crises, 251–55; race and diversity at Kartemquin, 255–57, 290; storytelling about race, 257–67, 290; struggling with the business model, 283–88; struggling with the conversation, 278–82, 290; struggling with the culture, 282–83, 290. *See also* challenges
Crisis to Crisis (series), 106, 113, 135
critical race theory, 255
Critics' Choice awards, 263
Crossroads Fund, 114, 120
crowdfunding, 276
Crundwell, Rita, 275, 276
cultural Marxism, 20, 23, 305n1
Cultural Revolution, 63
culture: changing of, 19; cultural creation, 19; cultural curiosity, 9; cultural hegemony, 22, 26; cultural production, 20–21, 22; cultural studies, 19, 305n1; cultural trends, 16; culture wars, 291; forming of, 19, 26; as habitus, 26; of Kartemquin, 285; shaping of, 19, 24; in social change, 15; struggling with changing culture, 282–83
CWLU (Chicago Women's Liberation Union). *See* Chicago Women's Liberation Union (CWLU)
cynicism, 133, 291

Daley, Richard, 13, 34, 49–50, 65, 120
Daniels, Rubin, Jr., 257, 264, 265, 270, 277, 280, 293
Daressa, Larry, 136
Davenport, Suzanne "Sue": *The Chicago Maternity Center Story* and, 84–90, 323; as collective member, 69; photos, 71*fig.*, 72*fig.*; *Refrigerator Mothers* and, 204; return to education, 292; Rohrer and, 77; social-justice missions and, 178
David and Reva Logan Family Foundation, 229
Dear White People (2017), 264
death penalty activism, 193–96
deaths of despair, 291
Debs, Eugene V., 116, 117
Deggans, Eric, 265
Delson, Susan, 69, 71*fig.*, 72*fig.*, 293
De Luna, Carlos, 194
De Mare, Ann, 237–40, 322
democracy: breakdown in, 291; citizen-led, 6; cynicism of libertarian elites, 291; democratic publics, 24–25, 30–31, 291;

democracy *(continued)*
  Dewey on, 25; documentary for, 233, 255, 289–95; fair use and, 143–44; humanist storytelling, 4; Kartemquin's dreams for, 15, 19, 255, 270, 291, 295; media production for, 4; shaping culture for stronger, 19; socialism and, 10; *In These Times* and, 15
democracy through documentary concept, 7, 9–10, 26, 166–67. *See also* mission of Kartemquin
Democratic Convention of 1968, 48, 68, 81, 108
Democratic Party, 20, 34, 48–49, 63, 120, 121, 148, 304n2
democratic socialism, 10, 20, 72, 95, 103, 152, 290, 304n2
Democratic Socialist Organizing Committee, 11, 12, 63, 72
DePaul University, 91, 268, 270, 275
Desai, Rehad, 206
Dewey, John: arguments of, 27, 108, 137; *Art as Experience*, 30, 157–58, 178; on art in society, 175; Carey and, 305n1; citizen agency, 146; faith in people, 256; Finitzo and, 200; Gilbert and, 107; *Hum 255* (1970) and, 58; Meyer and, 120; Mueller and, 161; as pragmatic philosopher and social activist, 24–25; on public education, 228–29; *The Public and Its Problems*, 30–31, 46, 248; Quinn and, 15, 25, 30, 43, 143, 152, 166. *See also* pragmatic philosophy, American
Deweyan philosophy: cinematic social inquiry and, 224; concept of art as experience, 178; concept of publicness, 25, 26–27, 101, 104, 110, 119, 126, 140–41, 177, 182; core public mission in tradition of, 121, 136, 265; engagement of viewers, 211; independent filmmakers and, 106; spirit of, 174; understanding of political agency, 124, 138, 182, 291; values and goals, 198, 274; vision of art, 158, 161, 224, 270, 289; vision of democracy, 126, 138, 161, 224, 270, 287, 289, 291
Dickson, Rachel, 139, 240, 242, 322
digital era, 142, 143–44, 148–49, 180, 182, 214
Digital Millennium Copyright Act (DMCA), 144
Dilemma of Desire (2020) (Finitzo), 229, 322

director(s), 5; Argentine directors, 64, 68; Blumenthal as, 188, 189; Bowman as, 242; Finitzo as, 232, 283; fundraising by, 267; Gilbert as, 188; James as, 5, 168; Kartemquin's directors, 68, 321–24; Quinn as, 40, 42, 188; Robinson as, 242; Simpson as, 203; Temaner as, 40, 42; white professionals as, 257. *See also specific directors*
Directors Guild, 191, 264
disabilities: Bettleheim and, 202; Beyond Blind (web resource), 293; disability rights advocates, 294; intersection with, 257; JJ's List, 203; Kartemquin physical plant as inaccessible, 217, 284; Lauterbach and issues of, 270, 293; making films about and with people with, 203–4, 257; ReelAbilities Disability Film Festival, 293; *Refrigerator Mothers* and, 202–5; *When Billy Broke His Head* and, 203
Discovery+/Discovery Channel, 180, 215, 215–16
disenfranchisement: experience of, 257; James and, 257–58; obstacles from, 267
Disney+/Disney Company, 184, 207, 215
distribution: awards of distributors, 290; California Newsreel and, 136; *Dilemma of Desire* and, 229; DIY distribution, 68; errors-and-omissions insurers and, 143; fair use and, 143; *Hard Earned* and, 232; *Hoop Dreams* and, 179; Horsburgh and, 222, 235, 238, 254, 270, 276; McCall and, 118; miniseries documentary format and, 263; Nagan and, 186; New Day Films, 90, 118; social media and, 222; veteran Kartemquin filmmakers and, 224. *See also* commercial providers
Diverse Voices in Documentary (DVID), 144, 214, 222, 248, 267–80, 281
diversity: DEI issues, 255; of filmmakers, 257; funding and, 257; *A Good Man* and, 224–25; *Hoop Dreams* and, 257; Horsburgh on, 281–82; Hulu partnership and, 233; limitations from lack of, 231; 371 Productions and, 214, 233, 247. *See also* James, Steve
Doc Films, 32, 36–38, 40, 45, 100
Documentary (Barnouw), 6, 303n1
Documentary Accountability Working Group, 256
Documentary Filmmakers' Statement of Best Practice of Fair Use, 143

Dont Look Back (1967) (Pennebacker), 39–40, 45
Doremus, Fenell: Blumenthal and, 155; as board member, 293; *Cooked* and, 236, 282; financial issues, 187, 284; *5 Girls* and, 199; freelancing, 212, 293; Hoffman and, 150; James and, 153; on Kartemquin, 154; Larson and, 184; *The New Americans* and, 207, 209*fig.*; Saedi and, 207; "Sweet Dreams" project, 177
Dornfeld, Barry, 178
Drew, Robert, 31, 33, 40
Dupont-Columbia award: *Hard Earned* and, 232; *The Interrupters* and, 260
DuVernay, Ava, 264
DVDs, 180, 180–81, 196, 215, 217, 222
DVID (Diverse Voices in Documentary), 214, 222, 248, 267–80, 281
Dylan, Bob, 36, 39–40, 45

Easy Rider (1969), 64
Eating Up Easter (2018) (Rapu and Rapu), 235, 322
Ebel Productions, 166
Ebert, Chaz, 227, 248
Ebert, Roger, 13, 14, 44, 153, 172, 226–27
Eckford, Matthew, 219*fig.*
Edith + Eddie (2017) (Checkoway), 236, 322
editing/editor(s): Daniels as, 265; edit room and equipment, 285; freelance work, 286; James as, 168, 265; Kaar as, 229, 235, 241; linear editing process, 163; Simmer as, 186, 201, 233, 236, 238; Simpson as, 189, 203, 224, 265; Suffredin as, 168; time needed for, 216; Weinberg as, 236; Wickenden as, 195, 228, 234, 283
education access channels, 140
Ehrenreich, Barbara, 87
Election Day (2006), 230
Ellis, Jack, 40
Emanuel, Rahm, 240
emerging filmmaker mentor programs, 252
Emmy Awards: *Abacus* and, 263; *City So Real* and, 266; *As Goes Janesville* and, 233; *The Homestretch* and, 239; *The Interrupters* and, 260; Kartemquin's films and, 2; *Life Itself* and, 227; *The Trials of Muhammad Ali* and, 234; *Vietnam, Long Time Coming* and, 191
encryption, 144–46
Encyclopedia Britannica, 220, 234
The End of the Nightstick (1994), 154, 155

engagement: campaigns, 181, 227, 236, 273; democracies and, 291; *The Homestretch* and, 237–40; Kartemquin and, 9; new technology and, 180–81; veteran Kartemquin filmmakers and, 224
English, Dierdre, 87
environmental movement, 63, 148, 181, 292
Epstein, Robert, 115
equity investment, 23, 241, 252
errors-and-omissions insurers, 143
Espinosa, Julio Garcia, 29
ethically grounded storytelling, 5, 197, 215–16, 228, 230–31, 271
executive director(s): Leonard as, 255; Nagan as, 218–21, 251, 283; Pinder, Jolene, 253–55; Revere as interim director, 253, 255; search for, 184, 217; Steinberg as, 247, 251, 286
experience: art as, 157, 225; capturing lived experience, 27; of disenfranchisement, 257; as heart of Kartemquin films, 224, 289. *See also* cinema verité genre
Eyes on the Prize series, 150, 187

Faber, Carolyn, 245, 247
Facets, 13, 14
fair use: application of, 204–5; copyright exception for, 289; *Documentary* Filmmakers' Statement of Best Practice of Fair Use, 204; national media policy initiatives and, 4; workshops, 220–21. *See also* copyright policy issues
Fanning, David, 135
Fanton, Jonathan, 2
Far from Poland (1984), 293
Farrakhan, Louis, 152
Federal Communications Commission (FCC), 33, 140
Fellini, Federico, 32
fellowships, 267, 268. *See also* DVID (Diverse Voices in Documentary)
feminism: after WWII, 8; Chicago Women's Liberation Union (CWLU), 72, 73, 77–78, 85, 89, 103; feminist activism, 64–65, 75, 132, 172, 174, 201; second-wave, 63; socialist feminist movements, 63
Ferraro, Geraldine, 120
Festival (1967) (Lerner), 40
festivals: *Abacus* and, 263; *All the Queen's Horses* and, 276; *On Beauty* and, 228; Cannes film festival, 227; *City So Real* and, 266; *Dilemma of Desire*, 229;

festivals *(continued)*
  Festival di Populi, 55; fiftieth anniversary and, 248; *In the Game* and, 229; *The Homestretch* and, 239; information on, 321; International Documentary Festival, 198; International Documentary Film Festival Amsterdam (IDFA), 198, 206, 234; *The Interrupters* and, 260; *For the Left Hand* and, 226; *Life Itself* and, 227; *Minding the Gap* and, 273; Montreal Film Festival, 37; Ohio Film Festival, 118; promotion at, 222; racial diversity workshops at, 256; *Raising Bertie* and, 236; ReelAbilities Disability Film Festival, 293; *Refrigerator Mothers* and, 205; Rotterdam Film Festival, 89; *Saving Mes Aynak* and, 234; South by Southwest (SXSW) Film Festival, 229, 278; *Stevie* and, 198; *Unapologetic* and, 277; Yamagata Film Festival, 198
Fetterley, Jim, 47, 150–51, 152, 155, 177, 180, 199, 292
Fielding, Stevie, 196, 197, 198
Fifer, Sally Jo, 137–38
The Fight for Life (1939) (Lorentz), 86, 87
FilmAid program, 294
Film Center of the Art Institute of Chicago, 65
film culture, 32, 64
filmmaker public formation and participation: building of filmmaker network, 4–5; as element of Kartemquin's work, 24, 126–29, 146, 290; fair use, 141–46; public access TV, 140–41; public broadcasting, 129–40
filmmakers: Arts Engine filmmakers, 214; arts organization model and, 285; of color, 214, 266–67, 272, 275, 276–77, 285; commitment of, 4; DVID and, 268; fundraising and, 238, 284; labor policies and, 23; nurturing of, 285; racial reckoning and, 266–67; resistance to authority, 8; resistance to propaganda, 8; screenings, 221; social movements and, 291; veteran Kartemquin filmmakers, 224–29; white legacy filmmakers, 231, 267, 280–81. *See also specific filmmakers*
film tax credit, 251
The Film Group, 48, 51
Finally Got the News (1970), 132
financial issues: accounting issues, 236, 251, 280; budgeting, 251; cash flow structure creation, 184; decisions over, 253; dependence on commercial work, 252; federal relief funds, 254; financial costs to a, 186–87; financial cost to accomplish dreams, 17, 290; insecure business model, 17; James and, 266; Larson and, 184; racial reckoning and, 284; restructuring of, 185, 188; staff layoffs, 253. *See also* funding; physical plant; revenues; staffing
Finding Yingying (2020) (Shi), 277–78, 321
Finitzo, Maria: *Dilemma of Desire* and, 228–29, 322; *5 Girls* and, 2, 198–99, 323; funding and, 187; *In the Game* and, 228–29, 272, 322; *Hard Earned* and, 232; *Mapping Stem Cell Research: Terra Incognita* and, 199–201, 202, 323; photo, 219*fig.*; Stocchetti and, 283
Firelight Media, 214
The First Step (2021) (Kramer), 236, 321
5 Girls (2001) (Finitzo), 2, 198–201, 323
Flag Protection Act, 152
Flaherty, Robert, 46, 162
Flamo, 259
Foner, Eric, 304n2
"For an Imperfect Cinema" (Espinosa), 29
Ford Foundation, 106, 128, 130, 132, 139, 181, 187, 213, 217
For the Left Hand (2020) (Simmer and Quinn), 156, 225–26, 321
foundations: access to resources of, 244, 267; Council on Foundations, 167, 181; Crossroads Fund, 120; family foundations, 205; Gates Foundation, 182; impact campaigns and, 182; Indiana Committee for the Humanities, 114; Kohl Foundation, 90–91; right-wing foundations, 183; Skoll Foundation, 182; smaller foundations, 205. *See also* community foundations; private foundations
founder syndrome, 213
Free Cinema, 28
freelance work: commercial freelance work, 17, 283; editors and, 286; for funding, 17, 290; at Kartemquin, 283
Freeman, Jo, 75, 307n1
free speech, 142–44
Free Spirit Media, 240, 279
Friedman, Milton, 12
From Bedside to Bargaining Table (1984) (Goldfarb), 110
Frontline (TV documentary series), 4, 106, 135, 260, 263
Fruchter, Norman, 81, 155

INDEX 335

Fuchs, Cynthia, 194
FullFrame Documentary Film Festival, 225
funding: in 1960s, 9; Bagwell and, 187; BBC, 196; cable programming and, 188–93; CBC, 196; commercial freelance work for, 17, 290; COVID-19 pandemic and, 290–91; The Crossroads Fund, 114; crowdfunding, 276; David and Reva Logan Family Foundation, 229; decease in, 252; diversity and, 257; of DVID mentees, 278; evolving, 205; for films, 275, 276, 277; *5 Girls* and, 199, 201; foundation, 181–82, 205, 228, 234, 237; fundraising, 156, 253, 267, 284; *In the Game* and, 228; government access channels, 140; government funding, 7–8, 23, 228, 289; *Hard Earned* and, 232; *Higher Goals* and, 167; *Home for Life* and, 245; *The Homestretch* and, 237; *Hoop Dreams* and, 163, 168; Illinois Humanities Council, 86, 205; Indiana Committee for the Humanities, 114; Indie Coalition, 139; individual donations, 289; individual funders, 205; *The Interrupters* and, 260; ITVS and, 203, 205, 224, 233, 263; MacArthur Foundation, 2, 143, 154, 167, 168, 175, 181, 182, 196, 205, 207, 213–14, 217, 221, 222, 234, 236, 237, 267; *Milking the Rhino* and, 205; National Endowment for the Arts (NEA), 129, 205; National Endowment for the Humanities, 105; *The New Americans* and, 207, 208, 211; for operations, 186; public funding, 181; public TV, 235; *Refrigerator Mothers* and, 205; right-wing foundations and, 183; Rockefeller Foundation, 142, 143, 181; Sage Foundation and, 221, 276, 277; *Saving Mes Aynak* and, 234; sources of, 23; *Stevie* and, 196; *Terra Incognita* and, 201; veteran Kartemquin filmmakers and, 224; white professionals and, 256–57. *See also* foundations; government funding; grants; private foundations; revenues
Furniss, Adrianne, 220

Gambach, Jennie, 219*fig*.
Gambrell, Ambrell, 277
Gates, William, 167
Gates Foundation, 182
gay rights movement, 63
gender power and privilege, 16–17
The Gender Gap (1984), 155

gentrification, 91
George, Amir, 288
Gerken, Meg, 15, 49–51, 52, 64, 65, 73, 292
German documentaries of 1930s, 8
Getino, Octávio, 29, 64, 68
Get Out (2017), 264
G Force (Anderson), 275
Gibney, Alex, 214–15
Gilbert, Peter: *American Dream* and, 107–8, 165; board and, 217; branding and, 219; *At the Death House Door* and, 185, 193–96, 221, 227, 230, 322; *In the Game* and, 229; *Golub* and, 162; HBO and, 183; *Hoop Dreams* and, 168, 169*fig*.; Jaffe and, 156; Kartemquin and, 107–8; Longshot Films, 184, 188, 206; *The New Americans* and, 207; Pinder and, 253; *Stevie* and, 196, 197; storytelling of, 175; *Vietnam, Long Time Coming* and, 188, 190–91, 217; Whisnant and, 188
Gilligan, Carol, 198
Glass, Philip, 58
Gleeson, Ryan, 222, 252, 283, 286, 293
Glick, Joshua, 216
globalization, 17, 95–96
The Godfather (1972) (Coppola), 64
Godmilow, Jill, 83, 174, 293
Goes Janesville (2012), 233
Goldfarb, Lyn, 110
Golfus, Billy, 203, 323
Golub (1988) (Quinn and Blumenthal), 156–62, 166, 167, 175, 225, 323
Golub, Leon, 156–62, 158*fig*.
Golub: Late Works Are the Catastrophes (2004) (Quinn and Blumenthal), 162, 323
Gomez-Mesquita, Laura, 269*fig*., 279, 280, 284
A Good Man (2011) (Hercules and Quinn), 5, 156, 224, 322
Good Jobs First, 292
government access channels, 140
government funding, 7–8, 23, 228, 289
Gramsci, Antonio, 19–20, 22, 26
grants: Chicago Filmmakers, 241; Corporation for Public Broadcasting (CPB), 199; development grants, 268; focus on, 252; Ford Foundation, 213, 217; Illinois Arts Council, 156, 163; institutional development grant, 187–88; MacArthur Foundation, 2, 154, 167, 168, 175, 181, 182, 196, 205, 207, 213–14, 217, 221, 222, 234, 236, 237, 267; National

336 INDEX

grants *(continued)*
   Endowment for the Arts (NEA) and, 105;
   National Endowment for the Humanities,
   156; National Film Preservation Founda-
   tion, 245; National Science Foundation
   (NSF), 59; planning for operating grants,
   278; programs requiring, 282; Sage
   Foundation funding, 221, 276, 277. *See
   also* DVID (Diverse Voices in
   Documentary)
Grassroots Chicago (1991) (James), 168, 323
grassroots politics, 38, 59, 63, 65, 66, 78–79,
   95–102, 104, 105, 154, 176, 262
Gravitas Ventures, 276
Gray, Mike, 47–48, 50–52, 120
Great Books Foundation, 193, 234
Great Migration, 11, 34, 39, 120
Great Performances, 106
Great Society, 14, 105, 109
Grieco, Greg, 69
Griego, Evangeline, 208, 209
Grierson, John, 7–8, 46
Groomer, Dorothy, 204
Grossman, Albert, 40
guerrilla television movement, 245
Guerrilla Theater Group, 60
Guggenheim, David, 215
Gully, Nora, 245
Gzech, Susan, 217

habitus, 22–23, 26
Haley, Martha, 201
Hall, Larry, 136, 137
Hall, Stuart, 19, 21
Hammer Channel, 293
The Hammer Museum, 292–93
Hampton, Fred, 11–12, 48, 51–52, 71, 102,
   120, 256
Hanley, JJ, 202-4
Happy Mother's Day (1963) (Chopra and
   Leacock), 37
Hard Earned (2015 miniseries) (Kaar and
   Simpson), 3, 210, 217, 230–32, 236,
   242, 263, 322
Harlan County, U. S. A. (1976) (Kopple),
   114
Hart, Emily, 227
Haugland, David, 295
Haugse, Bill, 109
Havel, Václav, 176
Hayden, Tom, 49
Haynes, Todd, 293
HBO Documentaries, 183, 215, 278

healthcare access, 23, 88, 90
Hedman, Lars, 47–48, 50
Helfand, Judith, 236, 322
Hercules, Bob, 224, 240, 287*fig*., 322
Higher Goals (1992) (James), 167, 323
History Channel, 180
Hobsbawm, Eric, 19
Hoffman, Abbie, 49, 68
Hoffman, Judy: alienation and, 84; Blumenthal and, 5, 76; as collective member, 69,
   77, 78–80; Doremus and, 150; Faber
   and, 245; Gilbert and, 108; *Golub* and,
   157; *HSA Strike '75* and, 323; IATSE
   member, 294; Insane Unknowns and, 93;
   The Last Pullman Car and, 121; Nagan
   and, 186; photos, 71*fig*., 115*fig*., 158*fig*.,
   287*fig*.; Scott and, 295; sense of alienation, 89; social-justice missions and, 178;
   Stocchetti and, 185, 283; Videopolis and,
   131; Weinberg and, 134; *What's Happening at Local 70?* and, 98–99, 323
Hollander, Nicole, 121–22, 122*fig*., 124
home computers, 16
Home for Life (1966) (Quinn and Temaner),
   40–45, 53, 218, 244, 324
The Homestretch (2014) (De Mare and
   Kelly), 2, 237–40, 322
honors, 1
Hooker, Evelyn, 295
hooks, bell, 172, 174
Hoop Dreams (1994) (James): Academy
   Award nominations, 227; character-
   driven narratives of, 2, 3, 59, 147, 175,
   178; discussions about, 150, 153; Doremus and, 150; Ebert and, 226; funding
   and, 167, 168, 175, 188, 196, 199; Godmilow on, 174; HBO and, 183; hooks on,
   172; influence of, 179, 233, 236, 238;
   James on, 164, 258–59; Madison and,
   149; making of, 162–75; marketing of,
   171; Oscar omission, 172, 173*fig*.; profit
   participation, 171; reviews, 171–74; success of, 166, 252, 257; Wideman on, 174
Horsburgh, Tim: on anniversary year, 249;
   on collective attitude, 284; departure of,
   281–82; distribution knowledge, 222,
   235, 238, 254, 270, 276; Firelight Media
   and, 214; *Hard Earned* and, 230; hiring
   of, 221–22; Indie Caucus and, 139;
   Minding the Gap and, 272, 273; National
   Geographic and, 293; photos, 249*fig*.,
   274*fig*.; Rapu and, 235; Stocchetti and,
   283; streaming platform creation, 248

INDEX   337

Horsfield, Kate, 78
Hour of the Furnaces (1968) (Solanas and Octávio), 64, 65, 68, 86
housing policies, 23, 291
HSA Strike '75 (1975) (Hoffman), 323
Hubbard, Gary, 128
Huffman, Brent, 234, 322
Hughes, Langston, 264
Hulu (streaming platform), 233, 266, 273
Hum 255 (1970) (Blumenthal, Kuttner, Litvin, Quinn, Temaner, and Thomas), 58, 324
humanist storytelling: evolving style of, 257, 289; James and, 258-59; network of, 5; pressure on local broadcasters, 4; television programming and, 16
Hungarian uprising, 10
Hutchins, Robert Maynard, 12

Iams, Beth, 217
IATSE (International Alliance of Theatrical Stage Employees), 154, 292, 294
identity politics, 63
IDFA (International Documentary Film Festival Amsterdam), 198, 206, 234
IFC (cable channel), 193, 198-99
Illinois Arts Council, 118, 156, 163
Illinois Caucus on Teenage Pregnancy (ICTP), 109
Illinois Film Office, 251
Illinois Humanities Council, 86, 205
Iltis, John, 170, 172
Image Union, 134
impact campaigns, 273; *In the Family* and, 185; *Hard Earned* and, 232; *The Homestretch* (2014), 237-40; James and, 258; *Life Itself* and, 227
Impact Partners, 215, 252
In a Different Voice (Gilligan), 198
Independent Feature Project, 84
independent filmmakers: activism and, 136; CPB and, 105, 135; mission shift of, 275; public TV and, 131, 132; social conscience of, 289
Independent Focus, 132
Independent Lens (TV documentary series), 4, 138-39, 200, 210
Independent Television Service (ITVS). *See* ITVS (Independent Television Service)
independent theaters, 8
The Independent (periodical), 308n1
Indie Coalition, 139
Industrial Areas Foundation (IAF), 11

Influence Film Club, 227
in media res, 110
In Performance at Wolf Trap, 131
Inquiring Nuns (1968) (Quinn and Temaner), 55-56, 58, 107, 253, 324
International Alliance of Theatrical Stage Employees (IATSE), 154, 292, 294
International Documentary Association, 230, 247-48
International Documentary Awards, 232, 248, 249*fig*.
International Documentary Festival, 198
International Documentary Film Festival Amsterdam (IDFA), 198, 206, 234
internet, 16, 32, 148, 152, 181
Internews, 294
internships: archives project and, 245; Daniels and, 257, 270; Doremus and, 150; fair use training and, 144; Fetterley and, 150-51; Gleeson and, 222; Kibbie and, 236; Liu and, 257, 271; mentoring through, 281; O'Shay and, 276; Quinn and, 153; Rana and, 268; revamping of, 220-21, 222; Scott and, 149-50; Simpson and, 189; Stocchetti and, 185
The Interrupters (2011) (James and Piper), 221, 227, 241, 259-60, 263, 282, 322
intersectionality, 264
In the Family (2008) (Rudnick), 185, 186, 201-2, 322
In the Game (2015) (Finitzo), 228-29, 272, 322
In These Times (periodical), 10-11, 12, 14-15, 44, 72, 82, 127, 136, 151, 152, 241, 304n2, 308n1
Iran-Contra scandal, 105, 159
"It's a Living" (1975), 79
It's a Wonderful Life (1946), 262-63
ITVS (Independent Television Service): allocated production funding, 136; creation of, 4, 106, 162; *Eating Up Easter* and, 235; funding by, 203, 207, 224, 233, 263; *As Goes Janesville* and, 233; *A Good Man* and, 224; *The Homestretch* and, 237, 238, 239, 240; *Independent Lens*, 4, 138-39, 200, 210; Lozano and, 230; *Minding the Gap* and, 272-74; missions and goals of, 137, 138; *The New Americans* and, 207, 210-11; OVEE online platform, 240; *Raising Bertie* and, 236; *Refrigerator Mothers* and, 205; Riggs and, 162; Saedi Kiely and, 294; series concept, 207; Siegel and, 233; support

338 INDEX

ITVS *(continued)*
for, 138; *Terra Incognita* and, 200; *The Trials of Muhammad Ali* and, 233-34; "When Art Makes a Difference" project, 175-76; *When Billy Broke His Heard* and, 203; Wickham and, 168
Ivens, Joris, 29
Iverson, Allen, 164, 258-59, 322

Jackson, Jesse, 48, 68, 152
Jackson State antiwar protests, 68, 102
Jacobs, Greg, 240, 322
Jaffe, Jack, 156
Jaffe's Focus/Infinity Fund, 156
James, Steve: *Abacus* and, 262-63, 322; academic analysis of, 5; *America to Me* and, 3, 61, 182, 210, 218, 263-65, 270, 272, 273, 286, 322; on business model, 285-86; *City So Real* and, 3, 182, 210, 265, 321; *A Compassionate Spy* and, 182, 321; *At the Death House Door* (2008) (James and Gilbert), 185, 193-96, 221, 227, 230, 322; DVID and, 268; *Grassroots Chicago* and, 168, 323; HBO and, 183; *Higher Goals* and, 323; *The Interrupters* and, 221, 227, 241, 259-60, 263, 282, 283, 322; *Joe and Max* and, 209; journalistic coverage of, 5; Kartemquinites and, 294; Kuttner and, 195; Larson and, 183; *Life Itself* and, 226-27, 322; Liu and, 272; Longshot Films, 184, 206; mentoring, 153; *The New Americans* and, 3-4, 154, 167, 181, 186, 206-12, 230, 231, 263, 286, 323; *No Crossover* and, 164, 258-59, 322; Participant Productions and, 182-83; *Passing Glory* and, 208; photos, 185*fig.*, 209*fig.*, 261*fig.*, 287*fig.*; *Stevie* and, 184, 196-98, 227, 323; storytelling about race, 257-67; white legacy filmmakers and, 231. *See also Hoop Dreams* (1994) (James)
Jarmusch, Jim, 163
Jaszi, Peter, 142-43
The Jeffersons, 64
Jensen, Shirlee, 65, 156
Jigsaw Productions, 214-15, 256
Jimenez, José Cha Cha, 50
JJ's List, 203
Jodorowsky, Alejandro, 32
Johnson, Kiere, 272*fig.*
Johnson, Morgan Elise, 41, 277, 293
Johnson administration, 14, 49, 53, 105
Jones, Bill T., 5, 224-25
Jones, Van, 236
journalistic documentaries, 215
Judas and the Black Messiah (2021) (King), 51
Judis, John, 304n2
Jump/Cut, 74, 82, 84

Kaar, Liz, 229, 235, 241, 249*fig.*, 293, 322
Karlin, Nurit, 172, 173*fig.*
Karp, Sharon, 69, 70, 76, 84-90, 98, 189, 293, 323
Kartemquin films: advocacy work, 9; as art form, 7; as character driven, 2; as complex works, 2; credibility of, 226; direct effects of, 17; early phase, 5; engagement work, 9; filmography, 321-24; as humanistic, real-life dramas, 2; late phase, 5; as nondidactic, 2; paucity of villains in, 2; subject matter, 16-17; television program production, 9; theatrical film production, 9; as tool for democratic discourse, 7; unjust systems, 2; as unsellable, 2; as unsentimental, 2. *See also specific films*
Kartemquin Films (book), 248
Kartemquin Films (company): Academy Award nominations, 1; accounting issues, 251; archives project and, 245-47; availability of DVDs of, 321; avoidance of celebrity, 6; avoidance of promotion, 6; awards, 1; board-run structure, 16; branding of, 186; business model, 184, 221, 251, 263, 283-88; Catholic films, 53-58; as center of activism, 4; changes in, 244-45; changing culture struggles at, 282-83; cinematic social inquiry goal of, 30-35; cinema verité within philosophy of, 27-30, 82, 86, 175; clubhouse and community, 212; collaborative mode of, 6; as collective, 6, 240-44; commercial work, 13; confronting power and privilege within, 16-17, 290; core assets, 254; core of, 12; core values, 1, 249; cultural mode creation, 17; as cultural network, 17; diversity and, 267; diversity program, 250, 268; Emmys, 2; equipment, 3*fig.*, 41, 59, 66, 285; ethos of, 226, 252; evolution of, 15-16, 26-27; in evolution of documentaries, 7; as family, 5; festival awards, 2; fiftieth anniversary, 245, 247-49; founding of, 6; honors, 1; humanist storytelling, 16; identifying slogan, 9-10; labor unions and, 16; launch of, 1; leaders of, 16-17, 213; as left-leaning, 10;

legacy of, 249, 287, 292; legacy projects, 267; local social movements and, 16; as media arts center, 282; mini-retrospective at The Hammer, 293; miniseries documentary format, 3-4; nonprofit projects, 58-61; as nonsectarian, 17; optimism of, 291-92; as overlooked, 5-6; Peabody Awards, 2; Peabody Awards institutional award (2019), 2; philosophy of, 1, 27-30; as political collective, 16; political polarization, 48-53; professional support of, 202, 238; progressive vision of social change, 17; resources of, 290; response to constraints, 16; response to opportunities, 16; restructuring of, 16, 188, 212, 216-24, 258, 267; social research beginnings, 16; storytelling styles, 4; Sundance Film Festival awards, 2; television program production, 16; vision of, 255, 290, 291; website, 321; work environment, 290; working conditions, 1; working mode of hope, 17

Kartemquinites: activism of, 24; afterlives of, 252, 292; altruism of, 292; arts and humanities councils and, 4; aspirations of, 17; change and, 269; cinema verité purity of, 58; in collective era, 280-81, 285; filmmaker public and, 24, 290; filmmaking of, 293; Free Spirit Media and, 279; nonprofit sector, 293; nonsectarian, progressive vision of social change of, 17; nonwhite, 263; optimism of, 291-92; on Quinn and Blumenthal, 153-54; screenings and, 221; shared ideals of, 17, 292; sweat equity, 199, 290; television and, 131. *See also specific Kartemquinites*

Kartemquin Labs, 214, 215, 221, 230, 234, 238, 248, 270, 278-79

Kartemquin's First Camera (2012 short) (Johnson), 41

Karter, Stan, 38, 45, 60, 242

Keep Talking (2017) (Weinberg), 236, 322

Kelly, Kirsten, 237-40, 322

Kennedy, Robert F., 49, 102

Kent State antiwar protests, 68, 102

Kerry, John, 188

Khrushchev, Nikita, 10

Kibbie, Ian, 236

Kiely, Gita Saedi. *See* Saedi Kiely, Gita

Kill the Documentary manifesto (Godmilow), 174

Kilmurry, Simon, 202, 244

Kindling Group, 214, 240

King, Allan, 81
King, Martin Luther, Jr., 102
King, Shaka, 51
Kirkman, Larry, 181
Klein, Jim, 83
Kleinhans, Chuck, 74
Kline, Kathy, 134
Kodiak Alutiiq (language), 236
Kohl Foundation, 90-91
Kopple, Barbara, 107-8, 114, 195, 207
Korsts, Anda, 79
Kotlowitz, Alex, 259, 261*fig.*, 263, 283
Kramer, Brandon, 156, 225-26, 236, 321
Kramer, Lance, 236
Kramer, Robert, 68
Krishnan, Indu, 207-8, 209*fig.*
Kupper, Dana, 196, 197, 227
Kurtis, Bill, 198
Kuttner, Peter, 69, 70, 80-81, 92-93, 108, 154-55, 195, 222, 280-81, 292, 323, 324
Kwakwaka'wakw nation, 294

labor issues: *Hard Earned* and, 3, 217, 230-32; *Harlan County, U. S. A.* and, 114; labor activism, 128, 132; labor conditions, 257; labor policies, 23; *The Last Pullman Car* and, 114-19; politics and, 109-19; progressive organizing in 1960s in Chicago and, 11

labor movements: activists, 79; *American Dream* and, 108, 110; history of, 304n2; Kartemquinites and, 72, 292

labor unions: *As Goes Janesville* and, 233; Kartemquin and, 16, 96-97; Kartemquinites and, 294; public TV sponsorship and, 131; *Taylor Chain I* and *II*, 110-14

La Leche League, 57

lantern slideshows, 7

Larson, Karen, 5, 184-85, 195

The Last Pullman Car (1983) (Quinn and Blumenthal), 9, 114-19, 121, 149, 163, 292, 323

Latin American cinema, 13, 64

Latinx people, 89; CCOM and, 128; *In the Game* and, 228-29; liberation theology, 53, 61; New Latin American Cinema, 64; Patlán, 94-95; in postwar Chicago, 11; solidarity among, 95; UnidosUS, 48; *Viva La Causa* (1974), 93-94; Young Lords Organization, 12, 48, 50, 61, 65, 80, 120

Lauterbach, Matt, 270, 293

Leacock, Richard, 31, 33, 36, 37, 40, 41, 46

Lear, Norman, 64
Learning Channel, 118
Lee, Grace, 21
Lee, Spike, 171
Left Hand (2020), 156, 225–26
the Left: Chuck Olin Association, 108; history of American left, 304n2; left-wing activist documentaries, 8; left-wing activists, 8, 50, 62, 83, 105, 120, 135–36; left-wing Democratic party, 20; mainstreaming of left-wing values, 64; UE and, 101
legacy projects, 267
Leitman, Ruth, 249*fig.*
LeMond, Greg, 188
Leonard, Betsy, 255
Lerner, Jack, 144
Lerner, Murray, 40
LeRoy, Greg, 114, 118, 119, 292
LeSage, Julia, 74, 77
Let the Little Light Shine (2022) (Shaw), 265
Lewis, Carolyn Herbst, 85
LGBT activism, 63, 84, 132, 133, 295
liberation theology, 53, 61
Lichtenstein, Brad, 214, 233, 247, 249*fig.*, 322
Life Itself (2018) (James), 226–27, 322
Lifetime, 123
Lincoln, Abraham, 224–25
Litvin, Jason, 324
Litwack, Leon, 304n2
Liu, Bing, 257, 263–64, 271–75, 280, 285, 287*fig.*, 322
Lonely Boy (1963), 37
Longshot Films, 184, 188, 206
"Looking for Democracy" project, 176–77
Lorentz, Pare, 86
Loxton, David, 106, 134
Lozano, Carrie, 230
Lumiere, 233
A Luta Continua (1972), 133
Lynd, Staughton, 95, 118
Lynn, Alice, 95
Lyon, Danny, 39

M*A*S*H, 64
MacArthur Foundation, 2, 80, 129, 139, 143, 154, 167, 168, 170, 175, 181, 182, 196, 200, 205, 207, 213–14, 217, 221, 222, 234, 236, 237, 267
MacDonald, Laquan, 255, 266
Magill, Jeannie R., 205, 322
Makavejev, Dušan, 32
Making a Murderer, 215
Malcolm X, 48, 102
Malone, Norman, 225–26
The Mandalorian, 215
Maoism, 63, 70, 72, 73
Mapping Stem Cell Research: Terra Incognita (2007) (Finitzo), 199–201, 202, 323
Marco (1970) (Quinn and Temaner), 56–58, 323
marginalized groups: creation of resources for filmmakers of, 4, 267; marginalized film participants, 9, 238; parity of conditions for, 24
Marker, Chris, 31
marketing, 171, 186, 270
Marshall Project, 242
Martens, Betsy, 69, 71*fig.*, 72, 292
Marx, Fred, 162–63, 165, 168–69
Marx, Karl, 24
Marxism: Black Panther Party and, 48, 51; cultural Marxism, 305n1; demonization of, 20; Dewey and, 24; Gramsci and, 22; white, working-class Marxist organizations and, 48, 51
The Mary Tyler Moore Show, 64
Marzyński, Marian, 189
Massiah, Louis, 214
Masterpiece Theater, 130
Mathews, Ameena, 248, 259, 261*fig.*
Matters of Life and Death . . . and Other Matters, 101, 113, 135
Matthews, Tracye, 242, 243*fig.*, 244, 322
Maysles, Al, 31, 33, 41, 66, 150
Maysles, David, 31, 33, 66
McCall, Marcy, 5, 108, 118, 127, 154, 164–65, 177, 185, 293–94
McCarter, Jeff, 322
McCarthyism, 46, 102
McDonald, Nancy, 245, 247
McGill, Jeannie, 205
McLuhan, Marshall, 53
Meadows, Tim, 167
media arts organization era: archives, 245–47; becoming a, 213–16; changes, 244–45; fiftieth anniversary, 247–49; *Hard Earned* (2015 miniseries), 230–32; *The Homestretch* (2014), 237–40; Kartemquin-based filmmakers, 224–29; partnering for impact, 237–40; partnering for productivity, 232–36; publicly defining as, 186; redefining as, 184; restructuring, 216–24; spirit of the collective, 240–44. *See also* crises

INDEX 341

Media Burn, 245
media industry scholarship, 19
Media Process Group, 214, 224, 240, 258
media reform movement: CCOM and, 128; Community Film Workshop, 82, 128, 177, 217, 267, 268, 295; fair use, 141–46; *Independent Focus*, 132; Kartemquin and, 127–29; media activists, 83; public access TV and, 140–41; public broadcasting and, 129–40
medical apartheid, 85
Medium Cool (1963) (Wexler), 50
mentoring: commitment to, 266–67; consistency in, 289; emerging filmmaker mentor programs, 252; expanding capacity for, 270; Kuttner's retiring from, 280–81; monetizing of, 284; Quinn's, 216–17, 218, 276. *See also* DVID (Diverse Voices in Documentary)
Merleau-Ponty, Maurice, 31
Mes Aynak (Afghanistan), 234
methodology, 18, 299–301
#MeToo movement, 293
Meyer, Nancy, 120–21, 123
Midwest Academy, 11
Midwest film culture, 5
Milk, Harvey, 294–95
Milking the Rhino (2008) (Simpson and Magill), 205–6, 322
Miller, Scharene, 86, 87
Minding the Gap (2018) (Liu), 271–74, 278, 322
miniseries documentary format, 3–4, 7, 230–32, 263
Minnesota Timberwolves, 167
Minow, Newton, 33
A Miracle on 19th Street (2021) (Mitten), 321
misogyny, 290, 293
mission-driven institutions, 68, 215, 250
mission of Kartemquin: aligning with, 263, 280; asserting of, 281; in broadcast and cable era, 179, 183; during collective era, 70, 82, 91; guidance of, 27; for-hire work and, 189; importance of, 1; insistence on, 6; post *Hoop Dreams* mission, 236; Quinn on, 248–49; supporters of, 154; Temaner on, 60; trust in, 217; unmade projects and, 175. *See also* cinematic social inquiry
Mitten, Mark, 321
Mondale, Walter, 120
Montreal Film Festival, 37

Moore, Michael, 2
Moran, Cyndi, 155
Morin, Edgar, 31, 55
Morris, Jeannie, 155
Morrissette, Jim: Byrne and, 235–36; Copyright Tribunal presentation, 144–45; departure of, 253, 283; *In the Game* and, 228–29; *Grassroots Chicago* and, 168; joining Kartemquin, 47; nonprofit and collaborative work, 154; sound and, 199; video and, 79, 149, 150, 163; "When Art Makes a Difference" project, 176
Moseley, Kelley, 219*fig.*
Moses, Bob, 240
Movement for Black Lives, 276
Moviola, 66
Moynihan, Daniel, 53
MTV Documentaries, 278
Mueller, Denis, 161
Mulligan, Zack, 272*fig.*
multiplicity of stories, 3–4
The Murder of Fred Hampton, 108, 181
Museum of Modern Art, 124
Myatt, Alyce, 168, 182
A Mystery to Me (2020) (Strang), 321

NAACP Image Award, 234
Nagan, Justine: archives project, 245; board and, 217–21, 267; boards and, 224; branding and, 186, 217, 219, 222, 247; departure of, 244–45, 251; fiftieth anniversary and, 247, 248; Finitzo and, 199; Firelight Media and, 214; *Hard Earned* and, 230, 231; *The Interrupters* and, 283; joining Kartemquin, 185–87; Kartemquin Labs and, 221; *Minding the Gap* and, 272; photos, 187*fig.*, 219*fig.*, 249*fig.*; *POV* and, 273, 293; revenues, 196, 268; *Sacred Transformation* and, 322; Stocchetti and, 283; *Typeface* and, 217, 322; visions of partnering, 232–33
'Namgis people of the Kwakwaka'wakw nation, 294
National Advocacy Video, 181
National Center for Outreach, 181
National Coalition of Independent Public Broadcasting Producers, 137
National Council of La Raza (UnidosUS), 48
National Educational Television (NET), 130, 132
National Endowment for the Arts (NEA), 105, 129

National Endowment for the Humanities, 105, 118, 156
National Film Preservation Foundation, 245
National Geographic Documentary Films, 180, 215, 282
National Guard, 50, 51, 68
national media: counterdiscourse to, 6; power relationships of, 8; prestige dailies, 8; TV networks, 8
National Organization for Women (NOW), 121, 124
National Science Foundation (NSF), 59
Native communities. See BIPOC issues
Nature, 131
NBC network, 191
The Negro Family (US Department of Labor), 53
Nelson, David K., Jr., 151
neoliberalism: in Clinton era, 148; feminism and, 119-25; in labor and politics, 109-19; in Reagan era, 104-6, 120, 122-23, 147; working-class groups and, 104-9. See also postcollective era of Kartemquin
Netflix (streaming platform), 215-16, 217, 234, 276, 278
Nevins, Sheila, 183, 278
New American Movement (NAM), 12, 63, 65
The New Americans (2003) (James, Saedi, and Quinn), 3-4, 154, 167, 181, 186, 206-12, 230, 231, 263, 286, 323
New Cinema, 68
New Day Films, 68, 84, 90, 118, 149
The New Explorer (documentary series), 198
New Latin American Cinema, 64
New Left: in Britain, 63; in Chicago, 11, 14-15; on cultural production, 20-21; Gramsci and, 22; Weinstein and, 10
New Left Review (periodical), 10, 15
New Orleans Film Society, 253
New Wave, 28, 36
New York Newsreel, 50, 55, 68, 81, 155
New York Women in Film and Television (NYWIFT), 124
Nightly Business Report, 131
Nixon, Richard, 128, 131-32, 134
No Crossover (2010) (James), 164, 258-59, 322
nonprofit sector: board members from, 217; consultants from, 187; dilemma of, 275; Kartemquinites in, 292, 293, 294; leader competition in, 217
nonsectarian approach, 6, 14, 17, 34, 52, 63, 73, 103

Now We Live on Clifton (1974) (Kartemquin Collective), 91-92, 323
Nyad, Diana, 188

Obama, Barack, 99
Ocasio-Cortez, Alexandria, 63
Office of Economic Opportunity, 128
Ohio Film Festival, 118
Olin, Chuck, 47, 89, 105, 120, 176, 294
On Beauty (2014) (Rudnick), 228, 322
One Day at a Time, 64
open access, 292
Operation PUSH, 152
organizations: producing with, 82-94; support programs from, 275
Orion Pictures, 293
Oscar awards: *The Times of Harvey Milk* (1984) (Schmeichen). See Academy Awards of Merit (Oscar awards)
O'Shay, Ashley, 276, 277, 280, 290, 293, 321
Our Bodies, Ourselves (Boston Women's Health Book Collective), 85
outreach: *Hard Earned* and, 232; *The Interrupters* and, 260; *The New Americans* and, 211; *Refrigerator Mothers* and, 205
OVEE online platform, 240
Ozu, Yasujirō, 32

Pacific Street Film, 83
Pack, Michael, 183
Paik, Nam June, 78
Parajanov, Sergei, 32
Parents (1968) (Quinn and Temaner), 54, 324
Paretzkin, Brita, 66
Parrish, Rebecca, 218, 263-64
Participant Productions, 182, 263, 265
participatory filmmaking: community engagement and, 9; *Hard Earned* and, 232; *The Homestretch* and, 238; *Hoop Dreams* and, 171; *Raising Bertie* and, 235; *Stevie* and, 198; *We Are Witnesses: Chicago 2019* and, 242; *When Billy Broke His Head* and, 203
partnerships: fiftieth anniversary and, 247; *The Homestretch* and, 237-40; with Hulu, 233; for impact, 237-40; with local broadcasters, 4; for productivity, 232-36; splits, 221
Pasolini, Pier Paolo, 32
Patel, Raj, 321
Patlán, Ray, 94-95

patterns of practice, 24
Paul Butterfield Blues Band, 13, 38, 40
Peabody Awards, 2, 200, 263
Pedraza, Linda, 201
Pennebaker, D. A. "Penny," 31, 33, 41, 45, 141
people of color: centering of experiences of, 236, 290; as directors, 290; as filmmakers, 214, 224, 242, 266–67, 272, 275, 276–77, 285; Free Spirit Media, 279; hiring of, 266–67; mentorship of, 266–67. *See also* BIPOC issues; Black people
Perdoux, Martin, 219*fig.*
The Perfumed Nightmare (1977) (Tahimik), 90
permissioned work, 143. *See also* fair use
phenomenological philosophy, 31
philosophy of Kartemquin: cinema verité within, 27–30; pragmatic philosophy and, 7, 17, 25, 72, 194, 270, 291–92. *See also* Dewey, John; Deweyan philosophy
physical plant: during COVID-19 pandemic, 254; expansion challenges, 283; in Hyde Park, 46, 59, 118; as inadequate, 17, 230; lack of disabled access, 217, 284; location of, 268; maintenance issues, 217, 220, 230, 251, 283–84; at Wellington Avenue, 66–67, 67*fig.*
Pickett, Carroll, 193, 194
Pierce Family Foundation, 237
Pill, Jeffrey, 323
Pillsbury, George, 86
Pimsleur, Julia, 214
Pinder, Jolene, 253–55, 263, 286, 291, 300
Pingatore, Gene, 165–66
Piper, Zak: afterlife of, 293; *The Ants & the Grasshopper* and, 321; archive project and, 245; on Blumenthal, 223; CeaseFire and, 259; *At the Death House Door* and, 195; as director, 321; *In the Family* and, 186; financial issues and, 187; *The Interrupters* and, 260, 261*fig.*, 283, 322; on Kartemquin's leaders, 198; *Let the Little Light Shine* and, 265; *Life Itself* and, 227; photos, 219*fig.*
Pitts, Brian, 165
Point of Order (1964) (Antonio), 31
political ideology: avoidance of rigidity in, 6; avoidance of sectarianism, 6, 14, 52–53, 70; challenges of political crisis, 291; change and, 24; labor and, 109–19; left-wing activist documentaries and, 8; political polarization, 48–53, 51; political trends, 16; publics and, 26; Republic Party, 122; role of, 19; two-party system, 10, 16. *See also* democratic socialism; the Left; Marxism; social movements; two-party system
The Politics of Documentary (Chanan), 6
Polk Bros. Foundation, 237
Pope, Kelly Richmond, 275–76, 322
The Popovich Brothers of South Chicago (1977) (Godmilow), 83
Portapak Revolution, 78, 79, 98, 99
positionality, 257
postcollective era of Kartemquin, 104–25; color work, 124–25; labor and politics, 109–19; neoliberalism and, 104–9; *Women's Voices: The Gender Gap* (1984), 119–24
postcolonial films, 29, 64, 133
postproduction, 186, 187, 222, 283
POV (TV documentary series), 4, 135, 139, 155, 199, 202, 236, 244, 272, 273, 277, 293
power: belief in powerful stories, 291; Bourdieu on, 22, 23; change and, 21; confronting of, 16–17, 294; cultural hegemony as, 26; Dewey on, 25; structures that channel, 23–24; struggle of different forces of, 19; working together and, 282
pragmatic philosophy, American, 7, 17, 25, 72, 194, 270, 291–92. *See also* Dewey, John; Deweyan philosophy
precarity: during COVID-19 pandemic, 254–55; of filmmakers, 239; of hard-working people, 231; Kartemquin's periods of, 186–87; as nerve-wracking, 154; of socially committed media, 214
Prisoner of Her Past (2010) (Quinn and Reich), 221, 223, 225, 322
private foundations: as anonymous donors, 139; BIPOC and, 284; Council on Foundations, 167, 181; as funding source, 23, 289; Jaffe's Focus/Infinity Fund, 156; Kohl Foundation, 91; public policy and, 289; relationships with, 179; *Saving Mes Aynak* and, 234. *See also* Annie E. Casey Foundation; Ford Foundation; MacArthur Foundation; Rockefeller Foundation
privilege: acknowledging, 239, 286; confronting of, 16–17; conversation struggles over, 278–79; working together and, 282

producer(s): Bowman, Maggie, 218; Bowman as, 230; Cole as, 235; Dickson as, 240, 242; Doremus as, 236, 282; James as, 265; Kibbie as, 236; LeRoy as, 115; Lozano as, 230; Piper as, 195, 265; Quon as, 225; Rohrer as, 115; Rudnick as, 224; Saedi as, 207; Scorsese as, 227; Singer as, 283; Whisnant as, 217
productivity, 232–36
profit participation, 283
propaganda, 7–8
public access cable: Cable Act of 1990, 309n1; CAN-TV, 140–41; creating and sustaining, 24; new opportunities in mediated storytelling in, 4; public access centers, 140; public access channels, 140
public broadcasting: independent filmmakers and, 308n1; legislation on, 129; national media policy initiatives and, 4; Republican hostility to, 105
Public Broadcasting Act, 130
Public Broadcasting Service (PBS): *American Masters*, 224, 225; CPB and, 106; *Eating Up Easter* and, 235; *In the Family* and, 202; *Frontline* (TV documentary series), 4, 260, 263; ITVS and, 138; *Minding the Gap* and, 273–74; *The New Americans* and, 208; *POV* (TV documentary series), 4, 199, 202, 236, 244, 272, 273, 277, 293; prioritizing series, 207; programming restatement, 139; program sharing, 131; *Raising Bertie* and, 236; *The Trials of Muhammad Ali* and, 234. *See also* ITVS (Independent Television Service)
publics: accountability and, 25; acting for change, 26; common problem-solving and, 25; communication processes and, 26; defined, 25–26; democratic publics, 24–25, 30–31; Deweyan concept of, 26; formation of, 25–26; as frail, 25
Public Television, A Program for Action (Carnegie Commission Report), 129
The Public and Its Problems (Dewey), 30–31, 46, 248
public TV: *American Masters*, 186, 224, 225; beginning of, 8–9; Black perspectives in programming, 64; competition for audiences and filmmakers, 180, 215; demands for funding and airtime from, 24; *The End of the Nightstick* and, 155; fair use and, 204; *In the Family* and, 201; fragility of, 131; funding, 235; *As Goes Janesville* and, 233; *Golub* and, 161; *The Homestretch* and, 239; ITVS (Independent Television Service), 176; *POV* (TV documentary series), 4, 155, 272, 273, 277, 293; public mission of, 136–37; as public policy, 289; *Refrigerator Mothers* and, 205; relationships with, 179; station KTCA, 167, 170; station WTTW, 33, 39, 79, 131, 134, 164, 209, 240, 241, 248; *Stranded by the State* and, 241; support from, 224, 233; *When Billy Broke His Head* and, 203
public TV activism. *See* filmmaker public formation and participation
The Color Purple (1985), 109

Queen Sugar (2016) (DuVernay), 264
Quinn, Gordon: Active Voice and, 181; advice of, 216, 235; advocacy of, 287; Alk and, 39–40; *Anonymous Artists of America* and, 323; archives project, 245, 247; as artistic director, 255; arts community meetings, 253; Becker and, 244; board and, 217; Boggs and, 21; Bowman and, 230; CAN-TV and, 140–41; career achievement award, 248; Chevigny and, 253; in Chicago, 12; *Chicago Crossings* and, 323; *The Chicago Maternity Center Story* and, 9, 46, 76, 84–90, 116, 117, 132–33, 141, 323; Citron and, 177; *City So Real* (2020 miniseries) and, 265; collaborative mode of, 224; as collective member, 69; *The College* (1964), 38; Copyright Tribunal presentation, 144–45; Cox and, 150; *At the Death House Door* and, 193; on democratic journalism, 10; on Dewey, 25, 152–53, 166; on diversity issue, 267; Doc Films, 32, 36–38, 100; *Dont Look Back* (1967), 39–40, 45; Dylan and, 39–40; *Edith + Eddie* and, 236; ethical compass of, 231; at ethnographic congress in Chicago, 79; as executive director, 183–84; fair use and, 143–46, 220–21; at festivals, 225; on filmmaker public, 24; on financial issues, 186–87; Finitzo and, 230; Firelight Media and, 214; *5 Girls* and, 199; forming Kartemquin team, 45–46; as founder, 1, 10; Gerken and, 49–51, 52, 64, 65; Gleeson and, 222; *Golub* and, 156, 159, 160–61, 166, 175, 323; *Golub: Late Works Are the Catastrophes* and, 162, 323; *A Good Man* (2011) and, 224, 322; *Grassroots Chicago* and, 168; Hanley and,

203, 204; Hoffman and, 157; *Home for Life* and, 40–45, 218, 244, 324; *Hoop Dreams* and, 163, 164, 166, 171, 172, 179; *Hum 255* and, 324; illness, 254; on inclusion, 280; *Inquiring Nuns* and, 55–56, 58, 324; Jewish culture and, 46–47; Kartemquinites and, 293, 294; KTCA negotiations, 167; Kuttner and, 195; Larson and, 183; *The Last Pullman Car* and, 9, 114–19, 121, 149, 163, 292, 323; Lichtenstein and, 233; *Life Itself* and, 227; Liu and, 272, 273; *Marco* and, 56–58, 323; Massiah and, 214; Mathews and, 259; mentoring, 153, 168–69, 201, 212, 216–17, 221, 236, 238, 270; *Milking the Rhino* and, 205; on mission, 27; at Montreal Film Festival, 37; Nagan and, 244; *The New Americans* and, 3–4, 154, 167, 181, 186, 206–12, 230, 231, 263, 286, 323; *Parents* and, 54, 324; photos, 3, 158*fig.*, 206*fig.*, 209*fig.*, 219*fig.*, 249*fig.*, 269*fig.*, 274*fig.*, 287*fig.*; policy work led by, 4; on politics, 74; Pope and, 275, 276; pressure campaign on CPB, 308n1; *Prisoner of Her Past* and, 221, 223, 225, 322; on public access and public TV, 127, 139–40; as resistant to marketing, 6; on role of culture in social change, 15; Rudnick and, 201–2; Sabu and, 270; *Saving Mes Aynak* and, 234; *The School Project* and, 240; as second father/family/friend, 5; as self-effacing, 6; senior thesis of, 30; Siegel and, 233, 234; *'63 Boycott* and, 38, 242, 244, 322; staff layoffs and, 253; *Stevie* and, 196, 197; story guidance, 226, 254; support of storytellers, 285; "Sweet Dreams" project, 177; *Taylor Chain I* and, 99, 110, 111, 112, 118, 149, 323; *Taylor Chain II* and, 99, 110–13, 118, 124, 131, 163, 323; television and, 33; Temaner and, 31; *And This Is Free* and, 38–39, 131; *Thumbs Down* and, 53–55, 324; *UE/Wells* and, 101–2, 323; at University of Chicago, 12–13, 29, 31, 32, 34; *Vietnam, Long Time Coming* and, 189–91, 323; vision of, 248–49, 291; Wellington Avenue building and, 67; *What the Fuck Are These Red Squares?* and, 67–68, 82, 151, 324; *Where's I. W. Abel?* and, 79, 96, 323; Whisnant and, 188; white legacy filmmakers and, 231; WTTW and, 134

Quon, Diane, 225, 272, 273, 278

race issues: Baldwin on reality in, 21–22; Black Lives Matter movement, 255, 277; confronting of, 290; confronting power and privilege of race, 16–17; *A Good Man* and, 224; institutional relationship with, 254–55; Jim Crow violence, 264; Movement for Black Lives, 276; storytelling about race, 257–67; veteran Kartemquin filmmakers and, 224; white nationalist organizing, 280, 291. *See also* James, Steve

racial injustice: documentaries and, 256; intersectionality and, 264; progressive organizing in 1960s in Chicago and, 11

racial justice: centering on, 255; Lichtenstein and, 233

racial reckoning: film and arts institutions and, 290; fundraising and, 284; internal process for action in, 254–55; national discourse on race as, 255; reparations framework, 281; white nationalist organizing and, 291

Rainbow Coalition, 12, 48, 50, 62–63, 71, 148, 256, 280

Rainbow Productions, 108

Raindance, 78

Raising Bertie (2016) (Byrne), 235–36, 322

Rana, Anuradha (Anu), 268–69, 269*fig.*, 279

Rapu, Elena, 235, 322

Rapu, Sergio, 235, 322

Raumer, Bruce, 241

Ray, Satyajit, 32

Reagan administration: neoliberalism and, 104–6, 120, 122–23, 147; public broadcasting and, 308n1; state media in, 183; women and, 122–23

reality: battle for, 19, 21; Bourdieu on, 22–23; complex reality, 9; cultural reality, 9, 26; in making of Kartemquin films, 7, 23; patterns of practice and shared, 24; as social construct, 22, 25, 26

Rech, Shawn, 215

Reddy, Helen, 64

Red Squad (1972), 49, 83

ReelAbilities Disability Film Festival, 293

Refrigerator Mothers (2002) (Simpson), 202–5, 323

Reich, Howard, 223, 225–26, 322

Reichert, Julia, 68, 83, 110

Represent (2020) (Bachelder), 252, 321

Republican National Committee, 122

resources: after restructuring, 267; commitment to overcome deficits in, 250; discussions over focus of, 252; for diverse talent, 256–57; Larson and, 183; sapping of, 212
Reveille for Radicals, 11
revenues: 50/50 split with filmmakers, 236; from commercial channels, 23; from *At the Death House Door* DVD, 196; educational sales, 215; equipment rental, 184; from *Hard Earned*, 232; from *Hoop Dreams*, 171; from ICTP project, 109; from *Life Itself*, 226; Nagan's vision for, 232–33; signature production revenue stream, 220; work-for-hire, 184
Revere, Elspeth, 168, 182, 205, 244, 249, 249*fig.*, 253, 255, 287
reviews: *Hard Earned* and, 232; *Hoop Dreams* and, 171; *Milking the Rhino* and, 206; *Raising Bertie* and, 236
Revolutionary Communist Party, 52, 63, 73
Rhoton, Rose, 194
Ribicoff, Abe, 50
Rich, B. Ruby, 64–65
Riggs, Marlon, 162
rights issues, 204
the Right: culture and, 151; right-wing organization, 8, 183; right-wing populists, 11, 20, 255–56. *See also* Reagan administration
Rising Up Angry (RUA), 48, 89, 90–93, 94*fig.*, 323
Roadrunner (2021), 215
Robé, Chris, 65
RogerEbert.com, 265, 274
Robinson, Stacy, 242, 322
Rockefeller Foundation, 12, 106, 142, 143, 181
Rocklin, William, 42
rock star profile genre, 37
Roettgen, Ingrid, 247, 252, 253, 293
Roger and Me (1989) (Moore), 2
Rohrer, Jenny: afterlife of, 294; *The Chicago Maternity Center Story* and, 84–90, 133, 323; as collective member, 69, 71*fig.*, 74–78; democratic socialism of, 72; *The Last Pullman Car* and, 115–16; mentoring by, 108, 294; New Day Films and, 118; at Quinn's farewell roast, 287*fig.*; return of, 107, 119; *Science Held Hostage* and, 155; *Women's Voices: The Gender Gap* and, 119–24, 323
Romero, George, 293

Rosenbaum, Jonathan, 161
Rosensweig, Roy, 304n2
Rotterdam Film Festival, 89
Rouch, Jean, 31, 46, 55, 79–80
Roundtable Media, 181
Rowe, Mike, 215
royalty payments, 184
Rubin, Jerry, 49
Rudnick, Joanna: *On Beauty* and, 228, 322; *Election Day* and, 230; *In the Family* and, 185, 186, 201–2, 322; funding, 217, 224; *A Good Man* and, 224; joining Kartemquin, 185–88; photo, 219*fig.*; *Prisoner of Her Past* and, 223
Rules for Radicals, 11
Rush, Bobby, 52
Rybicky, Dan, 228, 322

Sabu, Dinesh Das, 139, 144, 214, 219*fig.*, 220–21, 248, 252, 270–71, 322
Sacred Transformation (2010) (Nagan), 322
Saedi Kiely, Gita, 5, 154, 206–7, 209, 210, 283, 294, 300, 323
Sage Foundation, 221, 276, 277
SAIC (School of the Art Institute of Chicago), 78, 151–52, 176
Sanders, Bernie, 10, 39, 63, 243, 304n2
San Francisco Newsreel, 69
Sapadin, Larry, 136
Saturday Night Live, 13
Saving Mes Aynak (2014) (Huffman), 234, 322
scan conversion, 144
Scharres, Barbara, 35
Schwartzman, Stephan, 12
Schierbeek, Elise, 247
Schmeichen, Richard, 69, 73, 74, 84, 115, 294–95
Schneider, Ellen, 211
Scholl, Eric, 155
School of the Art Institute of Chicago (SAIC), 78, 151–52, 176
school reform movement, 292
The School Project (2014) (Siskel, Jacobs, and McCarter), 240–41, 322
Science Held Hostage (1992), 155
Scorsese, Martin, 227
Scott, Ed, 149–51, 152, 153, 155, 177, 212, 295
screenings, 221, 230, 239, 242, 244, 271
Scribe Video Center, 214
Second City, 13, 39, 249
sectarianism, 6, 14, 52–53, 70

INDEX 347

Seitz, Matt Stoller, 274
self-censorship, 143, 198
sentimentalism, 2, 4, 174, 289
Service Employees International Union, 110
Sexton, Robby, 219*fig.*
Shaw, Kevin, 263–64, 265
Shea, Mike: camera of, 41; Doc Films and, 38; Dylan and, 40; The Film Group and, 47–48; Kartemquinites and, 47; *'63 Boycott* and, 242; *And This Is Free* and, 39, 131
Shepherd, Cybil, 155
Shi, Jiayan "Jenny," 277, 321
Showtime, 229
Siegel, Bill, 233–34, 322
Simmer, Leslie, 186, 187, 191, 193, 201, 219*fig.*, 220, 225, 229, 235, 236, 238, 252, 264, 270, 286, 293; *As Goes Janesville* and, 233, 322
Simon, David, 258
Simpson, David E., 160, 189, 212, 220, 224, 227, 264, 265, 270, 286; *Hard Earned* and, 3, 210, 217, 230–32, 236, 242, 263, 322; *Milking the Rhino* and, 205–6, 322; *Refrigerator Mothers* and, 202–5, 323; *When Billy Broke His Head* (1995) (Simpson and Golfus), 189, 203, 323
Singer, Adam, 196, 197, 206, 281, 283
Siskel, Gene, 13, 153, 172, 227
Siskel, Jon, 240, 322
Siskel & Ebert & the Movies (TV show), 171–72
Siskel/Jacobs Productions, 240
Sisters in Cinema, 214
Sivak, Tom, 157
Six Degrees, 215
'63 Boycott (2017) (Dickson, Matthews, and Quinn), 157, 242–44, 322
Sklar, Martin, 304n2
Skolimowski, Jerzy, 32
Skoll Foundation, 182
Sloss, John, 170, 171, 196–97
Slutkin, Gary, 260
Smith, Janea, 265
social change, 5, 17, 19, 21, 103
social-issue documentaries: Aguayo on, 5; formulas for, 216; history of, 1, 6–10; Lumiere, 233; as persuasion projects, 9; roots of, 7–8; as sellable, 2–3
social media, 222
social movements: filmmakers' fate and, 291; formation of new, 24; history of, 304n2; as political trends, 16

Sojourner Truth Organization, 72
Solanas, Fernando, 29, 64, 68
Soloway, Jill (Joey), 149
Some Are/Summer Learning project, 60
A Song for You (2014) (Karp), 293
Soul! 64
South by Southwest (SXSW) Film Festival, 229, 278
Southern Regional Council (SRC), 233
Spero, Nancy, 156, 162
Spitz, Jeff, 134
Sports-Action Pro-files (1972) (Pill), 66, 323
staff/staffing: BIPOC staff, 280; departing staff, 252, 283, 286; discontent among, 251; diverse community of storytellers, 254; health insurance, 184; human relations policy, 184; insufficient levels of, 17; layoffs, 253; as overburdened, 230, 284; Paycheck Protection Program, 254; racial reckoning and, 254–55; as separate from talent, 219, 282; struggling with business model and, 283–88; struggling with changing culture and, 282–83; struggling with diversification and, 278–82. *See also* internships; Kartemquinites
Stalin, Josef, 10, 24
Stanton, Liz, 249*fig.*
Starr, Vicky, 155
STARZ, 209
Steenbecks, 66
Stehlik, Milos, 129
Steinberg, Betsy, 247, 248, 249*fig.*, 251, 252–53, 269*fig.*, 278, 286
Steinem, Gloria, 85
Steppenwolf Theatre Company, 13, 249
Sterne, Melissa, 240
Stevie (2002) (James), 184, 196–98, 227, 323
Stocchetti, Beckie, 185, 222, 252–53, 267, 283
Stonewall riots, 63
Stoney, George, 78–79, 233
storytelling: goals, 290; mediated storytelling opportunities, 4, 257–59; power of, 240; restructuring and, 218; as social justice, 247; storytelling styles, 4. *See also* humanist storytelling
Storyville series, 210–11
Stranded by the State (2016 miniseries) (Kaar), 241, 322
Strang, Ben, 321

streaming: Amazon Prime (streaming platform), 77; audiences, 257; era of, 222; Hulu (platform), 233, 266, 273; miniseries documentary format and, 3–4, 7; Netflix (platform), 215; as rival to cable and broadcast, 215; video on demand, 215
Street Level Youth Media, 295
student movements, 8, 11, 12, 34, 58–59. *See also* antiwar movement
Students for a Democratic Society, 11, 49, 63
The Subversive Imagination (Becker), 151
Suffredin, Susanne, 153, 185*fig.*
Summer '68 (1969) (Fruchter), 81
Sundance Film Festival: *All the Queen's Horses* and, 276; *America to Me* and, 265, 273; audience award for documentary, 2, 170; awards, 2; *City So Real* and, 265; *Hoop Dreams* and, 2, 163, 170, 172; *Life Itself* and, 227; *Minding the Gap* and, 273; Netflix and, 215; *Stevie* and, 198; *When Billy Broke His Head* and, 189, 203
Sundance Institute, 230, 237
Sung family, 262
sustainability, 217, 239
sweat equity, 199, 290
SXSW (South by Southwest) Film Festival, 229, 278
Szabo, David, 66

Taft-Hartley Act of 1947, 96
Tahimik, Kidlat, 90
Tajima-Peña, Renee, 110, 208, 209
tax exemptions, 289
Taylor, David Van, 233
Taylor, Jim "JT," 128
Taylor, Matt, 235
Taylor Chain I (1980) (Quinn and Blumenthal), 99, 110, 111, 112, 118, 149, 323
Taylor Chain II (1983) (Quinn and Blumenthal), 99, 110–13, 118, 124, 131, 163, 323
Tea Party movement, 11
technological trends: 1930s innovations, 8; adaptation to, 180; computers, 16, 149; DVDs, 180, 181; film project websites, 180; growth and change in response to, 16; internet, 16; Kartemquinites and, 16; leveraging for problemsolving, 16; VCRs, 16; World Wide Web, 16
television program production: distribution, 179; *Hoop Dreams* and, 257; Kartemquin and, 9, 16; technology and, 16

Temaner, Barbara, 56–58
Temaner, Gerald "Jerry": *Anonymous Artists of America* and, 323; Catholic films and, 53, 54; cinematic social inquiry style of, 38; *The College* (1964), 38; Doc Films, 32, 37, 100; ethnographic approach, 59; at ethnographic congress in Chicago, 79; forming Kartemquin, 45–46; Glass and, 58; Hoffman and, 78, 79; *Home for Life* and, 40–45, 218, 244, 324; *Hum 255* and, 324; *Inquiring Nuns* and, 55–56, 58, 324; Jewish culture of, 46–47; on Kartemquin's mission, 27, 60; *Marco* and, 56–58, 323; Mathews and, 259; Morrissette and, 47; *Parents* and, 54, 324; Quinn and, 31; *'63 Boycott* and, 38, 242; television and, 33; *Thumbs Down* and, 53–55, 324; at UICC, 61, 78, 79; at University of Chicago, 29, 31, 32, 34; vision of, 291; Wellington Avenue building and, 66–67
Terkel, Studs, 36, 44, 79, 131
theatrical film production, 7, 9
There Are No Children Here (Kotlowitz), 259
Third Cinema, 29, 68
third-party materials, 4, 142
Third World Newsreel, 68
30 for 30, 215
Thomas, Anthony, 324
Thomas, Isiah, 165, 167
371 Productions, 214, 233, 247
Thumbs Down (1968) (Quinn and Temaner), 53–55, 324
Tiger King (2020), 215
The Times of Harvey Milk (1984) (Schmeichen), 115, 294–95
TNT, 208
Tomlinson, Kenneth, 183
Toronto International Film Festival, 263
Tower Productions, 251
Toyota Motor Sales, 167
The Trials of Muhammad Ali (2013) (Siegel), 233–34, 322
Tribeca Film Festival, 234
Trick Bag (1974) (Kuttner), 9, 92–93, 94*fig.*, 141, 323
The Triibe (web-based platform), 41, 293
Trotskyist Spartacist League, 52
Turner Broadcasting Network, 155
Turner Classic Movies, 248
Tuss, Barbara, 123
TV Lab, 106, 115, 132

two-party system, 10, 16. *See also* political ideology
Tyler, "Dread" Scott, 152
Typeface (2009) (Nagan), 217, 221, 322

UE/Wells (1975) (Blumenthall, Quinn, and Brzostowski), 101–2, 109, 323
Unapologetic (2020) (O'Shay), 277, 280, 290, 293, 321
Unbroken Glass (2016) (Sabu), 248, 270–71, 322
UnidosUS (National Council of La Raza), 48
Union Maids (1976) (Reichert and Klein), 83, 132, 155
United Church of Christ, 15, 127
United Electrical Workers (UE), 96, 101, 102
Universal Declaration of Human Rights, 176
University of Chicago, 12–13, 60–61, 186, 217, 243, 294
Up the Yangtze (2007) (Yang), 278
Utopia Media, 229

Vachon, Christine, 293
Vance, Cyrus, Jr., 262
Vatican II, 53, 54
VCRs, 16, 106–7, 144
Velvet Revolution, 176
Vertov, Dziga, 31
VHS tapes, 144–45
Video Data Bank (VDB), 78, 292
Video Free America, 78
Videofreex, 79
Videopolis, 79, 131
Vietnam, Long Time Coming (1998) (Quinn, Blumenthal, and Gilbert), 188–93, 217, 230, 323
Vietnam War: effects of, 36, 103, 130; antiwar movement, 11, 12, 14, 34, 49, 58, 68, 158, 234; avoiding conscription, 34, 39, 45; *M*A*S*H* and, 64; *Thumbs Down*, 53–55; veterans of, 92, 132, 155, 188, 192*fig.*
Viva La Causa (1974) (Webb), 93–94, 323
Voice of America, 183
Voices from a Steeltown (1983) (Buba), 110
Voices of Cabrini (1999) (Hoffman and Bezalel), 134

Wales, Dirk, 108
Walker, Keith, 224, 257, 258–59
Walker, Scott, 233
Walmart, 285

War on Poverty, 53
Warrendale (1967), 81
Washington, Harold, 120, 151
Washington University, 247
WATCH (Women Act to Control Health Care), 85, 88, 89
Watchmen (2019), 264
Waxman, Henry, 136
We Are Witnesses (2019) (Bowman and Robinson), 242, 322
The Weather Underground (2004) (Siegel), 230, 233–34
Weather Underground, 52, 63, 81
Webb, Teena, 69, 70, 91, 93–94
Weinberg, Bertha, 42
Weinberg, Karen, 236
Weinberg, Tom, 79, 134
Weinstein, James, 10–12, 15, 304n2, 322
Weiss, Marc, 83, 132, 135
Welbon, Yvonne, 214, 267
Wertlake, Stephanie, 154
Westbrook, Robert, 305n1
Wexler, Haskell, 50, 107
Weyermann, Diane, 182–83
What's Happening at Local 70? (1975) (Hoffman), 98, 323
What the Fuck Are These Red Squares? (1970) (Quinn and Blumenthal), 67–68, 82, 151, 324
"When Art Makes a Difference" project, 175–76
When Billy Broke His Head (1995) (Simpson and Golfus), 189, 203, 323
Where's I. W. Abel? (1975) (Quinn), 79, 96, 323
Where's Joe? 97–98
Whisnant, Steve, 188, 190, 217
Who Killed Vincent Chin? (1987) (Choy and Tajima-Peña), 110
Wickenden, Aaron, 185, 195, 219*fig.*, 228, 234, 283, 322
Wickham, Woodward "Woody," 129, 167–68, 182, 196, 205, 244
Wideman, John Edgar, 174
Wilbur Wright College, 292
Williams, Kim, 167
Williams, Raymond, 19
Winfrey, Oprah, 109
Winnie Wright, Age 11 (1974) (Kartemquin Collective), 91–92, 323
Winter Soldier (1972), 132
Wisconsin Public Television, 186
Wiseman, Fred, 28–29

"Witches, Midwives and Nurses" (Ehrenreich and English), 87
With God on Our Side (1996) (Lichtenstein and Taylor), 233
WNET, 133, 134, 139
women: making films about and with, 257; misogyny, 290, 293; parity of conditions for, 24; women's rights, 257. *See also* feminism
Women Act to Control Health Care (WATCH), 85, 88, 89
Women's Film Restoration Fund, 124
Women's Issue Foundation, 155
Women's Voices: The Gender Gap (1984) (Rohrer), 119–24, 155, 204, 323
Woodlawn Organization, 60
Word Is Out (1977), 132
work-for-hire: focus on, 252; mission-aligned and, 189; as revenue source, 184; social inquiry cost and, 65–66; as supplemental income, 220; Walmart project, 285
Working (Terkel), 44, 79, 131
working-class groups: confronting contempt for, 290; feminist and revolutionary cinema, 90–95; *Hard Earned* and, 3, 217, 230–32; Marxism and, 48, 51; neoliberalism and, 104–9; *Now We Live on Clifton* (1974), 91–92; social dysfunction of, 291; *Thumbs Down* and, 53–58; *Trick Bag* (1974), 92; *Viva La Causa* (1974), 93–95; *Winnie Wright, Age 11* (1974), 91–92; Young Patriots, 48, 51. *See also* Rainbow Coalition; Rising Up Agency (RUA)
working conditions, 1, 23–24, 99, 232
World T. E. A. M. Sports, 188, 190
World Wide Web, 16, 148
WPA Film Library, 245
WTTW-TV, 33, 39, 79, 131, 134, 164, 209, 240, 241, 248
Wuhan Wuhan (2021) (Chang), 278, 321

Yamagata Film Festival, 198
Yates, Pamela, 157
Yippies, 49, 50, 68
Young Lords Organization, 12, 48, 50, 61, 65, 80, 120
Young Patriot Free Health Clinic, 89
Young Patriots, 48, 51
youth movements, 8, 28. *See also* student movements

Zaccardi, Denise, 109, 154, 214, 295
Zavattini, Cesare, 28
Zhang, Yingying, 277–78
Zimmermann, Patricia, 5–6, 245
Zimmermann, Vern, 38
Zones of Contention (Becker), 151

www.ingramcontent.com/pod-product-compliance
Lightning Source LLC
Chambersburg PA
CBHW020828160426
43192CB00007B/569